Invisible Fences

Invisible Fences

Prose Poetry
as a Genre
in French
and American
Literature

Steven Monte

University of
Nebraska Press
Lincoln & London

Publication of this book was assisted by a grant from The Andrew W. Mellon Foundation.

Manufactured in the United States of America
∞

PQ
491
.M66
2000

Library of Congress Cataloging-in-Publication Data
Monte, Steven, 1967–
    Invisible fences : prose poetry as a genre in French and American literature / Steven Monte
      p. cm.
    Includes bibliographical references and index.
    ISBN 0-8032-3211-x (cl : alk. paper)
    1. Prose poems, French—History and criticism.   2. French poetry—History and criticism.
    3. Prose poems, American—History and criticism.   4. American poetry—History and criticism. I. Title.
    PQ491 .M66   2000
    841—dc21
                             00-037426

Contents

Acknowledgments

A genre of sorts, acknowledgments give an author the opportunity to make visible the many contributors to the published work. I am grateful to John Shoptaw and Matt Greenfield for reading and commenting on individual chapters of my writing; to Lanny Hammer, David Quint, and Tyrus Miller, who read and commented on an earlier version of the entire work; and to my readers and the staff at the University of Nebraska Press, who helped me mold the book into its final shape. I am also grateful to John Hollander for his continual support for this project. He helped me frame the issues and directed me to source material in ways that cannot be expressed in notes, and he challenged and encouraged me throughout my research and writing. Special thanks go to Leah Price for the care with which she read the entire manuscript in its irregular installments and offered suggestions. Special thanks also go to Dave Southward for reading everything in one large installment and prodding me to make my arguments and writing clear without loss of nuance. Finally, I would like to thank the Camargo Foundation, at whose center in Cassis I was a fellow in 1995. The foundation allowed me that rare combination of productivity and relaxation, for which I owe the directors and the other fellows as much if not more than the surroundings.

Note on Terminology

I discuss terms like "genre" and "prose poetry" at length in chapters 1 and 5 and comment on their practical value in my introduction and conclusion. Though I have taken pains to use these terms clearly and precisely, consistent usage does not preclude some stylistic and argumentative play. "Generic," for example, sometimes hovers between its everyday meaning, "descriptive of a type," and its more technical sense, "adjective of genre." "Prose poem" and "poème en prose" are generally synonymous, but some occasions demand a distinction between what was being written in France and in America or the introduction of the phrase "poem in prose" when form rather than genre requires emphasis. Similarly, "genre" and "literary kind" are synonyms as a rule, but I occasionally use the latter as a more inclusive and deliberately less technical designation. Context will make the senses of these terms clear, but the reader should also keep in mind that shifts in meaning bear some relation to the progress of my argument. It is not until chapter 4 that I discuss at length the stakes of my distinction between form and genre and not until the conclusion that I place the distinction within the context of a general theory of reading.

Invisible Fences

Introduction

> I thought that if I could put it all down, that would be one way. And next the
> thought came to me that to leave all out would be another, and truer, way. —John
> Ashbery, *Three Poems*

By now every critic knows how to introduce his or her work: with an apology
for what could not be taken into consideration. Even in an age that looks
with suspicion on the comprehensive treatment, with all of its diagnostic,
medicinal, and positivistic connotations, most of us still feel the need to excuse
ourselves for our lack of it. What I have to say here is no exception to this rule.
In its most general trajectory, my work places prose poetry in historical and
theoretical perspective by comparing the form's development in French and
American literature. Needless to say, I discuss only a tiny fraction of the prose
poetry of the two literatures, but an international comparison is crucial to the
sorts of claims I make about how generic and literary-historical frameworks
influence readings of individual works. With regard to literary history, for
example, a comparative study helps one avoid reading a given author or poem
from within a single narrative of development. And comparing prose poems
written in different times and places forces one to be more circumspect about
describing what constitutes prose poetry as a literary kind.

From the moment I began working on *Invisible Fences*, I have been
repeatedly asked two related questions: "What is prose poetry?" and "Is *X*—
the questioner's pet text—a prose poem?" I do not attempt a direct answer
to either of these questions anywhere in my discussion. This may strike the
reader as odd; for me, it is the frequency with which I have been asked the
questions that is significant. Rephrasing my aims from a skeptical perspective
may help here: understanding prose poetry as a genre means exploring the
interpretive consequences of reading what has been called the *poème en*

prose, or prose poem, as if it were a genre. In other words, I am interested more in what prose poetry is and has been in specific historical and cultural contexts than in what prose poetry is in some normative sense. If a "What is . . . ?" question lies at the heart of my project, it is "What is genre?"— a concern that, I hope, adds to the general interest of my discussion. But the frequency with which I have been asked some variant of the question "What is prose poetry?" does more than indicate that "prose poetry" is a relatively unfamiliar term: it suggests that the desire for definition isn't shaken off so easily.

Why the desire for definition returns as if it were some repressed need is a subject of my conclusion. At the outset, it is worth sketching a few reasons why the approach to formal definition will either not take us very far or lead us down the wrong path entirely. The most foolproof definition of prose poetry, "poetry written in prose," sounds uncomfortably tautological. A glance at the French *poème en prose* clinches this reaction. The next best approach throws the question "What is prose poetry?" back at the questioner—"You tell me what 'prose' is and what 'poetry' is, and I will tell you what 'prose poetry' is"—to make the point that the two terms that constitute "prose poetry" are themselves difficult to define unambiguously. Recalling that prose poetry is or was once an oxymoron takes us in yet another direction: "prose poetry" is an abstraction meant to question generic boundaries and accordingly resists definition. But none of these approaches helps us much in recognizing a prose poem we might come across in our literary wandering, let alone help us read one. Maybe we are starting off too abstractly.

Let us try instead a kind of New Critical experiment and compare two works stripped of much of their context—author, title, publication date, and the like:

> It was near Lorient, the sun shone brightly and we used to go for walks, watching through those September days the sea rising, rising to cover woods, landscapes, cliffs. Soon there was nothing left to combat the blue sea but the meandering paths under the trees and the families drew closer together. Among us was a child in a sailor suit. He was sad and took me by the hand: "Sir," he said, "I have been in Naples; do you know that in Naples there are lots of little streets; in the streets you can stay all alone without anyone seeing you: it's not that there are more people in Naples but there are so many little streets that there is never more than one street for each person." "What stories is the child telling

you now," said the father. "He has never been to Naples." "Sir, your child is a poet." "That's all right, but if he is a man of letters I'll wring his neck." The meandering paths left dry by the sea had made him think of the streets of Naples.

Lazy and indifferent, shaking space easily from his wings, knowing his way, the heron passes over the church beneath the sky. White and distant, absorbed in itself, endlessly the sky covers and uncovers, moves and remains. A lake? Blot the shores of it out! A mountain? Oh, perfect—the sun gold on its slopes. Down that falls. Ferns then, or white feathers, for ever and ever—

Desiring truth, awaiting it, laboriously distilling a few words, for ever desiring—(a cry starts to the left, another to the right. Wheels strike divergently. Omnibuses conglomerate in conflict)—for ever desiring—(the clock asseverates with twelve distinct strokes that it is midday; light sheds gold scales; children swarm)—for ever desiring truth. Red is the dome; coins hang on the trees; smoke trails from the chimneys; bark, shout, cry "Iron for sale"—and truth?

Radiating to a point men's feet and women's feet, black or gold-encrusted—(This foggy weather—Sugar? No, thank you—The commonwealth of the future)—the firelight darting and making the room red, save for the black figures and their bright eyes, while outside a van discharges, Miss Thingummy drinks tea at her desk, and plateglass preserves fur coats—

Flaunted, leaf-light, drifting at corners, blown across the wheels, silver-splashed, home or not home, gathered, scattered, squandered in separate scales, swept up, down, torn, sunk, assembled—and truth?

Now to recollect by the fireside on the white square of marble. From ivory depths words rising shed their blackness, blossom and penetrate. Fallen the book; in the flame, in the smoke, in the momentary sparks—or now voyaging, the marble square pendant, minarets beneath the Indian seas, while space rushes blue and stars glint—truth? or now, content with closeness?

Lazy and indifferent the heron returns; the sky veils her stars; then bares them.

Does either of these texts in some fashion mark itself as a prose poem? The first prose piece is shorter than the second, limited in its time frame to something like a lyric moment, and makes suggestive use of the word "poet." It is also narrative, however, and might pass as a short short story or a parable. The second text is linguistically more dense than the first. Description dominates the short paragraphs, and subjective impressions overwhelm what hints at narrative exist in such details as the bits of overheard conversation and time passing from day to evening. The heron whose appearance opens and closes the piece points to self-conscious literary composition and may remind the reader familiar with modernist poetry of the seagull at the beginning of Hart Crane's "Proem: To Brooklyn Bridge"—especially given the atmosphere of a modern city, the fragmentation of impressions, and the discontinued sentences. The evidence is inconclusive, but based on text alone most of us would probably say that both pieces are potentially prose poems, and if we had to pick one over the other, the second is the more likely prose-poem candidate, if only because it is "laboriously distilling a few words."

But the experimental frame in which I have couched the comparison already argues that the opposite is true. And sure enough, it turns out that the first text is a prose poem and the second a piece of short fiction. Or rather the first selection is the poem "Littérature et Poésie" ("Literature and Poetry") from Max Jacob's *Le Cornet à dés* (*The Dice Cup*, 1917); the second the title story of Virginia Woolf's *Monday or Tuesday* (1921). Or even more precisely, the first prose piece is a John Ashbery translation of a Max Jacob poem from Paul Auster's edition of *The Random House Book of Twentieth-Century French Poetry* and the second a Virginia Woolf short story from Susan Dick's second edition of *The Complete Shorter Fiction of Virginia Woolf*. The moral here is that context, always an important consideration for genre, is especially important for the prose poem. Papyrus scraps of Greek dredged up in the Egyptian desert have proved more tractable to generic classification than prose poems stripped of their editorial context, or even some with their context. This is in part because prose poetry by definition resists definition in traditional formal terms (the oxymoron argument again), but the special case of the prose poem may help us rethink theories of genre and their use in interpreting literature. Publication context and readership, for example, may signal genre as much as a work's formal features, and "What does it mean to read X as a prose poem?" may turn out to be a more significant question than "Is X a prose poem?" Definitions can be helpful and may in some sense be necessary for interpretation, but attempts to formulate what constitutes a prose poem are outright misleading if, in the interests of all-inclusiveness, they ascend to a level of abstraction where they can describe everything but explain nothing. It is better to be "content with closeness," as the speaker in

"Monday or Tuesday" suggests at one point in her musings on truth, than to pretend to an impossibly comprehensive definition that may not even help with interpretation.

Considering the diversity and number of authors who have written poems in prose in the last century and a half, it is odd how little critical attention has, until recently, been given to prose poetry as a genre. In the French literary tradition, there is scarcely a major poet since Baudelaire who has not written some poems in prose: Rimbaud, Mallarmé, Valéry, Claudel, Jacob, Eluard, Reverdy, Perse, and Ponge only head the list. In the American tradition, poets as different as Eliot, Williams, Stein, Bishop, and Ashbery have all written prose poems. As might be expected given prose poetry's origins and continuous practice in France, what criticism exists on the subject has tended to discuss the French literary tradition, a fact that is particularly true of the first generation of prose-poetry critics. Franz Rauhut's *Das französische Prosagedicht* (1929), Vista Clayton's *The Prose Poem in French Literature of the Eighteenth Century* (1936), Albert Cherel's *La Prose poétique française* (1940), Suzanne Bernard's *Le Poème en prose de Baudelaire jusqu'à nos jours* (1959), and Monique Parent's *Saint-John Perse et quelques devanciers: Études sur le poème en prose* (1960) are all, as their titles more or less indicate, French-centered in their approach. Only John Simon's doctoral dissertation, *The Prose Poem as a Genre in Nineteenth-Century European Literature* (1959), is comparative in scope, and it is telling that this work became available as a book only in 1987.

The period beween 1960 and the late 1970s could be considered a gap in the history of prose poetry criticism. Outside of studies of individual works and scattered discussions in a few dissertations, the only book-length, or more accurately, pamphlet-sized treatment of prose poetry in this period is Ulrich Fülleborn's *Das deutsche Prosagedicht* (1970), a work that is obviously not comparative. It is only in the late 1970s and the 1980s that prose poetry criticism takes off. Beginning with Barbara Johnson's *Défigurations du langage poétique* (1979) and Mary Ann Caws and Hermine Riffaterre's edition of critical essays *The Prose Poem in France: Theory and Practice* (1983)—studies that, although French-oriented, contain theoretical treatments of the subject and leave room for some comparison—prose-poetry criticism receives a new impetus and direction. Since 1983 at least five academic books on prose poetry have been published in English alone: Stephen Fredman's *Poet's Prose: The Crisis in American Verse* (1983, 2nd ed. 1990), Stamos Metzidakis's *Repetition and Semiotics: Interpreting Prose Poems* (1986), Jonathan Monroe's *A Poverty of Objects: The Prose Poem and the Politics of Genre* (1987), Margueritte Murphy's *A Tradition of Subversion: The Prose Poem in English from Wilde to Ashbery* (1992), and Michel Delville's *The American Prose Poem: Poetic Form and the Boundaries of Genre* (1998). In addition, one useful, textbooklike study has been published in French, Michel Sandras's *Lire le poème en prose* (1995). There have also been numerous articles, half a dozen dissertations, and several theoretical books, such as Marjorie Perloff's *The Poetics of Indeterminacy: Rimbaud to Cage* (1981), Richard Terdiman's *Discourse/ Counter-Discourse: The Theory and Practice of Symbolic Resistance in Nineteenth-Century France* (1985), and Donald Wesling's *The New Poetries: Poetic Form since Coleridge and Wordsworth* (1985), which contain lengthy sections on prose poetry. Furthermore, as any MLA bibliography search will show, studies of individual prose poets and poems have been on the rise.

Even this cursory survey of the criticism makes it clear that academic interest in prose poetry has varied considerably over the years, as has the focus of its discussion. The current resurgence of interest in prose poetry has a lot to do with a renewed interest in the form among American poets— although it is not as if there has been a shortage of poets writing prose poems in English in the last century or so. The recent attention in America is especially intriguing in that much of it may be due to one poet, John Ashbery, and, even more specifically, to one work of his, *Three Poems* (1972). The increase in academic criticism of prose poetry corresponds neatly to the increased attention given to *Three Poems* in the early 1980s. In matters of influence and literary history, perception of continuity does count for reality to a certain extent, but the argument that Ashbery is a driving force behind the renewed interest in prose poetry—an argument that, whether true or not, is worth considering as a matter of reception history—begs further questions. Why Ashbery and why now? Is a work like *Three Poems* more or less sui generis, or are there literary or nonliterary texts to which it might be fruitfully compared? How does the recent Ashbery-influenced flurry of poetic and critical activity affect the status of prose poetry as a literary kind? Whatever the answer to these and other related questions, the term "prose poetry" has received new inflections. While it may still not be a household word in the English-speaking world (or even the English-speaking academic world), prose poetry is a literary form that many more poets and critics are at home with now.

Or at least more familiar with. As my opening remarks indicate, the difficulties in defining prose poetry remain notorious, and there is only a limited amount of critical consensus regarding the body of literature that the term denotes. While critics from Bernard to Caws can claim with some confidence that brevity is an essential trait of the prose poem, for a critic like Margueritte Murphy, writing in the wake of *Three Poems*, the length of a work is not necessarily a reliable generic marker. Michel Delville avoids the definitional dilemma by discussing works that have been received as prose poems and by privileging "generic intentionality." And while Stamos Metzidakis attempts to define prose poetry in relation to its internal linguistic structures, critics like Monroe and Terdiman are more concerned with how the language and subject matter of prose poetry relate to outside discourses, literary and extraliterary. In short, even if a good number of the disagreements among critics stem from methodological differences, it is nonetheless important to emphasize that prose poetry is a less well defined field of inquiry than other areas of study that exhibit the same variety of approaches and organize themselves around one literary kind.

My own approach at once takes part in and departs from the growing body of prose-poetry criticism. Like many of its recent critics, I am fascinated by the complex theoretical questions that the prose poem raises with regard to literary kinds and by the particular developments in the genre (always assuming prose poetry is a genre) in the last few decades. And like many of the first-generation critics, I consider certain literary-historical matters, such as the prose poem's origins, to be important in understanding what is at stake in the theoretical abstraction of the literary kind—that is, in the search for more precise terminology, what does not reduce to a mere definitional squabble or formal distinction approaching tautology. My study differs from the bulk of the criticism in that its point of departure is largely pragmatic: I am interested in prose poetry as an interpretive framework and not, in any direct way, as a pure theoretical category, a literary phenomenon with its own quasi-autonomous history, or an index of sociohistorical tensions. Inevitably I do discuss prose poetry as a "simple abstraction," a literary form with its own tradition and conventions, and a genre that issues from a particular historical and cultural milieu, but all of these concerns follow from my initial impulse toward interpretation. If I have in the end structured my study around "Prose Poetry as a Genre in French and American Literature," it is because I have come to realize that the prose poems of writers like Baudelaire and Ashbery gain something from the wider perspective.

But the most significant way in which my approach differs from virtually the entire corpus of prose-poetry criticism has to do with my views on the constraints of the genre. While many critics attempt to define the external and internal factors that help determine the form of the prose poem, they do so almost universally in the context of prose poetry's revolutionary or subversive impulse. It is as if one only bothers defining the prose poem's constraints in order to show more effectively how it violates them. I do not deny prose poetry revolutionary potential, but I am antiessentialist when it comes to questions of form or genre: the fact that a poem is written in prose does not necessarily mean it is subversive. To be sure, no one ever takes the extreme essentialist position on the matter. The claims that critics like Murphy, Terdiman, and Monroe make are more nuanced and always qualified by the historical fact of the prose poem's marginality. But even if, having evoked essentialism, one escapes from an extreme version of it, other versions are likely to arise that are potentially as reductive. In a sense it is not so much the positive claim of prose poetry's revolutionary status but its negative implications that I find most open to debate. Was verse poetry ever as single voiced or lacking in tension as some prose poets and critics would have us believe? Are the lyrics written in verse, free or otherwise, at the same time and after the arrival of the prose poem fossils and atavisms of literary history? Even when its claims are qualified, any approach investing heavily in prose poetry's subversive impulse begs these sorts of questions, if only by their ghost presence at an argumentative level. Finally, terms like "subversive" and "revolutionary" are somewhat slippery. If they do not reduce to "formally innovative" or covers for aesthetic judgments, these terms have to be related in some way to a work's impact on its readers and subsequent influence. By this logic *Les Fleurs du mal*, because of its trial, and *Uncle Tom's Cabin*, because of the controversy it provoked, would be more subversive than any prose poem—with the possible exception of Oscar Wilde's letter to Lord Alfred Douglas. One can of course speak of impact on a more narrow circle of readers (such as poets and critics) and influence that is gradual, less direct, and ultimately more profound: I would argue that, even from this perspective, prose poetry has been less revolutionary than most critics have asserted.

My general point is that prose poetry raises many questions that tend to get elided in the debate about its revolutionary character. Constraints can be thought of not only as restrictions to freedom or, conversely, as restrictions that enable freedom, but as generic signals that inform interpretation. If readers of prose poetry have been or become less aware of the genre's constraints, it is perhaps because so much of the rhetoric surrounding the prose poem has to do with its formal freedom. Or it may be that the illusion of no constraints is itself one of prose poetry's generic traits. In either case, these "invisible fences" that surround prose poetry are what I am trying to reconstruct on several levels throughout my discussion. Framed as an investigation of generic constraints with an aim toward interpretation of particular works, my study is necessarily concerned with the way literary-historical considerations affect how we read. My original point of departure was the observation that Baudelaire and Ashbery occupy similar, though by no means perfectly analogous, positions in their respective literary traditions with regard to prose poetry. Although Baudelaire and Ashbery were not the first to write prose poems in French and English, respectively, both poets have arguably put prose poetry on the map of their literatures from a historical perspective, and both have certainly been catalysts of prose-poetry activity.

Such contingent facts of literary history have important consequences. While not going so far as to argue that Baudelaire's and Ashbery's poems have determined the aesthetics of French and American prose poetry, I do find it suggestive that their work has occupied such a large space in the critical discussion of the genre. It is no accident, for example, that an aesthetic of brevity characterizes the "canonical" line of French prose poets often described as stretching back to Bertrand (Baudelaire's self-named precursor) and forward through the author of the *Petits Poëmes en prose* to Mallarmé, the Rimbaud of *Illuminations*, and Max Jacob. Nor is it by chance that this emphasis on brevity has prompted some critics either to exclude from consideration some longer poems (especially if they predate Baudelaire) or to judge them as aesthetically inferior—the more "anecdotal" poems of Baudelaire and Mallarmé included. Literary history may also be in part responsible for the impulse to read prose poetry as a revolutionary or evolutionary form. Writers like Baudelaire and Rimbaud started writing prose poems after they had written most of their lyrics in verse. In America, conversely, prose poetry has been an avant-garde gesture throughout most of its history. The relative success of Ashbery's work may mark the moment when the form enters a tradition on whose margins it has stood for a long time.

Though organized in a more or less chronological fashion, my study is not a history of the prose poem. In my first chapter I discuss the term "poème en prose," the significance of the form's origins, and genre theory. For historical background to the first usages of the term, I often draw on the work of early critics like Bernard and Simon, synthesizing points when necessary, and occasionally adding to and qualifying their findings in the light of new evidence. In general, I am interested in placing the eighteenth-century debates about the *poème en prose* (something very different from the modern kind) in theoretical and literary-historical perspective for the readings and the issues of reception I pursue later. The particular questions I explore include how and in what form eighteenth-century issues are carried over to the nineteenth century, the extent to which the controversies surrounding prose poetry are incarnations of long-standing or periodically recurring debates about tradition and modernity, and how the development of the *poème en prose* relates to the rise of the novel. In order to discuss genre, I make use of ideas and terminology developed by Alastair Fowler in his *Kinds of Literature: An Introduction to the Theory of Genres and Modes* (1982), in particular his discussions of genre, subgenre, and mode. Although I take issue with Fowler's view on the relationship between kind and mode, I am indebted to his analysis of genre as an interpretive much more than a classificatory framework. I am also indebted to a lesser extent to some genre criticism written since Fowler's book: Adena Rosmarin's *The Power of Genre* (1985), Ralph Cohen's "History and Genre" (1986), and David Fishelov's *Metaphors of Genre* (1993). My theoretical discussion argues that genres are negatively defined in relation to their neighboring genres rather than determined by a particular set of formal traits, so that at any given moment in our reading we identify only a handful of generic traits or contexts. Our sense of genre is therefore always "in progress," changing as we read onward and encounter new interpretive frameworks.

Of course, recognizing neighboring genres requires some familiarity with literary history. It is from this perspective, and not from some inherently literary-historical consideration, that my second chapter turns to the pre-history of prose poetry. Here I not only discuss texts that influence later prose poems, but also consider various works that resist traditional generic classification and that I believe either help indirectly to provide constraints for prose poetry, or serve as instructive counterexamples to it. My survey ranges from literary genres such as sermons and essays and quasi-literary writings like travelogues and prose descriptions of paintings to what are, historically speaking, nonliterary texts—physiologies and *chroniques* columns in magazines. Establishing the field of prosaic and poetic possibilities in existence before the first self-proclaimed prose poems is central to my approach. Although my critical sweep in this chapter is taxonomic in form, I do not intend it to be comprehensive in scope. Rather, through a procedure that has affinities to the act of reading, I shuttle constantly between interpretive framework and text, describing a range of categories through and against which individual prose poems, or prose-poem-like works, can be understood and gradually turn to the next logical focus of my discussion: the specific literary and historical conditions surrounding the first works that announce themselves as prose poems.

Chapter 3 centers on Baudelaire. Before pursuing a detailed reading of one of his first prose poems ("La Solitude"), I reevaluate Baudelaire's position within his literary and historical period, placing emphasis on his relationship to romanticism and the situations surrounding the publication of his prose poems. I furthermore reconsider Baudelaire's turn to prose poetry in the context of his poetic development. As with the prose poem's prehistory, I try to resist a teleological narrative here, arguing that the relation between *Les Fleurs du mal* and the *Petits Poëmes en prose* is not a one-way equation. Because many of Baudelaire's prose poems can be read as commentaries on his verse and the genre of lyric poetry, they alter in subtle ways how one reads the verse poems to which they are, for the most part, chronologically subsequent. My reading of "La Solitude" adds the more specific context surrounding the composition and publication of Baudelaire's first prose poems to the general background I discuss in the previous chapter. I pay particular attention to how the poem's obsession with being alone mirrors Baudelaire's attempts to position his *Petits Poëmes en prose* among other works in the literary marketplace and literary history. My general argument is that Baudelaire is not alone in his poetic enterprise, despite the relative success of his version of literary history in academic criticism of prose poetry. Other works and "outside" pressures, nowhere explicitly mentioned in "La Solitude" but crucial to its form and our understanding of the poem, offer an important perspective on the *poème en prose* and its generic constraints.

In my fourth chapter I am primarily interested in literary-historical questions, especially why the *poème en prose* was accepted in France relatively quickly—so much so that most poets at least attempt to write in the genre and some twentieth-century poets, like Perse and Ponge, become known especially for their prose poetry. As in chapter 2, I make gestures toward a typology of prose poems and prose-poem-like texts without seeking to be comprehensive. In fact, I am highly selective in my readings and examples here, concentrating on poets who wrote prose poems within a decade of Baudelaire's death—Rimbaud, Mallarmé, Lautréamont, Cazalis, and Cros—whose work sometimes attempts to differentiate itself from the paradigm set by the *Petits Poëmes en prose*. My aim is to show that while on the one hand certain generic traits of the "formally free" genre of the prose poem (such as brevity, concentration, and a less exclusively high-poetic diction) seem to be on their way to becoming quasi-normative features of the *poème en prose* in the late nineteenth century, on the other hand the notion of generic development in this period is informed by a particular narrative of literary history. Rimbaud, for instance (for some critics Mallarmé), can be seen as the figure who takes Baudelaire's blurring of genres an important step farther either by moving away from an aesthetic of coherence or by "deconstructing" the prose element of the *poème en prose* (Baudelaire, in this view, had deconstructed the poetry element)—thus exposing all generic constraints as mere constructs and bequeathing a legacy of difficulty and subversion to all future prose poets. My point is not that such a history is wrong—in fact, I find it in certain respects compelling—but rather that it is only one narrative and that it is often conservative in its very progressivism. Many histories of the *poème en prose* also ignore or treat as rare exceptions prose poems that violate the brevity aesthetic, like Lautréamont's *Chants du Maldoror*, a work likely to be excerpted for reasons that go beyond limitations of space in an anthology. I end chapter 4 with a reading of Claudel's "L'Heure Jaune," an analysis of Jacob's famous preface to *Le Cornet à dés*, and a brief discussion of trends in twentieth-century French poetry in order to place the issues I have raised in a broader literary-historical perspective.

Chapters 5 and 6 turn to prose poetry in nineteenth-century and modernist American literature. As with *poème en prose* in chapter 1, I begin with a history of the term "prose poem." This history, which necessarily involves some consideration of British literature, leads to an overview of prose poems and prose-poem-like works in the nineteenth century, parallel to the general prehistory of the *poème en prose* in chapter 2. The authors whose critical comments or works I discuss include Hunt, Poe, Hawthorne, Emerson, Lazarus, and Wilde. Through comparison and contrast to the French tradition, I situate the English-language prose poem within more general literary-historical trends. Chapter 6 discusses why the prose poem did not become as important in the American and British context as in the French. The reasons for prose poetry's failure to catch on in America and Britain are complicated; neither a purely formal explanation (the alexandrine was so strict a formal constraint French poets went to the extreme of prose poetry to break out of it) nor a purely historical explanation (Wilde's trial tainted prose poetry as decadent for Anglophone poets) suffices. The relative failure of the Anglophone prose poem had largely to do with the fact that other forms performed much of the poetic work for English-language poets that the *poème en prose* did for their French contemporaries. The prose poem was not avoided so much as not seen as missing, if seen at all. To develop more fully this point, I discuss some (mostly critical) writings of T. S. Eliot, placing particular importance on the relationship between the prose poem and the modern long poem. I conclude the chapter with a close reading of Eliot's prose poem "The Engine" in order to explore the significance of the labels "American" and "prose poem."

The seventh chapter continues discussing American prose poetry more as an interpretive framework than as a fact of literary history. My two test cases are Stein's *Tender Buttons* and Williams's *Kora in Hell: Improvisations*. The bulk of the chapter develops an approach to reading Stein and shows how her work asks us to reflect on composition. Since early discussions of Stein and automatic writing, critics have been interested in Stein's methods of composition, but they have not emphasized enough that *Tender Buttons* is a series of related experiments—that individual "descriptions" depend as much on what Stein has already written as on any inner or outer reality they supposedly represent. Critics tend to treat *Tender Buttons* as a collection of many discrete prose poems, concentrating on the titled pieces in the first two sections of the work to the neglect of the third section, "Rooms." While the conventional critical approach has its advantages, Stein's work is better viewed as a whole and outside a literary-historical narrative centered on the prose poem. The same holds true for *Kora in Hell*, though Williams was more intent on writing individual "improvisations." My argument emphasizes how literary history creates generic categories that then influence how we read.

In chapter 8 I discuss American prose poetry since the Second World War via John Ashbery's *Three Poems*. By concentrating on this work, I am purposefully being selective: readers looking for a survey of postwar trends would be better serviced by Delville's book. I focus on Ashbery's long prose poems in part to continue my reflections on the relationship between the modern long poem and prose poetry and in part to make a point about long prose poetry: *Three Poems* is not only living proof that long prose poems can be written, it is one of the most successful works of prose poetry in the language. In the course of my reading of *Three Poems*, I analyze various aspects of Ashbery's poetry and poetics. As with Baudelaire, I read one work within the context of a poet's œuvre; I also reevaluate Ashbery's position in literary-historical debates. In the current critical environment, Ashbery is generally read as one of the leading and most conspicuous examples of postmodernism, if not its paragon. I argue that Ashbery's work has significant affinities to modernism but try to avoid the old aporia of continuity versus change, as well as the semantic (read aesthetic and political) dispute over the term "postmodernity." Once again, my interest in literary history is oriented toward interpretation. By concentrating on cliché characteristics of postmodernism such as open-endedness and skepticism toward the authoritative, critics have helped make the poetry's constraints—its impulses toward closure in both the formal and the argumentative senses of the term—more invisible than they need be. Through analysis of the poetry's narratives and arguments and comparisons to other prose texts and poems, I offer a reading of *Three Poems* that emphasizes the work's "negative dialectics": its refusal to steer its meditations toward a fixed end that nevertheless, through a kind of tacking movement necessitated by moments of impasse, gives form and direction to the poem.

After a brief coda on formalist and experimentalist poetry, I conclude by revisiting the idea of prose poetry as a genre and putting the various questions I have raised into a broader theoretical perspective. I turn more specifically to the reception history of the prose poem as evidenced in anthologies, simultaneously building on observations I made in the preceding chapters and on my earlier arguments concerning the need to understand the category "prose poetry" by means of negative differentiation. Anthologies, even without their prefaces, are critical statements about literary history and genre. I tease out the interpretive implications of the dozen or so anthologies of the prose poem that have appeared in the last hundred years and then discuss the more general issue of audience. Audience is sometimes a more reliable generic marker than any set of formal or intentional features. Yet it may also indicate that the prose poem is, in the end, not a genre: to the extent that the prose poem succeeds in proving to its readership it is not merely experimental it tends to be incorporated into other genres, if not into "poetry" in general; to the extent that it fails it is more or less ignored. My theoretical discussion reaches its logical and pragmatic conclusion here, if only because further considerations of genre would be as a whole matters more of semantics than of substance, a return to the classificatory at the expense of the interpretive. My final remarks concern methodology. By evoking the notion of interpretive framework throughout my discussion, I have done more than redefine what is at stake with genre; I have in effect outlined a critical approach to reading. Needless to say, the label "genre" is itself neither superfluous nor neutral. It indicates the direction of my work as well as some of the considerations I inevitably leave out. The invisible question that should surround my study is whether, as Ashbery says, this leaving out is in fact another, and truer, way.

1. Origins of the Prose Poem and Theories of Genre

> Who among us, in his ambitious days, hasn't dreamed of the miracle of a poetic prose? —Baudelaire, dedicatory letter to Arsène Houssaye

Prose poetry may be a relatively recent literary phenomenon, but the idea of poetry in prose is not new.[1] The term "poème en prose" dates from at least the beginning of the eighteenth century, where it gained currency in a debate over the genre of Fénelon's *Télémaque* (1699).[2] Near the end of the first part of *Don Quixote* (1605), Cervantes has the canon remark to the curate, "the epic may be written in prose as well as verse."[3] The conversation between the curate and the canon is itself an allusion to and commentary on another debate—the Tasso-Ariosto controversy of the late sixteenth century—and that debate, like the later dispute over the genre of *Télémaque*, is a variation on the theme of ancients versus moderns, a quarrel that, in one form or another, goes at least as far back as the arguments concerning the use of the vernacular in fourteenth-century Italy. More and less ambiguous references to poetry in prose appear in works pertaining to each of these literary controversies, and the possibility of the *poème en prose* is arguably implicit in even earlier critical writings, such as Longinus's *On the Sublime*, where literature is evaluated more by the impact it produces on the reader than by formal criteria. In fact (but isn't this always the case with histories of ideas?), one can trace the notion of poetry in prose to a passage or two in Aristotle if one chooses to do so.[4]

The eighteenth-century *poème en prose*—to say nothing of its more remote ancestors—is admittedly very different from the modern literary kind, but it would be a mistake to consider the prose poem's early incarnations and the first usages of the term as unrelated to what followed. The mere fact that some version of the prose poem came into being during the *querelle des anciens et des modernes* is significant: perhaps the most persistent claim of the nineteenth-century *poème en prose* is that it is a form that somehow captures, or attempts to capture, a particularly modern experience. Moreover, the term's entry into wider usage parallels the rise of that historically more successful genre, the novel—a coincidence that has had lasting effects on the prose poem. For if the eighteenth-century *poème en prose* is itself a quasi-novel (a romance or epic written in prose), the success of the nineteenth-century novel exerts pressure on poets to remodel the traditional lyric. Neither the debate surrounding the term nor the rise of the novel made the modern prose poem inevitable per se, but they did influence its character. A partial transfer of generic traits is not only the effect of labeling a new form with an old name but also its cause: the lingering connotations of the eighteenth-century phrase "poème en prose" no doubt influenced Baudelaire's decision to identify his work as such and then helped determine the term's continued usage as a literal description rather than as a figure of speech.[5]

To analyze some of the factors in the appearance and the development of the *poème en prose*, it is necessary to do more than look at strictly literary debates and practices. When one tries to take into account the effect of the larger forces of history on eighteenth-century literature, however, it is difficult to avoid falling back on criticism's own usual suspects, such as the influence of empiricism, the gradual shift to a capitalist or market-based economy, the rise of the middle class, the spread of literacy (especially among the middle and lower classes), the evolution in thought from a theocentric to a secular worldview, and other interrelated developments that one finds in studies concerning the origins of the novel or, more generally, of modernity. Some combination of these factors would seem to explain the overall turn away from poetry to prose, if only because prose came to be associated with clarity, truth, naturalness, individual freedom, and economical expression in the eighteenth century.[6] But given that the form of prose is, in its own way, as conventional as that of poetry, such an explanation must remain contingent on the reasons for the new associations. General historical developments do not in any case explain the specific arrival of the *poème en prose*, especially considering that these developments are usually supposed to account for the rise of the novel. With regard to the evolution or revolution of the nineteenth-century prose poem, Richard Terdiman's analysis of its form as symbolic (though thereby no less real) resistance to a dominant bourgeois aesthetic and ideology is probably the best one can do short of writing a multivolume history of the period.[7]

Still remaining on a general level but retreating a little from history in its more global sense, it is possible to think of the prose poem as emerging in response to a gradual change in aesthetics. Instead of using the literary-historical terms "romanticism" and "classicism," it is perhaps better to speak here of an emphasis on affect over form. When the essence of poetry is no longer believed to reside in its external features but rather in the intensity of the response it elicits in the reader, the possibility exists for something like the prose poem. By 1800 Wordsworth could boldly assert that "there neither is, nor can be, any *essential* difference between the language of prose and metrical composition."[8] This shift in aesthetics goes a long way toward explaining the evolution of the eighteenth-century *poème en prose* into its nineteenth-century namesake, for the arguments and examples adduced for the possibility of writing poetry in prose are increasingly subsumed under issues of expression during the course of the eighteenth century. The long-term shift does not, however, explain the prose poem any more than the general historical developments in the period do, or why in particular vers libre did not develop before the *poème en prose* in France (see chapters 4 and 5). Furthermore, the aesthetic explanation begs its own explanation, leading once again to more general developments—only this time as often to the arguments of *The Mirror and the Lamp* as to those of *The Rise of the Novel*.[9]

If direct attempts to place the *poème en prose* in historical perspective are of limited use in explaining its origins, it may be helpful to return to the history of the term. For its eighteenth-century opponents, "poème en prose" was at best a bad figure of speech; for those who supported the idea of poetry in prose, the term was literal and signified removing merely one of the generic features of epic, the necessity of writing in verse. Though united in cause, the proponents of the *poème en prose* were of two very different camps. On the one hand, there were those who, like the philosophes, argued for prose in the name of truth; on the other, there were those who saw the issue as primarily one of taste.[10] The former group exerted little influence on later poets, except perhaps translators, mainly because they existed only as long as the *querelle* did. One also senses that some members of this group were not so much interested in the expressive possibilities of prose as they were in doing away with poetry in any form. Those who argued in the name of taste influenced profoundly the eighteenth and early-nineteenth-century *poème en prose*. Though their own poems strike the modern reader as almost parodies of poems with their apostrophe-filled and grandiose rhetoric, their general legacy is an aesthetic of unmediated expression. This aesthetic of the natural comes to be associated more and more with the primitive in the late eighteenth century, especially when combined with the vogue for Ossian following the first French translations (1760–62).[11] One can also associate this strain of thought with a variety of late-eighteenth-century trends—nature poetry, the fragment, dream literature, night poetry—anything, in short, that some critics label "preromanticism."[12]

Toward the end of the eighteenth century the term "poème en prose" already meant something slightly different than it did at the beginning of the century. Primarily it still designated long narrative works, such as Mamin's *Télémaque*-inspired *Ulysse dans l'île d'Aeaea* (1752) and Moutonnet Claifrons's *Les Îles fortunées* (1771), but it also referred to some nonnarrative works, such as the abbé de Reyrac's *Hymne au Soleil* (1776). In fact, the usage of the term had become widespread and the form recognizable enough for some readers to regard Marmontel's *Les Incas* (1777) as a *poème en prose* in spite of the author's explicit refusal to call his work a poem in the preface.[13] The varieties of the *poème en prose* had increased even more by the nineteenth century. One turn-of-the-century *poème en prose*, Cottin's *La Prise de Jéricho, ou la pecheresse convertie* (1803), is of particular interest for the history of the term. This biblical poem in prose is an amalgam of several genres. As its first title (*The Capture of Jericho*) indicates, its subject matter is epic in the manner of Tasso's *Jerusalem Delivered*, a work that, in prose and verse translations, was extremely popular in France at the time.[14] The poem's relatively small size (four *chants* of about fifteen pages each) and biblical subject matter make it something vaguely like Milton's *Paradise Regained*, a Christian epyllion. The alternative title, *The Converted Sinner*, gives the work a simultaneously didactic and confessional character. Finally, the poem itself, as its opening lines signal to the reader, is part prayer, part hymn, and part sermon: "Blessèd be the God of Israel! If his wrath is terrible for the wicked man who is hardened in his ways, his mercy is infinite for the repentant sinner. If we humble ourselves before him, he will turn his face toward us; if we shed tears on our sins, he will wash us of them; if we ask for grace, he will obtain it for us. For all the gifts he lavishes on us he only asks for our love—and is that not another gift?"[15]

The importance of *La Prise de Jéricho* for the history of the *poème en prose* does not really lie in the way in which it exemplifies a mixture of prose and poetic genres, however. Cottin's work is by no means the first prose poem to differ in subject matter and form from *Télémaque*, nor is it the first short *poème en prose*.[16] It is also not the first prose poem to make use of biblical language. Besides possible precursor poems like La Baume Desdossats's *La Christiade*, a work of 1753, prose translations of the psalms were used as far back as the *querelle* itself as *exempla* for the possibility of the *poème en prose*. But the reception of *La Prise de Jéricho* is worth pondering, especially as evidenced in the following introductions:

> In the first volume [of *Literary Miscellanies*] one will find a small poem in prose [*un petit poëme en prose*] entitled *The Capture of Jericho*, written by Madame Cottin, author of *Claire d'Albe, Malvina*, and *Amélie Mansfield*. The general and merited success which the three novels have procured renders praise of the author superfluous here. I will dare say, however, that a reading of *The Capture of Jericho* can add something more to the opinion that one should form of her rare talent. To the merit of an interesting story and the faithful and vivid portrayal of feelings and manners, this poem unites another, something that presupposes a good deal of taste: her having imitated with truth, but without exaggeration, the ornate, symbolic style which they call "oriental" and which characterizes the writings of the Hebrew nation that have come down to us. [from J. B. Suard's introduction to *Literary Miscellanies*, 1803][17]

> In an eight-year period, Madame Cottin published five novels. *The Capture of Jericho*, which appeared in 1802 [*sic*] in the *Literary Miscellanies* of M. Suard, should be considered the first work of this renowned woman, even if we do not know precisely when it was composed. It is a little poem in prose [*un petit poëme en prose*] that distinguishes itself by its style and details, but whose composition is feebly drawn and whose principal situations lack probability. No doubt it was one of those sketches Madame Cottin made in anonymity, before her friends revealed her genius to her, and to which she gave the finishing touches later on. "To the merit," writes M. Suard, "of an interesting story and the faithful and vivid portrayal of feelings and manners, this poem unites another, something that presupposes a good deal of taste: her having imitated with truth, but without exaggeration, the ornate, symbolic style which they call 'oriental' and which characterizes the writings of the Hebrew nation that have come down to us." The fault of the author is to have introduced love into a subject matter that could not allow it, both because of the prescribed length of the action and because of the position and the nature of the characters. [from an unsigned introduction to volume 1 of Cottin's works, 1824][18]

The phrase "un petit poëme en prose" stands out here even without my variant translations of it. In Suard's usage, the phrase is essentially descriptive: *La Prise de Jéricho* is a short epic in prose. The usage in the second passage is more ambiguous, however, perhaps because the anonymous writer's opinion of Cottin's work is not as high as that of Suard, whose praise is quoted as a preamble to criticism. Even supposing the anonymous writer does not intend any irony—the writer may be merely quoting Suard's description without indicating as much, after all—it is hard not to read condescension in the tone. In the writer's "Historical notice on the life and writings of Madame Cottin, followed by considerations on some *women authors*" (my emphasis), *La Prise de Jéricho* is not even among the better works. It is supposed to be an early composition in spite of the fact that the writer does not really know when it was composed, and it is faulted for breaches of *vraisemblance* and *bienséance*, curiously neoclassical criticisms that cannot apply directly to her novels.

For a mid–nineteenth-century reader like Baudelaire, it would probably be even more difficult not to read "petit poëme en prose" ironically. While there are about a dozen works in this period that literary historians have described as *poèmes en prose* (or precursors of prose poems), very few of them were given the label by their authors or readers, a fact that suggests the term was becoming archaic or no longer referred to a clearly defined genre, assuming it ever did. Sainte-Beuve labeled Bertrand's pieces in *Gaspard de la nuit* (1842) "ballades en prose"; Bertrand himself called them "fantaisies" or "un nouveau genre de prose."[19] Even the handful of works dubbed *poèmes en prose* by their authors are, like Aurevilly's *Amaïdée* (written around 1834, published in 1897) and Quinet's *Merlin l'enchanteur* (1860), published relatively late (that is, *after* Baudelaire's first prose poems) or, like De Cailleux's *Le Monde antédiluvien: Poème biblique en prose* (1845), far more obscure than their eighteenth-century namesakes.[20] Anyone in this period who was aware of the eighteenth-century sense of "poème en prose" and applied the label to a more recent work could not do so without at least considering its ironic potential and, if unaware or unconcerned with this sense of the phrase, would certainly risk an ironic reading with the addition of an adjective like "petit." Given that Cottin's works were best-sellers in the early nineteenth century, it is even possible that Baudelaire read one of the introductions quoted previously and was framing his own work as less ambitious—just some little poems— by labeling them "petits poëmes en prose."[21] For the poet who spent an enormous amount of effort correcting the punctuation and the typeface on the dedicatory page of *Les Fleurs du mal*, it would be enough to use a *tréma* instead of an *accent grave* over the first "e" of "poëme" to evoke the sense of an older or archaic form and then a "little" adjective to distance his own works from it.[22]

In short, the history of the term shows that "poème en prose" can simultaneously carry connotations of a modern and an archaic form for mid-nineteenth-century authors and readers. Because of the prose poem's relative lack of success in the early nineteenth century, it probably maintained somewhat of an experimental status.[23] It was at the very least an attractive possibility in an increasingly romantic age and a more feasible option than, say, free verse, if only because a century's worth of prose translations of poems would have prepared the French ear for it. It is difficult to gather precise statistics on the number of prose translations of poems in this period or even to say with certainty when poetry was first translated into prose—depending on what one means by "poetry" and "prose," one can go at least as far back as the twelfth century.[24] Nevertheless, a few general trends are clear. The fact that Dacier defended her prose translations of Anacreon and Sappho (1681) and the *Iliad* (1711) in her prefaces suggests something of the novelty of her method, and the philosophical and aesthetic values of the eighteenth century no doubt fostered an atmosphere conducive to prose translations in the name of clarity and truth.[25] By the time of the first Ossian translations in the 1760s, prose translation could even be called the vogue: not only were the first French translations of Macpherson's prose (those of Turgot, Huber, and Diderot) themselves in prose, but prose translations of the classics and more modern writers like Tasso, Ariosto, Milton, Pope, Thompson, Young, and Gray were common if not the norm.[26] Furthermore, what Suzanne Bernard calls "pseudo-translations"—prose works, like Parny's *Chansons madécasses* (1787), that frame themselves as translations of ancient or exotic, often fragmentary poems—abound in this period. By the nineteenth century, thanks to writers like Chateaubriand, the notion of "poetic prose" was widespread.[27]

Even given all of these literary and historical developments of the eighteenth and nineteenth centuries, the modern *poème en prose* would not be what it is without the particular directions that Baudelaire and later writers gave to it and which need to be examined individually. Baudelaire's reputation as a lyric poet played an important role in the subsequent perception of the originality of the *Petits Poëmes en prose*, especially the claim that he, or he and Bertrand, created the genre of prose poetry. (Baudelaire's antiromanticism and urban poetry continue to mark him as the first modern poet, and the desire to view the *Petits Poëmes en prose* as, in Barbara Johnson's phrase, the "second Baudelairean revolution" after *Les Fleurs du mal* has proved difficult to resist.) Two facts are indisputable: "poème en prose" takes on its modern sense after Baudelaire's usage, and with the relative stability of the term, it becomes easier to view prose poetry as a genre. Because of the contingency involved in the prose poem's development, it is again worth stressing that historical background may help explain the possibility of poetry in prose but does not determine the specific form of the *poème en prose*. If, as several critics have argued, the prose poem emerges at a particular historical moment because of its dialogic character, its open-endedness, and its inner freedom of form, it is hardly alone. Gerhard Hass has made similar remarks concerning the essay, and critics at least as far back as Bakhtin have claimed the same of the novel.[28]

Baudelaire's usage of "poème en prose" arguably marks the moment when, in Marxist terminology, the term enters the language as a "simple abstraction." As Michael McKeon explains in his study on the origins of the English novel, a simple abstraction is anything but simple. It is rather "a conceptualization whose experiential referent has a prehistory that is rich enough both to permit, and to require, the abstraction and the dominance of the general category itself."[29] In other words, a simple abstraction is a cover term for a category of historically associated, though potentially very different, phenomena, whose consistent usage "marks not the tentative inception, but the active dominance, of the category."[30] McKeon is, of course, interested more specifically in the emergence of "the novel" as an abstraction:

> The origins of the English novel occur at the end point of a long history of "novelistic usage"—at the moment when this usage has become sufficiently complex to permit a generalizing "indifference" to the specificity of usages and an abstraction of the category whose integrity is presupposed by that indifference. . . . To begin at the beginning therefore requires that we begin at the end. By the middle of the eighteenth century, the stabilizing of terminology—the increasing acceptance of "the novel" as a canonic term, so that contemporaries can "speak of it as such"—signals the stability of the conceptual category and of the class of literary products that it encloses.[31]

The origins of the *poème en prose* also occur at the end point of a long history of its usage. The stabilizing of the term, in its modern sense, occurs in the generation following Baudelaire. It is this relative stability of the category "poème en prose" that allows one to trace retrospectively the history of the form. In some ways a simple abstraction actually calls its history into being and determines some of the essential traits of its referent—such as whether the referent is to be thought of as a literary kind. Various questions inevitably arise. Is such a history a valid framework within which one can make sense of the abstraction? Which sorts of related kinds does the abstraction tend to exclude from its history? How do later manifestations of the kind reevaluate what is at stake in the abstraction and consequently rewrite its past? To answer these sorts of questions, it is necessary to turn to genre theory.[32]

• • •

Genre is often thought of as a formal category. Aristotelian definitions, Renaissance hierarchies of genres, and Northrop Frye's anatomies all contribute to this perception. Even attempts to link genre to history and culture, such as Fredric Jameson's *The Political Unconscious* (1981), tend to view literary kinds as fixed or would-be fixed entities (literary institutions and social contracts that "specify the proper use of a particular cultural artifact") insofar as they bypass literary history in their descriptions of what constitutes genre.[33] It may seem only natural that considerations of form have dominated discussions of genre, since the formal features of a work help signal genre and influence how we read. Yet the dangers of a strictly formal approach are also apparent, especially from a comparatist's perspective. Can Ashbery's *Three Poems* and Baudelaire's *Petits Poëmes en prose* be fruitfully compared or included under the same generic rubric merely because they are both collections of poems written in prose? There are probably many other texts, literary and otherwise, that show a closer family resemblance to either of these works. As a formal distinction, genre is an easy target for the theorist and an even easier target for the literary historian. And yet it also demands that form be taken into account somehow.

Prose poetry, like any other literary kind, has to be understood as constituting itself against or in relation to other kinds. This constitution not only implies a relationship to a prior "kind," poetry in general, but also hints at its own historical and cultural situation. Prose poetry must arise in a milieu in which prose and poetry exist in some sort of opposition. Furthermore, the continued existence of prose poetry as a literary kind would be predicated on such an opposition, though perhaps a modified or even very different version of the original one. Prose poetry has both formal and historical dimensions, neither of which alone describes the abstraction. Instead, they point to tensions in the term and its instability as a category.

It is here that genre theory can be of some use, especially when it concerns itself with interpretation more than classification. Though a large body of genre criticism exists, I will base my discussion primarily on Alastair Fowler's *Kinds of Literature: An Introduction to the Theory of Genres and Modes* and a few works that have appeared since its publication in 1982. My choice is dictated by more than matters of convenience: *Kinds of Literature* is one of those rare books that superannuates most of what preceded it. My discussion does not require the reader to agree with my assessment of Fowler's book, if only because I place his arguments and terms within an independent critical framework and do not assume their authority, but even an unsympathetic reader of Fowler would probably agree that his book corrects, synthesizes, and extends previous arguments in a thorough and lucid fashion.[34] Furthermore, my own thoughts on genre diverge from Fowler's on several important issues, though the fundamental premise of my approach is also his: genre is much more an interpretive framework than a category of classification.

As *Kinds of Literature* makes clear, this premise has far-reaching consequences:

> [G]enres have to do with identifying and communicating rather than with defining and classifying. We identify genre to interpret the exemplar.
>
> In literary communication, genres are functional: they actively form the experience of each work of literature. If we see *The Jew of Malta* as a savage farce, our response will not be the same as if we saw it as a tragedy. When we try to decide the genre of a work, then, our aim is to discover its meaning. Generic statements are instrumentally critical. . . . And when we investigate previous states of the type, it is to clarify meaningful departures that the work itself makes. It follows that genre theory, too, is properly concerned, in the main, with interpretation. It deals with principles of reconstruction and interpretation and (to some extent) evaluation of meaning. It does not deal much with classification.[35]

Genre functions in literature the way grammar functions in language: it is a set of interpretive guidelines that an act of communication presupposes rather than a schema imposed afterward onto a set of utterances in order to give them some coherence.[36] From this perspective, genre can be and often is a largely unconscious consideration. Even in a period like our own, where many readers associate genres with prescription and arbitrary rules, it is not possible to dispense with the notion of literary kinds. Novels, for example, "are quite commonly censured for defects of probability: a criticism that certainly implies normative ideas of genre. It is a rule of their genre that novels of a certain kind (but not other kinds) must maintain naturalistic probability."[37] One need only apply this observation to film reviews to get an idea of just how prevalent unacknowledged prescriptivism is today. More important, such a remark suggests how much interpretation and aesthetic evaluation rely on a familiarity with literary kinds.

Given that genre has more to do with interpretation than with classification, exclusively formal definitions of genre are especially suspect. The primary concern here is lack of explanatory power rather than lexical precision. One can imagine a sufficiently general definition of a genre that would include most of, if not all, the works of a kind, but such a definition would necessarily describe little more than the obvious, external features of that kind. More crucially, any new work that departed even the slightest from the requirements for this genre would raise serious doubts about the applicability of the definition. As Fowler puts it, "[T]heorists bent on defining have to elevate them [genres] to a level of very high abstraction, far removed from actual literature. We can arrive at permanent entities in that way, so long as we keep our descriptions vague. Then the genres remain in every age uniformly stable, equally tenuous, predictably inactive, like inert gases."[38] Another way of expressing this idea is to argue that any algorithmic definition, that is to say any definition based on abstracting the common qualities from a given set of examples, is unlikely to have much explanatory power.[39] It is not as if normative notions of kinds have no place in genre theory; rather, they enter into consideration indirectly. Insofar as such notions are operative in the historical and cultural milieu of an author or a reader, they are important generic signals. But genre criticism is, in general, more a reconstruction than a construction of a communicative code. In this respect it resembles reception theory more than structuralism.[40]

In the absence of timeless categories, what holds different works of a genre together and allows for meaningful comparison? Following several other critics, Fowler introduces the Wittgensteinian notion of family resemblance to cope with this problem: "Literary genre seems just the sort of concept with blurred edges that is suited to such an approach. Representatives of a genre may then be regarded as making up a family whose septs and individual members are related in various ways, without necessarily having any single feature shared in common by all."[41] The notion of family resemblance is in many respects compelling, but it needs some refining before it can be of use in interpretation. It is, in a sense, "a mere preliminary to definition": we should look for underlying causes for these resemblances, the literary equivalent of the biology behind shared traits.[42] We should also resist viewing literary kinds as existing only in direct lines of descent. Distant relations, atavisms, and polygenetic roots have to be allowed for.[43]

It is here, after Fowler's many qualifications, that the analogy starts to show signs of strain. The boundaries of genre, blurry as they are, exist only in relation to other kinds. Thus epic, considered in relation to romance, is perhaps very different from epic considered in relation to lyric. It is often difficult to say which other kinds are relevant to the makeup of a given genre. The status of a genre changes in time and according to cultural situation, within a single work even. The only way to arrive at a theory of genre oriented toward interpretation is to determine the operative contexts of a given literary kind. The notion of family resemblance emphasizes similarities and suggests that genre can be defined according to traits, even if no single trait or grouping of traits is necessary or sufficient for such a definition. My approach stresses difference and focuses on those generic traits that help determine this difference.

The basic insight of Fowler's theory of genre is the interplay of historical (diachronic) and ahistorical (synchronic) dimensions of literary kinds. Though by no means the first book to introduce this notion into genre study, *Kinds of Literature* may represent the first systematic treatment of genre that assigns it such a central role and explores in depth its practical and theoretical implications. Good criticism has arguably always taken diachronic and synchronic dimensions of genre into consideration implicitly, but most genre theory has unfortunately tended either toward speculation about permanent kinds or toward a "plodding chronicle history of individual genres that continually transform themselves without ever waiting long enough for generalization."[44] In general Fowler tries to position himself between the extremes of classificatory abstraction, especially as it relates to structuralism, and source hunting. From a theoretical perspective, this "polarity is the irreducible one of synchronicity versus diachronicity," but "good criticism will avoid or combine these opposites. It is a matter of tact in deciding where a historical accommodation is required, or when the broad generic outline may be treated as unchanged." I share the theoretical underpinning as well as the pragmatic impulse behind these words, but I would add that the sort of critical tact he speaks of is sometimes needed at the level of the individual work, perhaps even at the level of "unit of meaning" or affect. In its most general sense, genre criticism is concerned with the tension between interpretive framework and moment of reading. Equating literary kind with interpretive framework may seem to expand the concept of genre too much beyond our customary sense, and I will say more about this expansion of meaning later. For now it is enough to note that I am arguing for a dynamic relation between reading and interpretative frame.

For both theoretical and practical reasons, *Kinds of Literature* makes some important distinctions between "kind," "mode," and "subgenre":

> The terms for kind, perhaps in keeping with their obvious external em-bodiment, can always be put in noun form ("epigram"; "epic"), whereas modal terms tend to be adjectival. But the adjectival use of generic terms is a little complicated. Consider the expressions "comedy," "comic play," "comic." "Comic play" is nearly equivalent to "comedy." But "comic" is applied to kinds other than comedy, as when *Emma* is called a "comic novel." Thus we mean that *Emma* is by kind a novel, by mode comic. . . . The terms for modes are obviously applied more widely. And at first it seems that they must therefore be vague. However, they can be used exactly enough so long as the limits of their repertorial implication are kept in mind. In particular, modal terms never imply a complete external form. Modes have always an incomplete repertoire, a selection only of the corresponding kind's features, and one from which overall external structure is absent. Thus, to call Sidney's *Arcadia* pastoral conveys no information about its external form. . . . Similarly, a modal term implies nothing about size, so that there is no oddity in speaking of sonnets of Tasso's as heroic. In short, when a modal term is linked with the name of a kind, it refers to a combined genre, in which the overall form is determined by the kind alone.[45]

Modes, then, relate metonymically to kinds. Over time, of course, a mode's relation to its corresponding kind may become more remote, even change radically. Subgenres, however, are divisions of kinds "formed in just the opposite way from that which produces modes: subgenres have the common features of the kind—external forms and all—and, over and above these, add special substantive features."[46] From this point of view, a "piscatory or sea eclogue is just as much an eclogue as a pastoral one." Similarly, the Elizabethan love sonnet, "itself a subgenre, might easily be divided into secondary subgenres, and even tertiary ones." How far one subdivides would seem to be another matter of critical tact.[47]

The notions of kind, mode, and subgenre are intuitively clear and helpful for literary analysis. At least they prove to be so in Fowler's hands. Nevertheless, they need some refining in both a theoretical and a practical sense. As I have been arguing, kinds do not exist in and of themselves but in relation to other kinds.[48] Modes—and Fowler points this out emphatically—are also not discrete entities.[49] More important, the relationship between mode and kind is not necessarily one of part to whole or even subsequent to prior. If genres are negatively defined, the notion of a literary kind is an open-ended, partial one—partial, that is, to the mind's projection of a more fully defined notion. A literary kind therefore relates metonymically to a more complete version of itself. In short, a kind is much like a mode in this regard, and mode and kind are both interpretive frameworks in their most general formulations. What is more, it is arguably via mode rather than kind that the negative defining process of genre proceeds. Consider the example "epic as opposed to lyric." It would be possible to tally the similarities and differences between their respective generic repertoires and come to some conclusions about the nature of both. But differentiation, even if largely unconscious, does not proceed via an identification of anything resembling a full range of generic features. A reader identifies a handful of the more operative traits first, such as "long poem versus short poem" and "public voice versus private voice," then subsequently refines his or her views or perhaps revises them considerably after further reading or reflection. At any given moment our sense of a kind is therefore modal. Only in a restricted sense is mode antecedent to genre, since as soon as one tries to think of mode and genre in terms of ontological priority their meanings become considerably blurred. Genre and mode depend on each other like the chicken and the egg. It is better to say that a given genre presupposes a certain mode or modes and that a given mode has at least one corresponding genre. A genre then is an interpretive framework one projects based on modal knowledge, and a mode is a framework projected from generic knowledge.

•   •   •

A brief consideration of some genre criticism published since *Kinds of Literature* will help place my approach in perspective. As Adena Rosmarin points out in *The Power of Genre* (1985), twentieth-century genre criticism often finds itself caught between deductive (prescriptive) and inductive (descriptive) theories. With a few exceptions, like Northrop Frye, critics have avoided prescriptive theories, but prescription may have become unacknowledged, and the descriptive approach is not without its challenges. If one is merely describing or labeling types, how can genre have any explanatory power? Rosmarin suggests a pragmatic solution: we approach groups of texts "as if" they were a class.[50] We often, perhaps always, make mistakes in our groupings, but the process of grouping is itself inevitable. Above all, critics should acknowledge that readers always participate in both inductive and deductive approaches and are in this sense always erring.[51] (Rosmarin's approach thus represents a pragmatic response to deconstruction or a deconstructive perspective informed by pragmatism.) The problem can be restated in terms of the hermeneutic circle paradox: to understand the parts of a work we need to understand the whole, but to understand the whole we need to understand the parts.[52] This interpretive circle is not closed because we project or suppose some concept of the whole to make sense of the parts (or the reverse), then correct and refine our notions as we proceed. For Rosmarin, the "stopping place" of the critic's "schematic correction" will "vary from text to text, depending on its interpretive history and audience." The critic's aim is rhetorical: to persuade readers "that the posited genre is more 'like' the text than genres used to carry on previous discussions of the same text."[53]

My approach has several affinities to Rosmarin's: a strong pragmatic impulse, a belief that interpretation is inevitable rather than inevitably impossible, a view that comes close to equating genre with a general notion of interpretive framework, an investment in certain rhetorical aims of criticism, a reading process in which text and framework inform each other, and even a version of what she calls "as if" logic (my consideration of prose poetry "as if it were a genre"). But I do not share Rosmarin's view that the reason behind the genre critic's "pattern of reasoning" is "purely pragmatic," that is, "justified wholly insofar as it helps us make better or more convincing critical arguments, those that acknowledge their premises and whose reasoning is consistent with those premises."[54] Pragmatic considerations may help justify a given approach and acknowledging one's theoretical premises is often useful, but no considerations are purely pragmatic; it is conceivable, perhaps inevitable, that even the best theories do not acknowledge all of their premises. The reader's point of entry into and stopping place within the hermeneutic circle especially rely on considerations that go beyond the pragmatic or can only be called pragmatic by stretching the meaning of the term beyond its breaking point. Rosmarin herself allows for "interpretive history and audience," conditions that cannot be purely pragmatic because they are informed by historical developments. Linguistic and literary-historical considerations—to say nothing of aesthetic and other concerns—help shape our views of genre.

As I argue in my conclusion, such considerations also prevent genre from collapsing entirely into some general notion of interpretive framework.

Ralph Cohen's "History and Genre" (1986) presents an approach to genre very close to my own. Cohen, like Fowler, argues for a "regeneration" of genre theory in contemporary criticism. Cohen is especially intent on answering three common attacks against genre: "The claim that generic classes are indecipherable or indeterminate. . . . The claim that members of a genre share a common element or elements in consequence of which genre is an essentialist study. . . . The claim that genre cannot be a guide to interpretation."[55]

The first objection Cohen breaks into two charges of indecipherability and indeterminacy, as represented by some arguments of Foucault and Derrida: "Foucault states the general objection that dividing genre into groups like literature or philosophy is not useful since users of such distinctions no longer agree on how to take them. . . . Derrida argues, characteristically, for the need and futility of genre designation. He points out that any generic classification system is untenable because individual texts although participating in it cannot belong to it."[56] These charges are consistent on their own terms but lack perspective. True, genres do not seem to hold still long enough to allow for clear distinctions, and a text's "supplementary" trait of belonging to a genre arguably "does not properly pertain to any genre or class," as Derrida remarks.[57] Because difference inevitably reasserts itself when we designate different texts with one generic label, any individual text, Cohen notes, "will support the paradox of belonging and not belonging." But the charges of indecipherability and indeterminacy do not hold if one considers genres as processes rather than classifications based on fixed traits. The genre critic is interested in "the historical inquiry of the types of 'participation' involved in specific works."[58] Far from being a liability, the transformation or instability of literary kinds is an important area of study in genre criticism.

Cohen's approach comes closest to mine when he responds to the charge that genre theory is necessarily based on essentialist assumptions because members of a genre share a common element or elements. Cohen argues for a differential notion of literary kinds: "Genres do not exist by themselves; they are named and placed within hierarchies or systems of genres, and each is defined by reference to the system and its members. A genre, therefore, is to be understood in relation to other genres, so that its aims and purposes at a particular time are defined by its interrelation with and differentiation of others. . . . Only if one dehistoricizes genre does the notion of classification with one or more traits shared by each member become a problem. . . ."[59]

My approach places negative differentiation at the heart of genre theory. Cohen's argument is fundamentally the same, though he does not stress to the same degree the "negative" process of differentiation and thus might not share my view on "operative generic traits" and the reader's partial or "modal" sense of genre.[60] It is also difficult to determine the degree to which pragmatism informs Cohen's thinking. When summarizing his argument about genres, he writes, "Classifications are empirical, not logical. They are historical assumptions constructed by authors, audiences, and critics to serve communicative and aesthetic purposes. . . . Genres are open systems; they are groupings of texts by critics to fulfill certain ends."[61] Given the tenor of his argument and his use of literary history in the examples he cites, Cohen would probably not make the purely pragmatic claims of Rosmarin. After all, he emphasizes that genres are constructed to serve social and aesthetic functions and speaks of empirical classifications as though such groupings were more than a matter of critical convenience. Still, he leaves somewhat open the basis on which classes of texts are constructed and considers genres as "groupings of texts by critics to fulfill certain ends." Are such groupings ultimately ad hoc? In my view, literary, linguistic, and reception history play important roles in determining genres. The critic is not entirely free to make and unmake groupings.

Cohen breaks down the attack on genre as an interpretive guide into two charges: "a class generalization cannot help to interpret a specific member of the class" and "a specific text is indeterminate; thus no determinate statements are useful in its interpretation."[62] Cohen counters these charges by drawing on works by Elizabeth Bruss, Heather Dubrow, Hans Robert Jauss, and Gary Saul Morson, which argue that classes of texts provide expectations or conventions for interpretation and therefore "can help interpret any particular instance of that class."[63] Cohen's defense rests again on a process theory of genre, which does not require that texts or genres be determinate. He stresses that we cannot interpret texts without interpreting genre, arguing that even if "every text is self-contradictory" we would "still have to grant that types of contradiction exist and that such types . . . presuppose generic groupings."[64] Cohen thus comes close to equating genre with a general notion of interpretative framework, though in his reply to Dominick LaCapra's "Comment" on "History and Genre" he states that he conceives of genre "as a classification system and as a discursive institution."[65] Genre can have more than one function, of course, even within an approach emphasizing interpretation over classification.

David Fishelov's *Metaphors of Genre* (1993) presents a compelling case against the "neopragmatic" or "pragmatic-relativistic" view of literary kinds and reexamines the role genre plays in interpretation. Fishelov maintains that our understanding of genre works through analogy, and he identifies four of the most common and fruitful metaphors: the biological analogy, the family analogy, the institutional analogy, and the speech-act analogy. In this view, analogies are not ornamental; they constitute the core of our understanding. No single analogy defines genre, and there are advantages and disadvantages to each: the biological analogy is useful for questions of generic evolution and interrelationship, arguments based on family resemblance may offer an alternative to seeing genres as either prescriptive or descriptive, and the social-institution and speech-act analogies seem especially suited for dramatic and lyric genres, respectively. Fishelov's argument may thus appear to be pragmatic, but he in fact argues against such an approach insofar as it suggests "a picture of the critic, settled in his ivory tower, preoccupied in grouping and regrouping literary texts to achieve interesting . . . interpretations." The pragmatic approach is a useful corrective to essentialist views of literary kinds, but genre theory should not "overestimate the critic's role in 'constituting' genres" or underestimate the "historical evidence."[66]

Fishelov also warns against "assigning too great an interpretive weight to generic concepts," citing Fowler as a critic who has gone too far in that direction: "Although I believe that genres play an important role as orienting devices in literary history and communication, I think that Fowler loads a far greater burden onto genre than it can sustain. Genre as 'signal system,' producing and ensuring correct interpretations, is an unrealistic picture of how generic conventions function. We may approach a text with some assumptions about the generic tradition on which it relies, but there is always a *dialectical relationship* between these assumptions and expectations and what the text itself tells us."[67] Fishelov's point is well taken, though by drawing on arguments from Fowler's early article "The Life and Death of Literary Forms" (1971) instead of their reworked versions in *Kinds of Literature* he obscures the degree to which he agrees with Fowler.[68] The real question here regards the sense in which genre is an interpretive framework. I have been employing the term "interpretive framework" to stress that genres help us read individual texts. To say that literary kinds are an aid to interpretation or even that they are at some level necessary for interpretation is not the same as saying that they constitute the code regulating every aspect of interpretation. Fishelov's point still needs to be addressed, however, if only because of the degree to which I associate genre with interpretation and the degree to which I argue that genre, conceived in its most general sense, almost merges into the notion of interpretive framework. It may be that, in pursuing the logic that genre is primarily an interpretive framework, one tends to see genre increasingly in terms of a general hermeneutic process. This process may in fact help explain why the desire for generic definitions does not go away so easily: we do not stop searching for some holistic perspective in which we can better understand the parts. But whether my approach assigns too great an interpretive weight to generic concepts cannot really be decided in the abstract given the subjectivity of phrases like "too great" and "primarily an interpretive framework." To gain more perspective on this question, we will have to explore a specific case, prose poetry as a genre.

Though wary of arguing that genre is any one thing, Fishelov offers a preliminary definition: "I define genre as *a combination of prototypical, representative members, and a flexible set of constitutive rules that apply to some levels of literary texts, to some individual writers, usually to more than one literary period, and to more than one language and culture.*"[69] Though helpful and flexible, this definition is filled with enough qualifications to drain it of much of its explanatory power. In fairness to Fishelov, it is a working definition: it highlights some important elements of genre, in particular the idea of "prototypical, representative members." Here Fishelov draws on Thomas Kuhn's notion of paradigm as clarified by Margaret Masterman's analysis of *The Structure of Scientific Revolutions*; later on Fishelov mentions Roman Jakobson's idea of "the dominant."[70] (The term "prototype" or "prototypical" thus seems chosen to invoke but not require absolute theoretical commitment to Kuhn and Jakobson.) Without question prototypical or paradigmatic members have been historically important to certain genres (Homer's *Iliad* and *Odyssey* to epic, for example), but such a notion potentially commits the critic to essentialist or prescriptive literary kinds. Fishelov's disagreement with the pragmatist-relativistic view, for example, prompts him to adapt some ideas of Morris Weitz and Robert Elliot in the context of minimal conditions for genre. At first Fishelov seems to offer conditions for genre so minimal they approach tautology, as when Abel Chevalley defines the novel as "a fiction in prose of a certain extent."[71] But these conditions, Fishelov goes on to say, "cannot be dismissed as mere truisms, because they do have some informational value." In this way he narrowly avoids falling back on pragmatism.[72] Then, in order to avoid the opposite extreme, prescriptivism, Fishelov advocates Weitz's defense of "open concepts," where "different models of definition . . . not based on a closed set of necessary and sufficient conditions . . . nevertheless show different degrees of 'openness.' "[73] This last position arguably makes Fishelov something of a pragmatist in spite of himself.

In spite of itself or not, every genre theory, perhaps even hard-line pre-scriptivism, may be ultimately pragmatic. In order to assert that the groupings of texts called literary kinds are not purely or merely pragmatic, my approach emphasizes the roles literary, linguistic, and reception history play in the formation of genres. We can't just ignore words like "elegy" and "novel," pretend that traditions of writing and reading don't exist, or overlook the ways in which texts are packaged by editions, libraries, bookstores, course syllabi. But my approach inevitably begs questions about decisions made in every genre study. All genre studies require selection, and the principles upon which the selections are based, however historically and theoretically informed, cannot entirely be contained within the theory they help constitute. This lesson of deconstruction gets played out in a fairly immediate way in genre criticism, especially when the genre in question does not have a well-defined body of texts. Perhaps it is not accurate to call such decision-making pragmatic—critics of different persuasions might call it aesthetic or ideological, for example—but my point should be clear. In the end, the act of criticism is a rhetorical act. Groupings of texts are ultimately open-ended in a way Fishelov wants to avoid and critics like Derrida, Foucault, Jameson, and the latest writer of the "genre" entry in *The New Princeton Encyclopedia of Poetry and Poetics* believe discredits genre theory.[74] But open-ended groupings need not be a source of anxiety, and they do not point to theoretical bankruptcy: they underscore the need for a genre criticism based in literary history. They also urge us to question received histories of genre, to consider, for example, how our sense of prose poetry would change if its history did not have Baudelaire at its center or how our interpretation and evaluation of *Tender Buttons* would shift if we grouped it with works that are not generally considered prose poems. If I have made my case for genre, the reader will believe it is important to take generic considerations into account regardless of whether literary kinds are ultimately empirical or makeshift frameworks for interpretation.[75]

        •   •   •

Before exploring some of the practical implications of my approach to genre, I want to reexamine the term "prose poetry" in the light of the issues I have raised. Is prose poetry a genre, subgenre, or hodgepodge of mode and kind? It is difficult to say, a fact that itself suggests that there may be something missing from Fowler's account. Prose poetry (or a variant thereof) is mentioned in *Kinds of Literature*, once as a counterexample to a metrical definition of poetry and once as an example of a "short kind" in a discussion of how a work's size helps to determine its genre.[76] Fowler is not concluding it is a genre, however. Prose poetry seems to fit the definition of subgenre fairly well (it describes poems in prose, as the French expression makes clear), though it does not have all of what Fowler describes as "the common features of the kind—external forms and all."[77] It is perhaps possible to describe prose poetry as "prose in mode, lyric in kind," but surely such a description distorts Fowler's sense of mode.

There are several ways out of this dilemma. One is to evoke the notion of generic mixture or hybrid kinds. Fowler has an illuminating discussion of tragicomedy in these terms.[78] But in an analogous treatment of prose poetry, it would be difficult to maintain that prose is a genre. It is rather something more like what Jeffrey Kittay and Wlad Godzich term a "signifying practice," a formal trait shared by many genres.[79] Another way to approach the situation is from a literary-historical perspective, by evoking a version of the oxymoron argument. In the mid–nineteenth century "poème en prose" was a deliberate misnomer, a calling into question of generic categories, like Duchamps's urinal, which nevertheless does not transcend genre. Prose poetry may, in other words, approach the status of a literary kind in a particular time and place but then be absorbed into another genre at another time or in another cultural milieu.[80]

Another way of approaching the situation is to revisit the Derridean *supplement*, the extra or exceptional element in a set that reveals a more fundamental rule than the one it was supposed to prove. (This logic, of course, has always already been applied by Derrida in "The Law of Genre" in order to call into question the use of genre.) From this perspective, a genre does not simply gain a new member when a new work comes along: the very notion of what constitutes the genre is modified in the process. For purposes of reading, it would still be necessary to attempt to recover some notion of the original genre; interpretation is never a matter of complete disregard for older connotations of a generic label in favor of what it may now signify. In spite or perhaps because of the logic of the supplement then, it is important to note the similarities between reception history and genre criticism. A kind signifies in part what it has signified in the past modified through its present meaning. A theory of genre based on supplementarity is misleading to the extent that it implies a linear sequence of works that feed into a larger set that one calls the literary kind, independent of other layers of mediation.[81] As Fowler remarks, "No responsible critic feels free to play the trivial game of attaching interpretations at will, regardless of the original meaning."[82] Yet at the same time, "[i]t is right to bring one's own preoccupations to works of antiquity. In any case, part of the experience of an old work is precisely a sense of its distance, its alterity. For in interpretation—as distinct from construction—we do not suspend our sense of the present, but call up all the awareness we can muster of our own place in history."[83] The line between interpretation and construction may be more blurred than Fowler suggests, but his general point is important: no matter how lacking in historical perspective, the preoccupations we bring to a text need not be thought of as unfortunate biases, especially since they are never in any real sense our only concerns.

To the extent that supplementary logic itself leads the reader toward historical considerations, it works against some of Fowler's arguments, in particular the notion of subgenre. The subgenre's addition of "special substantive features" to a kind "over and above" such things as external form implies not so much a continuation of the kind under a new form but rather a realignment of generic identity, arguably even the creation of a new genre. Consider Fowler's example of piscatory eclogue. From some literary-historical perspectives—our own, for example—it does indeed appear to be a subgenre of eclogue. When Sannazaro wrote the first piscatory eclogues, however, many of his contemporaries refused to call them eclogues at all, not only on the basis of subject matter but also because they introduced work, a feature of georgic, into the *otium* of the pastoral world. Thus, although it is possible to make meaningful use of a term like subgenre, I prefer to stress that the notions of interpretive framework and negative differentiation are the fundamental principles involved in genre theory. Mode and kind are much more helpful abstractions than subgenre in this regard.

In the end, though, it is best to return to the important ways in which my approach resembles Fowler's. It would be incorrect to regard Fowler as anything but aware of the role played by historical perspective in establishing literary kinds:

> Whether or not it is meant to be innovative, the assembled form [of a kind] is apprehended as a new genre only from a subsequent perspective. This retrospective critical insight regroups individual works, and sees them now as belonging to the new genre, now anticipating

it, now differing in kind. In the eighteenth century, novels might be grouped with romances, or be seen as forming a new kind conceived in contradistinction to the romance. The Dedication to *The History of Pompey the Little* (1751) can still speak of Marivaux and Fielding as having brought "romance-writing" to perfection. It is only our point of view that Fielding's novels represent the infancy rather than the perfection of their kind. This introduces a concept of the first importance for understanding literary development. The earliest phase of every kind is the late phase of another, viewed from a different historical standpoint. Naturally we find it difficult to imagine any other groupings but our own. Nevertheless, it is fundamental to the appreciation of genre to grasp this principle of continuous movement of regrouping.[84]

Fowler's approach and my own both emphasize the need to construct, or reconstruct, more than one generic possibility. Historical considerations prevent us from making arbitrary divisions of literature into different genres, even as they allow for a certain amount of imaginative free play. What all of this means in practical terms for a reading of, say, the prose poems of Baudelaire is that it is necessary to approach the poetry from several critical directions at once or, rather, in succession. The desire to interpret prose poems leads us inevitably to the more abstract concerns of genre, literary history, and history in general but then, just as inevitably, brings us back to individual prose poems. Nor are the ways in which a genre constitutes itself *after* a work irrelevant. This last consideration raises an important issue that Fowler does not develop extensively: the role generic paradigms and reception history play in the formation of literary kinds.[85] Often a single work, because of its influence on later works, functions as a defining paradigm for a genre. A lack of such a paradigm in prose poetry—especially in the American tradition—may help account for its ambiguous generic status.

Whatever its intrinsic interest, genre theory ought to provide a foundation for the interpretation of literature. From this perspective, further theoretical discussion needs to be postponed until after a look at the history of a particular kind. The next three chapters examine the *poème en prose* and its neighboring genres from the period preceding Baudelaire to the late nineteenth century. An exhaustive literary-historical account is no more the ultimate aim of the following chapters than a comprehensive theory of genre is here. My analysis in fact alternates between aerial views of the landscapes of the *poème en prose* and close readings of specific works. This alternation follows logically from the above discussion of genre, for if genres are negatively defined, it is necessary to find out first what the *poème en prose* defines itself against, then explore how this framework informs interpretations of individual works. In chapter 5, I will turn to the American prose poem for more perspective on negative definition. At the end of chapter 4 and the beginning of chapter 5 I will also develop further some issues in genre theory and resume the history of terms like "prose poem." But for now more attention needs to be paid to the *poème en prose*.

2. A Wide Field of Prose Possibilities

The haze surrounding the origins of prose poetry is typical of that surrounding any genre or simple abstraction. Whether due to some postmodern condition or a critical environment that calls attention to the untidiness of life, indeterminacy has become the expected result rather than the exception with inquiries into origins. From a pragmatic point of view, indeterminacy is not so much a source of frustration or exhilaration as it is a call to shift interpretive efforts elsewhere. For if literary kinds exist only in relation to other kinds, understanding prose poetry as a genre necessarily involves establishing the field of generic possibilities from which it emerges and in which it continues to exist. Such a project is open-ended and potentially encyclopedic in scope. For purposes of interpretation, however, an examination of even a dozen or so genres that relate to the prose poem, if only as counterexamples, provides much of the necessary literary-historical context. In this chapter, I discuss various classes of prose works from the eighteenth and nineteenth centuries in an attempt to delineate some of the shifting and indefinite boundaries of prose poetry in the period. To resist a linear narrative of events, I do not exclusively examine works that influenced later prose poetry, although I frequently make comparisons to Baudelaire's prose poems. A knowledge of the roads not taken by the *poème en prose* is important not only in determining which roads and which byways prose poetry did take but also in clearing up some matters of reception—among other things, how novel or revolutionary prose poems would have seemed to contemporary readers.

• • •

As with attestations of the term "poème en prose," finding examples of poems in prose that predate Baudelaire's *Petits Poëmes en prose* is relatively easy. Suzanne Bernard and John Simon have in fact shown in some detail that there are a large number of pre-Bertrand and pre-Baudelaire works that resemble the later writers' prose poems on formal grounds.[1] Whether one should label these works prose poems is a largely academic question; the extent to which such works influenced the writing of the *poème en prose* a somewhat more important issue; and the manner in which they help negatively define the abstraction "prose poetry" a crucial matter. While an exhaustive treatment or typology of prose-poem-like works is beyond the scope of this discussion and in some ways inimical to its aims, it will be useful to examine some of these works at length before turning to the immediate literary and historical context of Baudelaire's *Petits Poëmes en prose*.

In the preceding chapter I remarked that prose translations of poems and pseudotranslations were commonplace in the late eighteenth century and may have helped prepare the French ear for prose poetry in the nineteenth century. The warrior's serenade to his mistress from Chateaubriand's *Atala* (1801) is typical of this sort of poetry:

> Je devancerai les pas du jour sur le sommet des montagnes, pour chercher ma colombe solitaire parmi les chênes de la forêt.
>
> J'ai attaché à son cou un collier de porcelaines; on y voit trois grains rouges pour mon amour, trois violets pour mes craintes, trois bleus pour mes espérances.
>
> Mila a les yeux d'une hermine et la chevelure légère d'un champ de riz; sa bouche est un coquillage rose, garni de perles; ses deux seins sont comme deux petits chevereaux sans taches nés au même jour d'une seule mère.
>
> Puisse Mila éteindre ce flambeau! Puisse sa bouche verser sur lui une ombre voluptueuse! Je fertiliserai son sein. L'espoir de la patrie pendra à sa mamelle féconde, et je fumerai mon calumet de paix sur le berceau de mon fils!
>
> Ah! laissez-moi devancer les pas du jour sur le sommet des montagnes, pour chercher ma colombe solitaire parmi les chênes de la fôret!
>
> [I shall walk in front of the footsteps of the day on the mountains' summits, to find my lonely dove among the oaks of the woods.
>
> I have tied a necklace of shells to her neck; you can see three red kernels for my love there, three violet ones for my fears, three blue ones for my hopes.

Mila has the eyes of an ermine and the light hair of a field of rice; her mouth is a pink shell adorned with pearls; her two breasts are like two little unblemished kids born on the same day from a single mother.

May Mila extinguish this torch! May her mouth pour a voluptuous shadow onto it! I will impregnate her bosom. The hope of the fatherland will hang from her fertile breast, and I will smoke my peace pipe over the cradle of my son!

Ah! let me walk in front of the footsteps of the day on the mountain summits, to find my lonely dove among the oaks of the woods!]²

The paragraph indentations and the blank spaces between stanzas are conventions of prose translations of poems. The line lengths are roughly those of a psalm verset and the brief blazon of the maiden is reminiscent of the Song of Songs. An imitation of verse or song rhythm is achieved through anaphora and parallelisms; closure through a near repetition of the opening line. In short, this pseudotranslation contains many conventional elements and clichés of those poems that are meant to be read as primitive, such as the Ossian fragments. Its rhetoric is as clearly marked as the broken English of an Indian chief in a 1950s western.

Most critics would consider the prose poems of Bertrand and Baudelaire as qualitatively different from this pretend primitive poetry. Baudelaire, after all, claimed he was writing a peculiarly modern poetry that had neither rhyme nor rhythm, and an ironic distance from subject matter is absent in poems like the warrior's serenade from *Atala*.³ The differences between a Baudelaire prose poem and the warrior's song by Chateaubriand are real and significant, but both writers are engaged in the activity of translating generic repertoires. Chateaubriand's translation is, from this perspective, more literal: versets, repetitions, anaphoras, and other traits of a certain kind of poetry are imported with minimal changes. Rhyme and meter are the only obvious external features that are lost in translation. Baudelaire's prose poems are less direct imitations of a variety of generic models. It is as if, having made the decision to write poems in prose, Baudelaire felt the need to tinker like a careful translator to find related but different forms capable of poetic expression.⁴ In general, primitive poetry and pseudotranslation represent an alternative path of development for the prose poem which, although noncanonical, does not suddenly end with Bertrand and Baudelaire or even with Mallarmé and Rimbaud: Judith Gautier's Chinese translations (*Le Livre de Jade*, 1867) were regarded by her contemporaries as prose poems, for example, and Pierre

Louÿs's *Les Chansons de Bilitis* (1894) present themselves as translations from the Greek. The first attempts at prose poetry in English by De Quincey and Wilde are also of this sort.

Prose translations need not always be read as caricatures of verse poems or gestures toward the primitive, the natural, or anything that a writer of Baudelaire's temperament would regard at best as an antimodel. Translations of contemporary poems into prose, such as Gérard de Nerval's versions of poems from Heine's *Buch der Lieder*, are much closer in spirit to *Petits Poëmes en prose*. Several of Nerval's translations have titles and subject matter nearly identical to those of Baudelaire prose poems ("Le Crépuscule," "Le Port"); others, like "Questions," are structurally and tonally similar to them:

> Au bord de la mer, au bord de la mer déserte et nocturne, se tient un jeune homme, la poitrine pleine de tristesse, la tête pleine de doute, et d'un air morne il dit aux flots:
>
> "Oh! expliquez moi l'énigme de la vie, la douloureuse et vieille énigme qui a tourmenté tant de têtes: têtes coiffées de mitres hiéroglyphiques, têtes en turbans et en bonnets carrés, têtes à perruques, et milles autres pauvres et bouillantes têtes humaines. Dites-moi ce que signifie l'homme? d'où il vient? où il va? qui habite là-haut au-dessus des étoiles dorées?"
>
> Les flots murmurent leur éternel murmure, le vent souffle, les nuages fuient, les étoiles scintillent, froides et indifférentes,—et un fou attend une réponse.
>
> [On the shore of the sea, on the shore of the deserted, nocturnal sea, a young man stands, his chest filled with sadness, his head filled with doubt, and he says to the waves in a dejected tone:
>
> "Oh! explain to me life's riddle, the painful and ancient riddle that has tormented so many heads: heads wearing hieroglyphic miters, heads in turbans and square bonnets, heads with wigs, and thousands of other poor and teeming human heads. Tell me what it means to be a man? Where does he come from? Where is he going? Who dwells up there above the gilded stars?"
>
> The waves are murmuring their eternal murmur, the wind is blowing, the clouds are flying away, the stars are twinkling coldly and indifferently,—and a madman is waiting for an answer.][5]

In this poem there is a distance between the poet and the young man that does not exist between the narrator and the warrior in the song from *Atala*. This distance is marked not only by a quotation surrounded by commentary but also by the young man's hyperbolic diction ("heads wearing hieroglyphic miters, heads in turbans and square bonnets . . .”). The poem's ironic tone, rhetorical buildup, and punchlinelike close are commonplace features of many of Baudelaire's prose poems, such as the ending of “Le Fou et la Vénus” (“The Fool and Venus”):

> Cependant, dans cette jouissance universelle, j'ai aperçu un être affligé.
>
> Aux pieds d'une colossale Vénus, un de ces fous artificiels, un de ces bouffons volontaires chargé de faire rire les rois quand le Remords ou l'Ennui les obsède, affublé d'un costume éclatant et ridicule, coiffé de cornes et de sonnettes, tout ramassé contre le piédestal, lève des yeux pleins de larmes vers l'immortelle Déesse.
>
> Et ses yeux disent:—“Je suis le dernier et le plus solitaire des humains, privé d'amour et d'amitié, et bien inférieur en cela au plus imparfait des animaux. Cependant je suis fait, moi aussi, pour comprendre et sentir l'immortelle Beauté! Ah! Déesse! ayez pitié de ma tristesse et de mon délire!”
>
> Mais l'implacable Vénus regarde au loin je ne sais quoi avec ses yeux de marbre.
>
> [And yet, amid this universal joy, I spied an afflicted being.
>
> At the feet of a colossal Venus, one of those artificial fools, one of those clowns on demand in charge of making kings laugh when Remorse or Boredom takes hold of them, decked out in a dazzling and ridiculous outfit, adorned with horns and tiny bells, completely curled up against the pedestal, is lifting his tear-filled eyes toward the immortal Goddess.
>
> And his eyes are saying: “I am the lowest and the loneliest human being, deprived of love and friendship, and far inferior with regard to that than the most imperfect animals. And yet I too was made to understand and to feel immortal Beauty! Ah Goddess! have pity on my sadness and on my delirium!”
>
> But the implacable Venus is looking into the distance at I'm not sure what with her marble eyes.][6]

Whatever the poet's relation to his subject matter—it is neither clear whether the fool acts out his role as a clown on demand when addressing the statue nor a given that the poet dislikes artifice—much of the poem's rhetorical force resides in its distanced tone and ambiguity. While not absent from the rhymed lyrics of *Les Fleurs du mal*, the deliberate distancing of poetic voice from subject matter is much more prevalent in *Petits Poëmes en prose*. It represents one of Baudelaire's main strategies of genre translation and suggests that in those works in which the abstraction "poème en prose" is an operative concern, the prose element and the poetry element are in dialogue.

Prose poems can, of course, be as much transformations of prose genres as they are translations of poetic genres. Instead of drawing on the resources of prose to reshape the lyric, prose poets can rework prose genres into poems (where "rework" need not imply a conscious, straightforward activity). The issue has more to do with interpretation than retracing the path of poetic creation. The *promenades* or *rêveries* of Rousseau (*Les Rêveries du promeneur solitaire*, 1782), for example, exerted some demonstrable influence on Baudelaire, but they are perhaps more important as an index of an aesthetic that becomes associated with the prose poem—the necessity for release from constraints.[7] In the first *promenade* Rousseau writes:

> Une situation si singulière mérite assurément d'être examinée et décrite, et c'est à cet examen que je consacre mes derniers loisirs. Pour le faire avec succès il y faudrait procéder avec ordre et méthode: mais je suis incapable de ce travail et même il m'écarterait de mon but qui est de me rendre compte des modifications de mon âme et de leurs successions. . . . Je me contenterai de tenir le registre des opérations sans chercher à les réduire en système. Je fais la même entreprise que Montaigne, mais avec un but tout contraire au sien: car il n'écrivait ses *Essais* que pour les autres, et je n'écris mes rêveries que pour moi.
> [Such a singular situation assuredly deserves to be examined and described, and it is to this examination that I am dedicating my last leisure moments. In order to do this successfully you have to proceed with order and method: but I am incapable of that sort of work and besides it would turn me aside from my aim, which is to make me aware of the alterations of my soul and what follows from them. . . . I will content myself to keep an account of the operations without seeking to reduce them to a system. I am engaging in the same enterprise as Montaigne, but with an aim entirely contrary to his: for he wrote his *Essays* only for other people, and I am writing my *rêveries* only for myself.][8]

Avoiding the systematic approach is a common *ars poetica* of prose poetry, from Baudelaire's dedicatory letter in *Petits Poëmes en prose* to Ashbery's "The System." In each case the necessity of finding a new method presents itself the moment the writer decides to abandon one group of restraints, if only because, as Rousseau admits, some aim remains. Rousseau's solution to the problem of translating the alterations of his soul onto paper is expressed in economic terms: he is content to "keep an account of the operations." Just as Montaigne, in his essays, transformed the religious meditation into a secular genre, Rousseau claims he is transforming the essay into a kind of internal meditation, though even the word "meditation" suggests more method than he believes lies behind his writing. "Sometimes my *rêveries* end in meditation, but more often my meditations end in reverie," he writes in the seventh *promenade*.[9] Rousseau's most extended allegory of his project occurs in the fifth *promenade*, when, like Thoreau on Walden Pond some years later, he describes rowing and letting go of the oars to float with the current:

> Le flux et reflux de cette eau, son bruit continu mais renflé par intervalles frappant sans relâche mon oreille et mes yeux, suppléaient aux mouvements internes que la rêverie éteignait en moi et suffisaient pour me faire sentir avec plaisir mon existence sans prendre la peine de penser. De temps à autre naissait quelque faible et courte réflexion sur l'instabilité des choses de ce monde dont la surface des eaux m'offrait l'image: mais bientôt ces impressions légères s'effaçaient dans l'uniformité du movement qui me berçait, et qui sans aucun concours actif de mon âme ne laissait pas de m'attacher au point qu'appelé par l'heure et par le signal convenu je ne pouvais m'arracher de là sans efforts.
>
> [The ebb and the flow of this water, its continuous yet occasionally swelling noise relentlessly striking my ear and my eyes, took the place of the internal movement which my reverie was extinguishing in me and was enough to make me sense my existence with pleasure without my taking the trouble to think. From time to time there arose in me some weak and short reflection on the instability of the things of this world of which the water's surface offered me the image: but soon these light impressions became blotted out in the uniformity of the movement that rocked me, and which, without any active cooperation of my soul, was not allowing me to fasten myself on anything to the point that, called by the hour and the appointed signal, I was unable to pull myself away from there without effort.][10]

For Rousseau, the *rêveries* are an attempt to get away from the intensely self-reflective writing of his *Confessions*. Paradoxically, Rousseau can only attempt such a project if he has more awareness than he could have possessed in writing the earlier work: a knowledge of how to induce a release from consciousness. For a mode of writing that supposedly follows an uncontrolled course, his prose is highly self-reflexive, both in content—the drifting boat as an allegory for reverie—and style—the sinuous sentences full of subordinate phrases mimicking the author's thought-process. In spite or because of their aesthetic of abandoning constraints, Rousseau's *rêveries* evidence an awareness of sophisticated formal considerations.

The literary kinds evoked by the labels Rousseau provides for his work, *rêverie* and *promenade*, have histories that intersect that of the prose poem at various points. Dream literature, such as selections from Nerval's *Aurélia* or De Quincey's *Confessions of an English Opium Eater* (1822), not only tends to show up in anthologies of prose poetry but is an important source of the prose poems of Lautréamont and the surrealists. The phantasmagoric elements of this literature also enter into the work of poets like Baudelaire and Rimbaud. The apparent lack of external or conscious constraints in a dream world is one of its significant features for prose poets, its subject matter another: dream accounts and fantastic subjects helped mark works as poetic in the early nineteenth century in the same way the appearance of a piece of fragmentary prose marks it as something other than ordinary prose. The *promenade*, however, becomes less literary and more journalistic, to judge by such works as Nerval's *Promenades et Souvenirs* (1854). Nerval's *promenades* are anecdotal; they read as abridged versions of the travelogues he and many of his contemporaries were writing, as do related works of his such as *Lorely* (1852), *Les Nuits d'Octobre* (1852), and *Petits Châteaux de Bohême* (1853). Like the chapters in Sterne's *A Sentimental Journey*, these anecdotes are often linked by tenuous narrative threads and seem more concerned with digressions and lighthearted morals than with continuing a story. And like Sterne's works, they are marked by sudden shifts in tone, sometimes as abrupt as the dashes in *Tristram Shandy*, sometimes relatively gentle, as in the opening of "Le Réalisme," the first section of *Les Nuits d'Octobre*:

> Avec le temps, la passion des grands voyages s'éteint, à moins qu'on n'ait voyagé assez longtemps pour devenir étranger à sa patrie. Le cercle se rétrécit de plus en plus, se rapprochant peu à peu du foyer. —Ne pouvant m'éloigner beaucoup cet automne, j'avais formé le projet d'un simple voyage à Meaux.
>
> Il faut dire que j'ai déjà vu Pontoise.
>
> J'aime assez ces petites villes qui s'écartent d'une dizaine de lieues du centre rayonnant de Paris, planètes modestes. Dix lieues, c'est assez loin pour qu'on ne soit pas tenté de revenir le soir,—pour qu'on soit sûr que la même sonnette ne vous réveillera pas le lendemain, pour qu'on se trouve entre deux jours affairés une matinée de calme.

Je plains ceux qui, cherchant le silence et la solitude, se réveillent
candidement à Asnières.

[With time, the passion for long voyages extinguishes itself, unless one
has traveled long enough to become a stranger in one's own land. The circle
contracts more and more, approaching little by little one's hearth. —Not being
able to remove myself far this autumn, I had formed the project of a simple trip
to Meaux.

I should say that I already saw Pontoise.

I quite like those small towns that stray about ten leagues from the radiating
center of Paris, modest planets. Ten leagues, that is far enough for one not to
be tempted to return in the evening, for one to be sure that the same little bell
will not wake one the next day, for one to find a morning of calm for oneself
between two busy days.

I pity those who, looking for silence and solitude, frankly wake up in
Asnières.][11]

By shifting between general reflections and comments on specific situations,
the narrator figures himself as alternatively rising above and falling back into
an urban reality. When he rises above reality, the writing is more philosophical,
even poetic ("With time, the passion for long voyages extinguishes itself,"
"towns that stray . . . from the radiating center," the repetition of the phrases
beginning "for one"). This language, unlike the pointed, journalistic phrases
that punctuate it, strays like the planetlike towns circling the epitome of the
real, Paris. The title of the section, "Realism," signals the literary dimension
of the debate played out on the level of language. After the narrator misses a
couple of trains and finishes reading "[l]a politique des journaux," he comes
across a translation of Dickens in the *Revue britannique* and exclaims:

Qu'ils sont heureux, les Anglais, de pouvoir écrire et lire des chapitres
d'observation dénués de tout alliage d'invention romanesque! À Paris,
on nous demanderait que cela fût semé d'anecdotes et d'histoires
sentimentales,—se terminant soit par une mort, soit par un mariage.
L'intelligence réaliste de nos voisins se contente du vrai absolu.

En effet, le roman rendra-t-il jamais l'effet des combinaisons bizarres
de la vie? Vous inventez l'homme, ne sachant pas l'observer. Quels sont
les romans préférables aux histoires comiques, ou tragiques d'un journal
de tribunaux?

[How happy they are, the English, to be able to write and read chapters
of observation denuded of every mixture of romantic invention! In Paris, they

would ask us to sow that with anecdotes and sentimental stories, either ending in a death or a marriage. The realist mind of our neighbors contents itself with absolute truth.

In reality, will the novel ever convey the effect of life's strange combinations? You invent the man without knowing how to observe him. Which novels are preferable to the comic, or the tragic, stories of a court of justice newspaper?][12]

The narrator puts the desirability of the real ("vrai absolu") into question by shifting from exclamation to rhetorical question in the second paragraph. He is also questioning the desirability of the novel as a genre and wonders—via a passing pun on "effet"—whether it is capable of representing some realities of life. Given the tone of the passage, Nerval is probably not seriously suggesting that short, journalistic writing like his own *Nuits* is preferable to a Dickens novel, but he does seem to be implying that there are some aspects of modern life the realist novel cannot capture.

As the titles of the various Nerval works attest, there are many labels for short, prose-poem-like genres in the nineteenth century: *promenades*, *Choses vues*, memories, rhapsodies, *Propos de table*, *Rondeaux parisiens*, impressions, *Intermèdes lycanthropiques*, nights, *Petits Châteaux*, curiosities, and fantasies represent only a fraction of the possibilities. As with *rêverie*, the labels often suggest vagueness, freedom from constraints, and open-endedness—all figured as necessary for articulating the experiences of a life in flux. While the assertion that new experiences necessitate new literary forms and genres is not new (there were sixteenth-century debates over epic and romance, for example), the nineteenth-century claims, especially those the poets make, are striking in their emphasis on the postlapsarian quality of the necessity.[13] For many poets, prose, especially journalistic prose, is a fall from poetry. Nerval even dedicates his *Petits Châteaux de Bohême* (subtitled "Prose et Poésie") to Arsène Houssaye by way of an apology:

> Mon ami, vous me demandez si je pourrais retrouver quelques-uns de mes anciens vers, et vous vous inquiétez même d'apprendre comment j'ai été poète, longtemps avant de devenir un humble prosateur.
>
> Je vous envoie les trois âges du poète—il n'y a plus en moi qu'un prosateur obstiné. J'ai fait les premiers vers par enthousiasme de je- unesse, les seconds par amour, les derniers par désespoir. La Muse est entrée dans mon cœur comme une déesse aux paroles dorées; elle s'en est échappée comme une pythie en jetant des cris de douleur. Seule- ment ses derniers accents se sont adoucis à mesure qu'elle s'éloignait.

Elle s'est détournée un instant, et j'ai revu comme en un mirage les traits adorés d'autrefois!

La vie d'un poète est celle de tous. Il est inutile d'en définir toutes les phases.

[My friend, you ask me if I could dredge up some of my old verses, and you are anxious even to learn how I was a poet a long time before becoming a humble prose writer.

I send along to you the three ages of the poet—there is no longer anything but an obstinate prose writer in me. I wrote my first verses out of youthful enthusiasm, the second ones out of love, the last out of despair. The Muse entered into my heart like a goddess with gilded words; she escaped from it like a Pythian priestess throwing out cries of pain. Yet her final tones softened to the degree that she distanced herself. She turned aside one moment, and I saw again the adored features of bygone days like a mirage!

The life of a poet is that of everyone. It is useless to define all the phases of it.][14]

The tone of this passage is not unlike that of another dedication to Arsène Houssaye, Baudelaire's prefatory letter to *Petits Poëmes en prose*. Nerval's mapping of the classical ages of the poet and the myth of Orpheus and Eurydice onto his own biography takes on a particular significance in the context of his œuvre, but the concerns he expresses are commonplace among writers of the period. Nerval goes so far as to suggest that the poet's situation is a general one: "The life of a poet is that of everyone." The domain of the modern poet is necessarily small ("petits châteaux"), probably illusory (the title recalls "castles of sand" and "châteaux en Espagne"), and, perhaps most significantly, marginalized: Houssaye and Nerval were formerly poets of Bohemian Paris.

For nineteenth-century French poets, journalistic prose did more than represent the reluctantly employed language of a fallen age; it helped determine some of the formal features and dialogic impulse of the *poème en prose*. The bantering tone of Baudelaire's prose poems and their appearance on the page in block paragraphs is in part a borrowing from, in part a deeply ambivalent comment on, journalism and journalism's effects on poetry. By the 1860s, as Graham Robb has pointed out, the mixture of low and high style in publications like *Le Figaro* and *La Presse* was widespread and one of the most frequent forms of Baudelaire's prose poetry, the anecdote with a moral, a readily recognizable genre.[15] Newspaper and magazine columns that listed and described events in quick succession (such as *Chroniques* and *Gravures du numéro*) also have some formal and stylistic affinities to the Baudelairean *poème en prose*. In *L'Artiste*, for example, a journal that published some of Baudelaire's prose poems, Pierre Dax regularly contributed a column consisting of experiences he heard of or claimed to have had walking around Paris. His description of his stroll to the Château-des-Fleurs is typical:

> J'entre au Château-des-Fleurs, parce que c'est parfois beau genre et qu'il fait beau ce soir, et je fredonne avec l'orchestre de Métra: "Amis, la matinée est belle." Il est bientôt minuit. Bravo! me dis-je: c'est ici le séjour des jeux et de l'insouciance! c'est ici qu'on se sent heureux de vivre pour s'amuser; ici qu'on dépenserait la moitié de sa vie et plus que la moitié de sa bourse; et par goût, j'aime la dépense et la variété, la variété surtout est mon élément. Je n'ai jamais compris l'antique Eden et ses monotones voluptés.
>
> Le Château-des-Fleurs est un chemin à l'atmosphère enflamée; si vous aimez les illuminations, vous aimez ce jardin étincelant; en face de cette estrade, qui est le pavillon d'Erato, comme disaient les Grecs, de sainte Cécile, comme disent les modernes, voyez: c'est le bal, le bal aux tourbilleux contours. Écoutons un instant les trente-six harmonies de cet orchestre, comme on écoute les trente-six histoires d'Arlequin. Ah! vous aimez les jolie femmes qui soient des femmes impossibles? Alors parcourons non-seulement le bal, mais jusqu'aux moindres sentiers du jardin. À ce jardin aussi la variété est dans son élément.
>
> La devise de notre siècle, c'est: Variété.
>
> [I go into the Château-des-Fleurs, because it's a pretty setting sometimes and it's nice out this evening, and I hum along with the orchestra of Metra: "Friends, the morning is beautiful." Soon it is midnight. Bravo! I say to myself: here is the place for games and carefree life! it is here that one feels happy to live to enjoy oneself; here that one spends half of one's life and more than half of one's purse. And, by inclination, I love spending and variety—variety especially is my element. I have never understood ancient Eden and its monotonous pleasures.
>
> The Château-des-Fleurs is a path to an inflamed atmosphere; if you like displays of lights, you'll like this sparkling garden. Opposite that dais which is the pavilion of Erato, as the Greeks say, or of Saint Cecilia, according to the moderns—look: it's the ballroom, the ballroom with whirling outlines. Let's listen a moment to this orchestra's thirty-six harmonies, the way one listens to Arlequin's thirty-six stories. Ah! you like pretty women who are impossible women? Then let us walk not only across the ballroom, but all the way to the

lesser paths of the garden. In this garden, variety is also in its element.
    The motto of our century is that: Variety.][16]

The familiar tone of the nighttime *flâneur*, the condensed anecdote, and
the intimation of a moral at the end do not mark this piece as Baudelairean
per se—they point instead to the conventional quality of many the of poems
in *Petits Poëmes en prose*. Without a consideration of particular poems and
readers, it is impossible to say whether Baudelaire's prose poems ultimately
undermine or are contained by these conventions. Revolutionary or not,
however, the first poems in prose tend to allegorize their internal division.
    One of the few journalistic genres Baudelaire could admire, caricature
writing, might serve as a metaphor for what results from the divisions in the
linguistic registers of many prose poems if only because, like the *poème en
prose*, it often relies on a distortion of accustomed modes of signification to
produce its effects.[17] The most popular form of caricature writing in the early
1840s was the *physiologie*, generally an inexpensive, pamphlet-sized book
with illustrations and text poking fun at social types or practices.[18] Subjects
could range from the *grisette* to the *voyage* and from Bohemia to the bourgeois
married man. Once the genre became established, there were physiologies
not only of people and daily activities but of inanimate objects and abstract
notions personified, such as *physiologies* of the quarters of Paris and of taste.
There was even a *Physiologie des physiologies*. Louis Huart's *Physiologie du
flâneur* (Physiology of the strolling man, 1841) is typical of the genre in that it
is divided into short chapters covering different topics (such as the pleasures
and dangers of *flânerie*) as if it were a kind of guidebook. Huart's second
chapter is especially Baudelairean in tone and subject matter:

CHAPITRE II: EST-IL DONNÉ À TOUT LE MONDE DE POUVOIR FLANER?
    "Rien de plus commun que le nom, rien de plus rare que la chose!"—
car il en est des flaneurs véritables tout comme des amis dont parle
La Fontaine, et si de notre définition de l'homme, donnée dans notre
chapitre précédent, on concluait que tous les hommes sont appelés à
flaner, on se tromperait étrangement.
    Il est des infortunés qui, par beaucoup de motifs différents, sont
privés de goûter ce plaisir que nous ne craignons pas de nommer celui
des dieux,—car les dieux de l'Olympe eux-mêmes ne faisaient rien autre
chose que de prendre une foule de travestissements pour pouvoir venir
flaner tranquillement sur la terre comme de bons petits rentiers, après
avoir pris leur demi-tasse d'Ambroisie, café de l'époque.

[CHAPTER II: IS EVERYONE GIVEN THE ABILITY TO STROLL THE STREETS?

"Nothing more common than the name, nothing more rare than the thing!"—for there exist true *flâneurs*, entirely like the friends La Fontaine speaks of, and if, from our definition of man given in the preceding chapter, you concluded that all men are called to stroll, you were strangely mistaken.

There are those unfortunates who, for a host of different reasons, are deprived of tasting this pleasure we aren't afraid to call the pleasure of the gods—because the gods of Olympus themselves did nothing other than assume a bunch of disguises in order to be able to stroll tranquilly on the earth like honest little landowners, after they had had their half cup of Ambrosia, the coffee of that age.][19]

The opening of Baudelaire's "Les Foules" (Crowds), for all it owes to Poe's "Man of the Crowd" and De Quincey's *Confessions of an English Opium Eater*, reads like an answer to the question posed at the beginning of this chapter of *Physiologie du flâneur*, "Est-il donné à chacun de flaner?":

Il n'est pas donné à chacun de prendre un bain de multitude: jouir de la foule est un art; et celui-là seul peut faire, aux dépens du genre humain, une ribote de vitalité, à qui une fée a insufflé dans son berceau le goût du travestissement et du masque, la haine du domicile et la passion du voyage.

[Not everyone can take a bath of multitude: playing the crowd is an art; and the only person who can, at the expense of the human race, have a drunken bout of vitality, is he to whom a fairy has, in his cradle, inspired the taste for disguise and the mask, the hatred of home and the passion for traveling.][20]

As described in the *physiologie*, the authentic *flâneur* is like the "active and fertile poet" of "Les Foules" or the speaker in the companion poem, "La Solitude," who defines himself against those who are "not able to put up with themselves": "The true *flâneur* never gets bored; he suffices to himself and finds nourishment for his mind in everything he encounters."[21] Caricature is an appropriate metaphor for Baudelairean and other prose poems in that the purposely distorted representations one finds in genres like the *physiologie* correspond to the clashing linguistic and generic registers of a *poème en prose*. The prose poem's play with generic expectations also has all the caricature's potential for humor and opens the possibility for ideological and aesthetic commentary, depending on how a poem allegorizes itself.[22]

• • •

From even the handful of examples discussed so far, it should come as no surprise that prose poems like Baudelaire's were not received with the sort of controversy surrounding *Les Fleurs du mal* or the intense discussion regarding the first poems in vers libre. This is not to say that *Petits Poëmes en prose* would have been thought of as unoriginal in comparison to what came before or coexisted with it. On the contrary: if any single person gave the *poème en prose* new life and a name, it was Baudelaire, and most histories of the prose poem are quite insistent about Baudelaire's originality. Drawing on Baudelaire's remarks in his dedicatory letter to Houssaye, many critics have compared *Petits Poëmes en prose* to its "mysterious and brilliant model," Bertrand's *Gaspard de la nuit: Fantaisies à la manière de Rembrandt et de Callot* (1842).[23] Bertrand's poem "Octobre" furnishes instructive material for such a comparison:

> Les petits Savoyards sont de retour, et déjà leur cri interroge l'écho sonore du quartier; comme les hirondelles suivent le printemps, ils précèdent l'hiver.
>
> Octobre, le courrier de l'hiver, heurte à la porte de nos demeures. Une pluie intermittante inonde la vitre offusquée, et le vent jonche des feuilles mortes du platane le perron solitaire.
>
> Voici venir les veillées de famille, si délicieuse quand tout au dehors est neige, verglas et brouillard, et que les jacinthes fleurissent sur la cheminée, à la tiède atmosphère du salon.
>
> Voici venir la Saint-Martin et ses brandons, Noël et ses bougies, le jour de l'an et ses joujoux, les Rois et leur fève, le carnaval et sa marotte.
>
> Et Pâques, enfin, Pâques aux hymnes matinales et joyeuse, Pâques dont les jeunes filles reçoivent la blanche hostie et les œufs rouges!
>
> Alors un peu de cendre aura effacé de nos fronts l'ennui de six mois d'hiver, et les petits Savoyards salueront du haut de la colline le hameau natal.
>
> [The little Savoyards are on their way home, and already their shouts question the resounding echo of the neighborhood. As the swallows follow the spring they come before the winter.
>
> October, the messenger of winter, is knocking at the doors of our homes. An intermittent rain floods the clouded window, and the wind strews the lonely stone steps with dead plane leaves.
>
> Here come the family evenings, so delicious when everything outside is snow, ice, and fog, and the hyacinths flower on the chimney, in the moist-warm atmosphere of the parlor.

Here comes the Feast of Saint Martin and its torches, Christmas and its candles, New Year's and its toys, the Three Kings and their bean-cake, Carnival and its costumes.

And Easter, finally, Easter with its matinal and joyous hymns, Easter when the little girls receive the white host and the red eggs!

And so a little ash will have wiped from our foreheads the boredom of six months of winter, and the little Savoyards will greet their native hamlet from the top of the hill.][24]

While the subject matter (autumn, coming of winter, the corner-by-the-fire theme) and some of the language ("Voici venir," "tiède atmosphère," "ennui") may remind one of Baudelaire, the differences between "Octobre" and *Petits Poëmes en prose* are much more striking. The versetlike strophes separated by blanks, the rhetorical crescendo ("Here come . . . Here comes . . . And Easter, finally . . .") followed by a varied repetition of the opening to lend the poem a sense of closure, and occasional inversions mark this prose as more akin to the warrior's song from *Atala* than to "Le Fou et la Vénus." Indeed, many of Bertrand's poems are even more balladlike than "Octobre" with their use of repetitions or refrains.

If, taking Baudelaire's hint, one rewards Bertrand with the title of the first prose poet, then it follows that Bertrand was doing something distinct from his precursors. Bertrand's often detailed descriptions and his somewhat distanced poetic voice alone would suffice to make this assertion plausible if one conceived of the *poème en prose* as a form that evolves toward a particular type: a brief, concentrated prose passage that resists the language and cadences of traditional verse and *poésie primitive*.[25] But the methodological assumptions behind a search for a unique, author-centered origin are highly questionable. Furthermore, such a history unnecessarily limits the possibilities of prose poetry and tends to obscure the importance of neighboring genres. If these considerations are not enough, Baudelaire may have been deliberately directing his readers' attention away from precursors who are more important than Bertrand. Several critics have pointed in particular to Jules Lefèvre (or Le Fèvre-Deumier), author of *Le Livre du promeneur, ou les mois et les jours* (1854).[26] This volume, consisting in its fiction of a year's worth of daily meditations or *promenades*, may be uneven from an aesthetic point of view, but it does contain poems that are as finished as Baudelaire's prose poems, such as the entry for 18 December, "Les Chemins de Fer" (Railway tracks):

Il m'est impossible de regarder, sans une sorte de tristesse, ces chemins merveilleux auxquels notre industrie semble donner des ailes. Je ne sais si c'est un progrès que de pouvoir fendre ainsi l'espace comme une flèche; mais ce qu'il y a de sûr, c'est que cela me rend plus sensible à la rapidité de la vie, qui avant notre invention l'était cependant bien assez. Ces rainures de fer où nous sommes forcés de courir sans dévier d'une ligne, emportés par une puissance aussi aveugle, presque aussi indomptable que la foudre; est-ce que ce n'est pas une image de cet implacable sort qui nous entraîne, et dont nous sommes les esclaves, alors même que nous croyons le maîtriser? On croit gagner du temps parce qu'on l'accélère! Mais ces voyages étourdissants ne font qu'abréger l'existence qui n'est elle-même qu'une traversée. Ils ne permettent pas la mémoire, le seul moyen qu'ait l'homme d'allonger et de doubler ses jours. L'unique souvenir qu'ils nous laissent, c'est qu'on va vite. Aller vite, c'est mourir plutôt.

[It is impossible for me to look, without a kind of sadness, at those marvelous tracks to which our industry seems to give wings. I don't know if being able to cut through space like an arrow is progress, but what *is* certain is that it makes me more sensitive to the swiftness of life, which was however swift enough before our invention. Those iron grooves in which we are forced to run without deviating one line, carried away as we are by a power that is as blind and almost as ungovernable as lighting—isn't all this an image of that unrelenting fate that drags us, and whose slaves we are even when we think we are mastering it? You think you are gaining time because you accelerate it! But these deafening excursions only help abridge an existence that is itself no more than a passing through. They don't allow for remembrance, the only means man has for increasing and doubling his days. The one memory that it leaves us with is that we go quickly. To go quickly is to die sooner.][27]

The reaction against the modern in "Chemins de Fer" may be a far cry from Baudelaire's determined embrace of it, but Lefèvre's attitude toward progress and the nostalgia informing his reflection are similar to those of the author of *Petits Poëmes en prose*. Moreover, *rêveries* or meditations with morals are Baudelairean, as is the sentence beginning with a deictic phrase ("Those iron grooves . . .") which, midway through, switches to a rhetorical question ("isn't all this an image . . . ?").[28] The possibility of influence here or with regard to the handful of Lefèvre poems with Baudelairean titles is secondary to the questions *Le Livre du promeneur* raises about the genre and reception of *Petits Poëmes en prose*. For if, in order to avoid the Scylla of the more cadenced poetry of Bertrand and the pseudotranslators, Baudelaire felt the need to create a "poetic prose" that was "musical without rhythm and rhyme" so as to distinguish his work from anything that resembled it but did not share its aims and effects, he needed to approach but not wreck himself on the Charybdis of journalistic prose—and insist on his modernity.[29] As I explain more fully in the next chapter, this process of negative differentiation takes on almost territorial connotations for Baudelaire: at one point he considered titling his book of prose poems *Le Promeneur solitaire*, presumably after Rousseau. As Robert Guiette has suggested, Baudelaire may have changed his mind upon noticing the similarity of this title to Lefèvre's *Le Livre du promeneur*.[30]

In histories, or prehistories, of the *poème en prose* like Bernard's, there are a handful of writers besides Bertrand who receive honorable mention. Houssaye, the only other precursor named in Baudelaire's dedicatory letter, published a number of short prose works under the title "La Poésie primitive" (book 4 of his *Œuvres poétiques*, 1857) from which his "La Chanson du vitrier" ("The Song of the Glazier") comes. Works like Alphonse Rabbe's *Album d'un pessimiste* (1834), Maurice de Guérin's "Le Centaure" (1840) and "La Bacchante" (1861), Champfleury's (Jules Fleury's) *Chien-Caillou. Fantaisies d'Hiver* (1847), Félicité-Robert de Lammenais's *Paroles d'un croyant* (1833), and Xavier Forneret's *Pièces de pièces, temps perdu* (1840) also receive their share of attention.[31] While it is worth speculating on why some of these works (Guérin's and Lammenais's, especially) end up in anthologies of the prose poem and why others do not, they are for the most part related to genres I have already discussed in this chapter. Guérin's "Le Centaure" and Rabbe's "La Pipe," for example, while arguably intended as prose poems in ways that, say, *Petits Châteaux de Bohême* was not, seem linguistically close to eighteenth-century pseudotranslations like the *Chansons madécasses* or perhaps the Ossian-influenced passages of Goethe's *Werther*:

> Pour moi, ô Mélampe! je décline dans la vieillesse, calme comme le coucher des constellations. Je garde encore assez de hardiesse pour gagner le haut des rochers où je m'attarde, soit à considérer les nuages sauvages et inquiets, soit à voir venir de l'horizon les hyades pluvieuses, les pléiades ou le grand Orion; mais je reconnais que je me réduis et me perds rapidement comme une neige flottant sur les eaux, et que prochainement j'irai me mêler aux fleuves qui coulent dans le vaste sein de la terre.

[As for me, oh Melampe! I am sinking into old age, calm as the setting of the constellations. I still possess enough daring to gain the top of the cliffs where I linger, either to consider the savage and restless clouds or to watch the rainy Hyades, the Pleiades, or the great Orion come from the horizon. But I recognize that I am dwindling away and vanishing rapidly like a snowflake on the waves, and that next I will go to blend myself into the rivers that flow into the vast womb of the earth.]

End of "Le Centaure"[32]

Jeune homme, allume ma pipe; allume et donne, pour que je chasse un peu l'ennui de vivre; pour que je me livre à l'oubli de toutes choses, tandis que ce peuple imbécile, avide de grossières émotions, précipite ses pas vers la pompeuse cérémonie du sacré cœur, dans l'opulente et superstitieuse Marseille.

Pour moi, je hais la multitude et son stupide empressement . . . .

Je périrai bientôt: tout ce qui compose mon être et le nom même dont on me nomme, disparaîtra comme cette légère fumée . . . Dans quelques jours, peut-être, à la place où j'écris, on ne saura pas même si j'ai jamais vécu . . . Mais, de ce corps si périssable, s'exhalera-t-il quelque chose qui ne périsse pas et s'élève en haut? Réside-t-il en effet dans l'homme une étincelle digne d'allumer le calumet des anges sur les parvis des cieux? . . .

O ma pipe! chasse, bannis ce désir ambitieux et funeste de l'inconnu, de l'impénétrable.

[Young man, light my pipe; light it and give it to me, so that I may chase away a little of the pain of living; so that I may devote myself to the forgetting of all things, while these foolish people, thirsting after coarse emotions, quicken their steps toward the pompous ceremony of the sacred heart in opulent and superstitious Marseilles.

As for me, I hate the multitude and its stupid hurrying . . . .

I will die soon: everything that makes up my being and even the name by which I am called will disappear like this thin smoke. . . . In a few days, perhaps, in the spot where I am writing, they will not even know if I ever lived. . . . But, from this so perishable body, will something be exhaled that does not perish and lifts itself on high? In truth does there reside in man a spark worthy of lighting the pipe of the angels on the outer sanctuaries of the heavens? . . .

Oh my pipe! chase away, banish this ambitious and disastrous desire for the unknown, for the impenetrable.]

beginning of "La Pipe" up to "hurrying"; end of "La Pipe" following[33]

"Le Centaure" takes the form of a brief *récit* of a life, but its manner of address suggests that the letter may be generically related to the prose poem. Guérin's blend of classical subject matter and romantic sentiment is more conventional than one might expect given the substantial place he occupies in most histories of the *poème en prose*. It may be that his poem, merely by its length (ten pages) and narrative quality, represents not so much a forerunner to the works of Baudelaire and Rimbaud as it does an alternative path— arguably a self-consciously pagan variation on the genre of Cottin's *La Prise de Jéricho*. "La Pipe," on the other hand, is very Baudelairean, from its subject matter and language down to its author's Horatian contempt for the crowd, though perhaps not in its attitude toward the unknown. Its inclusion in an "album" links it to genres as various as journal entries, meditations, *pensées*, and whatever one calls selections from commonplace books.

Houssaye's "La Chanson du vitrier," like "Le Centaure," is a work influenced by the tradition of *poésie primitive*. As even a few lines from its opening make clear, it is anything but formally innovative:

> Oh! vitrier!
>
> Je descendais la rue du Bac; j'écoutai,—moi seul au milieu de tous ces passants qui à pied ou en carrosse allaient au but,—à l'or, à l'amour, à la vanité,—j'écoutai cette chanson pleine de larmes.
>
> Oh! vitrier!
>
> C'était un homme de trente-cinq ans, grand, pâle, maigre, longs cheveux, barbe rousse:—Jésus-Christ et Paganini.—Il allait d'une porte à une autre, levant ses yeux abattus. Il était quatre heures. Le soleil couchant seul se montrait aux fenêtres. Pas une voix d'en haut ne descendait comme la manne sur celui qui était en bas. "Il faudra donc mourir de faim!" murmura-t-il entre ses dents.
>
> Oh! vitrier!

> [Oh! glazier!
>
> I was walking down the rue du Bac; I listened—me, alone, in the middle of all those passers-by who were going on foot or by carriage to their goals: to money, to love, to vanity—I listened to this tearful song.
>
> Oh! glazier!
>
> There was a thirty-five-year-old man, tall, pale, thin, with long hair, a red beard—Jesus Christ and Paganini. He was going from one door to another, lifting his dejected eyes. It was four o'clock. The setting sun alone showed itself in

the windows. Not one voice from above was coming down like manna on the one who was below. "I will have to die of hunger!" he murmured between his teeth. Oh! glazier!][34]

The most striking feature of this poem is its introduction of urban subject matter. Champfleury, the propagandist of realism and friend of Baudelaire, also wrote prose poems, or fantasies, with urban subjects. Some of his fantasies, such as "L'Hiver" ("Winter"), have refrains like the "Oh! vitrier!" of "La Chanson du vitrier"; others, such as "La Morgue," have lines about a sentence long each, a length apparently determined by the expression of a complete thought:

> Un bâtiment bourgeois et carré qui baigne ses pieds dans la Seine,— voilà la Morgue au dehors.
>
> Huits lits de pierre, huits cavaliers dessus, voilà la Morgue au dedans.
>
> La Morgue aime la Seine, car la Seine lui fournit des épaves humaines.
>
> Ce qu'elles consomment à elles deux, ces terribles recéleuses, on l'ignore; mais le nombre en est grand.
>
> Elles ne tiennent pas à avoir des amants beaux et coquets, roses et blonds. Ouich! elles veulent la quantité.
>
> Aussi la Morgue s'entend-elle avec la Seine pour défigurer les hommes, afin de les garder le plus temps possible.
>
> [A square bourgeois building that bathes its feet in the Seine—that is the Morgue from the outside.
>
> Eight stone beds, eight gentlemen on them: that is the Morgue on the inside.
>
> The Morgue likes the Seine, because the Seine furnishes it with human flotsam.
>
> Whatever it is that these two, these terrible black-market dealers, conclude between themselves, no one knows; but the number is great.
>
> They don't care about having beautiful, coquettish lovers, pink and blond. Bah! they want quantity.
>
> The Morgue also has an understanding with the Seine to disfigure men, in order to keep them for the longest possible time.][35]

Champfleury's deliberate cultivation of contemporary and traditionally antipoetic subjects in *Chien-Caillou* has obvious affinities to Baudelaire's aesthetics. The relatively unimpassioned tone of the piece combined with a lack of cadences that call attention to themselves and its refrains make it read more like a newspaper story than a pseudotranslation of a Greek fragment or an Indian song. Whatever their formal differences, "La Chanson du vitrier" and "La Morgue" have more than their urban subject matter in common: they were written by people whom Baudelaire knew. While Baudelaire may introduce the urban note into his poetry with more success than his contemporaries, he was no more the first poet to write lyrics about the modern city than he was the first prose poet, his subsequent literary reputation notwithstanding.[36]

From a consideration of formal constraints alone, many literary and nonliterary genres relevant to the nineteenth-century prose poem exist. In addition to the ones I have been discussing, these genres would include short stories (of the sort written by Hoffmann, Borel, Champfleury, and Poe), essays, journals (an important model for works like Mercier's *Mon Bonnet de nuit* and Lefèvre's *Le Livre du promeneur*), sermons (Bossuet), character sketches (La Bruyère), *pensées* (Pascal), religious meditations (the primary model for Lamennais's *Paroles d'un croyant*), fragments, serialized travelogues, fables, *Tableaux de Paris*, parables, and the kind of ekphrastic writing found in *Salons*.[37] Since the significance of any given genre is often poem-specific, no single kind or group of kinds is paradigmatic for the *poème en prose*, though there may be some general patterns. Margueritte Murphy's intriguing suggestion that prose poems tend toward either description (ekphrasis) or narrative (anecdote, journal entry) points to two of the most common translation and differentiation strategies of prose poets.[38] Ad hoc groupings and subdivisions of prose poems are more and less appropriate depending on the context, but the classifying impulse should not become an end in itself. Writing a history of the *poème en prose* backward from a given set of texts tends either to rule out certain works a priori from consideration or to make them less visible. Generally speaking, the notion of poetry in prose, as yet without a single label, was hardly foreign to the literary milieu of Baudelaire, and the dialogic features of the *poème en prose*, in particular its mixture of high and low language, were as potentially reaffirming as subversive of convention. Because the degree to which the prose poem was, became, or is revolutionary cannot be decided in a reliable way based on formal criteria alone, it is better to consider the question on a case-by-case basis and to emphasize the wide range of prose possibilities existing in the nineteenth century.

Yet, as astounding as this variety of generic influences is, there are very few if any features of the *poème en prose* that cannot, in principle, be found in a *poème en vers*. The sort of genre comparisons I have been making with prose poems could be extended to verse poems like Baudelaire's "Le Voyage" and "Un Voyage à Cythère," lyrics that owe something to the travelogue. "Le

Voyage," the final poem of the final section of *Les Fleurs du mal*, "La Mort,"
also borrows some of the features and tones of the sermon. A comparison of
the opening stanza of Baudelaire's poem to Bossuet's "Sermon sur la Mort"
makes this borrowing clear:

> Pour l'enfant, amoureux de cartes et d'estampes,
> L'univers est égal à son vaste appétit.
> Ah! que le monde est grand à la clarté des lampes!
> Aux yeux du souvenir que le monde est petit!

> Ah! vraiment l'homme passe de même qu'une ombre, ou de même
> qu'une image en figure; et comme lui-même n'est rien de solide, il ne
> poursuit aussi que des choses vaines, l'image de bien, et non le bien
> même. . . . Que la place est petite que nous occupons en ce monde! si
> petite certainement et si considérable, qu'il me semble que toute ma
> vie n'est qu'un songe.

> [For the child in love with maps and picture books
> The universe is as big as his appetite.
> Oh! how large the world is under lamplight!
> How small under the light of memory it looks!

> Ha! truly man passes like a shadow, or like an image in a picture; and just as he
> is nothing solid, he also pursues only vain things, the image of good, and not
> the good itself. . . . How small the space we occupy in this world is! so small
> certainly and so considerable, that it seems to me that my life is only a dream.][39]

The final section of "Le Voyage" may also owe something to sermons like
Bossuet's:

> Ô Mort, vieux capitaine, il est temps! levons l'ancre!
> Ce pays nous ennuie, ô Mort! Appareillons!
> Si le ciel et la mer sont noir comme de l'encre,
> Nos cœurs que tu connais sont remplis de rayons!
> . . . Verse-nous ton poison pour qu'il nous réconforte!

> O mort, nous te rendons grâces des lumières que tu répands sur notre
> ignorance: toi seule nous convaincs de notre bassesse, toi seule nous
> fais connaître notre dignité: si l'homme s'estime trop, tu sais déprimer
> son orgueil; si l'homme se méprise trop, tu sais relever son courage.

> [Oh Death, old captain, it's time! lift anchor!
> This land bores us, oh Death, let's set sail!
> If the sky and the sea are as black as ink,

Our hearts that you know are filled with rays of light!
. . . Pour us your poison so it fortifies us!

Oh Death, we give you thanks for the lights that you spread out over our ignorance: you alone convince us of our meanness, you alone make us know of our dignity. If man esteems himself too much, you know how to put down his pride; if man despises himself, you know how to raise his courage again.][40]

Baudelaire's late poems tend to show a wide variety of tones and diction and contain many enjambments that dislocate the rhythm of the metrical line.[41] These lyrics, in other words, apparently move in the direction of prose. Victor Hugo went so far as to assert that poetry in verse had annexed prose for its own purposes:

Oui, mon vers croit pouvoir, sans se mésallier,
Prendre à la prose un peu de son air familier.
[Yes, my verse believes it can, without marrying beneath itself,
Borrow from prose a little of its familiar tone.]
  "À André Chénier"

J'ai jeté le vers noble aux chiens noirs de la prose.
[I threw the noble line to the black dogs of prose.]
  "Réponse à un acte d'accusation"[42]

For Hugo, works like Marchagny's *Gaule poétique* (1813–17), a popular collection of pseudofolk poems in prose, were not only less revolutionary than his lyrics, they were outright reactionary: "Look out for Marchagny! Poetic prose / Is a beaten track in which the old lean Pegasus lies."[43] Poetic prose may be something different from prose poetry in this context, but Hugo's warning is still worth keeping in mind with the *poème en prose*.

It is commonplace to speak of the lyric since romanticism as moving toward prose or natural speech, and the history of the modern lyric—one need only contemplate Ashbery's *Flow Chart*—adds support to the notion that verse poetry is potentially as generically mixed or dialogic as the prose poem. Prose poems like Baudelaire's are nevertheless significantly different from the lyric poems of their period. As analyses such as Barbara Johnson's comparison of the verse and prose versions of Baudelaire's "L'Invitation au Voyage" have shown, *Petits Poëmes en prose* tends to draw on more linguistic registers than the lyrics of *Les Fleurs du mal*, generally presenting them in opposition to more traditional poetic discourses.[44] In this sense it is worth taking literally Baudelaire's own description of *Petits Poëmes en prose*: "In sum, it is *Les Fleurs du mal* again, only with more liberty, and more detail, and more bantering."[45] Additional linguistic registers do not in and of themselves guarantee a socially or an aesthetically more radical poem, however; to argue that they do is to strip from a work its publishing and historical context. Just as pseudotranslations, simply by framing themselves as translations rather than original work, reduced their shock value for an audience accustomed to prose translations of poems, Baudelaire's prose poems, by often appearing alongside of and mimicking journalistic genres in magazines and newspapers, risked a certain amount of invisibility. Shock value and visibility do not necessarily best indicate a work's power to transform society or aesthetics, of course: an innovative work disguised as a familiar one could possess a kind of fifth-column discourse capable of undermining its apparent master discourse from within. But even or especially by this logic, there is no reason to suppose that the lyrics of *Les Fleurs du mal* are not, after all, more radically subversive than *Petits Poëmes en prose*.

To recapitulate: the degree to which the prose poem is a revolutionary genre cannot be decided without a consideration of individual works. Nor can the matter be decided without reference to literary and reception history. Perhaps most importantly, the binary opposition of subversive versus nonsubversive is a frame of reference as potentially limiting as it is occasionally illuminating for interpreting and evaluating prose poetry. As the next chapter shows, there are important tensions in Baudelaire's prose poems besides their supposedly jarring formal and discursive features, especially when one pays attention to the shifting voices and genres of which the poems are comprised.

3. Poetry in a Prosaic World

Ah! why was I born in a century of prose! —Baudelaire, "Various Notes on *L'Art philosophique*"

It may be that all genres define themselves against other genres from a theoretical point of view; the *poème en prose* has the notion of differentiation built into its generic label. Baudelaire, who named the modern genre of prose poetry, was especially concerned with presenting his prose poems as different from whatever came before them. This concern is apparent in his dedication to Arsène Houssaye:

I have a little confession to make to you. It was in paging through, for the twentieth time at least, the famous *Gaspard de la nuit* of Aloysius Bertrand (doesn't a book known by you, me and some of our friends have every right to be called *famous*?) that the idea came to me to try to do something analogous, and to apply the process that he had applied to painting and ancient life, so strangely picturesque, to modern life, or rather *a* modern and more abstract life.

Who among us, in his ambitious days, hasn't dreamed of the miracle of a poetic prose, musical without rhythm and rhyme, flexible and choppy enough to adapt itself to the lyrical movements of the soul, to the undulations of reverie, to the somersaults of consciousness? . . . You yourself, my dear friend, haven't you tried to translate the strident shout of the *Glazier* into a *song* . . . ?

But, to tell the truth, I fear that my jealousy hasn't brought me happiness. As soon as I began the work, I noticed that I not only kept far away from my mysterious and brilliant model, but also was doing something (if it can be called *something*) strangely different, an accident which anyone other than me would no doubt be proud of, but which can only profoundly humiliate a mind which thinks that the greatest honor of a poet is to accomplish *exactly* what he set out to do.[1]

Whatever Baudelaire's prose poems are, they are not the same as Bertrand's and Houssaye's lyrics in prose. Unlike *Gaspard de la nuit, Petits Poëmes en prose* is not concerned with ancient life but modern; not with painting but music—music that does not have rhyme or rhythm, that is. Houssaye, like Baudelaire, chose to write about modern and urban experiences, but he unfortunately tried to translate the shouts of the glazier into song. Baudelaire's remarks about Bertrand and Houssaye are tinged with irony and, as several critics have noted, may be deliberately obscuring important predecessors like Jules Lefèvre.[2] Baudelaire's need to position his *Petits Poëmes en prose* against other works and authors—especially as revealed in "La Solitude," one of Baudelaire's first prose poems—points to tensions in his ideas about the *poème en prose*. These tensions shed some light on recurrent concerns of his œuvre, have immediate interpretive consequences for his prose poems, and offer insights into prose poetry as a genre.

. . .

Baudelaire believed strongly in poetic craft and had doubts about the prose poem on grounds of exactitude. Although he asserts he has written something distinct from the work of Bertrand and Houssaye, Baudelaire is unsure if his prose poetry is substantial ("if it can be called *something*"). His desire for "the miracle of a poetic prose," although at heart a desire for mastery, paradoxically requires the poet to relinquish some control. The primacy of poetic craft is never in doubt, however. In order to achieve the effect of *prose poétique*, Baudelaire chooses to write *poèmes en prose*. He presents his decision to find a new form as willful, not a simple letting go of the poetic reins. From this point of view, the *poème en prose* is more than a generic label: it connotes an approach to writing.

In his posthumous (1868) edition of Baudelaire's works, Théophile Gautier also presented the poet of *Les Fleurs du mal* as an artist always in control of his medium. Gautier's description of his younger contemporary deliberately counters such popular images as the Satanist, the opium-eater, and the sensualist.[3] But when he comes to the dedicatory letter to Houssaye, Gautier comments: "One sees that Baudelaire always pretended to lead inspiration by the will and to introduce a sort of infallible mathematics into art. He blamed himself for having produced something other than what he had resolved to do, even if it was, as in the present case, an original and powerful work."[4] The verb "pretended" is significant, even if the connotation of deceit is weaker in "prétendait" than its English equivalent. Gautier intimates that Baudelaire's dedication stresses artistic craft over spontaneous expression for reasons that may not correspond to the truth.[5] However much Baudelaire is arguing for the power of the will, he is at least as interested in arguing against something else that Gautier calls inspiration, evoking the ancient distinction between poetic skill and frenzy. Why did Baudelaire feel the need to define himself in this negative way?

Baudelaire's concern with the will is not a unique feature of his prose poems.[6] Whether, as in "Au Lecteur" ("To the Reader"), "the rich metal of our will / Is completely dissolved" by an alchemist-Satan figure, or, as in "Paysage" ("Landscape"), where the poet speaks of his ability "to conjure up Spring with the force of [his] will," Baudelaire aligns artistic creation on the side of the will and views a loss of this power as a fall from an ideal into a splenetic everyday existence.[7] Baudelaire's emphasis on the will is even played out on a syntactic level in some lyrics:

> Je veux, pour composer chastement mes églogues,
> Coucher auprès du ciel
> [I want, in order to compose my eclogues in a chaste way,
> To sleep under the sky]
>   *"Paysage"*

> Je la veux agiter dans l'air comme un mouchoir!
> [I want to shake it in the air like a handkerchief!]
>   *"La Chevelure"*[8]

In the opening line of "Paysage," the verb "want" is cut off from its infinite "to sleep" in such a way as to highlight the imposition of the artist's will. In "La Chevelure," the classical positioning of the object of "agiter" in front of the verb "veux" in the phrase "Ja la veux agiter" creates a similar effect; it also briefly suggests the readings "I want her" and "I want to shake her." Baudelaire figures the will, as well as analogues like artistic creation, as something that is distinct from, if potentially threatened by, its opposite—ideal versus reality ("Rêve Parisien"), solitude versus multitude ("Paysage"), masculine versus feminine ("Les Bijoux"), solid versus dissolved matter ("Au Lecteur," "Tristesses de la Lune"). From this perspective, the poetry and prose elements of *Petits Poëmes en prose* represent less a departure from *Les Fleurs du mal* than a new figuration of a recurrent concern.

Baudelaire's need to define his own position negatively is related to his con-cern with originality. In projected prefaces to *Les Fleurs du mal*, Baudelaire denounces imitations and diligently composes a "Note on the plagiarisms."[9] Writing prose poems would bring issues of originality to a head for Baudelaire, not simply because he was aware of some recent precursors to his work but because of the many generic and discursive models to which he was opening up the lyric. Was there anything left that was truly his own when, as he felt, he had prostituted himself by writing this sort of poetry? But once evoked, originality can become a mere label for the poetic tensions it supposedly helps explain. In order to tease out the significance of Baudelaire's tendency to define himself negatively, it is necessary to establish first what context—biographical, publishing, literary, and historical—surrounded and helped determine the kind of prose poetry and commentary he wrote. Some of this context Baudelaire erased or obscured in the act of writing his poems and criticism; most of it has become invisible since then.

Baudelaire and Sainte-Beuve
Baudelaire's letter to Houssaye reveals as much through what it does not mention as through what it does. When Baudelaire writes parenthetically, "doesn't a book known by you, me and some of our friends have every right to be called *famous?*", who are the friends he is speaking of, and why does he bother with the confidential aside? Baudelaire makes a similar comment in the final prose poem of the *Petits Poëmes en prose*, "Les Bons Chiens" ("The Good Dogs"): "'*Where do the dogs go?*' Nestor Roqueplan said at one time in an immortal feuilleton that he no doubt has forgotten, and that I alone, and perhaps Sainte-Beuve, we still remember today."[10] Sainte-Beuve is unquestionably one of the friends Baudelaire is referring to in his letter, since he wrote the preface to the 1842 *Gaspard de la nuit* and was instrumental in introducing this work to the literary world.[11] Sainte-Beuve was also someone with whom Baudelaire discussed his prose poems and whom he hoped would help insure a favorable critical reception of them. When seeking candidacy to the Académie Française, for example, Baudelaire wrote to Alfred de Vigny that his "new attempt" of prose poetry was something that "Jules Janin and Sainte-Beuve found some relish for."[12] Baudelaire's relations with Sainte-Beuve are complicated—they are as likely to be marked by calculated flattery as by genuine admiration, by playful banter as by deep respect—and would be beside the point here if they did not figure importantly in Baudelaire's presentation of *Petits Poëmes en prose* and, by extension, in readings of

the poems. To see how this is so is in part to understand what lies behind Baudelaire's negative positioning of his work.

Baudelaire was a long-time admirer of Sainte-Beuve's work, especially the *Poésies et Pensées de Joseph Delorme* and the novel *Volupté*. As early as 1844 or 1845 Baudelaire wrote an adulatory letter to the older writer; by 1856, he was referring to the author of the *Lundis* as "mon cher protecteur."[13] Indeed, Baudelaire sought Sainte-Beuve's protection after the seizure of the 1857 *Fleurs du mal*. As J. Kamerbeek Jr. has shown, Sainte-Beuve offered Baudelaire an argument for his defense:

> Everything had been taken in the domain of poetry.
> Lamartine had taken the *heavens*, Victor Hugo had taken the *earth* and more than the *earth*, Laprade had taken the *forests*. Musset had taken *passion* and the *dazzling orgy*. Others had taken the *hearth*, the *rustic life*, etc.
> Théophile Gautier had taken Spain and its high colors. What remained?
>
> What Baudelaire took—
> It was if he had been forced there.[14]

In a letter written shortly after the seizure, Sainte-Beuve proposed a similar argument by comparing Baudelaire's poetry to his:

> But we too, thirty years ago, sought poetry where we could. Many fields as well had already been harvested, and the most beautiful laurels had been cut. I remember the painful situation of mind and soul in which I wrote *Joseph Delorme*. . . . I was familiar with some of your poems from having read them in various collections; together, they produce a totally different effect. To tell you that this general effect is a sad one should not surprise you: it is what you wanted. To tell you that you haven't, in putting together your *Fleurs*, recoiled before any sort of image or color, no matter how frightening or distressing it was, you know better than I: it is again what you wanted. You are very much a poet of the school of art.[15]

In other words, Sainte-Beuve saw Baudelaire as a poet of the will negotiating grim historical conditions for poetry.

Sainte-Beuve and Baudelaire continued to discuss each other's poetry as late products of romanticism throughout the 1860s. Baudelaire wrote to

Sainte-Beuve on 15 March 1865, "[T]his evening, I reread *Joseph Delorme* with Malassis. You are decidedly right; *Joseph Delorme* is the *Fleurs du mal* of the day before. The comparison is glorious for me. You will have the kindness not to find it offensive for you."[16] During this period Baudelaire was trying hard to complete his collection of prose poems, if only because his editor would not publish another edition of *Les Fleurs du mal* until he finished this new work.[17] Although Baudelaire often refers to his prose poems in derogatory terms like "bagatelles" ("trifles"), he also complains to Sainte-Beuve of the work they require: "To write *one hundred* laborious bagatelles that demand a constant good humor . . . that is what I wanted to do! I'm only up to *sixty*, and I can't go further."[18] Baudelaire explicitly associates his prose poems, *Joseph Delorme*, and the need to walk outside in a crowd in his 15 January 1866 letter to Sainte-Beuve: "I have tried diving back into *Le Spleen de Paris* (poems in prose), for it's not finished. Finally, I hope to be able to show, one of these days, a new Joseph Delorme catching his rhapsodic thought on each accident of his strolling and pulling a disagreeable moral from every object. But how bagatelles, when one wants to express them in a manner that is at once penetrating and light, are difficult to write!"[19] While Baudelaire is guilty of some flattery and machination in his letters—when the Hugo family came to Brussels in late 1865, for example, Baudelaire acted as a kind of go-between for Sainte-Beuve and his former lover, Madame Hugo—he is nevertheless consistent in portraying *Petits Poëmes en prose* as a product of romanticism and promenades in the modern city.[20]

Baudelaire and Balzac

As Kamerbeek points out, Sainte-Beuve was not the only one to speak of the contemporary poetic milieu in territorial terms. In a scene in Balzac's *Illusions perdues*, Lucien de Rubempré prefaces reading from his collection of fifty sonnets with an explanation for his choice of form:

> The sonnet, sir, is one of the most difficult works of poetry. This little poem [*petit poëme*] has generally been abandoned. No one in France could rival Petrarch, whose language, infinitely more supple than ours, allows for plays of thought repelled by our *positivism*—excuse the term. It therefore seemed to me original to debut with a collection of sonnets. Victor Hugo took the ode, Canalis [a fictional poet] gives us fleeting poetry, Béranger monopolizes the Song, Casimir Delavigne corners Tragedy and Lamartine the Meditation.[21]

In the world of Balzac, Sainte-Beuve's feudal territories give way to capitalist shrinking markets ("monopolizes," "corners"), but otherwise the argument is the same. Many French poets in the first half of the nineteenth century used quasi-generic labels for their collections of poetry (meditations, consolations, contemplations), deliberately or in effect as marketing strategies. Baudelaire's gambit with and jealous guarding of the genre of prose poetry can be seen in this light. He in fact had high hopes for making money off of *Petits Poëmes en prose*.[22] The terms "genre" and "poetic form" are easily conflated in such an atmosphere.

If "uncle Beuve" was a kind of protector-figure for Baudelaire, Balzac was a model of the artist who had the will to carry through his projects. In letters to his mother, Baudelaire spoke of Balzac as an ideal to which he aspired:

> But he ALWAYS worked. It is no doubt very consoling to think that by working one acquires not only money but also an incontestable talent. But at the age of thirty, Balzac had for several years acquired the habit of permanent work, and up to now I have nothing in common with him except debts and projects.
>
> I don't have the courage, I don't have the genius of Balzac, and I have all of the embarrassing circumstances that made him so miserable.[23]

In an anecdote in *Les Paradis artificiels*, Baudelaire specifically makes the connection between Balzac and willpower:

> Balzac no doubt thought that there is no greater shame and no more intense suffering for a man than the abdication of his will. I saw him once, at a meeting in which the subject was the prodigious effects of hashish. He was listening and asking questions with an attention and a liveliness that were amusing. The people who knew him guess that he ought to be interested. But the idea of thinking in spite of himself shocked him greatly. He was presented with dawamesk; he looked at it, sniffed it, and handed it back without touching it. The struggle between his almost child-like curiosity and his repugnance for abdication betrayed itself in a striking way on his expressive face. Love of dignity won out. In effect, it is difficult to imagine the theoretician of the *will*, this spiritual twin of Louis Lambert, consenting to lose a particle of that precious *substance*.[24]

Baudelaire's portrait is based on his reading of *La Comédie humaine* and his personal acquaintance with Balzac. Louis Lambert, the protagonist of one of

Balzac's philosophical novels, writes a treatise on the will. Lambert is also an alchemist figure and may have come to Baudelaire's mind via a comparison of the will to a chemical substance.[25]

Baudelaire, Balzac, Sainte-Beuve, and Gautier

As Lucien de Rubempré's apology for the "little poem" indicates, few French poets wrote sonnets in the early nineteenth century. Sainte-Beuve was one of the poets responsible for the form's revival, asserting in one of his *Lundis*: "I flatter myself at being the first among us [French poets] who renewed the example of the sonnet in 1828."[26] Sainte-Beuve had in fact presented himself as the reviver of the form as early as his imitation of Wordsworth's "Scorn not the sonnet": "As for me, I want to rejuvenate the sweet sonnet in France."[27] Gautier was another poet who acquired a reputation as a sonneteer. One of the sonnets Lucien recites as his own, "La tulipe," is in fact a Gautier poem that Balzac inserted into the novel courtesy of his friend.[28] In the context of the recitation scene, the sonnet is implied to be a pure if somewhat precious poetic form. Lucien, the naive provincial poet in Paris, is soliciting advice from the street-wise journalist Lousteau to whom he reads his sonnets, each of which has a flower's name as a title. After hearing Lucien recite a few poems, Lousteau talks about the difficulties in selling this sort of work. Lucien's *fleurs* appear destined to make their author as little money as Baudelaire's did.

Baudelaire is yet another poet for whom the sonnet is an important form. Forty-five out of the one hundred poems of the 1857 *Fleurs du mal* are sonnets, and the poems' arrangement in some ways suggests a sonnet sequence. Twelve out of the first twenty poems are sonnets, including eight in a row starting with "La Muse malade," and the collection closes with five sonnets. Even the "birth to death of poet" narrative evoked by the poems' arrangement is sonnet-sequence-like. Baudelaire wrote Petrarchan sonnets, Shakespearean sonnets, sonnets comprised entirely of couplets, sonnets rhymed with lines of different lengths, sonnets in octosyllables and decasyllables, and sonnets in various nonce forms that do not lend themselves to succinct description. He also often grouped sonnets, whether by subject or theme within *Les Fleurs du mal* or by publishing several together in different journals, such as the seven that appear in the 12 January 1862 issue of *Le Boulevard*.

The sonnet, with its notoriously strict poetic constraints, seems the formal opposite of the prose poem. What is the relationship between Lucien's "petit poème" and Baudelaire's *Petits Poëmes en prose*? Baudelaire himself wrote a piece of prose fiction about a poet who wrote sonnets. The Balzac-influenced "La Fanfarlo" tells the story of Samuel Cramer, author of a collection of son- nets entitled *Orfraies* (Ospreys). The rare word "orfraie" appears in Gautier's *La Comédie de la mort* (1838) and *Albertus* (1833), Banville's *Les Cariatides* (1842), and Hugo's *Les Orientales* (1829). Baudelaire seems to have associated the word with the first-generation romantics: "*Orfraies*, a collection of sonnets like those we all wrote and read in the time when we had such short[-sighted] judgment and such long hair."[29] As Robert Kopp has noted, the word "orfraie" also appears in a striking context in Sainte-Beuve's introduction to Bertrand's *Gaspard de la nuit*:

> Now it must be shown by enough examples that the poetic movement of 1824–28 was not a simple infatuation of a coterie . . . . Two or three somewhat lively imaginations in each town sufficed to give the signal and sound the literary alarm bell. Things transpired in the same way as in the sixteenth century, starting with the poetic revolution proclaimed by Ronsard and Du Bellay: le Mans, Anger, Poitiers, Dijon had enlisted their recruits and supplied their contingent. Thus, in our time, the romantic eaglet (enemies would say osprey) seemed to fly rather rapidly from bell-tower to bell-tower, and, finally, to judge from the general result after fifteen or so years of occupation that is less and less disputed, it seems to have conquered.[30]

Baudelaire's choice of the word "osprey" indicates he was ambivalent about romanticism, a movement he associated with writers like Sainte-Beuve and Hugo.[31] By dedicating his *Petits Poëmes en prose* to Houssaye (another first-generation romantic) and asserting that his predecessor was Bertrand (whom Sainte-Beuve introduced as an important minor romantic), Baudelaire simultaneously declares his romantic lineage and distances himself from it. The sonnet and the prose poem are alike in at least one other respect: they are poetic forms which the most celebrated poets of romanticism—Lamartine, Hugo, and Vigny—did not cultivate, a point Sainte-Beuve explicitly makes of the sonnet in the *Lundis* where he claims to have renewed the form for French poets and implies with the prose poem in the introduction to *Gaspard de la nuit* by presenting Bertrand as a minor poet.[32]

Baudelaire and Hugo

Balzac and Sainte-Beuve mention several romantic poets who cornered poetic markets or occupied poetic territories but place special emphasis on Hugo.

For Sainte-Beuve, Hugo is the poet who has "taken the *earth* and more than the *earth*." Balzac dedicates *Illusions perdues* to Hugo, describing him as a poet who can take on the journalists of Paris and keep his integrity, someone who has "like Chateaubriand, like all true talents, struggled against the envious people lying in ambush behind the columns or the rugs in the undergrounds of the Newspaper."[33] He is therefore the opposite of Lucien, whom the world of journalism corrupts and who is, in Vautrin's words, "a poet without will."[34] Sainte-Beuve and Balzac are not the only writers to accord the poet of *Les Contemplations* this lofty status, of course. Throughout most of the nineteenth century, "Victor Hugo" was virtually synonymous with prolific writing of poems, novels, and plays; expansive vision; and commercial success.

Baudelaire's feelings about Hugo were, to put it mildly, mixed. On the one hand, he praises Hugo in works like "Reflections on some of my contemporaries":

> You say of the one [poet]: that's a poet of *interiors*, or of family; of another, that's a poet of love; and of another, that's a poet of glory. But by what right do you thus limit the range of the talents of each one? Do you want to assert that the one who has sung of glory was, *by that very fact*, unfit for celebrating love? You thus invalidate the universal meaning of the word *poetry*. If you do not want simply to make it understood that circumstances, which do not come from the poet, have, *up to the moment*, confined him in a specialty, I will always believe that you are speaking of a poor poet, an incomplete poet, however skillful he is in *his* genre.
>
> Ah! with Victor Hugo we do not have to draw these distinctions, for he is a genius without bounds.[35]

On the other hand, Baudelaire's private judgments of Hugo are harsh:

> [O]ne can simultaneously possess a *special genius* and be a fool. Victor Hugo has proved that well to us. —By the way, he is going to be living in Brussels. He bought a house in the Leopold quarter. It appears that he and the Ocean have quarreled. Either he did not have the energy to bear up with the Ocean, or the Ocean *itself* became bored with him.[36]

Baudelaire's ambivalent feelings about Hugo are analogous to his ambivalent feelings about prose poetry expressed in the dedication to Houssaye. For Baudelaire, incorporating aspects of more commercially successful writing into his own writing (Hugo's prosy lyrics or various prose genres) is a perilous if necessary adventure from about 1859 onward.[37] Baudelaire does not abandon small, "controlled" lyric forms like the sonnet, but he makes a concentrated effort to expand his poetic repertoire, even emulates Hugo in three of the *Tableaux Parisiens*. "Le Voyage," another long, Hugolian poem, also dates from this period. Besides their expansiveness, these four poems are marked by a greater use of enjambment, enumerations, and a tendency toward numbered subdivisions—all trademarks of Hugo's poetry. While it would be misleading to say that Baudelaire's roughly contemporaneous decision to write prose poetry corresponds to a gradual loosening of poetic form—some prose poems predate verse poems, and prose poetry is less a variation on a verse form than its own form—his formal experimentation is an index of his effort to open his poetry to new influences. Baudelaire is probably thinking of himself when he writes about the poet for whom "circumstances, which do not come from the poet, have, *up to the moment*, confined him in a specialty." He, too, is capable of writing in more than one genre.

Hugo is not just an expansive, insufferable, multifaceted genius for Baudelaire. He is the incarnation of romanticism:

> Today when we go through the recent poems of Victor Hugo, we see that just as he was he remains: a pensive walker, a man who is solitary but enthusiastic about life, a dreamy and questioning mind. But it is no longer in the wooded and flowered surroundings of the big city, on the broken quays of the Seine, among the promenades swarming with children, that he makes his feet and eyes wander. Like Demosthenes, he talks with the waves and the wind. At one time he prowled alone in places teeming with human life; today, he walks in solitudes peopled by his thoughts. In this way he is perhaps even more great and unusual. The colors of his reveries are tinged with solemnity, and his voice has deepened in rivaling that of the Ocean. But there, as here, he always appears to us as the walking statue of Meditation.[38]

While it is difficult not to read irony in phrases like "his voice has deepened in rivaling that of the Ocean," the most important criticism of Hugo is the unstated comparison between the country and the city *promeneur*. The romantic giant Hugo, living in exile, walks in solitude among nature, talking with the waves and the wind. Even when he lived in Paris he wandered "in the wooded and flowered surroundings of the big city, on the broken quays of the Seine, among the promenades swarming with children." Baudelaire is positioning the city walks of his prose poems against the nature walks of

Hugo, Rousseau, and Lefèvre. The *promenades* of Baudelaire and Hugo are alike, however, in that they represent the poet alone among multitudes.

Baudelaire and Jules Janin

Baudelaire was aware of at least one person who had written a book about a nighttime city walker. Jules Janin, the "prince of critics" much sought after by Baudelaire, was also the author of a book entitled *Le Gâteau des rois* (*The Cake of Kings*, 1847). As Jean-François Delesalle has argued, *Petits Poëmes en prose* may represent a reaction to and completion of a project "sketched and missed by Janin."[39] *Le Gâteau des rois* often digresses from its narrative and refers to its own generic status or lack thereof. What little narrative exists involves a young man who walks through Paris on the night of the Epiphany, the feast of kings, with a magic lantern that shows him different visions. The narrator of this story is fond of speaking of his writing as a kind of poem in prose:

> I am not unaware that prose is an outfit that does not go well with poetic things, and I don't know how to present myself to you, young colorists of the school of master Théodore de Banville . . . if you would lend me your rustic flute, Madame Desbordes-Valmore; accompany my loyal prose, oh you, Madame Tastu; and you as well. . . . [But] poetry doesn't come, and while I am invoking the alexandrine, see how pouting prose plants me there, indignant, in the middle of my song, and I find myself sitting on the ground.[40]

The narrator also plays with the idea that poetry, in its traditional sense, is dead, and that this death is more the fault of the poets than the age:

> And so, friend Fabius, if poetry is dead if the dream is no longer walking the streets, if the ideal hides itself the way a woman dressed in yesterday's fashion would, it's somewhat the fault of the time, I agree, but also very much the fault of the poets. You idle Pindars, admit it proudly: you are too occupied with form, you are too great lovers of rhyme, you completely intoxicate yourselves in the sonorous burst of your harmonious periods, and, during this time, you forget to mix, even out of charity, a story, a moral, an interest, a curiosity in your poems?[41]

In short, well before his angry response to Janin's 1865 article against melancholic and satanic poets, Baudelaire had some reasons for calling for an "éreintage absolu" (absolutely savage criticism) of Janin.[42] That Baudelaire for the most part refrained from publicly venting his anger against Janin can be attributed to his need for the critic's patronage. As Delesalle notes, Janin, for his part, tended to portray Baudelaire as a kind of wild man or curiosity in superficially positive criticism.[43]

One can gather Baudelaire's reaction to *Le Gâteau des rois* most directly from the opening of a review he never finished:

> In order to give immediately the reader who is not initiated into *the behind the scenes* of literature, who is not instructed in the preliminaries of reputations, a first idea of the real literary importance of those little books that are big on wit, poetry, and observations—let him know that the first among them, *Chien-Caillou: Fantaisies d'hiver*, was published at the same time as a book of a very famous man who, at the same time as Champfleury, had the idea of these quarterly publications. For, among the people for whom the sort of intelligence applied daily to produce books is more difficult than any other, Champfleury's book *absorbed* the book of the famous man. All those of whom I speak were familiar with *Le Gâteau des Rois*; they were familiar with it because their job is to be familiar with everything. *Le Gâteau des Rois*, a kind of *Christmas*, or Noël book, was above all a pretension clearly affirming to draw from the tongue all of the effects that a transcendent instrumentalist draws from his instrument. Play infinite variations on the dictionary! Displacement of efforts! Error of a weak mind! In this odd book ideas follow one another in haste, are spun out with the rapidity of sound supporting itself at random on infinitely subtle relations. The ideas connect among themselves by an excessively frail thread, according to a method of thought exactly analogous to that of those people they lock up for mental derangement—a vast current of involuntary ideas, a steeple-chase, an abnegation of the will.[44]

Baudelaire wishes to assert the priority and superiority of his friend Champfleury's work over Janin's: he awkwardly repeats the phrase "at the same time" as if to suggest that, even if *Chien-Caillou* was not written earlier than *Le Gâteau des rois*, it is still the more original book. Moreover, Janin's work is much more time-bound than Champfleury's: written by a journalistic intelligence capable of churning out books daily, *Le Gâteau des rois* is a kind of gift book, perhaps purposely written for the Christmas season given its subject matter. Baudelaire's most damning criticism of *Le Gâteau des rois*, however, is that its author abnegates his creative will. For the narrator of *Le Gâteau des rois* who complains of not being able to write in alexandrines, the poem in prose is, in Delesalle's phrase, "the last recourse of poetic impotence."[45] It may be that Baudelaire reacted so strongly against Janin because of his own anxiety about the fate of poetry in the modern world. In *Le Gâteau des rois*, Janin presents the contemporary period as the age of the novel: "Behold the reign, the true reign of the novel! Its day of universal domination has shone in the gladdened sky; Alexander the Great himself would never have dared dream of such a tyranny happily accepted by everyone. Deny it then, Mr. Hugo reigns by the novel he promises us entirely as much as by his past novels!"[46] In a 29 March 1862 letter, Baudelaire remarked to his mother: "Finally, I read at Flaubert's a few chapters of his next novel; it's admirable; I experienced a sentiment of invigorating envy. Hugo is going to publish his *Misérables*, a novel in ten vol[umes]. Yet another reason for my poor volumes, *Eureka, Poems in Prose*, and *Reflections on my contemporaries*, not to appear."[47] The prose poems of Baudelaire are not simply a response to *Le Gâteau des rois* any more than they are an offshoot of the rise of the novel. But neither would they be what they are without their author's obsessive need not to write in certain genres and forms.

• • •

Baudelaire's first prose poems were published in *Fontainebleau* (1855), a collection of "Landscapes, Legends, Memories, [and] Fantasies" issued as a benefit for and homage to C. F. Denecourt, caretaker of the forest of Fontainebleau. Presumably all of the verse and prose pieces in this collection were supposed to relate to forests. Baudelaire's decision to contribute "Les Deux Crépuscules"—the verse poems "Le Soir" and "Le Matin" along with the prose poems "Le Crépuscule du soir" and "La Solitude"—is therefore a pointed statement against the book's implied aesthetic of the natural.[48] As F. W. Leakey has pointed out, Baudelaire could have easily complied with the program of the book by sending a poem like "Correspondances."[49] Instead, he sent four urban poems with a letter, also published in *Fontainebleau*, to his friend who had solicited the poetry:

> My dear Desnoyers, you are asking me for some poems for your little volume, some poems on *Nature*, isn't that right? on woods, tall oaks, the greenness, the insects—the sun no doubt? But you know well that I am incapable of being moved by vegetables. . . . Given the impossibility of completely satisfying you according to the strict terms of the program, I send you along two poetic pieces that represent roughly the sum of

the reveries with which I am assailed during the twilight hours. In the depths of the woods, enclosed under those vaults that are like the vaults of sacristies and cathedrals, I think of our astonishing cities, and the prodigious music that rolls on the summits seems to me the translation of human lamentations.[50]

Baudelaire is not merely exercising a perverse temperament, he is showcasing his relatively new antinature aesthetic.[51] In the context of poems like Hugo's "À Albert Dürer," Baudelaire's twilight poems certainly stand out, but Baudelaire is not the only contributor who interprets the program of the collection in a personal way. Hippolyte Castille, for example, uses the experience of being alone in a forest as an excuse to write a philosophical reflection "On Solitude." While solitude is a topos of romantic nature poetry—the subject occurs in many contributions to *Fontainebleau*—Castille implies in a preliminary remark that he is doing something different from what writers in the romantic tradition have done, if only because "Zimmermann and Rousseau . . . have exhausted the physiology of the subject."[52] With its implied urban setting, Baudelaire's own reflection on solitude, like the dedication to Houssaye, displaces its romantic inheritance in the act of acknowledging it.

In its original published version, "La Solitude" makes a pair with "Le Crépuscule du soir." Baudelaire's contributions are placed between the poetry and the prose halves of *Fontainebleau*. His verse poems follow Gustave Mathieu's satire composed in "green solitudes . . . Far from the sales that one sees crawling in the city"; his prose poems come before George Sand's "Fragment d'une lettre."[53] The texts of the *Fontainebleau* "Le Crépuscule du soir" and "La Solitude" differ substantially from their later published versions. Most strikingly, they are written in paragraphs separated by blank spaces, like Bertrand's *fantaisies* in *Gaspard de la nuit*. They also call attention to their relation to each other.[54] The narrator of "Le Crépuscule du soir" describes the twilight manias of his "two friends"; "La Solitude" begins: "He—the second one—also told me that solitude was bad for people."[55] Significantly, the *Fontainebleau* versions are about half the size of their *Petits Poëmes en prose* namesakes, as if prose poems obeyed an inverse law of verse lyric economy and expanded with revision.

If only because of its position in *Fontainebleau* and status as one of Baudelaire's first prose poems, "La Solitude" can be read as a work that reflects on its generic identity. In spite or because of all of the revisions, the *Petits*

Poëmes en prose version of "La Solitude" is especially revealing of its author's mixed feelings about the genre of prose poetry:

Un gazetier philanthrope me dit que la solitude est mauvaise pour l'homme; et à l'appui de sa thèse, il cite, comme tous les incrédules, des paroles des Pères de l'Église.

Je sais que le Démon fréquente volontiers les lieux arides, et que l'Esprit de meurtre et de lubricité s'enflamme merveilleusement dans les solitudes. Mais il serait possible que cette solitude ne fût dangereuse que pour l'âme oisive et divagante qui la peuple de ses passions et de ses chimères.

Il est certain qu'un bavard, dont le suprême plaisir consiste à parler du haut d'une chaire ou d'une tribune, risquerait fort de devenir fou furieux dans l'île de Robinson. Je n'exige pas de mon gazetier les courageuses vertus de Crusoé, mais je demande qu'il ne décrète pas d'accusation les amoureux de la solitude et du mystère.

Il y a dans nos races jacassières des individus qui accepterait avec moins de répugnance le supplice suprême, s'il leur était permis de faire du haut de l'échafaud une copieuse harangue, sans craindre que les tambours de Santerre ne leur coupassent intempestivement la parole.

Je ne les plains pas, parce que je devine que leurs effusions oratoires leur procurent des voluptés égales à celles que d'autres tirent du silence et du recueillement; mais je les méprise.

Je désire surtout que mon maudit gazetier me laisse m'amuser à ma guise. "Vous n'éprouvez donc jamais,—me dit-il, avec un ton de nez très apostolique,—le besoin de partager vos jouissances?" Voyez-vous le subtil envieux! Il sait que je dédaigne les siennes, et il vient s'insinuer dans les miennes, le hideux trouble-fête!

"Ce grand malheur de ne pouvoir être seul! . . ." dit quelque part La Bruyère, comme pour faire honte à tous ceux qui courent s'oublier dans la foule, craignant sans doute de ne pouvoir se supporter eux-mêmes.

"Presque tous nos malheurs nous viennent de n'avoir pas su rester dans notre chambre", dit un autre sage, Pascal, je crois, rappelant ainsi dans la cellule du recueillement tous ces affolés qui cherchent le bonheur dans le mouvement et dans une prostitution que je pourrais appeler *fraternitaire*, si je voulais parler la belle langue de mon siècle.

[A philanthropic newsman tells me that solitude is bad for people; and in support of his thesis, like all unbelievers, he quotes sayings of the church fathers.

I know that the devil gladly frequents desert places, and that the spirit of murder and lust flares up marvelously well in solitudes. But it's possible that this solitude is only dangerous for idle and wandering souls who populate it with their passions and delusions.

Certainly a chatterbox, whose greatest pleasure consists in speaking from the height of a pulpit or a platform, would run a strong risk of going stark mad on Robinson's island. I don't ask my newsman to have Crusoe's courageous virtues, but I do ask him not to point a finger at those who love solitude and mystery.

Our talkative race includes individuals who would accept the death sentence less reluctantly, provided they were allowed to deliver a long harangue from the scaffold's heights without fearing that Santerre's drums might, at the wrong moment, cut short their words.

I don't pity them, because I suppose that their oratorical outpourings give them pleasures equal to those that others obtain from silence and meditation— but I do despise them.

Above all I want my damn newsman to let me enjoy myself as I please. "Then you'll never feel the need to share your delights?" he says to me in his most nasal and apostolic tone. Just imagine the subtlety and envy of the man! This disgusting stick in the mud—he knows that I look down on his pleasures, and so he comes worming his way into mine!

"That great misfortune of not being able to be alone! . . ." La Bruyère says somewhere, as if to shame all those people who rush to forget themselves in crowds, no doubt afraid they can't put up with themselves.

"Almost all of our misfortunes come to us from not having known how to stay in our room," says another wise man, Pascal, I believe, thereby summoning back to their cells of meditation all of those overwrought people who seek happiness in movement and a prostitution that I could call *fraternistic*, if I wanted to speak the sweet speech of my century.][56]

The opening of the poem makes the authority of different discourses an immediate issue: "A philanthropic newsman tells me that solitude is bad for people; and in support of his thesis, like all unbelievers, he quotes sayings of the church fathers." Delesalle suggests that Baudelaire had Janin in mind here, but regardless of any biographical reference, the speaker is positioning himself against the naïvely or falsely altruistic language of the "philanthropic newsman"—someone who is not convinced of his own assertions ("like all unbelievers") or is controlled by his language (he quotes out of habit).[57] Besides the diction and tone of everyday language, logical or persuasive rhetoric ("in support of his thesis") and religious discourse ("sayings of the church fathers") are evoked here, all of which are presented as being outside of the speaker's own language. The speaker never cites his own replies to the newsman. Instead, the reader must supply these retorts given the commentary of ideas that comes between the first paragraph and the next quoted remark of "my damn newsman." In short, the ability to use words effectively is a serious issue in "La Solitude."

From the outset, then, a poem called "La Solitude" offers a wide range of voices, but it is not so much the source of the voices as the rhetorical impact of alluding to outside voices that is immediately relevant and revealing. The different voices in "La Solitude" seem to be engaged in a debate over the advantages and disadvantages of solitude. Literary examples are mustered on the positive side of solitude: the character of Robinson Crusoe, the quotations purported to be from La Bruyère and Pascal. On the other side, images associated with institutions for the masses are given: "the sayings of church fathers" and the condemned person mounting the scaffold to address a crowd. The mention of "Santerre's drums" alludes to the execution of Louis XVI and may suggest the image of a democratic mob rule drowning out an individual voice. The expression "cut short their words" is used, half humorously, in conjunction with the guillotine and implied to be more devastating than it. But with digressive comments such as "I don't ask my newsman to have Crusoe's courageous virtues, but I do ask him not to point a finger at those who love solitude and mystery," there is a tension between what the speaker logically asserts and what his tone of understatement connotes. The discourse of reason or persuasion is being played with, shifting the focus of the argument away from the advantages and disadvantages of solitude. The individual's will is the determining factor in the argument, and the ability to exist in solitude is the telltale sign of a strong individual will—hence the speaker's need to be left alone to pursue goals as he pleases and his disdain of individuals who cannot act on their own will.

It is no accident that Baudelaire's concern with the will surfaces in one of his first prose poems, especially a poem in which the speaker places such high stakes on the ability to use, and not be used by, language. The speaker in "La Solitude" never quotes his own replies to the newsman's comments and questions, and he makes other people do the talking for him in a way that shows his own position does not depend on theirs. By saying that La Bruyère wrote "somewhere" about the "misfortune of not being able to be alone" and "another wise man, Pascal, I believe" wrote about not being able to sit quietly in one's room, the speaker is not quoting these writers as authority in the way the newsman quotes the sayings of the church fathers. And when the speaker asserts at the end of the poem that the actions of those people who need to lose themselves in a crowd is "a prostitution I could call *fratneristic*, if I wanted to speak the sweet speech of my century," he is making a sharp distinction between someone else's language and his own. He, or Baudelaire for that matter, is speaking the "sweet speech" of the nineteenth century, but through his use of the praeteritio "I *could* call . . . if I *wanted* to speak" he implies it is a matter of carefully selected rhetorical effect, not the result of unreflected impulses that control him.

In keeping outside linguistic registers at bay, the poet may be anxiously denying that his language relies on discourses he would distinguish from his own, but he parries this anxiety through narration, quotation, and indirect citation and misquotation. The La Bruyère aphorism "That great misfortune of not being able to be alone!" for example, is not exactly the same as the original passage in La Bruyère's *Les Caractères*.[58] As a number of critics have noted, disregarding the ellipsis and the exclamation point, Baudelaire's quotation is identical to the epigraph Poe uses for two of his short stories, "The Man of the Crowd" and "Metzengerstein."[59] The prose poem's additions to La Bruyère's lament give it a tone of exasperation.[60] The Pascal aphorism also differs from its original.[61] It is possible to interpret Baudelaire's misquotations as merely typical of an age in which the modern scholarly practice of supplying precise and footnoted quotations is not an operative concern, but "La Solitude" was revised over a period of several years. Baudelaire's manner of quotation also points to outside genres that inform his writing, such as the moral tale and the anecdote.

As several critics have suggested, one possible source of Baudelaire's Pascal is chapter 15 of Sainte-Beuve's *Volupté*.[62] At this point in the novel, the erotically frustrated narrator, Amaury, describes his struggles to come to terms with what he has been calling *volupté*, "voluptuousness" or "sensuality":

> La pauvre science, les livres négligés auxquels je revins, m'y aidèrent; je passais les soirs dans ma chambre: le malheur de beaucoup est de ne pas savoir passer les soirs dans sa chambre, Pascal a dit quelque chose d'approchant.
> [The poor knowledge, the neglected books to which I returned, helped me with this; I would spend my evenings in my room: the misfortune of much is not to know how to spend evenings in one's room, Pascal said something like that.][63]

The vagueness with which the narrator attributes the aphorism to Pascal is similar to the speaker's "Pascal, I believe" in "La Solitude." The context of the passage is even more suggestive. For Amaury, willpower is a kind of necessary but insufficient participant in the struggle with *volupté*: "Our will alone can do nothing, although without it Grace hardly ever descends or does not last."[64] Amaury compares the double necessity of grace and will to the *lisière* (leading string) parents sometimes attach to children when they are teaching them to walk. The string, grace, prevents the child from falling and, as the child vaguely senses, is always there even when he or she manages to walk alone. Ideally a double movement of grace and will characterizes the soul:

> Les plus saints sont ceux qui vont si également et si agilement, qu'on ne sait, à les voir de loin, s'ils marchent grâce à la vélocité de leurs pieds ou au soutien, au soulèvement continuel de la lisière; tant ce double mouvement chez eux est en harmonie et ne fait qu'un, les lisières ne les quittants plus, s'incorporant à leur épaule comme deux ailes immuables. [The most saintly are those who go so evenly and so nimbly that one does not know, seeing them from far away, whether they walk by the speed of their feet or by the support, the continual upward pull of the leading string—that is how much this double movement of theirs is in harmony and makes a whole, with the leading strings no longer leaving them but incorporating themselves into their shoulders like two immovable wings.][65]

In the 1861 version of "La Solitude," the line about solitude being only dangerous for those souls "who populate it with their passions and delusions" reads "which a despotic idea does not hold by the leading string."[66] Sainte-Beuve's image of ingrown *lisières* as angel wings is also similar to Baudelaire's description of the thrysus—the Bacchic emblem of fertility—in the prose poem "Le Thyrse":

> Le bâton, c'est votre volonté, droite, ferme et inébranlable; les fleurs, c'est la promenade de votre fantaisie autour de votre volonté; c'est l'élément féminin exécutant autour du mâle ses prestigieuses pirouettes. Ligne droite et ligne arabesque, intention et expression, roideur de la volonté, sinuosité du verbe, unité du but, variété des moyens, amalgame tout-puissant et indivisible du génie, quel analyste aura le détestable courage de vous diviser et de vous séparer?
> [The stick, that's your will, straight, firm, and unshakable; the flowers, that's the walk of your fancy around your will—it's the feminine element executing its marvelous pirouettes around the male element. Straight line and arabesque line, intention and expression, stiffness of the will, sinuosity of the verb, unity

of the aim, variety of the means, all powerful and indivisible amalgam of genius, what analyst will have the detestable courage to divide you and separate you?]⁶⁷

The Poe-resonant "arabesque" and the De Quincey-informed "amalgam" hint at Baudelaire's association of the indivisible mixture of will and fancy with the blending of personal and outside voices. "Amalgam" in particular is used in the *Confessions of an English Opium Eater* to describe situations in which one's own ideas mix with someone else's in such a way as to make them indistinguishable.

Another voice that blends almost indistinguishably into "La Solitude" is Balzac's. In a scene in *Illusions perdues* shortly before Lucien's talk with Lousteau, the young poet is waiting in a newspaper office to meet with an editor and notices nine different caricatures drawn in ink on a novel titled *Solitaire*, "a book whose unheard of success was being commended in Europe at the time and which necessarily irritated the journalists."⁶⁸ In the context of Balzac's novel, the sudden appearance of *Solitaire*, a real novel written by the vicomte d'Arlincourt, represents one last version of the warning d'Arthez has given Lucien to work in solitude, away from the world of journalism. Lucien later receives advice about solitude from a very different source, Vautrin: "[T]ake this in, engrave it in your still so malleable brain: man has a horror of solitude. And of all the solitudes [that exist], moral solitude is the one that terrifies him the most. . . . The first thought of man, whether he is a leper or a convict, infamous or sick, is to have an accomplice to his destiny. In order to satisfy this sentiment, which is life itself, he uses all of his energy, all of his power, his lifeblood. Without this sovereign desire, could Satan have been able to find companions?"⁶⁹ The ex-convict Vautrin is trying to convince Lucien to accompany him to Paris. Instead of using all of their energy to remain in their rooms, Vautrin claims people use every possible means not to be alone. As Lucien writes in a letter in *Splendeurs et misères des courtisanes*, Vautrin is "la poésie du mal," but he is also the figure who constantly makes fun of the idealism of poets: "As for you, my little one," Vautrin says to Lucien after having tutored him for a few years in the ways of Parisian life, "you are no longer such a poet that you will let yourself go to a new Coralie. We are going to make prose."⁷⁰ Toward the close of *Splendeurs et misères des courtisanes*, the narrator digresses to talk about the solitary confinement of the unconfessed condemned man:

Since the abolition of [physical] torture, public prosecutors, in the entirely natural desire to reassure the already very delicate consciences of the jurors, discovered the terrible resources that solitude gives justice against remorse. Solitude is emptiness, and moral nature is as afraid of it as physical nature is. Solitude is inhabitable only by the man of genius who fills it with his ideas, daughters of the world of the mind, or by the contemplator of divine works who finds it illuminated by the day of heaven, animated by the breath and the voice of God. . . . This sinister situation [of the solitary, unconfessed condemned man] which takes on such enormous proportions in certain cases . . . will have its story, in its place, in the *Comédie Humaine*.⁷¹

Baudelaire's speaker in "La Solitude" expresses a similar thought about the habitability of solitude, only in a negative, qualified way: "But it's possible that this solitude is only dangerous for idle and wandering souls who populate it with their passions and delusions." Balzac never did write the story about the condemned man in solitary confinement. Though Baudelaire's "La Solitude" is not in any direct sense the novel Balzac did not write, the *Petits Poëmes en prose* does represent an alternative to the Balzacian project. In a draft of the dedication to Houssaye, Baudelaire writes that his collection of prose poems "is worth more than an intrigue of 6000 pages."⁷² Insofar as an aesthetic of fragmentation is operative in *Petits Poëmes en prose*—"We can cut where we want," Baudelaire writes in the dedication to Houssaye, "me my reverie, you the manuscript, the reader his reading"—it is a work that positions itself against long narratives.⁷³ *Petits Poëmes en prose* is no more the novel of *La Comédie humaine* than it is the *petites epopées* (little epics) of Hugo's *La Légende des siècles*.

The final voice the speaker of "La Solitude" echoes is Baudelaire's own. The poem's deflating close "if I wanted to speak the sweet speech of my century" echoes a passage from one of Baudelaire's projected prefaces for the 1861 *Fleurs du mal*: "I know that the lover impassioned by beautiful style exposes himself to the hatred of the multitudes. But no human respect, no false modesty, no coalition, no universal suffrage will force me to speak the incomparable *patois* of this century, nor force me to confuse ink with virtue."⁷⁴ The similarity of the ending of "La Solitude" to this passage helps the reader identify the speaker in the poem with Baudelaire; it also calls attention to some of the ways in which *Petits Poëmes en prose* relates to *Les Fleurs du mal*. On the one hand, Baudelaire's prose poems represent a continued struggle against the poet's speaking the *belle langue* (sweet speech) of his century. On the other hand, it is obvious that *Petits Poëmes en prose* opens up Baudelaire's poetry to nineteenth-century discourses one finds less often, if at all, in his verse lyrics. Baudelaire offers various "solutions" to his self-posed dilemma, such as the image of the thyrsus, with its double movement of will and fancy, and the notion of the amalgam, where the controlling voice of the self is mixed with other voices yet remains autonomous—but in the end his gestures are essentially negative. He is not writing as Hugo writes, nor as Balzac writes, nor as Sainte-Beuve says Bertrand writes, and especially not as Janin writes. Although Baudelaire does manage to clear poetic space for himself in this way, he is not alone in his enterprise. As a close look at Baudelaire's "Solitude" shows, other voices, other genres are there—hidden and yet as present as a leading string.

My reading of Baudelaire's peopled "Solitude" may seem to argue that prose poetry, as a genre, tends to be many voiced, dialogic, and more open than verse poetry to discourses traditionally foreign to the lyric. Such is the consensus view on prose poetry, at least since Barbara Johnson's *Défigurations du langage poétique* (1979). While there is something to this idea, perhaps especially in regard to Baudelaire's work, poetry of the last hundred years (if not more) amply shows that there is nothing preventing verse poems from including all but maybe one feature of the prose poem, the absence of line breaks. Viewed in its literary-historical context, the *poème en prose* emerged when the lyric was undergoing changes necessitated by pressures, in part economic, that genres like the novel were exerting on it, but prose poetry is only one of many possible responses to these pressures, as its tardy development in England and America vis-à-vis free verse suggests. While Baudelaire's anxiety about the prose poem may be an index of the form's revolutionary potential, it may also reflect a more mundane sort of dissatisfaction—an artist casting a cold eye on his work.

Baudelaire's preoccupation with the will and artistic craft, coupled with his reputation as a lyric poet, helped and continues to help shape our view of the *poème en prose* as a genre. Baudelaire was hardly alone in writing prose poems in his time, and yet his name for the genre has stuck, and his history of the genre, going back to Bertrand, remains the standard version. We are so accustomed to locating Baudelaire as a starting point for poetic modernity that we are eager to attach his name to prose poetry and to consider the genre revolutionary or subversive. As the next chapter shows, looking back through a poet like Rimbaud makes the association even more tempting, but Rimbaud was not the only French writer writing prose poems in the decades following Baudelaire's death. By placing one of Baudelaire's first prose poems in literary-historical context, I hope to have made more visible the revolutionary (or evolutionary) narrative inherent in histories of the genre and to cast doubt on some of its aesthetic and theoretical implications. The prose poem need not be seen as exceptionally many voiced, and, insofar as Baudelaire's or any poet's work in this genre is exceptional, the prose poem's success need not depend on the number of voices or discourses it draws from, perhaps not even on the way in which it mixes them. Much criticism takes for granted the idea that all lyric poetry before some moment in the nineteenth century (or was it modernism or postmodernism?) is single voiced. We should not only question that perspective but also reexamine what we are objecting to in the first place. For if it turns out that any number of verse lyrics contain as many voices as Baudelaire's "Solitude," then maybe it is not so much the fact of many voices, or the illusion of a single voice, that matters so much as the way in which poets construct and disrupt voice.

4. The Makings of a Genre

If Baudelaire was somewhat tentative about writing poetry in prose, the generations of poets that followed him were not. Mallarmé was already writing and publishing his first prose poems in the 1860s, before Baudelaire's death. Lautréamont wrote his prose poems in the late 1860s; Rimbaud in the early 1870s. In different journals of the period one can find quite a few works that are arguably poems in prose, some labeled as such and some not. By the mid 1880s, as Suzanne Bernard has shown, the name if not the genre "poème en prose" had established itself in France: from the last decades of the nineteenth to the first decade of the twentieth century, there was a proliferation not only of collections of prose poems, but also of critical discussions of the *poème en prose* and related experiments in verse and prose forms.[1] When Max Jacob wrote his celebrated preface to *Le Cornet à dés* (*The Dice Cup*, 1917), a substantial tradition of prose poetry existed in France with and against which poets could align themselves.

Some of the appeal of the *poème en prose* in late nineteenth-century France can be attributed to the period's prevailing aesthetic climate. As a self-consciously modern form, the prose poem fit in well with one of Baudelaire's most important legacies, the artistic imperative to be modern. In an age in which music, in particular the synthesis of different media associated with Wagner, represented an ideal of expression, a generically mixed form that called into question boundaries between genres was bound to find its adherents.[2] To decadents like Des Esseintes, the hero of Huysmans's *À Rebours* (*Against Nature*, 1884), the prose poem represented the "ozmazome" of literature: a novel concentrated in a few pages, "a delectation offered to delicate people, accessible only to them," the essence of an age in decline comparable to the Roman empire before the barbarian invasions.[3] Add a political-historical dimension to these aesthetic considerations—the prose poem as a covert attack on "authoritative" prose discourses or a particular manifestation of different poets' reactions to the increasingly marginalized status of the lyric—and one arrives at a reasonable if general explanation of the rise of the genre in this period.

But even supposing the prose poem performed all of these potentially contradictory functions, late-nineteenth-century French poets had other options available that were capable of achieving the same or similar ends, such as free verse. As extraordinary as the increasing interest in the *poème en prose* is in the 1880s and 1890s, it is worth keeping in mind that the theoretical discussions and poetic experimentation in this period are much more preoccupied with verse, free and otherwise.[4] Mallarmé's famous essay *Crise de vers* (*Crisis of Verse*, 1886), for example, talks of a general trend toward poetic experimentation among French poets.[5] Outside of France, needless to say, there was even less prose-poetry activity. As LeRoy C. Breunig has pointed out, the relative increase of interest in the *poème en prose* during this period needs to be considered within its French context: "[T]hat the prose poem should have emerged from French soil is due in large measure—and not so paradoxically—to the very tyranny of French verse. Had it not been for Rimbaud's battle with the alexandrine, the *poème en prose* as we know it would probably not have been born."[6] In a logic reminiscent of Newton's third law of motion, the *poème en prose* develops in France before vers libre because it represents an equal and opposite reaction to the intense strictures of the alexandrine. While compelling insofar as it helps account for the relative lack of prose poetry in late-nineteenth- and early-twentieth-century Anglo-American literature ("There was no straightjacket to pull out of," Breunig remarks), such an explanation does not sufficiently take into consideration the "loosening" of the alexandrine already effected in French poetry by romantics like Hugo.[7] More important, it is by no means a given that prose poetry represents a more radical departure from the alexandrine than free verse. Gustave Kahn, the self-proclaimed French inventor of free verse, claimed in a preface to his *Premiers poèmes* (*First Poems*, 1897) that vers libre was "l'aboutissement nécessaire du poème en prose" (the necessary outcome of the prose poem), the form that would replace all forms.[8] The development of the *poème en prose* cannot, in short, be explained from a formal perspective any more than it can be explained solely in terms of a shift in aesthetics.

What makes the situation of the late-nineteenth-century French prose poem unique is the prestige accorded to the form by its practitioners. It is not necessary to evoke theories of poetic genius to argue that Baudelaire and Rimbaud, and to some extent Mallarmé, were more responsible for establishing the *poème en prose* in France than any general set of aesthetic theories or historical developments. The issue here has less to do with formal characteristics of the writing than with the frame: Baudelaire and Rimbaud stood for something larger than their poetry. *Petits Poëmes en prose* attracted more attention than all of the prose-poem experiments that preceded it because Baudelaire was, or became in retrospect, the harbinger of such modern literary movements as symbolism and decadence and was above all the author of *Les Fleurs du mal*. Rimbaud quickly became the archetype of the child genius revolting against authority and his prose poems the most extreme expression of his rebellion. Furthermore, both of these *poètes maudits*—here Verlaine might be invoked as an important filter for their literary reception—began their careers writing verse lyrics and therefore appeared to progress toward or to be forced into prose poetry by personal temperament and historical conditions. And though there is no apparent progression from verse to prose in the poetry of Mallarmé, the fact that this acknowledged master poet wrote poems in prose lent the form some prestige. The success of the *poème en prose* in this period has a lot to do with the success of its practitioners.

Given the even greater success the prose poem has had in twentieth-century French poetry and the subsequent histories of the genre that have been sketched by critics and poets alike, it is easy to regard the development of the post-Baudelairean *poème en prose* as both speedy and inevitable—neither of which appears to be the case if one does not from the outset focus on a particular line of poets. A few years after Baudelaire died, for example, Théodore de Banville wrote in his *Petit Traité de poésie française* (*Little Treatise of French Poetry*, 1872):

> Ceci tranche une question bien souvent controversée: Peut-il y avoir des poëmes en prose? Non, il ne peut y en avoir, malgré le *Télémaque* de Fénelon, les admirables *Poëmes en prose* de Charles Baudelaire et le *Gaspard de la nuit* de Louis Bertrand; car il est impossible d'imaginer une prose, si parfaite qu'elle soit, à laquelle on ne puisse, avec un effort surhumain, rien ajouter ou rien retrancher; elle est donc toujours à faire, et par conséquent n'est jamais la chose faite, le Ποίημα.
> [This decides a very often debated question: "Can there be prose poems?" No, there cannot be any, in spite of Fénelon's *Télémaque*, the admirable *Poëmes en prose* of Charles Baudelaire, and the *Gaspard de la nuit* of Louis Bertrand. For it is impossible to imagine a piece of prose, no matter how perfect, which one

might not be able, with a superhuman effort, to add something to or retract something from. (The prose poem) is therefore always something to be done and consequently never the finished thing, the *poiēma*.][9]

While it is easy enough to see that Banville's Parnassian bias informs his reasoning or to point out the irony of Banville himself publishing a volume of prose poems a decade or so later (*La Lanterne magique*, 1883), *Petit Traité de poésie française* cannot be summarily dismissed on the grounds that its author is out of touch with contemporary poetic taste or reality. In fact, prose poetry was a minor, fledgling form at this time regardless of the vigorous debates surrounding it. Banville's argument is also helpful in tracing two qualities many subsequent French poets and critics have claimed exist in the best prose poems: brevity and concentration. It is as if Baudelaire's anxieties about prose poetry and Banville's assertion of the genre's impossibility translate into later writers' needs for a formal aesthetic of the *poème en prose*. For some French poets, the prose poem proves less a release from constraints than a challenge to redraw the boundaries of the lyric.

Some general questions arise. Are there poets for whom the prose poem in fact represents a break from a poetics of the well-wrought urn in favor of what some critics would call a "poetics of indeterminacy"? Do considerations of whether prose poetry is an open form affect its status as a genre? How does the issue of indeterminacy inform readings of particular works? From the point of view of artistic intention, and often literary reception, the answer to the first question is yes. Writers like Rimbaud and Lautréamont certainly privileged indeterminacy, if not incoherence, as an aesthetic end, even when the means to this end might be calculated—as in Rimbaud's famous "long, immense and *reasoned* derangement of all the senses" (my emphasis).[10] As for the other two questions: provided a reader believes that a text is radically open-ended or that a given work is framed by such an aesthetic, the issue of indeterminacy will inform how he or she generically situates, interprets, and evaluates the work. The quasi-legendary status of Rimbaud's rebellious life, especially his abandonment of poetry at a young age, and the incredible number of biographical interpretations of his prose poems are proof enough of how perceived formal or formless qualities of a work can inflect a reading of it: the disorder of a life is expressed in the indeterminacy of the language; the open-ended form is an expression of a life lived in revolt. That such a mode of reasoning is largely circular should not obscure the significance of an author's—or for that matter a genre's—reception. To ignore how a work is framed is to ignore an important element of the reading experience. But an awareness of the rhetorical function of labels like "indeterminate" does qualify the framed reading. In order to discuss how the various developments in the late-nineteenth-century *poème en prose* adjust the notion of "prose poetry as a genre," it is necessary to look more closely at some poems.

• • •

For many critics Rimbaud represents one extreme in poetic writing. After giving an overview of Rimbaud criticism up to 1959, John Simon remarks: "What emerges from this is a picture of Rimbaud as innovator extraordinary whose work reaches an *Ultima Thule* beyond which—or even to which—no one has penetrated in the near century following; beyond which, indeed, there may be nothing."[11] Suzanne Bernard, writing in the same year as Simon, sees Rimbaud's (and Lautréamont's) experiments as the beginning of an oscillation in French prose poetry between anarchy and order.[12] Although more recent criticism is likely to speak of Rimbaud's achievement in somewhat different terms—Jonathan Monroe asserts that "Rimbaud carries forward the dialogical project of Baudelaire's *Petits poèmes en prose* to include a critique not only of conventional forms of verse lyric but of prose narrative as well"—there seems to be a consensus that his poetry, especially *Illuminations*, marks some sort of watershed in the French if not Western poetic tradition.[13] "Rimbaud" in this context may be a convenient label for broader changes in history and literature, like Boileau's "Enfin Malherbe vint" or Hugo's "Alors . . . je vins," but it is worth trying to tease out what qualities of Rimbaud's writing might account for his literary stature and influence, if only because his literary reputation has been closely linked with interpretations of his poems and the history of the *poème en prose*.[14]

"Après le Déluge" (After the Flood) reads as an announcement of new poetic possibilities in part because it is the opening poem of *Illuminations*:

> Aussitôt que l'idée du Déluge se fut rassise,
>   Un lièvre s'arrêta dans les sainfoins et les clochettes mouvantes et dit sa prière à l'arc-en-ciel à travers la toile de l'araignée.
>   Oh! les pierres précieuses qui se cachaient,—les fleurs qui regardaient déjà.
>   Dans la grande rue sale les étals se dressèrent, et l'on tira les barques vers la mer étagée là-haut comme sur les gravures.
>   Le sang coula, chez Barbe-Bleue,—aux abattoirs,—dans les cirques, où le sceau de Dieu blêmit les fenêtres. Le sang et le lait coulèrent.

Les castors bâtirent. Les "mazagrans" fumèrent dans les estaminets.

Dans la grande maison de vitres encore ruisselante les enfants en deuil regardèrent les merveilleuses images.

Une porte claqua,—et sur la place du hameau, l'enfant tourna ses bras, compris des girouettes et des coqs des clochers partout, sous l'éclatante giboulée.

Madame °°° établit un piano dans les Alpes. La messe et les premières communions se célébrèrent aux cent mille autels de la cathédrale.

Les caravanes partirent. Et le Splendide-Hôtel fut bâti dans le chaos de glaces et de nuit du pôle.

Depuis lors, la Lune entendit les chacals piaulant par les déserts de thym,—et les églogues en sabots grognant dans le verger. Puis, dans la futaie violette, bourgeonnante, Eucharis me dit que c'était le printemps.

—Sourds, étang,—Écume, roule sur le pont et pardessus les bois; — draps noirs et orgues,—éclairs et tonnerre,—montez et roulez;—Eaux et tristesses, montez et relevez les Déluges.

Car depuis qu'ils se sont dissipés,—oh les pierres précieuses s'enfouissant, et les fleurs ouvertes!—c'est un ennui! et la Reine, la Sorcière qui allume sa braise dans le pot de terre, ne voudra jamais nous raconter ce qu'elle sait, et que nous ignorons.

[As soon as the idea of the Flood had subsided,

A hare stopped among the clover patches and the swaying daffodils and said its prayer to the rainbow through the spider's web.

Oh! the precious stones that hid themselves—the flowers that were already looking around.

In the large dirty street butchers' stalls were set up, and small boats were dragged toward the sea rising in tiers as though in a print.

Blood flowed in Bluebeard's house—in the slaughterhouses—in the circuses, where the seal of God made the windows pale. Blood and milk flowed.

Beavers built. The "mazagrans" [coffee mixed with alcohol] steamed in bar rooms.

In the large house of windows that was still dripping children in mourning looked at marvelous pictures.

A door slammed, and on the village green the child spun around his arms—and was understood by the weathercocks and the cocks in steeples everywhere—under the dazzling downpour.

Madame °°° founded a piano in the Alps. Mass and first communion were celebrated at the hundred thousand altars of the cathedral.

Caravans departed. And the Hotel-Splendide was built in the polar chaos of ice and night.

Since then, the Moon has heard the jackals whining in the deserts of thyme,—and the wooden-shoed eclogues grumbling in the orchard. Then, among the violet and budding trees, Eucharis told me that it was spring.

—Spring forth, pond—Foam, roll on the bridge and over the woods; black shrouds and organs—lightning bolts and thunder—rise up and roll; Waters and sorrows, rise up and unleash the Floods again.

For ever since they were squandered—oh, the precious stones burying themselves, the opened flowers!—it has been unbearable! and the Queen, the Sorceress who lights her coals in earthen jugs, will never want to tell us what she knows, and what we are unaware of.][15]

Rhetorically at least, "Après le Déluge" is fairly straightforward. After the opening "As soon as the idea of the Flood had subsided," most of the poem settles into a series of short descriptive paragraphs detailing what occurs in the wake of the idea of the flood. There is some increase of tension in the paragraph that begins "Since then," a tension that is then released or perhaps climaxes with poem's only use of the first person in "Eucharis told me it was spring." The penultimate paragraph is incantatory, almost prayerlike, with its apostrophes and injunctions to the elements. The final paragraph-sentence is explanatory in form ("For ever since they were squandered . . . it has been unbearable! and the Queen") but alternatively filled with longing ("oh, the precious stones burying themselves, the opened flowers!"), dismissive ("it has been unbearable!"), and tinged with frustrated desire ("the Queen . . . will never want to tell us what she knows, and what we are unaware of"). Its interruptions both resist and lend a sense of closure to the poem.

The difficulty of "Après le Déluge" lies in the meanings of individual images and sentences and especially in their connection with one another—what, in short, the poem does or does not add up to. While some details arguably invite biographical explanations ("Madame °°°" standing in for the poet's mother, according to an anecdote of Ernest Létrange) or rely on literary allusions for some of their meaning ("Madame °°°" standing in for Madame Bovary, according to Nick Osmond), most of the images appear to be generated by a logic of associations.[16] An idyllic world (the various plants, the rainbow, the wooden-shoed eclogues), for example, is evoked in the same breath as the world of childhood (the talking hare, fairy tales like Bluebeard, the children looking at marvelous pictures, first communions). The details of childhood also seem linked with stories a child might know. Besides Bluebeard, the biblical tale of Noah and the Ark is alluded to in the poem (the poem's title, the rainbow image) along with an often-excerpted episode from Fénelon's *Télémaque*: Eucharis is the young, pure love of Telemachus in the popular prose epic or adventure story. Her sudden appearance in the poem may be linguistically motivated by the earlier line about first communions. Eucharis thus seems to suggest simultaneously an innocent, bucolic world and a fall into knowledge of the self and sexuality.[17] Her indirect address to the poet and mention of spring precipitate the incantatory penultimate paragraph and invite one to read the poet as a Telemachus figure, a boy on the verge of manhood.

Not all of the poem's logic of association is clear, however. The opening progression from flood to rainbow is familiar enough not to jar, and the link between "butchers' stalls" and "Bluebeard's house—in the slaughterhouses" fairly comprehensible. Linking the rainbow with the seal of God, or associating the rainfall, the flowing blood, and the still dripping house of windows requires a somewhat bolder intuitive leap.[18] Sometimes images and paragraphs do not seem to follow each other logically at all, except in the general sense that the entire poem may be a description of a world seen through a child's eyes. The cumulative impact of its series of disparate images is an important part of the poem's meaning. We alternatively grasp relations between images and are frustrated in our attempt to do so. As a result, we are pushed toward establishing a narrative or allegory within which the details of the poem make some sense: after an actual or metaphysical flood (emotional release? some biographical or historical event?) the world seems to be renewed; there is a surge of life and activity (erecting, dragging, constructing, founding, departing); in spite of all the vigorous activity, something is wrong or missing, and the poet calls for a new flood. If "Après le Déluge" does represent a child's view of the world, the poet may be describing events from a somewhat nostalgic, postlapsarian perspective. "Après le Déluge" has also been read as a reflection on the Paris Commune, an expression of dissatisfaction with certain bourgeois pursuits and values, a description of burgeoning sexual desire, and a combination of all of these.[19]

Regardless of its allegorical frame, one striking feature of the poem is the way in which it presents images at a remove. The opening line of the poem talks about "the idea" of the flood having subsided; the sea rises in tiers "as though in a print." It is difficult to say whether the poet, or especially the children in the poem, experiences this remove as a longing-filled distance from life, an enlivening of an otherwise boring reality, or some oscillation between or mixture of these two feelings. Likewise it is difficult to say whether the childhood purity the flood restores is something the poem presents in a positive light or as an inevitably dull, naive, and bourgeois view of the world— or perhaps it is something fleeting that must be constantly renewed. By the end of the poem the remove evoked in the opening idea of the subsiding flood has increased: the exclamation "Oh! the precious stones that hid themselves— the flowers that were already looking around" becomes "oh, the precious stones burying themselves, the opened flowers!" as if to suggest that what is valuable is now farther away than ever and what is beautiful has already blossomed. The negative phrasing in the poem's close is potentially even more devastating: "the Queen, the Sorceress who lights her coals in earthen jugs, will never want to tell us what she knows, and what we are unaware of." The closing words "que nous ignorons" (what we are unaware of) are almost logically superfluous, since "ignorer" is an antonym of "savoir," the verb "to know." "Que nous ignorons" thus not only emphasizes the distance between the Queen-Sorceress and the simultaneously generalized and personal "we," it also suggests the misreading "we are not even aware of our own lack of knowledge," a self-deconstructing notion, like the paradox of the Cretan liar. How can one lament the lack of knowing something unless one is aware of the lack? Instead of removing the frustration of not being in on the secret, such a contradiction heightens the impasse at which the poem has arrived. The idea that potential energy is building to be released, like water behind a dam, is strengthened by the echo in the poem's title of Madame de Pompadour's fabled words, "Après nous, le déluge" (After us, the flood). Rimbaud represents the coming flood as *rising*.[20]

In general then, "Après le Déluge" announces itself as revolutionary both with regard to content and form. Its title and placement at the head of *Illuminations*, its invocation of a new flood, and its disjunctive images apparently aimed at frustrating reading expectations all invite such an interpretation.[21] Given the context of the other *Illuminations* and Rimbaud's literary reputation, the poem might even be said to frame itself as radically open-ended and written in a language that resists assimilation. Whereas the Baudelairean *poème en prose* disguises itself as some more familiar genre, the Rimbaudian prose poem calls immediate attention to its not being ordinary prose via its language, images, and gestures toward incoherence. It is even possible to argue that the interpretive drive to find coherence in a poem like "Après le Déluge" is at some level, perhaps fundamentally, misguided, that part of the poem's meaning is that it resists meaning. From a perspective outside the framed interpretation, however, the poem's aesthetic of indeterminacy is a rhetorical construct. As Albert Sonnenfeld has shown, even with a poet as apparently incoherent as Rimbaud, the prose poem "remains largely faithful to typographical linearity, to accepted syntax, and, above all, to clearly marked boundaries. It retains its composure, in other words."[22] If some aspects of Rimbaud prose poems are in fact semantically indeterminate, meaning depends on affect at least as much as semantics, and thus the poems remain interpretable on that level. If a work is disorienting, one can always analyze what causes the disorientation.

Of course, it is also possible to consider *Illuminations* indeterminate relative to other poems of the period in the same way that it can be argued that Baudelaire's *Petit Poëmes en prose* was revolutionary for its time. Yet even this qualified claim needs to be qualified. The logic of poetic progression on which the assertion relies points to a narrative imposed in retrospect and perhaps to formal essentialism. Moreover, if such a claim bestows upon a work a secure place in literary history, this position may come at the expense of aesthetic value: the work is important for what it helped bring about in the past, and even then it may have only served a symbolic function. In Rimbaud's case at least, it is especially the reception of his work that has played a significant role in diffusing ideas about the possibilities of poetic language. When Mallarmé and Valéry praise Rimbaud, for example, they tend to cite a handful of verse lyrics (especially certain stanzas of "Le Bateau ivre") and mention *Illuminations* only by title and with reference to its overall impact.[23] Rimbaud's poems may thus have given prose poetry a flavor of liberation regardless of whether they are in fact revolutionary, and perhaps *Illuminations* helped promote the idea that prose poems should be short and concentrated, though such an argument depends to a certain extent on a teleological view of literary history.[24] It is worth recalling that for a long time *Une Saison en enfer*, not *Illuminations*, was believed to be Rimbaud's poetic last word and that Rimbaud was initially associated with Lautréamont, primarily on the grounds that both writers took poetic language to new extremes in gestures of liberation.[25] The long *poème en prose* was no less highly regarded than the short by the end of this period.

Like Rimbaud, Lautréamont acquired the reputation of being a radically innovative poet because of the extremes to which he took the French language and the lyric. Indeed, given the size and divisions of *Les Chants du Maldoror* (1869), it is debatable whether the term lyric accurately describes his prose poetry. Even individual strophe of *Maldoror*'s six *chants* are longer than most nineteenth-century prose poems. The fourth strophe of the fourth book is one of the shortest in the poem:

Je suis sale. Les poux me rongent. Les pourceaux, quand ils me regardent, vomissent. Les croûtes et les escarres de la lèpre ont écaillé ma peau, couverte de pus jaunâtre. Je ne connais pas l'eau des fleuves, ni la rosée des nuages. Sur ma nuque, comme sur un fumier, pousse un énorme champignon, aux pédoncules ombellifères. Assis sur un meuble informe, je n'ai pas bougé mes membres depuis quatres siècles. Mes pieds ont pris racine dans le sol et composent, jusqu'à mon ventre, une sorte de végétation vivace, remplie d'ignobles parasites, qui ne dérive pas encore de la plante, et qui n'est plus de la chair. Cependant mon cœur bat. Mais comment battrait-il, si la pourriture et les exhalaisons de mon cadavre (je n'ose pas dire corps) ne le nourissaient abondamment? Sous mon aisselle gauche, une famille de crapauds a pris résidence, et, quand l'un d'eux remue, il me fait des chatouilles. Prenez garde qu'il ne s'en échappe un, et ne vienne gratter, avec sa bouche, le dedans de votre oreille: il serait ensuite capable d'entrer dans votre cervelle. Sous mon aisselle droite, il y a un caméléon qui leur fait une chasse perpétuelle, afin de ne pas mourir de faim: il faut que chacun vive. Mais, quand un parti déjoue complètement les ruses de l'autre, ils ne trouvent rien de mieux que de ne pas se gêner, et sucent la graisse délicate qui couvre mes côtes: j'y suis habitué. Une vipère méchante a dévoré ma verge et a pris sa place: elle m'a rendu eunuque, cette infâme. Oh! si j'avais pu me défendre avec mes bras paralysés; mais, je crois plutôt qu'ils se sont changés en bûches. Quoi qu'il en soit, il importe de constater que le sang ne vient plus y promener sa rougeur. Deux petites hérissons, qui ne croissent plus, ont jeté à un chien, qui n'a pas refusé, l'intérieur de mes testicules: l'épiderme, soigneusement lavé, ils ont logé dedans. L'anus a été intercepté par un crabe; encouragé par mon inertie, il garde l'entrée avec ses pinces, et me fait beaucoup de mal! Deux méduses ont franchi les mers, immédiatement alléchées par un espoir qui ne fut pas trompé. Elles ont regardé avec attention les deux parties charnues qui forment le derrière humain, et, se cramponnant à leur galbe convexe, elles les ont tellement écrasées par une pression constante, que les deux morceaux de chair ont disparu, tandis qu'il est resté deux monstres, sortis du royaume de la viscosité, égaux par la couleur, la forme et la férocité. Ne parlez pas de ma colonne vertébrale, puisque c'est un glaive. Oui, oui . . . je n'y faisais pas attention . . . votre demande est juste. Vous désirez savoir, n'est-ce pas, comment il se trouve implanté verticalement dans mes reins? Moi-même, je ne me décide à prendre pour un souvenir ce qui n'est peut-être qu'un rêve, sachez que l'homme, quand il a su que j'avais fait vœu de vivre avec la maladie et l'immobilité jusqu'à ce que j'eusse vaincu le Créateur, marcha, derrière moi, sur la pointe des pieds, mais, non pas si doucement, que je ne l'entendisse. Je ne perçus plus rien, pendant un instant qui ne fut pas long. Ce poignard aigu s'enfonça, jusqu'au manche, entre les deux épaules du taureau des fêtes, et son ossature frisonna, comme un tremblement de terre. La lame adhère au corps, que personne, jusqu'ici, n'a pu l'extraire. Les athlètes, les mécaniciens, les philosophes, les médecins ont essayé, tour à tour, les moyens les plus divers. Ils ne savaient pas que le mal qu'a fait l'homme ne peut plus se défaire! J'ai pardonné à la profondeur de leur ignorance native, et je les ai salués des paupières de mes yeux. Voyageur, quand tu passeras près du moi, ne m'adresse pas, je t'en supplie, le moindre mot de consolation: tu affaiblirais mon courage. Laisse-moi réchauffer ma ténacité à la flamme du martyre volontaire. Va-t'en . . . que je ne t'inspire aucune pitié. La haine est plus bizarre que tu ne le penses; sa conduite est inexplicable, comme l'apparence brisée d'un bâton enfoncé dans l'eau. Tel que tu me vois, je puis encore faire des excursions jusqu'aux murailles du ciel, à la tête d'une légion d'assassins, et revenir prendre cette posture, pour méditer, de nouveau, sur les nobles projets de la vengeance. Adieu, je ne te retarderai pas davantage; et pour t'instruire et te préserver, réfléchis au sort fatal qui m'a conduit à la révolte, quand peut-être j'étais né bon! Tu raconteras à ton fils ce que tu as vu; et, le prenant par la main, fais-lui admirer la beauté des étoiles et les merveilles de l'univers, le nid du rouge-gorge et les temples du Seigneur. Tu seras étonné de le voir si docile aux conseils de la paternité, et tu le récompenseras par un sourire. Mais, quand il apprendra qu'il n'est pas observé, jette les yeux sur lui, et tu le verras cracher sa bave sur la vertu; il t'a trompé, celui qui est descendu de la race humaine, mais, il ne te trompera plus: tu sauras désormais ce qu'il deviendra. Ô père infortuné, prépare, pour accompagner les pas de ta vieillesse, l'échafaud ineffaçable qui tranchera la tête d'un criminel précoce, et la douleur qui te montrera le chemin qui conduit à la tombe.

[I am filthy. I am riddled with lice. Hogs, when they look at me, vomit. My skin is encrusted with the scabs and scales of leprosy, and covered with yellowish pus. I know neither the water of rivers nor the dew of clouds. An enormous mushroom with umbelliferous stalks is growing on my nape, as on a dunghill. Sitting on a shapeless piece of furniture, I have not moved my limbs now for four centuries. My feet have taken root in the ground; up to my belly, they form a sort of tenacious vegetation, full of filthy parasites; this vegetation no longer has anything in common with other plants, nor is it flesh. And yet my heart beats. How could it beat, if the rottenness and miasmata of my corpse (I dare not say my body), did not nourish it abundantly? A family of toads has taken up residence in my left armpit and, when one of them moves, it tickles. Mind one of them does not escape and come and scratch the inside of your ear with its mouth; for it would then be able to enter your brain. In my right armpit there is a chameleon which is perpetually chasing them, to avoid starving to death: everyone must live. But when one party has completely foiled the cunning tricks of the other, they like nothing better than to leave one another in peace and suck the delicate fat which covers my sides: I am used to it. An evil snake has eaten my cock and taken its place; the filthy creature has made me a eunuch. Oh if only I could have defended myself with my paralyzed hands; but I rather think they have changed into logs. However that may be, it is important to state that my red blood no longer flows there. Two little hedgehogs, which have stopped gnawing, threw the inside of my testicles to a dog, who did not turn up his nose at it: and they lodged inside the carefully washed epidermis. My anus has been penetrated by a crab; encouraged by my sluggishness, he guards the entrance with his pincers, and causes me a lot of pain! Two medusae crossed the seas, immediately enticed by a hope which was not disappointed. They looked attentively at the two fleshy parts which form the human backside, and, clinging on to their convex curve, they so crushed them by constant pressure that the two lumps of flesh have disappeared, while two monsters from the realm of viscosity remain, equal in color, shape, and ferocity. Do not speak of my spinal column, as it is a sword. . . . Yes, yes . . . I was not paying attention . . . your request is a fair one. You wished to know, did you not, how it came to be implanted vertically in my back. I cannot remember very clearly; however, if I decide to take for a memory what was perhaps only a dream, I can tell you that man, when he found out that I had vowed to live disease-ridden and motionless until I had conquered the Creator, crept up behind me on tiptoe, but not so quietly that I did not hear him. For a short moment, I felt nothing. This sword was buried up to the hilt between the shoulder blades of the festive bull, and his bones shuddered like an earthquake. Athletes, mechanical experts, philosophers and doctors have tried, in turn, all kinds of methods. They did not know that the evil man has done cannot be undone! I forgave them for the depth of their native ignorance, and acknowledged them with a slow movement of my eyelids. Traveler, when you pass near me, do not address the least word of consolation to me, I implore you. You will weaken my courage. Leave me to kindle my tenacity at the flame of voluntary martyrdom. Go away . . . let me not inspire in you any pity. Hatred is stranger than you think; its action is inexplicable, like the broken appearance of a stick in water. Such as you see me, I can still make sorties as far as the walls of heaven at the head of a legion of murderers, and then come back and, resuming this posture, meditate again on noble projects of vengeance. Adieu, I shall delay you no longer; and, so that you may learn a lesson and preserve yourself, reflect on the fatal destiny which led me to revolt, when I was perhaps born good! You will tell your son what you have seen; and, taking him by the hand, you will make him admire the beauty of the stars and the wonders of the universe, the robin's nest and the temples of the Lord. And you will be surprised to see how amenable he is to your paternal advice, and you will reward him with a smile. But as soon as he knows he is unobserved, take a look at him and you will see him spitting his slime on virtue; he has deceived you, he who is descended from the human race, but he will deceive you no longer; thenceforward you will know what is to become of him. Oh unfortunate father, prepare, in order to accompany the steps of your age, the ineffaceable guillotine which will cut off the head of a precocious criminal, and the sorrow which will show you the way which leads to the grave.][26]

For readers today, Lautréamont's lurid descriptions can border on the comical. Extremely graphic, they seem calculated to offend the sensibilities of the poem's contemporary readers. Lautréamont's matter-of-fact tone when describing horrific situations, his lengthy digressions that do not always return to their original topic, and his mixture of such seemingly opposed discourses as the prophetic ("Oh unfortunate father, prepare") and the scientific ("An enormous mushroom with umbelliferous stalks") flaunt nineteenth-century reading conventions and senses of propriety. The occasional addresses to the reader ("Yes, yes . . . I was not paying attention . . . your request is a fair one"; "Traveler, when you pass near me, do not address the least word of consolation to me, I implore you") are simultaneously alienating and conspiratorial. Lautréamont often shows his contempt for the reader of bourgeois morality, such as the advice-giving father whom he addresses in the familiar form, but also, like Baudelaire with his "hyprocrite lecteur," gestures toward the reader who can understand him, the "hardened and momentarily ferocious" person of the opening lines of the poem.[27] Because *Maldoror* is a work of revolt both against the self and society, it is highly aware of its audience.

Les Chants du Maldoror is perhaps more self-consciously revolutionary than even *Illuminations*, but as with *Illuminations*, it is difficult to say in what the revolutionary dimension of the work consists. Even without modern editors parsing the poem into numbered strophes, *Les Chants du Maldoror* lends itself to being read in familiar interpretive modes, such as a series of antifables or allegories. In the selection quoted here, the poet offers advice to the traveler-reader at the close of the strophe in what reads rhetorically as a moral of the previous narration. Whether this advice follows logically from what precedes it is debatable, but it does close the passage in a conventional way. The question of whether a piece of writing is revolutionary will seem unanswerable when considered from an exclusively formal perspective. Flaunting formal conventions is moreover a gesture with its own conventions, and it may be that many of the traits we now associate with avant-garde writing have their origin in the late nineteenth century.[28] The question can be partially adjudicated via reception history. Though *Maldoror* was published in 1869, the first editions of the work were not distributed for sale until 1874. It was not until the 1890 edition (and the 1891 edition of Rimbaud's *Illuminations*) that Lautréamont became widely known. Lautréamont was especially lionized in France after the First World War.[29] In other words, by the time writers like Rimbaud and Lautréamont reached a relatively large audience, many of the formal elements of their prose poems that earn them the label "revolutionary" had become clichés. Although it is likely that works like *Illuminations* and *Les Chants du Maldoror* helped enlarge the sensibility of poets and readers to the point where formerly forbidden poetic gestures became a matter of course, once again the revolutionary status of a writer potentially comes at the expense of aesthetic value.

Rimbaud and Lautréamont by no means represent the only direction of the prose poem in late-nineteenth-century France. Mallarmé's first prose poems, for example, are recognizably Baudelairean. "Le Phénomène futur" and "Pauvre Enfant Pâle" (The future phenomenon and Poor, pale child), both written in 1864, have Baudelairean subjects, beauty in a fallen age and an outcast figure of the modern city. "Plainte d'automne," "Frisson d'hiver," and "La Pipe" (Autumn lament, Winter shiver, and The pipe), all written in 1864, have titles almost straight out of *Les Fleurs du mal*. Even the tinge of Bertrand some critics have detected in these early poems can be attributed to Baudelaire's guidance via his dedicatory letter to Houssaye published in *La Presse* in 1862.[30] Mallarmé's initial interest in the *poème en prose* as a form thus has everything to do with his interest in Baudelaire as a poet. This is not to say that Mallarmé's prose poems are slavish imitations of the *Petits*

Poëmes en prose; far from it. Baudelaire himself sensed there was a difference between his and Mallarmé's aesthetics if we can judge from his comments in *Pauvre Belgique!*:

> Un jeune écrivain a eu récemment une conception ingénieuse, mais non absolument juste. Le monde va finir. L'humanité est décrépite. Un Barnum de l'avenir montre aux hommes dégradés de son temps une belle femme des anciens âges artificiellement conservée. "Eh! quoi! disent-ils, l'humanité a pu être aussi belle que cela?" Je dis que cela n'est pas vrai. L'homme dégradé s'admirerait et appellerait la beauté laideur.
>
> [A young writer recently had an ingenious idea, but not absolutely correct. The world is going to end. Humanity is worn out. A Barnum of the future shows the degraded men of his age a beautiful woman of ancient times artificially preserved. "Eh! what!" they say, "humanity could be as beautiful as that?" I say that that is not true. Degraded men would admire themselves and call beauty ugliness.][31]

Baudelaire believes that beauty possesses a transient component, like the fashions he discusses in *The Painter of Modern Life*.[32] As the final paragraph of "Le Phénomène futur" makes clear, the differences between the prose poems of Baudelaire and Mallarmé are also stylistic:

> Quand tous auront contemplé la noble créature, vestige de quelque époque déjà maudite, les uns indifférents, car ils n'auront pas eu la force de comprendre, mais d'autres navrés et la paupière humide de larmes résignées se regarderont; tandis que les poëtes de ces temps, sentant se rallumer leurs yeux éteints, s'achemineront vers leur lampe, le cerveau ivre un instant d'une gloire confuse, hantés du Rythme et dans l'oubli d'exister à une époque qui survit à la beauté.
>
> [When they all have contemplated the noble creature, a vestige of some already cursed age, some of them indifferent, for they will not have the strength to understand, but others distressed and their eyes watering with tears of resignation will look at each other; while the poets of those times, sensing their extinguished eyes being rekindled, will head toward their lamps, their brains drunk for an instant with a confused glory, haunted by the Rhythm and in the oblivion of existing in an age which has outlived beauty.][33]

While Baudelairean in its general theme and tone, the syntax of the poem, albeit tame in comparison with Mallarmé's later prose poems, is sinuous and extended in a manner in which most of the prose of *Petits Poëmes en prose* is not. The last paragraph of "Le Phénomène futur" is one long sentence. Baudelaire's self-described staccato, surprise-oriented prose gives way to a sentence drawn out in such a way as to enact on the level of language the longing that the future poets feel for the vanished beauty of their time. The reference to poets at the end of the poem is self-referential in another sense: one gets the feeling that the future the poem speaks of is either not very distant or already arrived. The capitalization of "Rhythm" is also self-reflexive. While the prose of Mallarmé is certainly not without rhythm, the context of the passage and the author's placement of the poem at the beginning of both *Pages* (1891) and the *Anecdotes ou poëmes* of *Divagations* (1896) encourage reading "Le Phénomène futur" as a commentary on writing poetry that is not in verse.[34] "Rhythm" may in this respect stand in for "Verse" or "Poetry." As with Baudelaire's first prose poems, the prose element of "Le Phénomène futur" is figured as a fall from an ideal.

The mixture of Baudelaire and Bertrand elements can also be found in the prose poems of less canonical poets writing at this time. Daniel Cazalis, Mallarmé's close friend, published four "Poésies en Prose" in the 15 September 1864 edition of *L'Artiste*, a journal in which Baudelaire had published some prose poems. The first of these poems, "Divan," is typical:

> Amour, vin étrange, ceux que tu désaltères ont toujours plus soif après qu'ils ont bu.
>
> Si je pouvais comme Dieu étreindre l'infini! Si je pouvais comme Dieu étreindre tous les mondes! Si je pouvais comme Dieu couvrir toutes les âmes de l'immense azur de ma joie.
>
> La nuit apaise l'âme et le corps, versant sur le fini le calme de l'infini.
>
> Vois toutes choses s'unir, ivres de volupté, et ainsi d'âge en âge se prolonger les noces éternelles.
>
> Ce n'est pas seulement dans les yeux des femmes qu'est le paradis, mais il est aussi dans l'amour qu'à certaines heures la nature verse aux choses.
>
> L'extase est une mort qui te transfigure, et, tout transfiguré, t'emporte dans la lumière.
>
> [Love, strange wine, those whom you quench the thirst of are always more thirsty after they have drunk.

If I could only, like God, embrace infinity! If I could only, like God, embrace every world! If I could only, like God, cover every soul with the vast azure of my joy.

Night calms the soul and the body, pouring on the finite infinity's calm.

Watch all things unite, drunk with sensuality, and in this way the eternal wedding prolong itself from age to age.

Paradise is not only in women's eyes, but also in the love that nature pours on things at certain hours.

Ecstasy is a death that transfigures you, and, completely transfigured, carries you into the light.][35]

The versetlike lines of "Divan" are perhaps reminiscent of Bertrand, but the heavy use of apostrophe and subjunctives that express impossible wishes points more toward the tradition of *poésie primitive*. In a similar way, the subject matter and epigrammatic close of the poem are vaguely Baudelairean, but the lack of ironic distancing and lines such as "Paradise is . . . also in the love that nature pours on things" suggest a more general romantic inheritance.[36] But even if his prose poems are rhetorically conventional, Cazalis shares the drive of many of his contemporaries for innovation via mixing genres and different artistic media, as evidenced in the title of another of his prose poems, "Musica dans le mode mineur" (A piece of music in the minor mode). His use of odd, thought-interrupting punctuation in "Semper Eadem"—there are twelve dashes and four ellipses in this eighteen-line prose poem—points to a certain amount of experimentation with typography for various effects.

A poet of more strikingly original work, Charles Cros, was writing prose poetry at the same time Rimbaud was writing his *Illuminations*. While not without touches of Baudelaire and Mallarmé, Cros's prose poems, such as "Effarement" (Affright), have a surrealist quality:

Au milieu de la nuit, un rêve. Une gare de chemin de fer. Des employés portant des caractères cabalistiques sur leurs casquettes administratives. Des wagons à claire-voie chargés de dames-jeannes en fer battu. Les brouettes ferrées roulent avec des colis qu'on arrime dans les voitures du train.

Une voix de sous-chef crie: La raison de M. Igitur, à destination de la lune! Un manœuvre vient et appose une étiquette sur le colis désigné—

une dame-jeanne semblable à celles des wagons à claire-voie. Et, après la pesée à la bascule, on embarque. Le coup de sifflet du départ résonne, aigu, vertigineux et prolongé.

Réveil subit. Le coup de sifflet se termine en miaulement de chat de gouttière. M. Igitur s'élance, crève la vitre et plonge son regard dans le bleu sombre où plane la face narquoise de la lune.

[In the middle of the night, a dream. A railway station. Employees wearing cabalistic characters on their administrative caps. Open-grated cars filled with demijohns built out of steel. The clunky iron cars roll with pieces of cargo that are stowed in the train.

A supervisor's voice shouts: "The reason of Mr. Igitur, destination the moon!" A manual worker comes and affixes a label on the designated package—a demijohn like those in the open-grated cars. And after the weighing at the balance-scale, the train sets off. The whistle-blow of departure resounds, shrill, dizzying, and prolonged.

Sudden awakening. The whistle-blow ends in a meow of a cat in the gutter. Mr. Igitur starts up, breaks open the window and sinks his gaze into the dark blue through which the teasing face of the moon is gliding.][37]

Though framed in *Le Coffret de santal* (*The Sandalwood Gift Box*, 1873) as a description of one of three aquatints by Cros's brother, Henry, "Effarement" is not easily reconstructed as a piece of ekphrastic writing.[38] The many narrative elements of the second and third paragraphs of "Effarement"—the shout, the weighing, the train setting off, the whistle-blow, the meow, the waking up, the breaking open of the window, the gaze at the moon—may correspond to visual representations of action in an etching but may also be part of the poet's interpretation of the portrayed scene. Because it is difficult to tell where description ends and interpretation begins, to read the prose as ekphrasis is to engage in provisional speculations about such particulars as the primary focus of the aquatint—the whistle turning into a meow? Mr. Igitur starting up in bed?—and, in general, to assume that the poet's voice is somewhat removed from the action described. These indeterminate signals and the poem's dream images lend "Effarement" its surrealist air.

• • •

If prose poems as different as Rimbaud's, Lautréamont's, Mallarmé's, Cazalis's, and Cros's could be written within a decade of each other and Baudelaire's death, poetry in prose was certainly a recognizable option among poets. Apparently, by the law of need expanding to fill resources, poets were quick to experiment with the form once the notion of "prose poetry" became current in the late nineteenth century. As with the *poème en prose* before Baudelaire, a literary-historical overview of this period is potentially encyclopedic in scope, but even the preceding examples from the 1860s and 1870s should help readjust the notion that prose poetry was developing along some inevitable course. This general perspective is in many ways more important to my discussion than a laundry list of authors and their works. Given that a variety of prose poets and poems established the form in the French imagination, the issue of genre now becomes one of literary history and reception. To what extent was the late-nineteenth-century *poème en prose* a genre or at least perceived of as such?

In order to answer this question, we first need to jump from the 1880s to the twentieth century. Judging from the statements and editorial practices of twentieth-century critics and anthologists, a normative or ideal type of prose poem slowly emerged in the late nineteenth century: the brief and intense lyric in prose. Perhaps the best example of this type of prose poem is Paul Claudel's "L'Heure jaune" (The yellow hour), from *Connaissance de l'Est* (1905), a book whose title means "knowledge of" (or "acquaintance with" or "getting to know") "the East":

> De toute l'année voici l'heure la plus jaune! comme l'agriculteur à la fin des saisons réalise les fruits de son travail et en recueille le prix, le temps vient en or que tout y soit transmué, au ciel et sur la terre. Je chemine jusqu'au cou dans la fissure de la moisson; je pose le menton sur la table qu'illumine le soleil à son bout, du champ; passant aux monts, je surmonte la mer des graines. Entres ses rives d'herbes, l'immense flamme sèche de la plaine couleur de jour, où est l'ancienne terre obscure? L'eau s'est changée en vin; l'orange s'allume dans le branchage silent. Tout est mûr, grain et paille, et le fruit avec la feuille. C'est bien de l'or; tout fini, je vois que tout est vrai. Dans le fervent travail de l'année évaporant toute couleur, à mes yeux tout à coup le monde comme un soleil! Moi! que je ne périsse pas avant l'heure la plus jaune.
>
> [The yellowest hour of the year is here! As the farmer at the end of the season realizes the fruits of his toil and gathers in the prize, the time arrives in a gold into which everything in the sky and on the earth is transmuted. I wander up to my neck in the lanes of the harvest. I rest my chin on the table of the field flashing in the sunlight to its farthest boundary. Passing to the mountains, I rise above a sea of grain. Between the banks of herbs—that immense, dry flame of the plain colored like day—where is the dark and ancient earth? The water

has changed into wine; orange catches fire in the silent branches. Everything is ripe: the grain and straw, the fruit with its leaves. Yes, it is gold. And as it all ends, I see it all is true. In the boiling activity of the year every color evaporates, and suddenly, in my eyes, the world is like a sun! Oh, may I not die before the yellowest hour!][39]

"L'Heure jaune" epitomizes the short, undeniably lyrical prose poem. Even its title, which seems a cross between Cros's fantasy in prose "L'Heure froide" (The cold hour) and Sainte-Beuve's verse poem "Les Rayons jaunes" (The yellow rays), evokes the idea of a lyric moment. The romanticism of "L'Heure jaune" is also evident in the descriptive details of the harvest and the poem's steadily building emotional intensity. Though eminently excerptable for an anthology, the poem gains something from being read in the context of *Connaissance de l'Est*. "L'Heure jaune" is the penultimate piece in a collection of poems arranged as a travelogue or journal of experiences in the East. The harvest and the ending of the day and year thus carry overtones of the close of a period in the poet's life and the "harvesting" of or bringing to a close a book of poems. As the final exclamation of the poem makes explicit, reflections on mortality are almost inevitable with this conjunction of moods and images. "L'Heure jaune" is, in other words, a poem written with a sense of a matured poetic tradition behind it, a self-consciously late-romantic work. Its appearance in a collection composed entirely of prose poems is also an indirect comment on how well the *poème en prose* had been incorporated into the French poetic tradition by the turn of the century.[40] For later poets and critics, Claudel's poems are recognizably written in the genre of the prose lyric.

While many turn-of-the-century poets wrote short and intense prose poems "in the genre" of "L'Heure jaune," the most distinctive feature of the late-nineteenth-century *poème en prose* is its lack of distinctive features. Although it is still possible to distinguish different types of prose poems, categorization of works in this period elides the important development toward a variety of styles. Bernard attempts to describe some prose poems in terms of the prose genres they approach (Retté and Schwob with the "poetic novel"; Rachilde, Gourmont, and de Régnier with the "story-poem") but in the end refers to the very late nineteenth century as "a period of out-and-out individualism" and emphasizes the widespread experimentation in poetic forms. If the literary historian needs to speak of a Parnassian prose poem, a symbolist prose poem, a decadent prose poem, and prose poems that approach fables, novels, hymns, and the like, he or she risks simply listing authors and their works. Bernard's notion of an oscillation between order and anarchy represents a possible solution to the problem of categorizing prose poems, but it also points to the limits of the approach. To the extent that the *poème en prose* became a widely accepted but diversely practiced form by the 1890s, it lost many of the specific traits that a few practitioners or a few prototypical examples might have given it. Alternatively, one can argue that, like other genres, the prose poem was beginning to spawn subgenres or new literary kinds. To gain perspective on the matter, we have to keep in mind the subsequent or reception history of the *poème en prose*.

Little was inevitable about the prose poem's development in late-nineteenth-century France, except diversification (one is tempted to say deversification) coupled with the rhetoric that poets were in need of new forms or genres. As I discussed in chapter 1, the term "poème en prose" became a simple abstraction in this period with the growing reputation of Baudelaire, and once the notion became operative it did not take long for poets to start exploring the prose poem's formal possibilities. The imperative for novelty is especially obvious in poets like Rimbaud and Lautréamont, but it is no less present in the early prose poems of Mallarmé or even in the poems of Cazalis. The *poème en prose* was well on its way to becoming a widely accepted form by the end of this period as a result of vigorous experimentation and was thus gradually incorporated into a more general poetic tradition. All of the developments that give the form the makings of a genre potentially unmade it as a genre. The prose poem is only one example of the period's generally felt need to revamp the lyric by experimenting with new poetic forms. Like a well-marketed product, it created some of the need for itself. If poets like Baudelaire and Rimbaud initially leant the prose poem some prestige, a critical mass of poets writing prose poetry helped make it a viable literary possibility, if not part of a tradition. By the twentieth century the *poème en prose* became such an important fixture of French literature that some poets' reputations were based exclusively on their writings in the form.[41]

Yet for all of these considerations, there is at least one important sense in which the prose poem of late-nineteenth-century France was a genre: some poets and readers thought of it as such. Des Esseintes's discussion of prose poetry and short anthology in Huysmans's novel *À Rebours* indicate that the *poème en prose* had found a kind of cult audience, thereby distinguishing itself somewhat from other genres. As the existence of some parodies in the early 1890s attests, the decadent prose poem had acquired a certain reputation among French poets.[42] Bernard argues persuasively that this sort of *poème en prose* reached the height of its popularity among young poets in the mid 1880s, after which the vogue for vers libre dominated and mixed and hybrid forms of all sorts proliferated.[43] To the extent that the phrase "poème en prose" became associated with the symbolist and decadent prose poem, a recognizable genre existed throughout the 1890s with which prose poetry had to contend, whether it fit the model or not.

But even the assertion that the *poème en prose* was a recognized genre requires one to be specific about time and place and poetic circle. The poetry fashions of Paris, like the clothing styles of the capital, took some time to reach other centers of French culture, such as Belgium, and warring schools of poets had different perspectives on prose poetry. The name and the form "poème en prose" nevertheless outlasted fin de siècle poetic styles, in part because prose poetry had diversified—it was not merely a symbolist form— and in part because it could, in spite of its diversification, continue to be associated with a line of prestige poets. By the early twentieth century, Max Jacob could routinely refer to the prose poets he liked and disliked in a preface to his own book of prose poems, *Le Cornet à dés*, and discuss the *poème en prose* in a way that assumes the reader is familiar with the body of literature it denotes. But widespread recognition of a poetic type and familiarity with its history are not always sufficient indications of genre. As the case of *poème en prose* suggests, genres can blend into other genres over time or become mostly formal distinctions.

• • •

Jacob's famous preface to *Le Cornet à dés* is at once a culmination of an important strain of thinking about the prose poem and a wonderfully biased view of the tradition, and may thus shed some light on the generic status of the prose poem. It may also help prevent the distinction between form and genre from becoming only a matter of semantics. If nothing else, the preface marks a moment when poets were gaining some perspective on the prose poetry already written in France:

> On a beaucoup écrit de poèmes en prose depuis trente ou quarante ans; je ne connais guère de poète qui ait compris de quoi il s'agissait et qui ait su sacrifier ses ambitions d'auteur à la constitution formelle du poème en prose. La dimension n'est rien pour la beauté de l'œuvre, sa situation et son style y sont tout.
> [Many prose poems have been written in the last thirty or forty years; I know of hardly any poet who understood what it was about and who knew how to sacrifice his ambitions as an author to the formal composition of the *poème en*

prose. Dimension is nothing for the beauty of the work: its situation and its style are everything.][44]

Jacob, above all interested in the "formal composition of the *poème en prose*," stresses that the size of a work has nothing to do with its aesthetic value. Instead he emphasizes situation and style, terms he considers to have very specific meanings. "Le style est la volonté de s'extérioriser par des moyens choisis" (Style is the will to make oneself exterior though chosen means), not to be confused with "language," the sense of "style" in Buffon's celebrated phrase, "Style is the man himself."[45] Style is, in this view, art.[46] As for situation, Jacob explains what he means somewhat more indirectly:

[L]'œuvre d'art doit être éloignée du sujet. C'est pourquoi elle doit être *située*. On pourrait rencontrer ici la théorie de Baudelaire sur la surprise: cette théorie est un peu grosse. Baudelaire comprenait le mot "distraction" dans son sens le plus ordinaire. Surprendre est peu de chose, il faut *transplanter*.

[The work of art has to be distanced from its subject. That is why it has to be *situated*. One might be reminded here of Baudelaire's theory on surprise: that theory is a bit coarse. Baudelaire understood the word "distraction" in its most ordinary sense. To surprise isn't much, one must *transplant*.][47]

In order to be situated, a work must defamiliarize its subject matter by placing it in an unexpected context. An example of this kind of displacement might be Jacob's own "Roman Feuilleton," a one-paragraph poem that purports to be a serial novel, or his various prose poems entitled "Poème dans un goût qui n'est pas le mien" (Poem in a taste that isn't mine) dedicated to Rimbaud, Baudelaire, and other prose poets, which frame a set of reading expectations that are not always matched in the body of text, even as parody. If style is will, situation is emotion: the authorial and the readerly components of a work, roughly speaking.[48] Style and situation can also be distinguished by function:

Distinguons le style d'une œuvre de sa situation. Le style ou volonté crée, c'est-à-dire sépare. La situation éloigne, c'est-à-dire excite à l'émotion artistique; on reconnaît qu'une œuvre a du style à ceci qu'elle donne la sensation du fermé; on reconnaît qu'elle est située au petit choc qu'on en reçoit ou encore à la marge qui l'entoure, à l'atmosphère spéciale où elle se meut.

[Let us distinguish the style of a work from its situation. The style or will creates, that is to say separates. The situation distances, that is to say excites toward the artistic emotion. One is aware that a work has style in that it gives the sensation of a closed thing; one is aware that it is situated in the little shock that one receives or even more in the margin that surrounds it, in the special atmosphere in which it moves.[49]

For Jacob, a work of art is objectlike, ideally giving the reader the "sensation of a closed thing." As he says a little later in the preface, "The poem is a constructed object, not a jeweler's display . . . the prose poem is a jewel."[50]

Jacob's arguments are partly informed by his own tastes, or rather distastes—Flaubert has style but no situation; Musset has situation but no style; Mallarmé has style and situation, but is affected and obscure; and Rimbaud has neither style nor situation.[51] Though his harshest criticisms are generally reserved for Rimbaud, Jacob lets no prose poet off easy:

> Rimbaud a élargi le champ de la sensibilité et tous les littérateurs lui doivent de la reconnaissance, mais les auteurs de poèmes en prose ne peuvent le prendre pour modèle . . . Rimbaud ne conduit qu'au désordre et à l'exaspération. Le poème en prose doit aussi éviter les paraboles baudelairiennes et mallarméennes, s'il veut se distinguer de la fable.
>
> [Rimbaud has enlarged the field of sensitivity and all writers of literature owe him thanks, but authors of prose poems cannot take him as a model . . . Rimbaud only leads to disorder and exasperation. The prose poem should also avoid the Baudelairean and Mallarmean parables, if it wishes to distinguish itself from the fable.][52]

In light of the qualities for which Jacob argues, some of his criticisms seem misdirected. Who, if not the Rimbaud of *Illuminations*, wrote short, concentrated poems aimed at defamiliarizing language and experience? Who, if not Baudelaire, emphasized the power of the will in artistic creation? However much Jacob may be inferring methods of writing from poetic results, his criticisms and arguments about the nature of the *poème en prose* are as negatively defined as Baudelaire's.[53] (Ironically, his own emphasis on artistic will points to a Baudelairean inheritance.) Jacob speaks of genres the prose poem must "avoid" or "distinguish itself from," and there is no poet, even among those he praises, who is not reproached for some failing.

As I discuss in my concluding chapter, some editors have used Jacob's notion of the prose poem to decide which works should be included in anthologies. The question worth raising here is the degree to which some of the qualities Jacob stresses, such as brevity and the lapidary nature of the prose poem, come to be seen as normative qualities of the French *poème en prose*. From the point of view of poetic practice, nothing could be farther from the truth: as I have been arguing, prose poems of many different varieties were not only being written in this period but admired, and in the twentieth century there has been, if anything, more variety. From the point of view of reception history, however, the issue is somewhat muddled. Prescriptive notions of the prose poem bearing some resemblance to Jacob's ideas continue to appear in anthologies and much of the critical literature on the *poème en prose* and certainly existed in the minds of some poets and readers in the early twentieth century. When Louis de Gonzague-Frick, a "Parisian aesthete," made a formal "inquiry into the prose poem" in 1919, for example, the fifty or so responses he received from writers often made reference to the prose poem as a "bijou ciselé" (chiseled jewel).[54] The symbolist inheritance of the prose poem was something poets either accepted or struggled against.

An exploration into the historical associations of "poème en prose" has implications for the term itself and helps continue a discussion begun in chapter 1. How has the usage of "poème en prose" shifted in the twentieth century? In his *Lire le poème en prose*, Michel Sandras provides a concise overview:

> It's to Baudelaire that we are indebted for having imposed, with fanfare but not without hesitation, the title "poème en prose" on an installment of short prose pieces in the November 1, 1861, issue of *La Revue fantaisiste*. This expression, whose usage spreads between 1860 and 1920, tends to disappear in the following decades, before making a comeback, at least among readers, due to the publication of brief prose pieces in Gallimard's "Poetry" series. If the expression has a fragrance of disuse today, the object which it designates is still very much alive, but as difficult to grasp as it was at the time of the *Spleen de Paris* [*Petits Poëmes en prose*].[55]

He adds in a later passage: "The œuvres of Saint-John Perse, Michaux, Char, and Ponge have helped modify the image of poetry. In the 60s, prose was not only recognized as one of the possible modes of writing a poem, but as the major form of poetic expression. And writers do not feel it necessary to specify on the cover of the work whether it is in verse or prose. . . . Today, the situation is no longer the same. In the last twenty years, verse has made a comeback."[56] Sandras also points out that some poets, like Perse and Ponge, preferred not to call their works prose poems. The Gallimard poetry series may well have contributed to the comeback of the term among readers, but if so it has also helped make prose poetry part of a general poetic tradition and less of a separate genre. The familiar white-cover editions with multiple color pictures of the poet on the front and back covers do not discriminate between prose poets and verse poets and are in fact often shelved as a group in bookstores. "Poème en prose" has virtually become a formal distinction.[57]

The sorties of the previous chapters into literary history also have implications for genre theory. How does the distinction between form and genre affect my earlier discussion of literary kinds? Comparing the prose poem to a verse form like the sonnet goes a long way toward answering this question. Most of the genre critics I discuss in chapter 1 would consider the sonnet a genre without a second thought. Thus, Fishelov argues that "literary genres whose organizing principles are basically thematic or rhetorical (e.g., satire) enjoy greater flexibility than those with conspicuous formal organizing principles (e.g., the sonnet)."[58] And even Fowler speaks of the "Elizabethan love sonnet" as a subgenre that "might be easily divided into secondary subgenres, and even tertiary ones," implying that either the love sonnet or the sonnet is a genre.[59] The issue is not so cut-and-dried for me. Assume for sake of argument that some formally defined or designated class of texts like "the sonnet" is a genre within a certain cultural milieu and over a certain period of time. As the genre diversifies, taking on new subject matter (from Petrarch's love regrets to Du Bellay's regrets of exile), groupings (the sonnet sequence, the corona), metrical forms (Petrarchan sonnets, Elizabethan sonnets, sonnets with sestets and octaves reversed), and whatever else, including the removal and transformation of traits, it becomes possible to talk of subgenres or new genres. But in the process of doing so, what happens to the old designation? To the extent that the term becomes more and more associated with external form, it is likely to become less useful as a generic label and distinction. Insofar as "the sonnet" refers only or mostly to a poem in fourteen lines of rhyming verse, the term "form" seems more appropriate than "genre," especially in a time like our own where formal considerations alone are less likely to suffice in determining genre. A case can still be made for the sonnet as a genre, particularly if one's view of genre is invested more in pragmatic than in historically based groupings, but some distinctions are necessary if one wishes to maintain that genre is the kind of interpretive framework I have been arguing it is. Like the sonnet, perhaps, the *poème en prose* has been a genre at some historical moment or moments and may no longer be one in a significant sense.

The history of the sonnet may not be typical, however. A comparison between the novel and the sonnet shows that there can be instances in which a generic label still designates a literary kind after the original genre has diversified. There are arguably more varieties of the novel than of the sonnet, and yet most of us would consider the novel a genre. Designations like "the Gothic novel," "the romance novel," or "the Gothic romance novel" also strike us as generic, to the point where we do not really think of them as subgenres of the novel (as evidenced by the shortened labels "romance" and "Gothic romance"). In this way we use generic labels to designate relatively large groupings of texts ("dramas" and "poems") as well as groupings we might almost consider subsets of the large classes of texts ("tragedies" and "elegies"). I say "almost" because, as several critics have pointed out, we should not be misled by the implied analogy of literary kind to biological species: individuals belong to one species, whereas texts generally belong to or participate in more than one genre; more often than not, interbreeding is precluded among species, whereas genres commonly diversify by mixing with other genres and producing "hybrids." In short, "the novel" has not become a term as heavily associated with external form as "the sonnet," though it remains both a formal and a generic label. Based on these examples, it is possible to argue that formal designations are less likely to endure as generic labels but also to draw from them a cautionary tale against generalizing. We are again reminded that linguistic, literary, and reception history has at least as much to do with our sense of genre as do formal considerations, though the latter may be an important driving force behind the former.

From a generic perspective, the history of the *poème en prose* is more analogous to that of the sonnet than that of the novel. Like "sonnet," "poème en prose" may have some air of a literary kind about it, but the increased variety of types the label now designates has reinforced the formal meaning, "poem in prose," at the expense of the generic "prose poem." Genres of the *poème en prose* may exist, such as the long travelogue or quest poem exemplified by Michaux's *Au Pays de la magie* or even Perse's *Anabase*, but we can only talk in a qualified sense of the *poème en prose* as a genre.[60] Situations may arise in which it is appropriate or useful to speak of prose poetry as a genre, whether for some conjunction of historical and pragmatic reasons or in casual conversation. But the conceptual distinction between form and genre should not be overlooked or undervalued. Formal considerations may provide an interpretive framework for reading; generic considerations always will.

Poetry in prose has a different history in the English-speaking world than the French, and its fortunes and misfortunes raise new questions about genre. As the next chapters show, English-language poets had not only to contend with native traditions of poetic prose and prose poetry but also to come to terms with a French inheritance.

5. The Emergence of
Prose Poetry in English

Among other things, this chapter and the next reflect on historical contingency. Why does prose poetry become an important part of the French poetic tradition by the turn of the twentieth century and yet emerge so sporadically in English? One answer, not easily bettered, is "because it did." The happenstances of history cannot always be explained in terms of inevitabilities or even probabilities, and when faced with less than inevitable developments, we fall back on phrases like "contingent on many circumstances." But since contingency can quickly become a catchall explanation, a metaphor for the inexplicable that does not acknowledge itself as such, it begs its own explanations in the end. If a set of historical contexts fails to account for cultural differences, one should neither halt nor infinitely defer exploring the reasons for the differences but rather, as the next chapter will argue, reexamine the comparison. In the meantime, this chapter provides some of the background necessary for a comparison between the developments of the *poème en prose* and the prose poem. The first half continues the history of the term "prose poem" begun in chapter 1 with "poème en prose." The second half parallels chapter 2 in that it provides examples of prose poems and prose-poem-like works written before prose poetry gained something approaching name recognition among poets. Though oriented toward American prose poetry, the historical overviews of this chapter are not limited to American authors and works. In order to come to terms with prose poetry in America, it is necessary to refer to the French literary tradition and discuss British authors. In what follows I will do both, beginning with the usage of "prose poem."

• • •

The earliest reference in the OED to a variant of "prose poem" occurs in a passage written by Anthony, earl of Shaftesbury in 1711:

But with poets and philosophers 'tis a known case:

> Aut insanit homo, aut versus fuit.
> [The man is either raving or composing.]

> Composing and raving must necessarily, we see, bear a resemblance.
> And for those composers who deal in systems and airy speculations, they
> have vulgarly pass'd for a sort of prose poets.[1]

The phrase "a sort of prose poets" is clearly derogatory in this context. It refers to prose writers who have a tendency to be rhapsodic. While not a term referring to a recognizable genre of literature, the prose poem implied in this passage is nevertheless comparable to its French counterpart in that it is an emerging phenomenon that crosses generic boundaries, in the process raising the eyebrows of critics such as the earl of Shaftesbury. Eighteenth-century British writers, like their contemporaries in France, sometimes labeled novels "epics in prose" or "poems in prose," as when Henry Fielding called *Joseph Andrews* (1742) a "comic epic poem in prose" in his preface to that work.[2] Though there is no English-language equivalent of *Télémaque* in eighteenth-century Britain, there are suggestive analogues, such as the Ossian poems and other "preromantic" prose texts. There are also works that are poetic in intent and not written in metered verse: Christopher Smart's "Jubilate Agno" ("finished" in 1763, first published in full in 1939), for example, is a poem in versets. Some prose works, such as Coleridge's "The Wanderings of Cain" (written in 1798), are even included in collections of poems.[3]

"Prose poem" continues to be used mainly as a figure of speech in the nineteenth century, as evidenced by the reflections of the narrator in Charles Kingsley's novel *Alton Locke* (1850): "[T]o speak first of the highest, I know no book, always excepting Milton, which at once so quickened and exalted my poetical view of man and his history, as that great prose poem, the single epic of modern days, Thomas Carlyle's 'French Revolution.'"[4] Alexander Main uses a similar sense of the term in his 3 June 1872 letter to John Blackwood: "[*Middlemarch*] is really a prose-poem much more than a novel in the ordinary sense of the word."[5] Now and then "poet in prose" or "prose poet" is used in a sense that hovers between literal and figurative. In 1834, for example, a reviewer of *The Poetical Works of Anne Radcliffe* claimed that Radcliffe was among writers "who are poets in prose, but whose poetry forsakes them the moment they attempt to embody their ideas in verse."[6] And Emerson writes in his journal in April 1846: "Yes, we want a poet, the genuine poet of our time, no parrot, and no child. The poets that we praise, or try to, the Brownings, Barretts, Bryants, Tennysons,—are all abortive Homers; they at least show tendency, the direction of Nature to the star in Lyra. Boys still whistle, and every newspaper and girl's album attest the ineradicable appetite for melody. Oh, no, we have not done with music, nor must we console ourselves with prose poets."⁷ "Prose poets" may refer to writers who set out to write poetry in prose, though Emerson is more likely giving "prose" the force of an adjective: the poets of the silver age of the nineteenth century are mere "prose poets." As with the French writers of midcentury, Emerson is portraying prose poetry as a fall away from an ideal.

An apparent exception to the metaphoric use of "prose poem" occurs in a review by Edgar Allan Poe in the January 1842 issue of *Graham's Magazine*: "Criticism is *not*, we think, an essay, nor a sermon, nor an oration, nor a chapter in history, nor a philosophical speculation, nor a prose-poem, nor an art novel, nor a dialogue. In fact, it *can be* nothing in the world but—a criticism."⁸ Poe's placement of the word "prose-poem" within a list of genres suggests it has a like status. But on closer examination of the context of the passage, it turns out that Poe is returning, almost word for word except in the negative, a remark of the critic Cornelius Matthews cited earlier in the review. Whatever Matthews's investment in the term, Poe seems only concerned with not confusing criticism with other types of writing. Another indication that Poe is not concerned with prose poetry as a genre occurs in his preface to *Eureka, Poem in Prose* (1848)—a long cosmological piece—where he claims that he added the subtitle "Poem in Prose" in the hope that readers would judge the work not as philosophy but as a poetry.⁹

Matthews's own sense of "prose-poem" can be gathered from the context in which Poe frames the original remark:

"But *now*" (the emphasis on the *now* is our own)—"But *now*," says Mr. Matthews, in the preface to the first volume of his journal, "criticism has a wider scope and a universal interest. It dismisses errors of grammar, and hands over an imperfect rhyme or a false quantity to the proof-reader; it looks *now* to the heart of the subject and the author's design. It is a test of opinion. . . . Good criticism may well be asked for, since it is the type of the literature of the day. It gives method to the universal inquisitiveness on every topic relating to life or action. A criticism, *now*, includes every form of literature, except perhaps the imaginative and the strictly dramatic. It is an essay, a sermon, an oration, a chapter in history, a philosophical speculation, a prose-poem, an art-novel, a dialogue; it admits of humor, pathos, the personal feelings of auto-biography, the broadest views of statesmanship. As the ballad and the epic were the productions of the days of Homer, the review is the native characteristic growth of the nineteenth century."[10]

Matthews's argument that modern criticism "includes every form of litera-ture, except perhaps the imaginative and the strictly dramatic" is sufficiently vague to allow for nongeneric explanations of his usage of "prose-poem." In particular his choice of the word "form" (as opposed to "genre" or "kind" or even "type"), such nongeneric examples as "a chapter in history" and "a philosophical speculation," and his comment that criticism "admits of humor, pathos, the personal feelings of autobiography, the broadest views of statesmanship" suggest that Matthews is concerned more with modern criticism's wide range of formal features than its status among genres. It is possible that he is referring to the eighteenth- and early-nineteenth-century varieties of the *poème en prose*, but it is more likely that he is using the term as a figure of speech, like the earl of Shaftesbury, in order to denote a certain type of prose writing. Even the twentieth-century usage of "prose poem" to denote a genre is confined largely to critics and poets, and yet the term is not so technical that most readers could not use or make some sense of it, especially given an appropriate context. Since form has historically been seen as the primary indicator of genre, "prose poem" lends itself to usage in contexts involving literary kinds.

Matthews's use of "prose poem" hovers somewhere between literal and figurative because an atmosphere for prose poetry already existed by the early nineteenth century, and yet influential examples of the form are conspicuously absent. In theoretical terms, there is no clear referent or "simple abstraction" for prose poetry. One can nevertheless unearth "prose poems" from journals of the period if one wishes to make a case for a native English-language tradition. Charles Dickens even subtitled his "The Old Church-yard Tree" "A Prose Poem" when he published it in the 13 July 1850 issue of his weekly journal *Household Words*. As the opening of this short prose work makes clear, English-language prose poems of this period are as filled with awkward gestures toward the poetic as their French counterparts of the late eighteenth and early nineteenth centuries:

> There is an old yew tree which stands by the wall in a dark quiet corner of the church-yard.

And a child was at play beneath its wide-spreading branches, one fine day in the early spring. He had his lap full of flowers, which the fields and lanes had supplied him with, and he was humming a tune to himself as he wove them into garlands.

And a little girl at play among the tombstones crept near to listen; but the boy was so intent upon his garland, that he did not hear the gentle footsteps, as they trod softly over the fresh green grass. When his work was finished, and all the flowers that were in his lap were woven together in one long wreath, he started up to measure its length upon the ground, and then he saw the little girl, as she stood with her eyes fixed upon him. He did not move or speak, but thought to himself that she looked very beautiful as she stood there with her flaxen ringlets hanging down upon her neck. The little girl was so startled by his sudden movement, that she let fall all the flowers she had collected in her apron, and ran away as fast as she could. But the boy was older and taller than she, and soon caught her, and coaxed her to come back and play with him, and help him make more garlands; and from that time they saw each other nearly every day, and became great friends.

Twenty years passed away. Again, he was seated beneath the old yew tree in the church-yard.[11]

Though narrative in form, "The Old Church-yard Tree" marks itself as something other than an anecdote or a short story through its language and formal features. The three short paragraphs surrounding the long narrative section, the repetition of the opening phrase "And a," frequent uses of the preposition "upon," and adjective phrases like "flaxen ringlets" signal the reader that this piece of prose aspires to poetry, or at least the poetic. Whatever its clumsiness and sentimentality, the prose also points to a design, especially in its handling of temporality. "The Old Church-yard Tree" falls into four sections that chart the course of the lives of a couple and their son; each section corresponds to a season, from spring to winter. Short paragraphs punctuate the beginnings and endings of these sections, until the final paragraph obliquely urges an allegorical interpretation, even as it concludes with a reference to the title of the poem:

Grief and old age had seized upon the father, and worn out his life; and premature decay soon seized upon the son, and gnawed away his vain ambition, and his useless strength, till he prayed to be borne, not the way yonder that was most opposite to his father and his mother, but even the same way they had gone—the way which leads to the Old Church-yard Tree.[12]

The capitalization of the "Old Church-yard Tree" at the end adds a final touch of self-reference, which points toward a metaphorical or poetic function of language. In other words, "the way which leads to the Old Church-yard Tree" asks for a moral.

Though typical of a species of writing in the mid-nineteenth century, "The Old Church-yard Tree" is a rarity in that it labels itself a prose poem. Again, it is the figurative sense of "prose poem" that predominates in the nineteenth century. This sense also persists into the twentieth century. In Willa Cather's novel *The Professor's House* (1925), one of the professor's sons-in-law describes some of his journalistic writing as prose poetry:

> Unless I keep my nose to the grindstone, I'm too damned spontaneous and tell the truth, and the public won't stand for it. It's not an editorial I have to finish, it's the daily prose poem I do for the syndicate, for which I get twenty-five beans. This is the motif:
>
> > When your pocket is under-moneyed and your fancy is over-girled, you'll have to admit while you're cursing it, it's a mighty darned good old world.
>
> Bang, bang![13]

In spite or perhaps because of the motif's rhyme ("over-girled . . . good old world"), the use of "prose poem" here to describe the daily column is tongue in cheek. We can take "the daily prose poem" to refer to the son-in-law's scornful label for his work or to the title of the column, or to both. This ironic use is as figurative as Main's dubbing *Middlemarch* a "prose-poem," only now the phrase deflates the importance of the work in question.

Virginia Woolf's use of "prose poem" in her biography of Roger Fry (1940) is also somewhat derogatory: "Nor was Roger Fry a born writer. Compared with Symonds and Pater he was an amateur, doing his best with a medium for which he had no instinctive affection. For that very reason perhaps he was saved from some of their temptations. He was not led away to write prose poems, or to make the picture a text for a dissertation upon life. He wrote of pictures as if they were pictures, and nothing else."[14] In this context, "prose poem" comes close to meaning purple prose. For Woolf, Victorian writers like Symonds and Pater wrote in a style that she admires only from a distance.

Nevertheless, Woolf's use of prose poem approaches a literal meaning: she is associating a certain tradition of writing essays with writing prose poetry. It is as if, after enough time has gone by in which writers have thrown "prose poem" around in various figurative senses, some literal meanings begin to stick. When Edmund Wilson discusses the "magnificent poetry" of Joyce's *Ulysses* and calls Flaubert "the great prose poet of Naturalism" (*Axel's Castle*, 1931), for example, he is speaking less figuratively than when Kingsley spoke of "that great prose poem . . . Carlyle's 'French Revolution'."[15] Needless to say, these new meanings do not prevent some figurative senses from persisting or being reinvented later.

"Prose poem" did not really take on its modern sense until English-language writers became aware of the *poème en prose*. The French influence is evident in late-nineteenth-century England and America in that writers like Oscar Wilde and Emma Lazarus title or subtitle some of their work "poems in prose." Variants on the phrase such as Ernest Dowson's *Decorations in Prose* (1899) and Stuart Merrill's *Pastels in Prose* (1890) also indicate descent from the *poème en prose*.[16] As William Dean Howells's introduction to *Pastels in Prose*, "The Prose Poem," makes clear, "prose poem" and "poem in prose" were somewhat interchangeable terms by the 1890s:

> In a measure the whole Bible is a prose poem in our version, and in the Bible Job and Ecclesiastes are notable prose poems. . . . In fact, every strain of eloquence is a strain of poetry; every impassioned plea or oration is a poem in prose.

> Indeed, some writers have intentionally imparted to their prose the flow of verse, as if one would modulate his walk to a dancing step, and have produced a vicious kind in literature, which is as different as possible from the Poem in Prose as the French have cultivated it.

> I do not know whether Tourguénief, in his Prose Poems . . . received or gave an impulse in this irregular species of composition. . . .

> I do not know the history of the French Poem in Prose, but I am sure that, as we say in our graphic slang, it has come to stay.[17]

While "poem in prose," especially when capitalized, seems to describe the genre as practiced in France, Howells is not consistent in his usage. On the one hand, the "poem in prose" may mean anything written according to Baudelaire's injunction "without rhyme or rhythm"; on the other hand, "every impassioned plea or oration is a poem in prose." Despite his speculations about the Bible, emotionally intense prose passages, and the writings of Turgenev, Howells's main point is that the prose poem is "a peculiarly modern invention" whose origins are French (to judge from the anthology itself if not his orthography of the Russian writer's name).[18] At the same time, however, Howells's mixture of the terms "prose poem" and "poem in prose" suggests that there may exist in the future, and possibly already existed in embryo, differences between the English-language prose poem and the French model.

By the modernist period, the category "prose poetry" was widely recognized even though the usage of the term was still in flux. The three essays of the April 1921 *The Chapbook* (*A Monthly Miscellany*) are all, according to the magazine's stated format, devoted to "Poetry in Prose," but there is no consensus among the authors regarding the term.[19] T. S. Eliot uses "prose-poetry" and "prose poem" (the former generally with a hyphen and latter without) and evidently sees "poem in prose" as a target for criticism when he writes, "I have not yet been given any definition of the prose poem, which appears more than a tautology or a contradiction."[20] The other contributors to *The Chapbook*, Frederic Manning and Richard Aldington, prefer "poem in prose," though Aldington acknowledges the currency of both terms.[21] The prose poems appearing in various journals of the period are sometimes labeled "poems in prose" or "prose poems," as in John Rodker's "Prose Poems" (*The Little Review*, October 1918), and sometimes given quasi-generic titles or subtitles, as in Rodker's "Three Nightpieces" (*The Little Review*, July 1917). Most prose poems have no overt generic label and rely on the framework of the journal and the audience's familiarity with the form for recognition.

It was perhaps not until the 1960s and the work of poets as various as Russell Edson, Robert Bly, and Karl Shapiro that "prose poem" received a kind of consensus preference over "poem in prose."[22] "Poem in prose" appeared prominently as late as 1953 in Charles Henri Ford's "A Little Anthology of the Poem in Prose" (*New Directions* 14), but all English-language anthologies since have been "of the prose poem."[23] Academic criticism in English on the subject, coming into its own in the 1970s and 1980s, has decidedly favored "prose poem," with the notable exception of Stephen Fredman's polemical "poet's prose." (The tentative hyphen that occasionally appeared in "prose-poem" seems to have disappeared from use, as what was once a neologism has gradually become a more widely accepted term.) But if "prose poem" is preferable to "poem in prose" today, the former existence of a split between the two terms is revealing, both of the French origins of Anglophone experimentation and of the desire of English-language poets to distance themselves from these origins. From this point of view, William Carlos Williams's decision to call his prose poems "improvisations" and Fredman's move to use "poet's prose" are only manifestations in an extreme form of a recurrent preoccupation among American poets and critics.[24]

•   •   •

As with the French *poème en prose*, it is possible to speak of English-language prose poems or prose-poem-like texts in existence before the term itself took on its modern sense or before anything approaching a genre came into being. A long tradition of "poetic prose" stretches at least as far back as the Renaissance, depending on how continuous one considers its history to be. In his 1912 history of English prose rhythm, George Saintsbury effectively allows for the possibility that all artfully composed prose is potential poetry. Walter De la Mare, in his 1935 Warton lecture on English poetry, defines prose poetry as "*fine* writing *in excelsis*" and suggests including the prose of "Sir Thomas Browne, Francis Bacon, Fuller, Jeremy Taylor, Burton, Ruskin, Lamb, . . . Jonson, Traherne, Milton, Dryden, Landor, Hardy, Doughty."[25] Such prose arguably does not belong to the genre this study is concerned with—if anything, the essay is the privileged genre—but the existence of a tradition of poetic prose is important to the prose poem on several counts. Some writers, like De Quincey in "Suspiria de profundis" (first published in 1856 as an appendix of "dream fugues" to the *Confessions of an English Opium Eater*), wrote prose pieces that, if not in intent, were later read as prose poetry.[26] With the passage of time, the prose stylist was arguably crowned with some of the poet's laurels, as attested by Woolf's remark about Symonds and Pater and by Yeats's famous inclusion of Pater's "Mona Lisa" in a poetry anthology.[27]

Parallel, once again, to the French tradition, a host of English-language works in neighboring genres (meditations, anecdotes, sermons) might qualify as prose poems from a formal perspective. The Hawthorne sketch entitled "An Afternoon Scene" (1835) is an instructive example:

> There had not been a more delicious afternoon than this, in all the train of summer—the air being a sunny perfume, made up of balm and warmth and gentle brightness. The oak and walnut trees, over my head, retained their deep masses of foliage, and the grass, though for months the pasturage of stray cattle, had been revived with the freshness of early June, by the autumnal rains of the preceding week.

The garb of Autumn indeed resembled that of Spring. Dandelions and buttercups were sprinkled along the roadside, like drops of brightest gold in greenest grass; and a star-shaped little flower, with a golden centre. In a rocky spot, and rooted under the stone-wall, there was one wild rose-bush, bearing three roses, very faintly tinted, but blessed with a spicy fragrance. The same tokens would have announced that the year was brightening into the glow of summer. There were violets, too, though few and pale ones. But the breath of September was diffused through the mild air, whenever a little breeze shook out the latent coolness.[28]

The small size of the piece and its tendency toward description mark it as lyric. If it were framed differently, say by a subtitle or by appearance in a journal devoted exclusively to poetry, "An Afternoon Scene" would probably pass for a prose poem. Hawthorne published a number of "American sketches" in journals like the *New England Magazine* and the *American Monthly Magazine* in the late 1830s. Some of these pieces he later included in *Mosses from Old Manse* (1854). "An Afternoon Scene" was published first in a group of "Sketches from Memory by a Pedestrian" (1835) and later among "Fragments from the Journal of a Solitary Man" (1837).[29] The different labels under which "An Afternoon Scene" was published indicate that they do not necessarily indicate genre. As with the *fantaisie* or the promenade in France, "sketch" or "fragment" serves to reduce readerly expectations of a finished piece of writing in a way in which "poem" might not.

It is possible to go on indefinitely with examples of prose-poem-like works *avant la lettre*. The genres bordering on the prose poem are important to an understanding of the prose poem, if only because they help negatively define it. But as soon as the principle of differentiation is established, the relevance of any one neighboring genre to the prose poem is best determined in relation to specific poems. Only a few works framed themselves as prose poems in the period before "prose poetry" became a term with a clear referent. Leigh Hunt's "Dreams on the Borders of the Land of Poetry" (from *The Keepsake of 1828*) qualifies, if not by its title announcing its marginal existence as poetry then by its author's complaints about the difficulties of writing verse and his confession: "But I have the wish to be a poet, and thoughts will arise within me as painful not to express as a lover's. I therefore write memorandums for verse;—thoughts that might perhaps be worthy of putting into that shape, if they could be properly developed;—hints, and shadows of something poetical, that have the same relationship to actual poetry, as the little unborn spirits that perish by the waters of Lethe have to the souls that visit us, and become immortal."[30] While excusing himself for writing not poetry but "memorandums for verse," Hunt also expresses a desire that his "dreams" be read as poems. The dreams generally consist of a series of short prose paragraphs on romantic or classical subjects ("My Bower"; "On a Bust of Bacchus"). Perhaps the most interesting of the dreams, "An Evening Landscape," plays with typographical conventions:

> Did anybody ever think of painting a picture in writing? I mean literally so, marking the localities as in a map.
>
> The other evening I sat in a landscape that would have enchanted Cuyp.
>
> Scene—a broken heath, with hills in the distance. The immediate picture stood thus, the top and the bottom of it being nearly on a level in the perspective:

> Trees in a sunset, at no great distance from the foreground.
> A group of cattle under them, party-coloured,
> principally red, standing on a small landing place;
> the Sun coming upon them through the trees.
> A rising ground   A rising ground
> Broken ground.
> with trees.   with trees.
> Another landing place, nearly on a level
> with the cows, the spectator sitting and looking at them.

> The Sun came warm and serious on the glowing red of the cattle, as if recognizing their evening hues; and every thing appeared full of that quiet spirit of consciousness, with which Nature seems rewarded at the close of its day labours.[31]

The poem painted in spatially placed phrases is framed by the box traced around it and by the text that precedes and follows it. At a further remove, "An Evening Landscape" is framed by the series of dreams opened by the author's apologies and by the dreams' appearance in *The Keepsake*, a miscellany. These different frameworks cushion the reader's response to the unconventional typography. In contrast to literary works that present themselves as something new—say, Baudelaire's *Petits Poëmes en prose* or

Apollinaire's *Calligrammes*—Hunt's "Dreams" are everywhere marked as slight and marginal, a typical feature of prose poems *avant la lettre* and even of some *après*.

Emerson's prose poem "Woods, A Prose sonnet" has an even more oblique relationship to its readership than Hunt's "Dreams." Written in 1839, it appears in one of Emerson's journals but was not published until 1969:

> Wise are ye, O ancient woods! wiser than man. Whoso goeth in your paths or into your thickets where no paths are, readeth the same cheerful lesson whether he be a young child or a hundred years old. I cannot In Comes he in good fortune or bad, ye say the same things, & from age to age. Ever the needles of the pine grow & fall, the acorns on the oak, the maples redden in autumn, & at all times of the year the ground pine & the pyrola bud & root under foot. What is called fortune & what is called Time by men—ye know them not. Men have not language to describe one moment of your eternal life. This I would ask of you, o sacred Woods, when ye shall next give me somewhat to say, give me also the tune wherein to say it. Give me a tune of your own like your winds or rains or brooks or birds; for the tunes songs of men grow old when they have been often repeated, but yours, though a man have heard them for seventy years, are never the same, but always new, like time itself, or like love.[32]

The sub- or alternate title, "A Prose sonnet," is an instruction on how to read what follows. In some sense, "Woods" must be sonnetlike. But how? Though it lacks rhymes, line breaks, and stanza divisions, the poem is roughly the length of a sonnet. Furthermore, the phrase beginning "This I would ask of you, o sacred Woods" functions somewhat like a turn after an octave in an Italian sonnet. It is even possible to rewrite the entire poem with line and stanza divisions, as though its structure and development corresponded closely to that of a verse sonnet:

> Wise are ye, O ancient woods! wiser than man.
> Whoso goeth in your paths or into your thickets where no paths are,
>   readeth the same cheerful lesson whether he be a young child or a
>   hundred years old.
> Comes he in good fortune or bad, ye say the same things, & from age
>   to age.

Ever the needles of the pine grow & fall, the acorns on the oak, the
 maples redden in autumn,
& at all times of the year the ground pine & the pyrola bud & root under
 foot.
What is called fortune & what is called Time by men—ye know them
 not.
Men have not language to describe one moment of your eternal life.

This I would ask of you, o sacred Woods,
when ye shall next give me somewhat to say, give me also the tune
 wherein to say it.
Give me a tune of your own like your winds or rains or brooks or birds;

for the songs of men grow old when they have been often repeated, but
 yours,
though a man have heard them for seventy years, are never the same,
but always new, like time itself, or like love.

Rewriting "Woods" in this way may be too literal an application of "A Prose
sonnet," but the subtitle encourages readings of this sort. Regardless of
whether a given text is or is not a prose poem in some normative sense,
the reader's consideration of it as such has interpretive consequences.

Hunt's and Emerson's prose poems present themselves as resulting from
the author's inability to write in verse. Hunt overtly laments this fact, albeit
in a lighthearted way. In his journals, Emerson often complains or speculates
about his inability to write verses and quotes from Herrick's "Not Every Day
Fit for Verse" in the entry that immediately precedes "Woods."[33] This mode
of defense contrasts to the bolder claim, explicit or implicit in the work of
many nineteenth-century French poets and some British and American poets
of the modernist period, that the prose poem enables the writer to express
aspects of modern experience that traditional verse poems cannot. The two
claims are more similar than they may at first appear, however. They both
issue from a romantic aesthetic in which expression has a privileged position.

By the time Emma Lazarus published her prose poems "By the Waters of
Babylon" (first published in 1887 in the *Century Magazine* and then in 1888
in the posthumous *The Poems of Emma Lazarus in Two Volumes*), the French
prose poem had made its appearance. Lazarus, best known as the author of
a sonnet commissioned for the Statue of Liberty, "The New Colossus," had

traveled in France and was probably aware of the existence of the *poème en prose*. "By the Waters of Babylon" in fact carries the Baudelairean subtitle "Little Poems in Prose." Lazarus's prose poems, such as "The Exodus (August 3, 1492)," nevertheless owe more to the Bible and Whitman than they do to the *poème en prose*:

1. The Spanish noon is a blaze of azure fire, and the dusty pilgrims crawl like an endless serpent along treeless plains and bleached highroads, through rock-split ravines and castellated, cathedral-shadowed towns.

2. The hoary patriarch, wrinkled as an almond shell, bows painfully upon his staff. The beautiful young mother, ivory-pale, well-nigh swoons beneath her burden; in her large enfolding arms nestles her sleeping babe, round her knees flock her little ones with bruised and bleeding feet. "Mother, shall we soon be there?"

3. The youth with Christ-like countenance speaks comfortably to father and brother, to maiden and wife. In his breast, his own heart is broken.

4. The halt, the blind, are amid the train. Sturdy pack-horses laboriously drag the tented wagons wherein lie the sick athirst with fever.

5. The panting mules are urged forward with spur and goad; stuffed are the heavy saddlebags with the wreckage of ruined homes.

6. Hark to the tinkling silver bells that adorn the tenderly-carried silken scrolls.

7. In the fierce noon-glare a lad bears a kindled lamp; behind its network of bronze the airs of heaven breathe not upon its faint purple star.

8. Noble and abject, learned and simple, illustrious and obscure, plod side by side, all brothers now, all merged in one routed army of misfortune.

9. Woe to the straggler who falls by the wayside! no friend shall close his eyes.

10. They leave behind, the grape, the olive, and the fig; the vines they planted, the corn they sowed, the garden-cities of Andalusia, and Aragon, Estremadura and La Mancha, of Granada and Castile; the altar, the hearth, and the grave of their fathers.

11. The townsman spits at their garments, the shepherd quits his flock, the peasant his plow, to pelt with curses and stones; the villager sets on their trail his yelping cur.

12. Oh the weary march, oh the uptorn roots of home, oh the blankness of the receding goal!

13. Listen to their lamentation: *They that ate dainty food are desolate in the streets; they that were reared in scarlet embrace dunghills. They flee away and wander about. Men say among the nations, they shall no more sojourn there; our end is near, our days are full, our doom is come.*

14. Wither shall they turn? for the West hath cast them out, and the East refuseth to receive.

15. O bird of the air, whisper to the despairing exiles, that to-day, to-day, from the many-masted, gayly-bannered port of Palos, sails the world-unveiling Genoese, to unlock the golden gates of sunset and bequeath a Continent to Freedom![34]

As the sequence title "By the Waters of Babylon" suggests, "Exodus" relies on the Psalms for some of its formal features—its versetlike lines, numbered verses, and language. Most of the dramatic effect of the poem comes from its stated and unstated comparisons between biblical and historical events. The sequence titles and the poem title link the Babylonian captivity of the Jews in ancient times and the expulsion of the Jews from Spain in 1492, which is, of course, the year that Columbus ("the world-unveiling Genoese") discovered the New World, an event the poem connects to the eventual founding of the United States. Columbus is then linked back to Moses via the title "Exodus," which on first reading may seem to convey something like exile rather than flight out of captivity to a promised land.

Like Lazarus's prose poems, Oscar Wilde's *Poems in Prose* (1894) rely on the Bible for certain linguistic and formal features. "The Disciple" is typical in that it takes the form of a parable:

When Narcissus died, the pool of his pleasure changed from a cup of sweet waters into a cup of salt tears, and the Oreads came weeping through the woodland that they might sing to the pool and give it comfort.

And when they saw that the pool had changed from a cup of sweet waters into a cup of salt tears, they loosened the green tresses of their hair, and cried to the pool, and said: "We do not wonder that you should mourn in this manner for Narcissus, so beautiful was he."

"But was Narcissus beautiful?" said the pool.

"Who should know better than you?" answered the Oreads. "Us did he ever pass by, but you he sought for, and would lie on your banks and

look down at you, and in the mirror of your waters he would mirror his
own beauty."

And the pool answered: "But I loved Narcissus because, as he lay on
my banks and looked down at me, in the mirror of his eyes I saw my
own beauty mirrored."[35]

The pool's narcissism illustrates how self-love may be the feeling that moti-
vates all lovers, not just a certain type of individual. This twist in the Ovidian
tale makes everyone a potential disciple of Narcissus. "The Disciple" may also
bring out the homoerotic elements latent in the myth: Echo is no where to
be seen or heard in Wilde's continuation of the story, and the pool is male, to
judge by what it believes to be its reflection.

It is appropriate to conclude a survey of nineteenth-century prose poems
with Wilde if only because some critics have argued that his trials gave
the term "prose poem" a French and decadent tinge for twentieth-century
writers. But before turning to this claim, it is worth considering some of this
chapter's arguments in light of the general aims of this study. The histories
of terms and works traced here "from poem in prose to prose poem" are not
ends in themselves: they follow from the theoretical concerns addressed in
the introduction and the first chapter, which in turn follow from the initial
focus on prose poetry as a genre. In other words, theoretical and literary-
historical—or, for that matter, philological—concerns are intimately linked.
My emphasis on unacknowledged constraints guarantees some consideration
of literary history, but even if my discussion were centered on genre theory
rather than "Prose Poetry as a Genre in French and American literature,"
the theoretical issues would require literary history to be made sense of and
acquire relevance. You can't have literary kinds unless you have a body of
literature that gives rise to them, and a body of literature implies at least one
narrative—a history—that organizes it.

The literary-historical discussions presented here should also point to the
ways in which abstractions like genre help create literary histories. Once it
becomes possible to speak of a specific kind such as prose poetry, its history
and the history of neighboring genres take on new forms and meanings.
This dialectical relationship between the theory and the history of literature
ultimately informs the terms within which the discussion itself takes place. In
particular, the significance or texture of "genre" will have altered from being
passed back and forth between the hands of literary history and theory. In

the conclusion I will say more about the significance of the term "genre," but the direction of my argument should already be clear. Shuttling between the perspectives of literary theory and history makes visible the outlines and limitations of both and their dependence on each other. "Genre" helps us see this interrelationship.

6. The Idea of an American Prose Poem, Take One

To judge from the remarks of various American critics and poets, the French *poème en prose* and the American prose poem are not the same thing. Irked by Ezra Pound's charges of provincialism and quips such as "what the French real reader would say to your *Improvisations* is Voui, ç(h)a j(h)ai déjà (f)vu ç(h)a ç(h)a c'est de R(h)imb(h)aud!!" William Carlos Williams wrote in his 1918 prologue to *Kora in Hell*, "I was familiar with the typically French prose poem, its pace was not the same as my own compositions."[1] Russell Edson stated in 1976 that "the prose poem comes to us [Americans] not so much from the idea of the *poème en prose*, but out of modern poetry itself. . . . I don't think a line of European virtuosos is necessary to find the availability of the prose poem in America."[2] Stephen Fredman argues in *Poet's Prose* that whereas the French *poème en prose* is "a highly aestheticized, subjective, idiolectical artifact, a paean to the isolated genius," the American prose poem tends to "interrogate the realm of truth" and thus clear the way for "a union of fact and imagination."[3] Fredman goes as far as to suggest that the term "poet's prose" is preferable to "prose poem" because the latter is "an oxymoron aimed at defamiliarizing lyric poetry, and it remains redolent with the atmospheric sentiment of French Symbolism."[4] Even John Ashbery, who acknowledges some debt to French poets, remarked in a 1971 interview that "there's something very self-consciously poetic about French prose poetry which I wanted to avoid [in *Three Poems*] and which I guess is what I found disappointing in my earlier prose poems; it's very difficult to avoid a posture, a certain rhetorical tone."[5]

From a formal perspective, the differences that exist between the French and the American prose poem are either limited to narrow historical periods or nonexistent. A wide range of types exists in both literatures—long and short prose poems; ekphrastic, anecdotal, and surrealist prose poetry; poems that use versetlike lines; poems written in block paragraphs—making it easy to locate exceptions to any simple notion of "Frenchness" or "Americanness." It may be that American poets and critics, especially those who are noticeably defensive, have based their claims on a single type of French poem or a straw-man symbolist poem.[6] The idea of an American prose poem is no less real as a result, but it needs to be considered from a literary-historical rather than a formal perspective. At certain times and in certain places, poets, editors, and readers have had some stake in the idea of an American prose poem, and our understanding of the poetry they wrote, published, and read should take their perspectives into account. Regardless of its taxonomic value, "American" is potentially an important interpretive framework for some prose poems. To evaluate the importance of the frame, this chapter focuses on the situation of the prose poem during the modernist period. The first section provides a general overview of the prose poetry written in the first decades of the twentieth century, the middle sections discuss the relative neglect of the English-language prose poem, and the final section pursues a reading of T. S. Eliot's "The Engine" in light of the framework "American prose poem."

• • •

In the modernist period, many expatriate American writers, like T. S. Eliot and Gertrude Stein, were living in Europe, and a few, like Stuart Merrill, were writing in French. Nevertheless, much of the prose poetry published in these years is different from the earlier "poeticized prose" of Wilde and Dowson written under the shadow of French symbolism.[7] The few Anglophone poets who labeled some works "poems in prose" (such as the British writers Aldous Huxley and Richard Aldington) arguably descend from the writers of the nineties, but many poets simply did not label their work prose poetry or, as with Williams in his *Improvisations*, actively defined their work against the *poème en prose*. For better or worse, the French prose poem was in the air, to be emulated, elided, or denounced by English-language poets. In the modernist period, the idea of writing poetry in prose gained some impetus from the *poème en prose*, yet prose poetry as such did not gain widespread acceptance. Between 1910 and 1930, most prose poems were published in journals or anthologies among verse poems and in some cases later included in collections of verse poems. Eliot's "Hysteria," for example, was first published in the *Catholic Anthology, 1914–15*, then later in *Prufrock and Other Observations* (1917). Only a few collections of poetry from this period, such as Stein's *Tender Buttons* (1914) and Williams's *Kora in Hell* (1920), are comprised exclusively of prose poems.

The American prose poem of the modernist period can be compared to the *poème en prose* before Baudelaire in that prose poetry was not a preferred genre among poets and did not attract a wide audience. How little inroad the prose poem made into Anglophone poetry can be illustrated via a sampling of critical remarks made before, during, after, and well after the modernist period:

> The so-called prose-poem is very rarely attempted.
>   Daily Chronicle, *15 January 1906*

> It has not yet been proved—in spite of many interesting attempts which have been made, chiefly in France, in spite of *Gaspard de la Nuit*, Baudelaire's *Petits Poèmes en Prose*, and Mallarmé's jeweled fragments—that prose can, quite legitimately, be written in this de-tached, poetic way, as if one were writing sonnets.
>   *Arthur Symons, 1923*

> Indeed, the number of English masters of poetic prose is legion. . . . But you can count on the fingers of one hand the prose poets, and if you wanted to count the writers of great prose poems, you might as well keep that hand in your pocket. Consequently, the notions of rhythmical prose and prose rhythm have become extremely familiar ones . . . , whereas the very term "prose poetry" remains unfamiliar to many English and American ears.
>   *John Simon, 1959*

> For Baudelaire, who had always made his poems in verse, it was a startling notion that poetry might also be made from prose. But now, more than a hundred years later, this can hardly be news. Yet, in some quarters the poem in prose is treated like a door suddenly opened.
>   *Russell Edson, 1976*[8]

The *Daily Chronicle* comment is intended as a statement of fact, in spite of its author's use of the phrase "so-called prose-poem": in 1906 the prose poem was rarely attempted. Symons's remark, however, is made against the background of modernist experimentation with the form. It is comparable to Banville's argument, in his 1872 treatise on French poetry, that the prose poem does not exist, in spite of the admirable efforts of different poets.[9] Simon, unlike Symons, does not call the existence of the prose poem into doubt, but he is aesthetically dissatisfied with the prose poems that have been written in English. Edson is simply surprised that the prose poem has not, after so many years of existence, become a commonplace notion. Like the prose poem in France before Baudelaire, the English-language prose poem undeniably exists as a form but is of marginal interest to most poets and readers.

The modernist prose poem is also like the pre-Baudelairean *poème en prose* with regard to some forms in which it manifested itself. Many prose poems of the early twentieth century presented themselves as translations or primitive lyrics, comparable to the pseudotranslations and works written deliberately as *poésie primitive* in eighteenth- and early-nineteenth-century France.[10] Allen Upward's "Scented Leaves—From a Chinese Jar," for example, was laid out in the September 1913 issue of *Poetry* as a series of translations, opening with "Kublai and the Linnet": "It is told that the great emperor Kublai, listening one day in his garden, condescended to praise the song of the common brown linnet. Do thou, O high-born scholar, who mayest overlook these clumsily written trifles, be not less gracious than that great emperor, Kublai!"[11] "Scented Leaves" was accompanied by a notice that the individual sections were not direct translations but paraphrases from the Chinese.[12] The result is a work not unlike Stevens's "Thirteen Ways of Looking at a Blackbird" in its imagistic quality and vaguely philosophical speculation. (This was also the heyday of imagism, a movement with which Upward was associated.) The prose poems in *Poetry* could, like "Scented Leaves," approach pseudotranslation or present themselves as actual translations, as in the following piece by the Bengalese author Rabindranath Tagore:

> Over the green and yellow rice fields sweep the shadows of the autumn clouds, followed by the swift-chasing sun.
> The bees forget to sip their honey; drunken with the light they foolishly hum and hover; and the ducks in the sandy riverbank clamour in joy for mere nothing.
> None shall go back home, brothers, this morning, none shall go to work.
> We will take the blue sky by storm and plunder the space as we run.
> Laughters fly floating in the air like foams in the flood.
> Brothers, we shall squander our morning in futile songs.[13]

One biographical note accompanying Tagore's poems in effect packages them as exotic primitive songs. It mentions that his lyrics "are sung throughout

Bengal by the people, and many of them form part of the simple ritual of the Brahma Somaj church."[14]

Alternatively, or in addition, modernist prose poems can frame themselves as experimental. From this perspective, the situation of the modernist prose poem can be likened to that of the post-Baudelairean *poème en prose*. Both Anglo-American modernism and the literary milieu of late-nineteenth-century France are periods marked by widespread formal experimentation. In such an environment, the prose poem tends to become one form among many new poetic forms rather than its own genre. This tendency is especially pronounced in Britain and America, where the "make it new" spirit dominated in certain circles and the question of which direction poetry should be taking was a special concern of poets like Ezra Pound, William Carlos Williams, and Amy Lowell. The majority of prose poems written in this period were in fact published in the more experimental, and often obscure, journals, like *Broom*, *Pagany*, *The Little Review*, *transition*, *The Double Dealer*, and *Blues: A Magazine of New Rhythms*. These prose poems therefore appeared among the free-verse poems of Cummings and Zukovsky, the prose of Stein and Joyce, and pieces of very short fiction and mixtures of prose and verse.[15] Though some prose poems, like Stein's "Advertisement!," deliberately obscured their generic identity by announcing themselves as something other than poetry, most prose poems were generically ambiguous by virtue of the contexts in which they were published.[16] As the parallel with the late nineteenth-century *poème en prose* might suggest, poets also began to theorize some about new experimental forms. Criticism devoted exclusively to the prose poem was the exception, but prose poetry was discussed along with other poetic forms, especially free verse, in articles like Alice Corbin Henderson's "Poetic Prose and Vers Libre," Amy Lowell's "Vers Libre and Metrical Prose," and John Gould Fletcher's review of *Sword-blades and Poppy Seed*, "Miss Lowell's Discovery: Polyphonic Prose."[17]

• • •

Why was the prose poem, as a whole, a neglected form? This question assumes more than may at first be apparent. It most obviously presupposes that the prose poem *was* neglected by American and British modernists. Yet if one judges cultivation of a form by publications such as those previously mentioned, the prose poem arguably makes a respectable showing. The American neglect of the form is relative and only becomes conspicuous when one compares the prose poem to the *poème en prose*. The *poème en prose* of the early twentieth century had a pedigree that could be traced back to

Mallarmé, Rimbaud, and Baudelaire and had the contemporary sanction of poets like Claudel, Jacob, and Reverdy. In France, poets would soon be able to establish their reputations by writing poetry solely or primarily in prose. No comparable trend exists in English-language poetry. In fact, "prose poetry" has yet to become a common expression.

So the question should be rephrased. Why did the prose poem not catch on the way the *poème en prose* did? This question assumes that French and American poets had similar poetic concerns. One might after all argue that the French and American poetic traditions are simply different—that there is literally no comparison. But an assumption of similar concerns seems reasonable given the otherwise strong influence of nineteenth-century French poetry on Anglo-American modernism. And the discrepancy between French cultivation and Anglophone neglect of prose poetry is so marked as to merit at least a developmental comparison of the two traditions. The possibility that French and American poetry "just happened to develop differently" needs to be explored further, since arguing for difference in the name of historical contingency does not release one from concerns of literary history and history in general; it merely shifts the burden of explanation. The happenings of literary history are informed by the happenings that surround and precede them, and these may help put matters in some perspective, if not explain them.

The question remains: Why did the prose poem not catch on the way the *poème en prose* did? Several critics have already posed and tried to answer this question, and two basic explanations have emerged. As I discussed in chapter 4, the first approach accounts for the differences in the poetic traditions in strictly formal terms, with vague cultural overtones. The revolutionary attitude emerges in France due to a reaction against the rigid strictures of alexandrine, and the evolutionary attitude emerges in England and America due to the existence of less dictatorial poetic forms like blank verse. But this "straitjacket" argument is ultimately based on an essentializing logic. What one poet sees as strict another may see as free. Even if one poetic tradition tends to view prose poetry as a revolutionary innovation, the "straitjacket" explanation does not make the *poème en prose* inevitable. Prose poetry would be only one option for poets, perhaps one among many.

The other explanation turns away from form toward history. The phrases "prose sonnet" and "prose poems" were used in Oscar Wilde's trials to designate the alleged letters of seduction to Lord Alfred Douglas. These usages—so the argument runs—and the prose poem's general air of French decadence tainted the form for English-language poets. John Simon was the first critic to suggest this possibility:

> Wilde's failure to endear the prose poem to readers and writers is regrettable, because, I repeat, the age was ripe for this art form. . . . But Wilde, not content with doing the cause of prose poetry no service, managed, I fear, to do it a major disservice.
>
> If anything beyond the name of Oscar Wilde was besmirched in the Wilde-Queensberry scandal, it was, I suspect, the name of the prose poem.[18]

Margueritte Murphy gives a more developed version of the argument:

> How did [Wilde's trial and its aftermath] affect the fate of the prose poem? Clearly, the genre gained notoriety as the genre par excellence of homosexual decadence, hiding abominations behind its already damning veneer of "art for art's sake." Furthermore, it was hopelessly "French" at a time of growing English nationalism. But would such prejudices affect those most likely to produce prose poems, poets like Wilde? Indeed, Dowson's prose poems appeared in 1899, four years after Wilde's trials. Yet the stigma of effeminacy, of a lack of strength and virility, remained with the form, if Irving Babbitt's condemnation of mixed genres, including the prose poem, is typical of the intellectual and literary reaction to Wilde's generation.[19]

Some early-twentieth-century reactions of British and American writers can be used to support this "stigma" argument. In 1921, for example, Aldington lamented in his *Chapbook* article on prose poetry: "The words 'prose poem' and 'poem in prose' seem to suggest to most people something impotent or unwholesome."[20]

Even more revealing is Walter De la Mare's 1935 Warton lecture, "Poetry in Prose." De la Mare, in spite of familiarity with French literature and contemporary experiments in English-language poetry, barely acknowledges prose poetry as a genre. For him, poetry in prose certainly exists, but prose poetry is, however harmless, at best a decadent activity: "[W]hatever its defects may be, prose poetry is usually innocent enough in intention, springing perhaps from a misconception, from extreme sensitiveness or self-consciousness or vanity, and then, pose, pretence, flattery. It may, too, be the fine flower of a genuine delight in the rich, ornate, exquisite, and lavish."[21] De la Mare finds this usage confirmed in a contemporary *Dictionary of Modern English Usage*, which without making "specific reference to it" would seem to be implied by the author's "remarks on genteelisms, gallicisms, poeticisms, purisms, 'the tuppence coloured', the stylish, and elsewhere."[22] At its worst, prose poetry is feminizing and easily assimilated into the language of advertising. For De la Mare, there is a variety of prose poetry which "chiefly frequents the Woman's Page, but its dulcet persuasions haunt also the wine merchant's or house-agent's list and the company promoter's prospectus, the wooings of the tailor, or the purveyor of patent medicines, every seedsman's catalogue."[23] De la Mare's remarks, coming in 1935, represent a conservative and British response concerned with defending a native tradition of "poetry in prose." From this perspective, "The style [of prose poetry] smells of the lamp, and the oil is scented."

Though it may help explain some of the reasons why the English-language prose poem failed to catch on, the stigma argument is not entirely satisfactory. As Murphy notes, explaining why some poets and readers would have shied away from the form does not explain why "those most likely to produce prose poems" did not write them—or why the prose poem did not, by virtue of its notoriety, attract certain poets and readers, especially in the long run. If one qualifies the argument, it may help explain why the prose poem did not gain general acceptance, but prose poetry continued to be largely ignored by American poets and readers well after the modernist period. In a sense, the prose poem was for many years not so much reacted against as seen as unimportant, if seen at all.

There is a more fundamental reason why the stigma explanation is insufficient, however: it confuses form with function. Assuming once again that French and American poets had similar poetic concerns, there is no reason why different poetic forms could not perform the same or similar poetic functions. In this sense, an English-language tradition of free verse may help explain why American poets did not feel a need to write poems in prose, though not simply due to a perceived lack of formal constraints, the missing straitjacket. Free and other verse forms may have developed in such a way as to allow modernist poets most of the expressive possibilities associated with the prose poem. As will gradually become clear, this functional explanation relies on some notion of historical contingency, but first the explanation needs some documentary support.

• • •

In order to understand the modernists' relative neglect of the prose poem, we need to reexamine the terms of the argument, in particular "poème en prose" and "prose poem." Eliot's writings on prose poetry and the long poem provide a useful point of departure for this reexamination, for he not only wrote and translated poetry in prose but also knew the French tradition well. In addition, Eliot is a focal point in Murphy's stigma argument. After analyzing Eliot's prose poem "Hysteria," she remarks:

> Eliot himself tried no more original prose poems, struggling instead to bring more of prose, and of "life" into his verse. One cannot help wondering whether Eliot's memories of Professor Babbitt's stern warnings to the Harvard undergraduates of the dangers of feminizing mixed genres deterred the young poet from further experiments, particularly for one in the grip of his own "hysterical" sexual anxieties, his fear of engulfment and unmanning by the woman.
>
> Given Eliot's stature and influence over his generation of poets and critics, and over subsequent generations of professors of English, I wonder, too, whether his lack of sustained interest in the prose poem, as well as Ezra Pound's, helped keep the form at the margins of modernist poetry in English.[24]

Murphy keenly argues that the hysterical scenes in "Hysteria," "Sweeney Erect," and *The Waste Land* are inflected by sexual anxieties, but the speculations in the preceding passage are less compelling. Even if one grants that Babbitt's views on genre are Eliot's, any lack of interest shown by Eliot or the age toward prose poetry may point more to a scarcity of successful practitioners than to a critical atmosphere emanating from him. In other words, Eliot's poetry and critical views need to be examined in more detail and with more perspective if they are going to comment meaningfully on American prose poetry in the modernist period.

Eliot wrote three critical pieces on the subject of prose poetry: his 1917 review article "The Borderline of Prose"; his 1921 article in *The Chapbook*, "Prose and Verse"; and his 1938 preface to his translation of Perse's *Anabasis*. In the first article, Eliot argues for a fairly strict separation of prose and poetry: "The distinction between poetry and prose must be a technical distinction; and future refinement of both poetry and prose can only draw the distinction more clearly."[25] He never argues, however, that poems written in prose do not or should not exist; on the contrary, he is especially intent on distinguishing between what he considers successes (Rimbaud's *Illuminations*, Claudel's *Connaissance de l'Est*) and failures (Mallarmé's *Divagations*, Aldington's prose poems). His main point is that "whichever we are writing," verse or prose, "there are moments when we simply have to conform to the limitations of the medium we have chosen." In short, "There could be no prose equivalent for *The Rape of the Lock*. There could be no verse equivalent for *Madame Bovary* or *Bubu de Montparnasse*."[26] The failure of a given prose poem is due not so much to the category "prose poetry" but to those criteria for good writing that all prose works share.

In the *Chapbook* article, Eliot is primarily concerned with disputing exclusively formal definitions of prose poetry. His argument is straightforward: all formal definitions of prose poetry are either trivial ("poetry in prose") or inadequate because contradictory.[27] Most of the article consists of considerations of, and counterexamples to, different possible formal criteria of the prose poem: length, intensity, concentration, and so forth. Eliot registers his dislike of the term "prose poetry" rather than the phenomenon of poetry written in prose: "I object to the term 'prose-poetry' because it seems to imply a sharp distinction between 'poetry' and 'prose' which I do not admit."[28] This position is already a modification of the idea that the distinction between poetry and prose is a "technical distinction" that future refinement will only draw more clearly. Some of Eliot's tastes have also changed: "But we must remember, on the one hand, that verse is always struggling, while remaining verse, to take up to itself more and more of what is prose, to take something more from life and turn it into 'play.' Seen from this angle, the labour of Mallarmé with the French language becomes something very important; every battle he fought with syntax represents the effort to transmute lead into gold, ordinary language into poetry."[29] Eliot had remarked in "The Borderline of Prose": "Beside the prose of Rimbaud, the laboured opacity of Mallarmé fades colourless and dead."[30] While his later remarks probably refer to Mallarmé's verse, Eliot is nevertheless refining his views according to his lifetime preoccupation with the relationship between poetry and ordinary speech—a Wordsworthian inheritance, though he may not have acknowledged it as such. This preoccupation receives perhaps its most intense articulation in "Little Gidding" (*Four Quartets*, 1942), in the passage where the poet meets his "dead master" who explains how poets have and must continue "To purify the dialect of the tribe / And urge the mind to aftersight and foresight."[31] "Little Gidding" is the quartet whose presiding element is fire, so Eliot's lines, even as they paraphrase a line from Mallarmé's sonnet to Poe, are a kind of shorthand for the refining or alchemical process of transmuting ordinary speech into poetry.[32] The Eliot of 1921 is like the Eliot of 1942 in that he is not as concerned with prose poetry's stigma of decadence as he is with the historical fates of prose and verse: "The real decadence in literature occurs when both verse and prose cease their effort . . . when verse becomes a language, a set of feelings, a style quite remote from life, and when prose becomes a mere practical vehicle."[33]

Eliot's dissatisfactions with the term "prose poetry" and absolute distinctions between prose and verse continue in his preface to *Anabasis*: "I refer to this poem as a poem. It would be convenient if poetry were always verse—either accented, alliterative, or quantitative; but that is not true. Poetry may occur, within a definite limit on one side, at any point along a line of which the formal limits are 'verse' and 'prose.' . . . 'Poetry' introduces a distinction between good verse and bad verse; but we have no one word to separate bad prose from good prose. As a matter of fact, much bad prose is poetic prose; and only a very small part of bad verse is bad because it is prosaic."[34] Eliot never uses the term "prose poetry" but more than grants that poems can be written in prose, going as far as to assert that it is generally beneficial to use elements of prose in verse. The relative good of introducing prose into poetry and the relative danger of an emphasis on the "poetic" are constants in Eliot's criticism. In "Prose and Verse," Eliot had not only asserted the principle that verse takes up to itself "more and more of what is prose," he also observed, "We seem to see clearly enough that prose is allowed to be 'poetic'; we appear to have overlooked the right of poetry to be 'prosaic.'"[35] In other writings, the potentially dangerous opposite of "prose" is an exclusive reliance on the musical element of poetry, or in Valéry's analogy "Poetry : Prose :: Dancing : Walking," whatever corresponds to dancing in poetry.[36] The latter argument, from 1958, complements Eliot's three earlier pieces on prose poetry and reveals best his underlying concerns. The issue is no longer a matter of proving or disproving a sharp distinction between poetry and prose but a concern with "a tendency, which is very much favored by [Valéry's] account of prose and poetry, to approve a difference of vocabulary and idiom between poetry and prose."[37]

Eliot's ideas on the long poem dovetail with his ideas on prose poetry. His most elaborate defense of the modern long poem occurs in his essay "From Poe to Valéry" (1948):

> Poe has a remarkable passage about the impossibility of writing a long poem—for a long poem, he holds, is at best a series of short poems strung together. What we have to bear in mind is that he himself was incapable of writing a long poem. He could conceive only a poem which

was a single simple effect: for him, the whole of a poem had to be in one mood. Yet it is only in a poem of some length that a variety of moods can be expressed; for a variety of moods requires a number of different themes or subjects, related either in themselves or in the mind of the poet. These parts can form a whole which is more than the sum of the parts; a whole such that the pleasure we derive from the reading of any part is enhanced by our grasp of the whole. It follows also that in a long poem some parts may be deliberately planned to be less 'poetic' than others: these passages may show no lustre when extracted, but may be intended to elicit, by contrast, the significance of other parts, and to unite them into a whole more significant than any of the parts.[38]

This passage is self-conscious in the extreme: Eliot is apparently defending his own poetic practice by pointing out the limitations of another poet's defense of his poetry.[39] Eliot's argument is most concisely expressed in the two related propositions that a long poem "is more than the sum of the parts" and that some of the parts of a long poem are necessarily "less 'poetic' than others." The poet who proves this theory best for Eliot is Dante. Poe represents the opposite view: he is not only upbraided for generalizing from his personal inability to write long poems, he is also chided, in a passage preceding the one cited here, for words he apparently chose for their sound-value without regard to their sense.[40]

Eliot discusses the long poem in scattered places throughout his criticism, suggestively broaching the subject in his *Chapbook* article on prose poetry:

No long work can maintain the same high tension throughout. . . . This leads us to Poe's law: that no poem should be more than 100 lines. . . . We are, most of us, inclined to agree with him: we do not like long poems. This dislike is due, I believe, partly with the taste of the day, which will pass, and partly to the abuse of the long poem in the hands of distinguished persons who did not know how to use it. . . . Any long poem will contain certain matter of ephemeral interest, like some of Dante's divine processions, but this does not imply that the long poem should not have been written—that, in other words, it should have been composed as a number of short poems.[41]

This passage is remarkably similar to the later passage in "From Poe to Valéry." Between 1921 and 1948, Eliot had published his two long poems, *The Waste Land* (1922) and *Four Quartets* (1943). In both the *Chapbook* article and the

Poe lecture, Eliot emphasized the necessarily "less poetic" moments of the long poem and Poe and Dante, representatives of the different sides of the issue. In "Prose and Verse" and other essays, Dante is further contrasted to Milton, the poet who maximally distorts ordinary speech, and, at the opposite pole of diction, to Wordsworth, the poet who can be pedestrian to a fault.[42] The ideal situation, as Eliot describes it in "Little Gidding," has "The common word exact without vulgarity, / The formal word precise but not pedantic, / The complete consort dancing together." Dante's, and therefore Eliot's, allowance of philosophical material in a long poem should also be placed in this constellation of concerns, and writers who, like Poe, sometimes place too much emphasis on the musical quality of language and pure verbal beauty are numerous in Eliot's criticism: they literally run from Poe to Valéry and include the likes of Swinburne and Pater.[43]

The drift of my argument should be clear: the long poem provided Eliot ample opportunity for introducing the prosaic into poetry. There is every reason to believe that other modernist poets felt similarly about the long poem, if only because Eliot's poetry provided a model or an antimodel.[44] Williams's *Paterson*, for example, an anti-Eliot work if there ever was one, includes prose passages in its verse narrative.[45] What is more, the modernist long poem has been successful, as evidenced by not only *The Waste Land* and *Four Quartets* but also through the works of poets as diverse as Pound, H. D., Crane, Williams, and Stevens. As Margaret Dickie has argued, American modernism can virtually be defined by the writing of long poems.[46] It is also clear from the philosophical language of Stevens's *Notes toward a Supreme Fiction* or the letters, historical anecdotes, and interviews inserted into Williams's *Paterson* that the American long poem introduced more prose discourses into poetry. Nor need we stop with the modern long poem in pursuing the logic of function and form. Other verse experiments of the modernist period introduced the prosaic into poetry, whether through everyday conversation in poems like Frost's "Home Burial" and "The Death of the Hired Man" (blank verse), via the use of bureaucratic language in collections such as Auden's *The Orators* (part verse, part prose), or in the quasi-encyclopedic language and the use of quotations in discursive lyrics like Moore's "The Pangolin" and "The Frigate Pelican" (syllabics).

•   •   •

Understanding that English-language modernists did not so much react against poetry in prose as have no pressing need for it places some of the age's literary experiments into perspective yet at the same time raises questions about historical contingency. How should we understand events like the success or failure of a genre, which may have been likely but not inevitable? The prestige of poets like Baudelaire and Rimbaud contributed to the widespread interest in the *poème en prose* in late-nineteenth-century France. Poets like Stevens and Eliot arguably gave a comparable boost to the modernist long poem. Free verse happened to develop before prose poetry in America; in France, the reverse is true. And so on. Arguing that some events need not have happened is neither an assertion of randomness nor a covert way of reinstating the idea of the romantic genius in order to explain the discontinuities of literary history. It instead points to the shortcomings of both exclusively formal approaches and approaches that would bypass literary history altogether in the name of culture and history. Moreover, such explanations should point toward reception history and further inquiry into why national literatures have developed in the directions they have. "Contingency" is at once a dose of skepticism and pragmatism.

By describing the problem of explanation in this way, I do not wish to short circuit such questions as whether literary genres are informed by aesthetic and ideological currents of their times (clearly they are) but rather to argue that it is often worth looking to literary history for perspective on these matters. In the preceding discussion, neither the formal "straitjacket" explanation nor the historical "stigma" explanation was able, by itself, to provide a compelling argument for the neglect of prose poetry among English-language modernists. The former focus seemed too narrow; the latter, too wide; and the question itself misconceived. A wide-angle view of modernism's literary experiments helps place the question of neglect into perspective. This perspective in turn deepens our understanding of modernism's formal and stylistic tendencies, especially toward the "prosaic" in poetry, and places us in position to make meaningful connections between the prose poem and its historical context. Literary history may not fill the gulf that seems to divide formal and historical arguments, but it can throw a rope bridge across it.

In a study that explores how generic frameworks affect interpretation, contingency should not be viewed as a stopgap explanation pending more thorough investigations of cultural and historical contexts. When explanations for why the prose poem and the *poème en prose* developed differently begin to reach a level of abstraction or historical detail in which the original interpretive questions (What does it mean to read *X* as a prose poem? What does it mean to read *X* as an American prose poem?) have receded, it is time to shift the focus back to individual works. When it comes to interpreting prose poems, perceived differences between the French and American traditions often matter more than the explanations for the differences or whether the differences are real. Interpretation, after all, never consists solely in establishing historically accurate readings of works, however historically minded we may be. (If we didn't read works of the past out of some contemporary need, why would we bother?) But some consideration of reception history is always present: we read a work from our vantage point in time mediated through our imaginative reconstruction of what it would have meant in its own context. Knowing that the work was written by someone who lived in a time—a place, a culture—different from our own, we construct some version of the work "on its own terms," no matter how centered on our terms and concerns the reconstruction may turn out to be. With these considerations in mind, we can explore the interpretive consequences of reading a few modernist works as prose poems or even—when the context encourages it—reading them as American prose poems.

Eliot's "The Engine" provides a convenient place to start:

I

The engine hammered and hummed. Flat faces of American business men lay along the tiers of chairs in one plane, broken only by the salient of a brown cigar and the red angle of a six-penny magazine. The machine was hard, deliberate, and alert; having chosen with motives and ends unknown to cut through the fog it pursued its course; the life of the deck stirred and was silent like a restless scale on the smooth surface. The machine was certain and sufficient as a rose bush, indifferently justifying the aimless parasite.

II

After the engine stopped, I lay in bed listening while the wash subsided and the scuffle of feet died out. The music ceased, but a mouth organ from the steerage picked up the tune. I switched on the light, only to see on the wall a spider taut as a drumhead, the life of endless geological periods concentrated into a small spot of intense apathy at my feet. "And if the ship goes down" I thought drowsily "he is prepared and will somehow persist, for he is very old. But the flat faces . . ." I tried to assemble these nebulae into one pattern. Failing, I roused myself to hear the machine recommence, and then the music, and the feet upon the deck.[47]

This poem was written sometime in the 1910s; it was not published until 1996. "The Engine" resembles the one prose poem Eliot published in his lifetime, "Hysteria," in that its anxious narrator attempts unsuccessfully to come to terms with an experience. But the anxieties of "Hysteria" are primarily sexual; those of "The Engine" are difficult to attribute to a single cause. The narrator of "The Engine" sets himself apart from the "flat faces of American business men" and yet is potentially more like them than either the decisive, autonomous ship or the old but resilient spider. The threat of lifelessness or extinction obsesses him, blown up to evolutionary proportions ("endless geological periods") by the second section of the poem. Because the source of the anxiety cannot be pinpointed, the poem forces us into a situation analogous to that of the narrator: we want to but cannot easily assimilate the disparate materials of our reading experience, and the encountered resistance to meaning creates some uneasiness.

Much of the meaning of the poem issues from its rhetorical effects. The poem's sentences are generally short: multiple phrases and subordinate clauses are the exceptions. Parataxis dominates. Assertions such as "The engine hammered and hummed" and "The machine was hard, deliberate, and alert" seem determinedly prosaic in their straightforward tone and verbal economy, but this determined quality also rhetorically enacts the content, an effect reinforced by alliteration (in the case of the verbs) and enumeration (the adjectives). The similes and metaphors achieve their effects by reversing expected directions of comparison. The "engine," an inanimate object, hammers and hums. The "machine"—the narrator significantly avoids a word like "boat" here—chooses its course direction "with motives and ends unknown" and then is likened to a rosebush possessing the human qualities of certainty and sufficiency. The faces of the human businessmen, meanwhile, are flattened into a plane from which only a magazine and a cigar protrude, and even their collective "life" suggests a "restless scale" on a "smooth surface." They are the parasites on the life-giving ship. The narrator's inability to take the scene in whole is conveyed via the synecdoche of the businessmen's faces, themselves featureless, which are in turn represented by synecdoches, the cigar and the magazine.

In retrospect, the narrator's anxiety about humankind's place in the world begins with the comparison of the businessmen to insects on a rosebush—a connection we must read back through the more immediate comparison of machine to bush. By the second half of the poem, the narrator has gone below deck, to his cabin, and the section break marks the moment when he registers the relative quiet of his surroundings after the engine has stopped. The emotional and auditory respite is brief, however: as soon as "the music" ceases, "a mouth organ from the steerage" picks up "the tune." Presumably a dance on the deck above has ended ("the scuffle of feet died out") and someone who can only afford the cheapest accommodations ("from the steerage") is playing a harmonica. But the opening phrase "After the engine stopped" and the metonymic reduction of human beings to "the scuffle of feet" and "a mouth organ" tempt one to read "The music ceased" and "a mouth organ from the steerage picked up the tune" as indications of a sound akin to the humming of the engine now starting up in some instrument in the helm of the ship. The perceived aimlessness of human activity causes the narrator to reflect on the "spider taut as a drumhead" appearing when he turns on the light, an appropriate enough image given the parasites on the rosebush and the recent music. All of the "endless" years of evolution (the *Bildung* of the narrator? the history of humankind?) lead to "a small spot of intense apathy": the inactive spider, perhaps also the narrator's state of mind or view of the world. The narrator's drowsy thought then provides a lens, albeit a blurry one, through which we can view his anxiety: "And if the ship goes down . . . [the spider] is prepared and will somehow persist, for he is very old. But the flat faces. . . ." The spider, for all of its apathy, is better equipped to survive a disaster—better equipped than the narrator, we expect to hear, only to be brought up short by the phrase "But the flat faces" trailing off into ellipsis.[48] The thought is either too painful or too complicated for him in his present state of mind. The featureless American businessmen, traveling to Europe no doubt, are relatively new and unprepared in comparison with "the spider." According to the narrator's dream logic, the aged spider (European tradition?) perpetuates itself either through Darwinian fitness or inertia. But the narrator cannot draw complete conclusions, even as he tries "to assemble these nebulae into one pattern." As he fails to organize his thoughts, he temporarily rouses himself to hear "the machine"—the engine apparently, not the whole boat—start up again, "and then the music, and the feet upon the deck." The "and . . . and" in the last sentence rhetorically enacts the concatenation, as opposed to assimilation, of the narrator's sensory experiences.

The question worth raising here is whether the poem's effects rely on our reading it as a prose poem. Phrased in this way, and in a critical study, the question may be superfluous. To interpret in critical detail any work is, in a sense, already to read it as a poem. Even the argument that certain texts, such as "The Engine," urge us to reread and pay close attention to detail may not prevent the question from becoming trivial. If a text resists interpretation and happens to be written in prose, we may in effect be reading it as a prose poem, but issues of genre threaten to disappear in the process. For the question "What does it mean to read X as a prose poem?" to be meaningful, "prose poem" must signify more than a poem that happens to be written in prose and must be more than a consideration that comes around eventually on the hermeneutic circle. Considerations of genre, to be truly generic, must help determine at a more basic level what modes of interpretation are appropriate. Do the effects and meanings of "The Engine" depend in any significant way on prose poetry as interpretive framework?

"The Engine" is a good test case in part because it was not published during Eliot's lifetime. We, of course, do not need the editorial context of the publication in which "The Engine" appears, *Inventions of the March Hare, Poems 1909–1917*, in order to read the text as a poem. It is enough to know that "The Engine" comes from one of Eliot's notebooks of poems. It may even be enough to know that Eliot wrote the text or that "The Engine" was written in the early twentieth century. Still, an editorial apparatus inevitably suggests some interpretive frameworks. Without the editor telling us we might already know that Eliot was familiar with the *poème en prose* and consider "The Engine" in that context. The editor's copious notes also tell us that Eliot may have recently been reading Charles Vildrac's prose poems.[49] Do facts like these significantly change our perspective on the poem? Similarities in style need not imply generic influence, and while the generic models for "The Engine" may well be French (among prose poets, Rimbaud comes to mind), Eliot is only in a very general sense writing in the genre of the *poème en prose*. As his refusal to embrace the term "prose poem" indicates, Eliot would not have thought of the prose poem as its own genre.

But still, we might say, neither an editor's packaging of a text nor an author's intention alone determines genre. If we wished to we could set up Eliot as a symbolist straw man, or even, following the lead of William Carlos Williams, as an essentially European poet. The real question is whether these labels affect our interpretation of the poetry. On the one hand, it seems self-evident that such considerations as an author's literary tradition and national identity inform our reading. On the other hand, these "generic" considerations seem little more than background information once we attempt to describe the ways in which a text achieves its effects (rhetorical analysis), though they may influence our interpretations obliquely (the American businessmen in my reading of "The Engine"). It may help here to recall that generic signals can and often are communicated on an unconscious level or taken into account implicitly in our evaluations. The invisibility of the fence should not cause us to forget that the fence exists.

If nothing else, packaging or considering a text as a prose poem makes the work itself less invisible. Recent interest in prose poetry means an interest in overlooked poems and new evaluations of texts previously not seen as prose poems. As Baudelaire suspected, presenting a body of work as a new genre has some market value. A focus on prose poetry as a genre makes us seek out and analyze texts like "The Engine" in the first place. So if the question "What does it mean to read *X* as a prose poem?" seems confusing in the American context, it is perhaps because prose poetry is only a genre in a nebulous sense. Given the focus of this study and today's critical climate, the more difficult task may be to resist reading certain works as prose poems. In other words, "What would it mean *not* to read *X* as a prose poem?" may turn out to be the more important question in some cases. What would it mean to read Stein's *Tender Buttons* or Williams's *Kora in Hell* outside a tradition of prose poetry?

7. The Idea of an American Prose Poem, Take Two

Constructing a history of American prose poetry from a late-twentieth-century perspective, it might seem natural to give prominence to Stein and Williams in the same way that it seems natural to think of Bertrand and Baudelaire as the first prose poets in France. After all, *Tender Buttons* and *Kora in Hell* are two of the very few collections of modernist poetry written entirely in prose, Stein and Williams have become fairly famous, and like Bertrand and Baudelaire, Stein and Williams arguably mark a break with most of the poetry in prose written before them. In comparison with the prose poems of Tagore, Wilde, and Lazarus, *Tender Buttons* and *Kora in Hell* seem almost antipoetic. They refuse or use ironically such "high lyric" gestures as addresses to inanimate objects, employ American slang and diction not found in most poems before them, and undermine whatever allegories they inadvertently or purposely elicit. Perhaps most tellingly, the authors themselves thought of their work as something new. Stein presented *Tender Buttons* as experimental and commented on her techniques in several lectures, while Williams's preface to *Kora in Hell* distances his "improvisations" from French prose poems and contemporary American poetry.

But such a construction of literary history would be just that, a construction. Whatever value the literary-historical frame possesses lies in the perspective it brings to works like *Tender Buttons*, *Kora in Hell*, and the prose poems that come after them. Stein's and Williams's collections are best evaluated in light of other works they wrote and against the backdrop of the period's formal experimentation. Both writers were intensely interested in exploring the boundaries of prose and poetry and deeply concerned with Americanness in literature. In this context, the phrase "American prose poetry" may be more or less inevitable, but the generic label is in the end too generic. Like Bertrand

and Baudelaire, Stein and Williams were not alone in their enterprise, but their enterprise was tightly linked with other literary developments, personal and otherwise.

• • •

As Stein remarked on a number of occasions, *Tender Buttons* can and even ought to be read as a step in her development as a writer. In "Portraits and Repetition," for example, she reviews her progress as a portrait writer:

> So here we have it. There was the period of The Making of Americans portraiture, when by listening and talking I conceived at every moment that I had the existence of that one inside me until I had completely emptied myself of this that I had had as a portrait of that one. . . . Then as I said I had the feeling that something should be included and that something was looking, and so concentrating on looking I did the Tender Buttons because it was easier to do objects than people if you were just looking. Then I began to do plays to make the looking have in it an element of moving and during this time I also did portraits that did the same thing.[1]

Some critics have followed Stein's lead. Michael Hoffman presents a useful and lucid account of Stein's "development of abstractionism" from her earliest works up to and culminating in *Tender Buttons*. As he explains it, "If Gertrude Stein has," in her works up to about 1913, "abolished from her writing story, setting, movement, subject matter, analyses, and meaning, it would seem that there is only one thing further that she can do in the way of abstractionism other than ceasing to put letters together into words, words into an order, or merely leaving the page blank. She must shift her gaze away from the world of people completely to focus on things. This is what she does in her next creation, *Tender Buttons*."[2] *Tender Buttons*, in this view, is a product of continuous experimentation in writing, especially in portraiture and abstraction. Considering the work as an isolated example of American prose poetry is therefore potentially misleading.

Though Stein did not set out to write American prose poems, her critical views on prose, poetry, and American writing dovetail so well that it would be wrong to ignore their interrelation in her work. To understand how these views comment on each other, it helps to consider her *Lectures in America* as a series of related arguments. More specifically, the first and last lectures have overlapping concerns, as their opening sentences illustrate:

One cannot come back too often to the question what is knowledge and to the answer knowledge is what one knows.

What is English literature that is to say what do I know about it, that is to say what is it.

"What Is English Literature"

What is poetry and if you know what poetry is what is prose.

There is no use in telling more than you know, no not even if you do not know it.

"Poetry and Grammar"[3]

Viewed together, these four sentences form a chiastic pattern of inquiry that proceeds from a general statement about knowledge to specific questions, then back to a general assertion about knowing. While Stein's repetitious mode of procedure guarantees some patterning of this sort, here the repetition signals a return to concerns raised in the earlier lecture. "Prose" and "poetry" appear more often as "What Is English Literature" progresses; in "Poetry and Grammar," issues of Englishness and Americanness gradually emerge.

Near the beginning of "What Is English Literature," Stein asserts that "by English literature" she means "American literature too," only to drive a wedge between the two traditions shortly afterward: "To be sure it has been more or less truly said about English literature that until about fifty years ago a first class English writer appeared almost every ten years, since that time it has been necessary to very much help if not replace it by American literature."[4] Continuity between English and American literature becomes relative within Stein's narrative of literary evolution or revolution. Stein especially wants to explore how formal innovations in literature relate to internal and external developments:

> In English literature there is a great deal of poetry and there is a great deal of prose and sometimes the poetry and the prose has something to do with the other and very often not. Besides this there has been again and again in English literature the question can one serve god and mammon, and the further question if one can should one. But the important question can remain and does remain what is god and mammon insofar as it concerns English literature. Has this question to do with prose and with poetry as both or as either one. I wish to very

largely go into this because in it is the whole description of the whole
of English literature and with it and after it although not entirely out of
it comes American literature.[5]

The answers Stein goes on to give are in a sense less important than the
way she frames the questions: from the outset Stein is wondering about the
differences between English and American literature, how cultural factors
played a role in their developments, and what all this has to do with prose
and poetry.

Stein's answers are, in fact, couched in metaphors and terms whose significance only gradually surfaces. With regard to English literature, for example,
she often speaks of the English "daily island life" and its effects on writing,
and in her brief history of English literature, she argues that the Elizabethans
had a choice between writing styles and "god and mammon," that sentences
are not emotional and paragraphs are, and that eighteenth-century literature
lives by sentences, nineteenth-century by phrases, and twentieth-century
by paragraphs. In general terms, Stein presents a history distantly akin to
Eliot's dissociation of sensibility, though the "confusion" and "separation" she
speaks of usually refer to the writer's relationship with words, their adequacy
or inadequacy to express an inner state. Stein's criticism of early-twentieth-
century British writers, a generation "doing the second class writing of the
past generation," seems to owe something to Woolf insofar as it singles out
"Wells, Galsworthy, Bennett, etc." as its target.[6]

By "daily island life" Stein approximately means a situation where no
outside reality forces the writer to choose between styles of writing, or if
it does the writer is not conscious of having to choose. Poetry written in such
an environment is not what the poets "lose or what they feel but is the things
with which they are shut up, that is shut in."[7] It may be that the English,
even in Chaucer's time, were not living a completely hermetic existence. The
situation was definitely breaking down by the Elizabethan period, where the
choice between "god and mammon" is in itself significant: "In a true daily
island life a choice is not the thing."[8] By "god and mammon" Stein does
not mean religion and money per se; nor does she exactly refer to a struggle
between an ideal mode of writing and the sort of work imposed upon the writer
by economic circumstances. It is more an issue of freedom and constraint,
of unself-conscious expression and composing with an aim toward effect.
Stein speaks of using words "directly" and "indirectly."[9] When the writer is
consciously thinking, trying to arrange words in order to move or persuade

an audience rather then finding them adequate to his or her needs, he or she is serving mammon. By the nineteenth century, this situation is the norm. It is an age in which explanations about writing proliferate, and the twentieth century may still be in its shadow.

There are fuzzy moments in Stein's argument, but at least two clear ideas emerge from her narrative: American literature is related to but qualitatively different from English literature, and the modern artist has very little choice about genre or mode of writing. For Stein, "American literature all the nineteenth century went on by itself and although it might seem to have been doing the same thing as English literature it really was not and it really was not for an excellent reason it was not leading a daily island life."[10] The circumstances for writing were already changing in England around the turn of the century when "Victoria was over and the Boer war," when "daily life was ceasing to be quite so daily," and when the English "were beginning not to know everything about owning everything that was existing outside of their daily living"—when, in short, England could no longer incorporate easily the outside world into its sense of self and self-sufficiency. Stein claims that all of these developments relate to phrasing in literature, a phenomenon she traces through Browning, Swinburne, and Meredith and which she claims culminates in the late writings of James, "who being American knew was he was doing." At this point, "even phrases were no longer necessary to make emotion emotion to make explaining explaining." What is more, words, sentences, and choosing do not exist "for themselves" in the twentieth century. Historical developments had "created the need for paragraphing."[11]

When tracing Stein's literary-historical argument in "What Is English Literature," one tends to forget that she began her inquiry into the relationship of "god and mammon" and English and American literature in the context of what they have to do "with prose and with poetry as both or as either one." "Prose" and "poetry" appear throughout the lecture but are generally considered together as "literature" or forms of writing equally affected by cultural developments. Stein nevertheless associates poetry more than prose with the English way of life, for she stresses that England produced much poetry, that English poetry mentions "things" in a "simple intense certain way" unlike the poetry in other countries, and that this simple intense quality comes from the English being "shut in in their daily, completely daily island life."[12] Because Stein's thoughts on prose and poetry remain for the most part submerged in the lecture, it is difficult to say whether she intended to draw a parallel between the twentieth-century "need for paragraphing" and twentieth-century uses of prose and poetry. But it is also difficult not to consider this possibility. If the modern paragraph is not a matter of writerly choice, perhaps new and hybrid genres are also a historical inevitability. Such an argument resembles Baudelaire's economic rationale for the *poème en prose*.

Stein returns to issues of paragraphs, Americanness, and literary evolution periodically throughout *Lectures in America* but discusses prose and poetry in light of these concerns at length only in the final lecture, "Poetry and Grammar," which makes distinctions between poetry and prose via grammar. Stein begins by explaining why she believes that nouns and adjectives are not very exciting, pronouns only a little better, and verbs and adverbs a whole notch more interesting, if only because verbs and adverbs "make mistakes," "change," and are "on the move" in ways that nouns and adjectives don't, can't, and aren't.[13] Later in the lecture she associates poetry with nouns and adjectives and links prose, "really great written prose," with "verbs adverbs prepositions prepositional clauses and conjunctions."[14] In the meantime, she has returned to the narrative of her development first intimated in "What Is English Literature" and stated more explicitly in "The Gradual Making of the Making of Americans" and "Portraits and Repetition." The twentieth century created a need for paragraphing, and Stein herself needed to go beyond late James to a new kind of organization based neither on the sentence nor the paragraph. As she tells the story, *The Making of Americans* was her first success in "creating a balance that was neither the balance of the sentence nor the balance of the paragraph." Afterward she created "a new balance that had to do with a sense of movement of time included in a given space . . . an American thing."[15] As is typical in Stein's narrative, the matter of personal or literary-historical development is culturally inflected. But how does her use of prose and poetry in *Tender Buttons* relate to all of this?

For Stein, the poetry in prose of *Tender Buttons* was virtually inevitable given her cultural situation and personal and literary-historical developments. Stein's narratives progress dialectically, though the outcome of the dialectic stays somewhat open-ended. Words and sentences give way to phrases, which in turn give way to paragraphs and then a balance neither of the sentence nor the paragraph. American literature both opposes and issues from English literature. The portraiture of movement in *The Making of Americans* anticipates and helps produce the still lives of *Tender Buttons*; the latter help bring about the period of *Geography and Plays* when Stein becomes enchanted by the sounds of words, slowly losing the sense of "a thing contained within itself," which she had in the portraits. Eventually she feels a need to return to the earlier style but with a difference.[16] Stein tells several versions of her development, sometimes even contradicts herself, but the dialectical pattern remains consistent, along with the story's general outlines. In the narrative leading up to her explanation of *Tender Buttons*, Stein concentrates on showing how poetry, because it involves naming, needs nouns. First she writes: "Nouns are the name of anything and anything is named, that is what Adam and Eve did and if you like it is what anybody does."[17] Then when defining poetry she notes that the vocabulary of poetry is "entirely based on the noun" and that poetry is "concerned with using and with abusing, with losing and wanting, with denying with avoiding with adoring with replacing the noun."[18] Prose, in the meantime, is "the emotional balance that makes the reality of paragraphs and the unemotional balance that makes the reality of sentences"; it can also be "the essential balance that is made inside something that combines the sentence and the paragraph."[19]

Stein suggests that *Tender Buttons* represents a kind of resolution of these opposing tendencies:

> I was writing The Making of Americans, I was completely obsessed by the inner life of everything including generations of everybody's living and I was writing prose, prose that had to do with the balancing the inner balancing of everything. I have already told you all about that.
>
> And then, something happened and I began to discover the names of things, that is not discover the names but discover the things the things to see the things to look at and in so doing I had of course to name them not to give them new names but to see that I could find out how to know that they were there by their names or by replacing their names. And how was I to do so. They had their names and naturally I called them by the names they had and in doing so having begun looking at them I called them by their names with passion and that made poetry, I did not mean it to make poetry but it did, it made the Tender Buttons, and the Tender Buttons was very good poetry.[20]

A language of inner compulsion ("I did not mean it to make poetry but it did, it made Tender Buttons") overlays a narrative of original creation ("how was I to do so") in which the narrator, like the God of Genesis, looks back and sees that what came out of the creation was good. The fissure that has developed between the noun and the object it names, exemplified in Stein's famous "a rose is a rose is a rose," asks to be closed through repeated naming or naming via replacement, a new form of poetry.

The dialectical progression of Stein's arguments ensures that they rely heavily on the narrative they are embedded in. Thus, when she comes around to the often cited assertion, "in Tender Buttons and then on and on I struggled with the ridding myself of nouns," her meaning risks distortion when her words are taken out of context.[21] Stein is not exactly saying that she tried from this point on in her life to rid herself of nouns, though that may have been her preoccupation during the *Tender Buttons* period and for some time afterward. Even during the period in question, Stein is struggling as much with "the ridding" as with "ridding" herself of nouns, that is, the theory behind avoiding nouns as well as the practice, and as Stein recognizes, even her avoidance of nouns in *Tender Buttons* is a relative aim or achievement. She immediately adds to her assertion about ridding herself of nouns that she "knew nouns must go into poetry as they had gone into prose if anything that is everything was to go on meaning something." Stein's narrative emphasizes her struggles more than anything else, the dilemmas produced by a confluence of ideas, experiments, cultural circumstances, and literary-historical developments in respect to which *Tender Buttons* represents both a solution and a document to what remains unresolved.[22]

Ideally, *Tender Buttons* represents a new poetry of inclusion. For Stein, poetry once upon a time, in Chaucer's age and Homer's, "practically included everything." It included "narrative and feelings and excitements and nouns so many nouns and all emotions." This state of affairs was natural "because then everything including what was happening could be made real to anyone by just naming what was happening in other words by doing what poetry always must do by living in nouns."[23] The situation is changed now: poetry no longer includes narrative, for example, and many nouns through repetition have lost something of their power to name. Poetry still needs to name, use nouns, and repeat, but it must do so in new ways. Whitman's *Leaves of Grass* is perhaps the first modern poetry that attempts to reinvest names and the things they name with a thrill—the kind of thrill children feel in words. *Tender Buttons* continues the Whitmanian project with the realization that poets cannot simply invent new names but "must stay with the language their language that has come to be spoken and written and which has in it all the history of its intellectual recreation." In the attempt to "constantly realize the thing" so that she can "recreate that thing," Stein feels herself constrained by personal and historical developments—invisible but very real barriers.[24]

• • •

Stein narrates her development retrospectively; the story her lectures tell may be more teleological and seamless than the actual writing process or the process we as readers construct to understand her work. Nevertheless, her explanations provide important frameworks within which we can test interpretations of *Tender Buttons*. In Stein's account, the poetry in prose of *Tender Buttons* issues from circumstances particular to the modern age, the history of English and American literature, and her own philosophical preoccupations and experiments with writing. (Prose poetry does not, in this version, come out of the *poème en prose*; Stein claimed that she never read French literature.)[25] The model here is one of inner necessity and dialectical progression: something like *Tender Buttons* was inevitable given the conditions within which Stein was writing. Whether this claim is true, false, or partly true and partly false, it alerts us to an important dimension of *Tender Buttons*, the way in which the process of writing influences the writing itself.

Interpretations of *Tender Buttons* founder in a variety of ways. Stein's notorious difficulty gives some critics free rein to interpret, urges others to stand outside the hermeneutic process or question its appropriateness to the work, and causes still others, the majority, to limit their readings to a few passages and heavily qualify their findings.[26] *Tender Buttons* does not lend itself to easy interpretation, and the conscientious critic must inevitably say something about the limitations of his or her approach and perhaps of the work itself. But if *Tender Buttons* often frustrates interpretation, it may be because there is something unresolved at the core of Stein's prose poetry. Stein's narratives of her development hint at a lack of resolution via their emphasis on what I have called dialectical progression. Paying attention to the ways in which *Tender Buttons* progresses—formally and rhetorically when we are confronted with logical nonsequiturs—helps put the work in some perspective. Even this approach has its limitations, of course. However much the process of writing figures into the writing itself, the work does not unfold according to some inexorable logic or toward some inevitable goal. Attention to process may help us avoid some pitfalls of interpretation but may open up new interpretive traps in the process.

My aim is neither to present a lengthy close reading of *Tender Buttons* nor to claim that the interpretive framework I am bringing to the poetry accounts for all or even most moments in the text resistant to interpretation. When interpreting *Tender Buttons*, it helps to view it as a whole, though not as an organic whole. Form merges into content in *Tender Buttons* at least as much through self-referential gestures as through local effects of verbal mimicry and punning—the text is often "aware" of its own process of becoming, and this awareness influences how it proceeds. I use the verb "influences" here rather than "determines" in order to stress the open-endedness of the poetry's progression; by "progression" I refer to the way the prose moves forward, not its narrative or argumentative progress. Stein's concerns are many, though her interest in composition frequently seems uppermost. In general, the work's struggle with expression and meaning is part of its meaning. It is through our own struggle with Stein's text that we can gain some perspective not only on what it means and how much it means to mean but also on the degree to which our understanding of the work must take issues of Americanness and prose poetry into account.

In varying degrees, critics have already commented on process and progression in *Tender Buttons*. Richard Bridgman notes that "the book's tripartite structure is unusually suggestive. 'Objects'—what we perceive outside us. 'Food'—what we absorb. 'Rooms'—what encloses us."[27] Pamela Hadas presents a strong case that *Tender Buttons* gains from being read as a kind of story, at least "in the broad context of the differences sought by and between Gertrude Stein and her brother [Leo], of an immanent change in their living arrangements, of a change which includes Alice Toklas."[28] Even critics who resist extracting narratives from *Tender Buttons* tend to rely on narratives extrinsic to the work to organize their interpretations. Thus Marianne DeKoven, who does not think "it matters that the work contains these particular words in this particular order," takes pains to argue that the "Rooms" section was composed "in the 1911, transitional style" whereas "Objects" and "Food" "accelerate steadily through the middle style toward the extreme style of 1913."[29] Margueritte Murphy, whose compelling comparison of "Food" to cookbooks contemporary with *Tender Buttons* is based on nonnarrative frameworks of interpretation (household advice and the recipe), intimates a narrative of formal progression in which Stein's prose poetry represents "an experiment in prose even more radically disorienting than the *Improvisations*" and where Stein's and Williams's prose experiments are themselves more disruptive "on the level of grammar, syntax, [and] semantics" than Eliot's prose poetry.[30]

It may be that *Tender Buttons* creates a desire for argumentative and narrative frameworks, and it may be possible to find a narrative in every interpretive framework. The progression I wish to trace in Stein's work is nevertheless best described as nonnarrative. *Tender Buttons* urges the reader to consider its own process of composition. Here it is important to emphasize the experimental quality of Stein's prose. In contrast to the prose portraits Stein previously wrote, *Tender Buttons* is a series of still lives. Furthermore, there are many shifts in procedure within the collection that indicate Stein is writing in response to what she is writing. Most obvious is the tripartite division Bridgman describes, which could suggest a progression of concerns that is neither argumentative nor narrative. Even within the first section, "Objects," there is a gradual introduction of abstract items, including "A frightful release," "More," "A time to eat," "In between," and a self-reflective description titled "Objects." The progression of headings cannot be reduced to a clear narrative, but there is nevertheless a noticeable shift between the first titles ("A carafe, that is a blind glass," "Glazed Glitter," and "A substance in a cushion") and the last ("Peeled pencil, choke," "It was black, black took," and "This is this dress, aider"). The progression of headings in "Food" approaches narrative only to turn away from it. As Bridgman points out, this section "possesses a basic coherence. Among its fifty-one items are 'Breakfast,' 'Lunch,' and 'Dinner' in that order. Each meal is surrounded by food appropriate to it, lunch being the main meal of the day."[31] Stein seems to have planned her organization of "Food" in a quasi-narrative way, only to play with it later: the items listed do not always match the headings in the text. Some foods drop out, some are added, and some are repeated, occasionally to humorous effect. Immediately following "Cooking," for example, "Chicken" is listed four times with short descriptions, as if to indicate steps in the process of cooking chicken, different methods of preparing chicken, or the boredom of having chicken, chicken, chicken, and still more chicken.

Insofar as progression exists in *Tender Buttons*, it is formal and rhetorical. No clear narrative or argument emerges, because the ways in which the text shifts and the motivations for the shifts are generally unpredictable. It is a given that Stein's writing will change in response to itself; it is harder to view as inevitable how and when it will change. Such a quirky progression may call into question the idea of progression or the appropriateness of the label, but *Tender Buttons* contains enough examples to compel our recognition that the order of the prose matters and possesses a significance that goes beyond whatever will to coherence we bring to the text. Even the sizes of the paragraphs and passages beneath the headings in "Objects" and "Food" hint at progression. "Objects" opens with a single paragraph titled "A carafe, that is a blind glass," followed by two descriptions each slightly larger than the last, then shifts back to a one-paragraph description ("A box") before moving to a long description, a series of five one-paragraph descriptions, and another long description (also titled "A box").[32] This not-quite-random procedure suggests that Stein wrote as much in response to formal patterns as according to a philosophy of description. Later in "Objects" she experiments with one-sentence descriptions and abstract objects. It thus appears as if the "Objects" section ends when one set of experiments or variations has played itself out. "Food" then begins with a slightly different subject matter and approach, including several descriptions longer than anything that has come before. Eventually middle-sized and short descriptions return, but perhaps this set of experiments also plays itself out by the end of the section, for the continuous series of paragraphs and lack of titles in the final section of *Tender Buttons*, "Rooms," contrasts sharply with the formal structure of "Food." At the same time, the opening line of "Rooms," "Act so there is no use in a center," seems to follow from the last title in "Food," "A center in a table."

Because *Tender Buttons* foregrounds process, it may turn out to matter, for example, whether "Rooms" was composed earlier than "Objects" and "Food" as DeKoven argues. But Stein's actual process of writing—whatever that may be—is not a privileged vantage point from which to view the work as a whole, only a perspective that asks to be considered along with a host of other perspectives. This process, insofar as it can be reconstructed, is important in ways a reading of the published text at best only hints at. Ulla Dydo has shown how an examination of Stein's manuscripts and typescripts can illuminate passages in her published work.[33] Stein sometimes comments on the physical features of the notebook in which she is writing, for example, or makes use of line lengths and notebook lengths as structural principles. Michael Hoffman has compared Stein's method of composition to Joyce's in *Finnegans Wake*, where the author incorporates into the writing distractions such as those occasioned by a visitor.[34] Stein's immediate surroundings— objects, food, and rooms—would have been likely to find their way into *Tender Buttons* if only because they presumably served as points of departure for Stein's descriptions. Such considerations of process help account for some of the difficult passages in Stein. They also invite us to consider composition as content.

Stein's three notebooks for *Tender Buttons* (corresponding to "Objects," "Food," and "Rooms") do not resolve the question of dating, though they do contain enough evidence of continuous writing to argue for linear composition within the sections.[35] The neatness and darkness of the handwriting vary some-what, apparently according to when Stein broke off composing or copying a passage. More important, the notebooks are filled with text on every other page from front to back and on the opposite pages starting from the back, indicating that Stein turned the notebooks over when she reached the end and kept composing linearly. Only the "Rooms" notebook is entirely filled, as if Stein had run out of not only rooms but room.[36] The pun lingers in the section's title for which Stein considered such variants as "Some Rooms" and "Rooms Number one" before crossing them out. (At some point, she may have considered writing a second notebook of "Rooms.") There might even be a pun in the phrase "not/ passed uselessly" (in the paragraph beginning "A tribune"), which marks the center or halfway point at which Stein turned over the "Rooms" notebook and began writing back to front.[37]

The three notebooks could have been written simultaneously or in any order; the evidence seems almost deliberately confusing. As several critics have pointed out, Stein contradicts herself in *The Autobiography of Alice B. Toklas*. She writes first that "she [Stein] stayed with her task, although after the return to Paris she described objects, she described rooms and objects, which joined with her first experiments done in Spain, made the volume Tender Buttons."[38] Later on she asserts that, of the three manuscripts sent to her publisher, "two had been written on our [Toklas and Stein's] first trip into Spain and Food, Rooms etcetera, immediately on our return."[39] Should we conclude that "Rooms" at least was composed in Paris? Some passages in this section seem to correspond to details of Stein's home at 27 rue de Fleurus or refer to her separation from her brother, Leo, and the new living arrangements made with Toklas.[40] As if to obscure the matter further, the typescripts are bound in the order "Rooms," "Objects," "Food," but the table of contents lists "Tender Buttons. Food Rooms Objects." Perhaps Stein wanted to confuse the evidence, perhaps she could not remember exactly the order of composition, or perhaps the mislabeling comes from Toklas or whoever bound the typescripts.[41] In any case, we seem urged to return to the sections in their published order.

Explicitly or implicitly, readings of *Tender Buttons* have responded to the work's emphasis on process all along. In 1934, the behavioral psychol-ogist B. F. Skinner argued that *Tender Buttons* was composed by automatic writing, opening a debate whose effects still linger in critical discussions of Stein.[42] Today the blunt question of whether Stein's writing was automatic seems a red herring: it is either false (as Stein herself insisted) or, if true or partly true, does not release or prevent the reader from finding meaning in the work. It may not even change substantially the reader's approach to meaning, depending on what that approach is. The arguments over meaning and nonsense in Stein have not abated, however. The critical literature has therefore paid increasing attention to composition and not simply in studies of Stein's development. DeKoven's insistence on not interpreting *Tender Buttons* with the aim of generating conventional coherence, for example, is itself an interpretation ultimately based on arguments about Stein's aims and methods of composition.

Considerations of method or process of composition figure perhaps most importantly into evaluations of *Tender Buttons*. When interpretation shifts toward composition, the form and gestures of the prose tend to become its privileged qualities. Though critics generally intend to point to Stein's achievement in such instances, attention to form in *Tender Buttons* potentially comes at the expense of aesthetic value:

> As gestures toward content, the subtitles of *Tender Buttons* make as well as mock meaning. They divide the work, however arbitrarily, into sections, making it much more manageable, less intimidating, than it would be otherwise. . . . On the whole, "Objects" and "Food" are more successful than "Rooms" precisely because they are divided into short, titled fragments.
> *Marianne DeKoven*

> [B]y virtue of their conspicuous fragmentation at the level of form, the discrete, monadic, objectlike texts in the "Objects" section violently resist any totalization that might imply existing conflicts have already been resolved. "Rooms," by contrast—with its much smoother flow of language, the absence of titles to break up discrete texts such as one finds in both "Objects" and "Food"—suggests an aspiration toward the unbroken continuum of prose, or what in Adorno's terms might be called a "non-violent integration of divergences."
> *Jonathan Monroe*

> "Rooms," the final section of *Tender Buttons*, [was] written in 1911 during the same period as "Portrait of Constance Fletcher." . . . "Rooms" has often been overlooked in readings of *Tender Buttons* because the other two sections of the prose poem appear to be more interestingly experimental. But "Rooms" has its own power as an early and quite

successful effort to find a language that could both express and conceal lesbian eroticism.

   Margaret Dickie

Stein disrupts her voices and interior world so fundamentally as to achieve an opacity unmatched by Williams's *Kora* with its disjointed phrases and oblique scenarios from small-town America. Difficulty for difficulty's sake is hardly laudable; the charm of *Tender Buttons* does not lie simply in its attack on the English language and on normal modes of writing, but in its playfulness, inviting the reader to put the pieces back together again.

   Margueritte Murphy[43]

DeKoven and Monroe find the "Rooms" section of *Tender Buttons* the least compelling on formal grounds. For DeKoven, the "senseless and yet signifying" quality of Stein's prose is best served in small doses; for Monroe, "the discrete, monadic, objectlike texts" in the early section of *Tender Buttons* resist accommodation. Dickie recuperates "Rooms" somewhat through reference to its homoerotic subtext but more or less concedes that the other sections are more linguistically experimental and takes it as a given that "Rooms" was composed earlier than "Objects" and "Food." Murphy, like Monroe, points to disruption and difficulty in Stein, though she allows for more playfulness and believes that the text invites the reader "to put the pieces back together again." Whatever their differences, all four critics are interested in the form and gestures of Stein's prose. This emphasis is understandable and in some ways inevitable, though it risks reducing *Tender Buttons* itself to a gesture—as if the work's compositional principle mattered more than the reader's experience of it. Given Stein's own emphasis on the experimental quality of her work, such a conclusion may turn out, after all, to be correct, but in the meantime we should at least try to see how far interpretation which resists evaluation can take us.

   • • •

Considerations of how *Tender Buttons* was composed do not remove the critic from responsibility to local meanings in it. As many interpretations of the work have shown, close readings of selected passages yield results that encourage us to pay some attention to semantics. The kind and the degree of attention we should pay to semantics depend on which passage we are looking at as much as on our critical approach and endurance. Knowing that Stein is describing a mixture of inner and outer realities takes us only so far even in the "Objects" and "Food" sections, where titles promise some focus on representation. In the long "Rooms" section, it is even easier to lose track of the representational gestures in the prose. If we focus on the sounds of words along with their meanings, we can sometimes make more headway. Thus, critics like William Gass and Richard Bridgman can read the title "This is this dress, aider" as, resepectively, "This is Distress, Aid her" and "This is distress, Ada," alerting us to threatening and playful sexual dimensions in the prose. And John Shoptaw can read "A carafe, that is a blind glass" as a title which via "blind" suggests "glasses" of the sort that help one see, dark glasses such as those worn by blind people, opaque glass, and clear glass that appears opaque because it is filled with a dark liquid like red table wine. For some moments in *Tender Buttons*, interpretive ingenuity pays off.[44]

For "Objects" and "Food" at least, a fairly straightforward strategy of inter-pretation can be formulated: think of the relationship between the individual title and description as potentially pointing toward the representation of inner and outer realities, but be prepared for moments when word choice, syntax, and other stylistic decisions are motivated either in an obscure manner or along lines that relate more to composition than description. Sometimes the discrepancy between title and description is deliberate. This strategy also works for "Rooms" insofar as prose descriptions of objects, passageways, arrangements in space, and other features that might qualify as inner or outer realities can be identified in its prose. But taken as a whole, this section distracts us from its representational project, if only because its length makes it difficult to keep our attention focused on it. On these grounds, "Rooms" might be touted as the most radically disruptive section of *Tender Buttons*, except that such a conclusion draws on an essentializing logic as problematic as one that argues that "Objects" and "Food" are more subversive. The three sections of *Tender Buttons* are best viewed as parts of a larger project of experimen-tation. In Stein's own description of her development, she stumbled onto the poetry in prose of *Tender Buttons*. Toward the end of "Poetry and Grammar," she even raises the question "will poetry continue to be necessarily short as it has been," indicating that her experimentation with poetry in prose has inclined her to think that prose poetry, or poetry in general, now needs to be long.[45] Whether "Rooms" was composed last or first or whether it represents a less or more radical experiment than "Objects" or "Food" is unimportant from this perspective. As the third section of *Tender Buttons* differing in form from the earlier sections, "Rooms" occupies the position of an experiment in long poetry in prose generated in part from the shorter pieces.

An interpretive strategy for *Tender Buttons* needs to combine considerations of composition with local semantics. As *Lectures in America* intimates, Stein's experiment can be thought of as a working through of problems faced by a modern and American writer. For Stein, nouns are associated with poetry, but her decision to rid herself of nouns paradoxically requires her to foreground them in her prose, either via the titles in "Objects" and "Food" or through the repetitions of nouns throughout *Tender Buttons*, which increase in frequency at the beginnings of paragraphs in "Rooms." Some series of paragraphs are particularly repetitious in their opening lines:

> A tribune, a tribune . . .
> A success, a success . . .
> One taste one tack, one taste one bottle, one taste one fish . . .
> Any smile is stern and any coat is a sample . . .
> Cadences, real cadences, real cadences . . .
> A line in life, a single line . . .
> Star-light, what is star-light, star-light is a little light . . .
> Why is the name changed. The name is changed because . . .
> Why is there education, there is education because . . .
> A curtain, a curtain . . .
> Climate, climate . . .
> China is not down when there are plates . . .
> Currents, currents . . .
> A religion, almost a religion, any religion, a quintal in religion[46]

The repetitions both point toward and distance the prose from representation. If Stein's description of her own development is accurate, repetitions of this sort drove her toward portraits like "Susie Asado" and "Preciosilla," where sound overwhelms sense. The act of repeating the name of an object helps the reader feel or remember that there is no intrinsic relation between object and name. In *Tender Buttons*, Stein wants to use this "a rose is a rose is a rose" effect point out and bridge the gaps between inner and outer realities.

Stein's repetitions not only riddle the relations between nouns and the objects they name but also reveal some of her recurrent concerns. A key word search of *Tender Buttons* helps us approach meaning indirectly, as Bridgman has shown:

> In *Tender Buttons* specifically, colors predominate, especially versions of red—pink, scarlet, crimson, rose. There are also words of transparency: glass, spectacle, eye glasses, carafe. Images of opening are

common: gate, window. There are also ones of closing and obscurity: glaze, dusty, curtain, cover. One cluster of words concerns polishing and its effect: rubbing, shining, glittering. There are numerous receptacles: cups, plates, sacks. And there are images of breakage: crack, separate, shatter. These images of unity and separation, of obscurity and dirt, or clear vision and cleanliness, of blockage and of opening, of containers and of holders are all involved in the thematic development of *Tender Buttons*.[47]

One can agree with Bridgman's general approach without sharing his optimism that Stein's book "will yield its meanings as readers grow more familiar with it." Some meanings emerge, at any rate. In the "Rooms" section, for example, a list of key words and concepts might include center, climate, substitution, change, replacement, arranging, positioning, whole and pieces, fitting, order, disorder, measure, windows, decision, words beginning with "ex," why, and question.[48] While some of these words seem inevitable given the section's emphasis on rooms, the list also suggests concerns that go beyond arranging furniture and living spaces. There are metaphysical and autobiographical overtones in Stein's preoccupations with the ways in which experience receives organization and meaning via essentially arbitrary centers and arrangements. In addition to any allusion to domestic settlements with her brother and Toklas, arranging can refer to negotiating societal expectations such as marriage, which is, in its own way, an arrangement. Stein associates marriage with patriarchy and pokes fun at both:

> The sister was not a mister. Was this a surprise. It was. The conclusion came when there was no arrangement.
>
> Startling a starving husband is not disagreeable.
>
> Then there is a way of earning a living. Who is a man.[49]

Even comments such as "Why is the name changed" can suggest marriage in this context.[50] As the discussion of the relationship between nouns and poetry in "Poetry in Grammar" shows, naming has a particular significance for Stein. More specifically, Stein's attempts to rid herself of nouns and her decision to write poetry in prose have political implications. Later, in "Patriarchal Poetry" (written 1927), Stein writes "A Sonnet" about marriage centered around a happy husband, then glosses it: "Patriarchal poetry makes no mistake makes no mistake in estimating the value to be placed upon the best and most arranged of considerations."[51]

Perhaps the most important word in "Rooms" is "center." From the opening sentence of the section, Stein instructs us, or herself, to "Act so that there
is no use in a center." Her phrasing suggests that we may not be able to
avoid centering, but there is value in the attempt to avoid a fixed point of
reference or a single object of attention such as the focus supplied by each
title in "Objects" and "Food." Stein also associates center with custom (see
"What is the custom, the custom is in the center" in "Food"), enabling us to
read political overtones in "center" similar to those in "arrangement."[52] As
with "arrangement," it is tempting to align the command "Act so that there
is no use in a center" with Stein's concern with ridding herself of nouns. The
noun is a kind of center that organizes other parts of speech around it. The
word "center," and variants of it, appear often at the beginning of "Rooms"
and periodically throughout:

> Act so that there is no use in a center . . .
> A whole center and a border make hanging a way of dressing . . .
> Any change was in the ends of the center . . .
> If the center has the place then there is distribution . . .
> . . . there comes to be both sides and the center . . .
> . . . the shape is there and the color and the outline and the miserable
> center . . .
> . . . it is not very likely that there is a center . . .
> . . . and the center having spelling . . .
> . . . and the single surface centered . . .
> . . . why is not disturbing a center no virtue . . .
> . . . lover sermon lover, center no distractor, all order is in a measure . .
> . . . if flowers are abundant then they are lilac, if they are not they are
> white in the center . . .
> . . . a wideness makes an active center.

Stein is especially concerned with displacing the center—"why is not disturbing a center no virtue"—even as she relies on the concept of center as a point
of reference. She strives for an active or wide center instead of a fixed point
or singularity, desires a change of center when faced with the impossibility of
doing away with centering, and is interested as much in a center's purposes
or goals as its margins ("the ends of the center").

"Center," "position," "arrangement," "replace," and like words appear
often enough in "Rooms" to put pressure on other words close in meaning or
sound. Stein frequently uses such words as "suppose" (with its etymological

sense "place under"), "middle," and "singularity," for example. Sometimes her puns on "center" are clearly audible: "So the shape [of a hill] is there and the color and the outline and the miserable center, it is not likely that there is a center, a hill is a hill and no hill is contained in a pink tender descender."53 Stein's decentering of the center is played out in the phrase "pink tender descender." "Tender" and "pink" recall the title Stein imposed on her work after finishing it, *Tender Buttons*. As several critics have pointed out, there are erotic connotations in "tender buttons" (*bouton* can mean "nipple"; "tender buttons" suggests soft and hard), adding support to the idea that the decentering alluded to in "pink tender descender" is from male to female and away from a single center or erogenous zone. Passages like this also alert the reader to submerged puns, such as the "her" sound often audible in words ending in "er"—a sound that potentially changes nouns into verbs, as with "aider" and "muncher" in "This is this dress, aider," the final description of "Objects."54

Though it may be difficult to decide how important a word like "center" is to an interpretation of any given passage in *Tender Buttons*, it helps to look at key words in context and think about progression. The phrases "the center having spelling" and "why is not disturbing a center no virtue," for example, occur in the middle of an unusual sentence, which is also a paragraph, in the middle of "Rooms":

> A religion, almost a religion, any religion, a quintal in religion, a relying and a surface and a service in indecision and a creature and a question and a syllable in answer and more counting and no quarrel and a single scientific statement and no darkness and no question and an earned administration and a single set of sisters and an outline and no blisters and the section seeing yellow and the center having spelling and no solitude and no quaintness and yet solid quite so solid and the single surface centered and the question in the placard and the singularity, is there a singularity, and the singularity, why is there a question and the singularity why is the surface outrageous, why is it beautiful why is it not when there is no doubt, why is anything vacant, why is not disturbing a center no virtue, why is it when it is and why is it when it is and there is no doubt, there is no doubt that the singularity shows.55

In a work consisting largely of flat expository assertions, this sentence stands out. Perhaps two earlier paragraphs in "Rooms" ("Blind and weak and organized"; "Why is pale white not paler than blue") produce something of the effect of this run-on sentence, but the only paragraph that rivals it in intensity is the very last in the book, with its long sentence beginning "The sensible decision was that notwithstanding."[56] The word "center," so prominent at the beginning of "Rooms," does not appear in the pages immediately preceding the paragraph just cited, as if centering were a repressed concern making its reappearance here with a vengeance. Apparently, fixed beliefs and singularities are the targets of the outburst, but doubt and indecision pervade a paragraph that seeks to make disturbing centers a virtue without raising this principle to the status of a fixed belief. What begins as some kind of statement about religion transforms itself into a list of nouns, presumably characteristics of the religion being described (including rituals), but as the list continues the reader loses any clear sense of description. At one point the list seems mostly determined by rhythms, especially trochaic tetrameter, and rhyming sounds: "and a single set of sisters and an outline and no blisters and the section seeing yellow and the center having spelling." The sentence then turns into a series of "why" questions before finally returning to the initial mode of assertion, except that now we are bound to wonder just how assertive the statement is meant to be. The phrase "there is no doubt, there is no doubt that the singularity shows" may be more an uncertain stutter than assertion, more hypothesis than conclusion. Intentionally or not, the statement "there is no doubt" suggests that there is doubt. Even the statement "there is no doubt that the singularity shows" is ambiguous. Does Stein mean that the singularity shows us something definitive (that disturbing a center is a virtue, for instance), that it hides its doubts by not showing them, or merely that it makes its appearance felt? Given all the "whys" and the negatives of the sentence, especially "why is not disturbing a center no virtue," one senses that Stein is weighing the ethical ramifications of confrontation, perhaps in reference to some personal decision. Such odd moments of urgency amid otherwise flat prose hint at something beyond description of inner and outer realities. At the end of "Rooms" Stein asks, "Why is there so much useless suffering. Why is there," then refers to "the sensible decision" that seems to resolve the dilemma that has been prompting her questioning all along.[57] With enough interpretive coaxing, we can find some narrative in *Tender Buttons* after all.[58]

This interpretive approach to *Tender Buttons* is meant to give the reader direction, not provide comprehensive solutions to problems of meaning in Stein. One last series of examples will demonstrate some of the advantages and limitations of the approach. As mentioned, the final description of "Food,"

"A center in a table," effectively sets the table for "Rooms" via its concerns with centering. The closing sentences of this description are especially rich in puns, though it is difficult to know what to make of the wordplay: "Next to me next to a folder, next to a folder some waiter, next to a foldersome waiter and re letter and read her. Read her with her for less."[59] Stein seems to become more self-referential as she approaches the end of the section. It is as if she were describing the table at which she is sitting along with a folder and either some water or someone waiting nearby. Stein's instructions to "Read her" are apparently directed to the "reader," be this Toklas, the reader in general, or Stein herself (a reminder to read the manuscript with Toklas or revise what she has written). Once we are aware of the potential puns on "her," we can speculate some more. Is Stein directing us to hidden meanings by commanding us to read "her" into her prose? Should we imagine someone like Toklas waiting nearby, perhaps busy reading a letter or folding a letter to put into an envelope? Is the scene in fact a restaurant, and would Stein rather go home and eat ("read") with Toklas at less expense? Maybe whoever is waiting wants Stein to read the letter or else "let her" read it—a letter lying on the table and acting as the scene's center of attention? (In this reading the "center" in a table could refer to a letter "sent [to] her" on the table.) Is there a joke on excessive attention in the "foldersome"—that is, fulsome and bothersome—waiter? Stein may even be directing our attention to spelling in the phrase "waiter and re letter and read her." By separating "re" from "letter," Stein causes us to stop short. Perhaps "re" points to the contents of the letter, as in a memorandum, or literally appears on the envelope. At first we expect a noun—"next to a waiter, a letter"; "her letter"—only to read "re letter" as an imperative in retrospect. We might then be tempted to turn "foldersome waiter" into some kind of imperative—"wait here"; "give her some water"— though once we have gone this far, we might be better off dowsing ourselves with some water. Are we still with Stein at this point? More or less. Or so she seems to reassure even as she admonishes: "Read her with her for less." Stein might as well be telling us "less is more," for her economically worded command paradoxically encourages us to read more into her prose, as well as onward in it, to "Rooms."

Stein's prose invites speculation of this sort in part because it presents itself as experimental. Whether it is a successful experiment is immaterial: *Tender Buttons* asks to be read as poetry in prose, and this perspective affects how we make sense of its use of nouns and titles and even the length of "Rooms." There remains the question of Americanness: does *Tender Buttons* ask to be read as an American prose poem? The answer is yes, at least in the same sense that it and Stein's lectures encourage us to read "Act so that there is no use in a center" as an impulse to decenter nouns and poetry with verbs and prose. Stein's narratives of development posit that American literature decenters or recenters English literature by becoming part of it, allowing us to interpret the claims made in "Rooms" about change and replacement as references to her ideas about literary history. Stein may even have left a trace of her views on English and American literature in the spelling of center. In all published texts of *Tender Buttons* except the Library of America edition I have been quoting from—which is based on the typescript—center is spelled "centre" throughout until the very last use toward the end of "Rooms," "a wideness makes an active center."[60] *Tender Buttons* seems to enact on a textual level the desire to create an active and American center. Such an idea is, at the very least, consonant with Stein's view that "a movement of time included in a given space . . . is a definitely American thing." The manuscript evidence is ambiguous, however: the difference in spelling may simply be due to a printer's error. But given Stein's puns on words ending in "er," the attention she calls to lettering (and "re" lettering), and the reference in "Rooms" to "the center having spelling," the different spellings of center arguably ought to be retained, printer's error or not.[61]

•   •   •

Given a general sense of how to approach *Tender Buttons*, we can step back and reflect on what it means to read the text outside a tradition of American prose poetry. *Tender Buttons* is not only a book of poetry in prose written by an American but also a work concerned with issues of prose, poetry, and Americanness. At the same time, it can be misleading to label *Tender Buttons* a collection of individual prose poems, if only because it asks to be read as a series of related experiments—the individual titles in "Objects" and "Food" notwithstanding. The label "prose poetry" can be meaningfully applied to the work, but there is an important sense in which other frameworks of interpretation are just as, if not more, relevant—Stein's narrative of development, for instance, or the modernist impulse to blur generic distinctions, or perhaps the modernist long poem. (It is telling that the long section "Rooms" tends to get slighted in criticism of prose poetry dealing with Stein.) Even the label "American" risks irrelevance or circularity in logic: knowing that Stein was concerned with Americanness helps us locate suggestive moments throughout her writings and then connect them to passages in *Tender Buttons*. Again, reading the work as an American prose poem is not wrong per se, but we should be conscious of the role literary history plays in our perspectives, how it gives a center to our interpretations. In the late twentieth century we cannot ignore the term "prose poem," but it is sometimes worth acting as if there were no use in it. Just as we look at *Robinson Crusoe* differently once we are aware that its label "novel" came later and its generic sources include travel writing, spiritual autobiography, and the Puritan guide tradition, so our perspective on *Tender Buttons* shifts somewhat when we consider Stein's work within narratives not centered on the prose poem.

A similar claim can be made of interpretations of Williams's *Kora in Hell*. One can certainly treat *Kora in Hell* as a collection of prose poems, in spite of Williams's ardent defense of "improvisation" against "the typically French prose poem" in his prologue to the City Lights Edition. Williams in fact published other short pieces of prose called "improvisations" in publications like *transition*, the journal that reprinted *Tender Buttons* in 1928. But while the numbered pieces in *Kora in Hell* may possess more autonomy than the titled descriptions in *Tender Buttons*, Williams's work also asks to be read as a kind of sequence: the improvisations are organized into twenty-seven groups of three, and many are followed by glosses in italics. In his preface, Williams speaks of a "fragmentary argument." Perhaps most crucially, the collection gains something when considered in light of other poetic works Williams was writing at the time. (It is no accident that *Kora in Hell* is now published in the collection *Imaginations*, a book that includes Williams's experimental work written between 1920 and 1932.) Like Stein's studies in description, Williams's improvisations form part of a larger project, and they issue as much from personal stylistic developments as the period's tendencies toward formal experimentation.

None of these considerations prevent us from exploring how *Kora in Hell* fits into a tradition of prose poetry, but they do suggest that there are some attractive alternatives. Studying prose poetry in the modernist period can mean looking at the general role prose plays in poetry, for instance. Williams's own œuvre provides an instructive example. Readers familiar with Williams's poems from anthologies, selected works, and collected volumes may be surprised to find that some of the most famous verse lyrics from *Spring and All* are surrounded by prose passages in their original publications. These prose passages sometimes function like the glosses in *Kora in Hell*, commenting however obliquely on the poems and presenting a fragmentary argument. Sometimes Williams uses the expository prose to announce, rhetorically and literally, the next lyric. Before "By the road to the contagious hospital," for example, Williams speaks of "The Traditionalists of Plagiarism" and asserts:

> Now at last that process of miraculous verisimilitude, that great copying which evolution has followed, repeating move for every move that it made in the past—is approaching the end.
> Suddenly it is at an end. THE WORLD IS NEW.[62]

In this context, "By the road to the contagious hospital" heralds more than spring: it announces a new kind of poetry.

Moreover, the prose of *Spring and All* discusses the relationship between prose and poetry and even compares its experiments with those of *Kora in Hell*:

> The *Improvisations*—coming at a time when I was trying to remain firm at great cost—I had recourse to the expedient of letting life go completely in order to live in the world of my choice. . . . Now I have come to a different condition. I find that the values there discovered can be extended. I find myself extending the understanding to the work of others and other things— . . .
>
> Or better: prose has to do with the fact of an emotion; poetry has to do with the dynamization of emotion into a separate form. This is the force of the imagination.
> prose: statement of facts concerning emotions, intellectual states, data of all sorts—technical expositions, jargon of all sorts—fictional and other—
> poetry: new form dealt with as reality itself. . . .
>
> I can go no further than to say that poetry feeds the imagination and prose the emotions, poetry liberates the words from their emotional implications, prose confirms them in it.[63]

Prose has a mixed function in *Kora in Hell*; *Spring and All* divides the labor of prose and poetry. Given the obscurity of many glosses and the occasional intrusion of italics into the improvisations, even the division between the improvisations and glosses is blurred in *Kora in Hell*. The *Spring and All* pattern continues in Williams's later books like *Paterson*, but in all of his works the dialogue between exposition and expression collapses some differences between prose and poetry in the act of reinforcing them. The middle passage cited here, for example, follows the poem "The pure products of America

/ go crazy." The prose argument up to this point has centered on copying, originality, and "the feeling of reality" we draw from art. When this prose passage begins "Or better: prose has to do with the fact of an emotion," the reader cannot directly connect the argument with the prose that has come before and is thus urged to think of the poem as an illustration of or comment on the prose. In this way the functions of the verse and prose are not entirely distinguishable.

The most obvious feature of *Kora in Hell* that Williams may have thought distinguished it from "the typical French prose poem" is its frequent use of American slang and subject matter. From the outset Williams floods the reader with many voices, most of them recognizably American:

> For what it's worth: Jacob Louslinger, white haired, stinking, dirty bearded, cross eyed, stammer tongued, broken voiced, bent backed, ball kneed, cave bellied, mucous faced—deathling,—found lying in the weed "up there by the cemetery." "Looks to me as if he'd been bumming around the meadows for a couple of weeks."[64]

Even in those improvisations in which the subject matter is not American, the point of view and the energetic tone of the prose seem meant to signal Americanness:

> Ha! the dark canals [of Amsterdam] are whistling, whistling for who will cross to the other side. If I remain with hands in pocket leaning upon my lamppost—why—I bring curses to a hag's lips and her daughter on her arms knows better than I can tell you—best to blush and out with it than back beaten after.[65]

Considering all of these markers of Americanness, one almost gets the sense that Williams wants readers to believe that writing poetry in prose is somehow American.

Even more quickly than with Eliot and Stein, we have arrived at the familiar impasse: when it comes to interpretation, how much do abstractions like "American" and "prose poem" really matter? Perhaps now it is possible to provide a more general answer to this question and put the idea of an American prose poem in a larger perspective. Poetic genres are creations of literary history: they can be born, grow up or regress, die, and be reborn. We make these literary-historical narratives, they are made for us, or they are half-created and half-given—the important point is that they can to some extent be remade. My readings of Eliot, Stein, and Williams point not only to ways in which the idea of an American prose poem is often a retrospective framework but also to circumstances in which the idea can be outright misleading. My skepticism regarding the labels "American" and "prose poem" should not obscure the usefulness of such terms—the important point is that literary-historical narratives can be remade. Works like *Tender Buttons* and *Kora in Hell* might, or might soon, be best described as collections of prose poems. Up to now, however, the near invisibility of the American prose poem has helped it blend in with a more general poetic tradition. There is, in short, a sense in which prose poetry has never been a genre, but this perspective can only come to light in a meaningful way by engaging with prose poetry as a genre.

A comparative study of American and French prose poetry does more than provide perspective on the cultivation and neglect of the prose poem in different literary traditions. From a purely formal perspective, a discussion of the American prose poem, especially of the modernist prose poem, would have been concerned with a much wider range of examples. What, for example, are to be made of Hemingway's first versions of the stories of *In Our Time* (1924), which he described as prose poems? Is Hart Crane's late work "Havana Rose" (1933) a prose poem? What is the status of Jean Toomer's "Nora," a prose piece published on its own in a 1922 issue of *The Double Dealer*, then reprinted as "Calling Jesus" in the novel *Cane* (1923)?[66] But this narrow sense of boundaries for the American prose poem leads at best to a catalogue of types, at worst to a misrepresentation of the form's significance.

The idea of an American prose poem can instead be regarded as an interpretive framework and its significance examined accordingly. Beyond the propaganda value of this idea—not to be underestimated—its importance must be viewed in light of other strains in modern American poetry, especially the drive to bring poetry closer to ordinary speech (whose roots go at least back to romanticism) and the development of the modern long poem. The relationship between everyday speech in poetry and an American prose poem is fairly straightforward: whatever formal similarities the prose poem and the *poème en prose* may have, each (so the argument would run) is distinguished via the untranslatable element of idiom. Williams's annoyance with Pound's comparison of *Kora in Hell* to the *Illuminations*, for example, both arose from and accounts for some of Williams's determination to introduce a recognizably American idiom into his poems. Russell Edson's comment that the prose poem comes to Americans "out of modern poetry itself" can also be read in this light, for as *Tender Buttons* and "The River" section of *The Bridge* indicate, the introduction of an American idiom into poetry was often the result of writing in a self-consciously modern way, whether in prose or verse. The relationship between the modern long poem and American prose poetry is somewhat more difficult to explain. As Eliot observed, there may be something about writing a long poem that tends to introduce the prosaic into poetry. But it is not really accurate to assert that length and expansion are specifically American traits, archetypically American examples like Walt Whitman notwithstanding. Nor are brevity and concentration necessarily French traits, as Lautréamont and twentieth-century writers such as Henri Michaux prove. If there is a grain of truth in the association of certain poetic traits with nationalities, it would seem to result from cultural preconceptions that then influence poetic practice and critical thinking—Williams's overtly American *Improvisations*, Fredman's location of Frenchness in a particular mode of symbolism. In other words, national difference can be a self-fulfilling prophecy. Americans who set out to write long prose poems in order to avoid writing artifact-like *poèmes en prose* may help create some of the differences they posit as preexisting. Even this picture, however, requires a careful selection of poets and poems, whatever its usefulness in identifying one strain in American poetry. The American prose poem and long poem are related historically through figures like Eliot, Stein, and Williams, or for that matter the Ashbery of *Three Poems*.

8. Negative Dialectics

This is the only way in which new lives—not ours—can ever begin again. But the thought haunts me—will they be defined in terms of what we never were? Will the negative outlines of our never doing define their being, a repoussoir, and so enmesh themselves even more disastrously with their warning to become? If that were the case it would be better to stop right here, in this room . . . —John Ashbery, "The New Spirit"

Prose poetry in America is not a continuous tradition. It is not a tradition at all, really, in spite of the number and variety of poets who have written in the form. At most an intermittent stream of prose-poetry experiments has remained a familiar feature on the poetic landscape: just as modernists like Eliot, Stein, and Williams tried their hand at poetry in prose, many poets of the postwar period—Elizabeth Bishop, James Merrill, W. S. Merwin, Robert Creeley, and Mark Strand, to name a few—have written prose poems yet remain better known for their poetry in verse. Robert Bly and Russell Edson are possible exceptions to the rule of writing prose poetry on the side in that they have both published several volumes of prose poems and called some attention to their choice of poetic form.[1] On the whole, however, the prose poem has not fared particularly well in American poetry, at least until recent years.

John Ashbery's *Three Poems* (1972) marks a turning point in the story of the American prose poem. To place such importance on a single collection of poems risks misunderstanding: Ashbery is not the only important poet writing prose poems, nor does he represent the culmination of a particular trend in the form, nor has his influence since the publication of *Three Poems* determined the direction of American prose poetry. The reception poets and critics have given his prose poems is unique, however. *Three Poems* has not only received Harold Bloom's blessing as canonical and exerted the sort of influence that makes Marjorie Perloff call it "a startling precursor of the 'new poetry' of the 1980s," it has also functioned as a catalyst for prose-poetry activity.[2] Ron Silliman's bibliography of "recent" literature in the form, compiled in 1986, suggests that there have been over fifty prose-poetry books published since *Three Poems*.[3] Some of these books descend recognizably from Ashbery, but even when Ashbery's influence is not an issue, the success of *Three Poems* is arguably performing for the American prose poem the same service that the prestige of Baudelaire and Rimbaud performed for the *poème en prose*.

If the success of Ashbery's *Three Poems* marks the beginning of the end of prose poetry's marginal status in America, it is also contributing to the dissolution of the prose poem as a distinct genre. Again, a comparison to the development of the *poème en prose* is helpful. In France the prose poem became a widely accepted poetic form—one color of poetry's palette, so to speak—by the early twentieth century. In a similar way, the American prose poem of today seems to be on its way to becoming one form among many. This is not to say that choosing to write poems in prose is now a neutral aesthetic decision. Like "free verse," "prose poetry" covers a wide variety of poetic forms, and any given form has the potential to take on special significance to the extent that it becomes associated with the work of a particular group of poets or through the development of additional, subgeneric features. Types of prose poems are no doubt already emerging or will soon be recognizable as such in retrospect. Nevertheless, the fact that different sorts of poets are writing prose poems alongside poems in a wide variety of verse forms indicates the degree to which prose poetry is becoming part of a general "lyric" tradition. In the short run at least, Ashbery's work has helped supply the impetus for exploring the expressive possibilities of a form. Ashbery's *Three Poems* also prefigures its own reception by poetically enacting, in a kind of systole-diastole movement, the establishment and dissolution of form.

•   •   •

Before pursuing a reading of *Three Poems*, it is useful to consider the book in the context of Ashbery's œuvre and in relation to what different critics have written about it. In retrospect, it seems no accident that Ashbery wrote and published *Three Poems* after the long poem "Fragment" from *The Double Dream of Spring* (1970) and before "Self-Portrait in a Convex Mirror" from the collection of the same name (1975). The meditative prose of *Three Poems* seems both an antidote to the intricate *dizains* of the former and a foreshadowing of the discursive arguments of the latter. As several critics have pointed out, *Three Poems* is also worth comparing to Ashbery's earlier

long poem, "The Skaters" (*Rivers and Mountains*, 1966) in that both poems
make mention of the problem of selectivity, the "leaving-out business."[4] At
the very least, the different long poems relate to each other via a kind of
negatively determined progression: Ashbery's desire to avoid repeating what
he has done.[5] Change in direction resulting from a temporary dead-end in
development, a more or less dialectical movement when continued over a
series of instances, is thus already present at a general level in *Three Poems*.

A negative dialectic also makes itself felt in an immediate way in Ashbery's
long poems via the frequent appearance of contrasting logical connectives—
"yets," "buts, "howevers, and similar expressions:

> Nothing anybody says can make a difference; *inversely*
> You are a victim of their lack of consequence
> Buffeted by invisible winds, *or yet* a flame yourself
> Without meaning, *yet* drawing satisfaction
> From the crevices of that wind, living
> In that flame's idealized shape and duration.
>
> *Whereas* through an act of bunching this black kite
> Webs all around you with coal light
>   *"Fragment," my emphasis*

> This is not easy. And already something like envy is lurking there,
> ready to destroy the whole solid but fragile mass with just a push too
> much. The whole structure must be subtracted from harm's way. It
> is better to take in a third person as a confidant, *but since* there is
> nothing to confide. . . . *But how much more prudent* to have begun the
> thing in a different spirit, manfully, crossing each bridge as you came
> to it, flattening obstacles. . . . *But there is no help for it* and it must
> be remembered that the halfhearted, seemingly lazy way of moving
> forward is both the impetus and the nature of the work.
>   *"The New Spirit," my emphasis*[6]

Contrasting adverbs and conjunctions often occur in the long poems of Wallace Stevens, especially when used to mark transitions between stanzas and
sections, and Ashbery's connectives probably owe something to them.[7] More
abrupt rhetorical shifts, such as the midsentence "but since there is nothing
to confide" in the passage from "The New Spirit," are quintessential Ashbery.
Generally, they indicate that the poet is unsaying, though not necessarily
canceling, a thing as he says it.

Whether following from their discursive mode or interrupting it, the rhetorically signaled shifts in Ashbery's long poems help create the impression of a mind meditating on experience as it occurs. Ashbery has commented on the mimetic character of his long poems:

> It seems quite obvious to me that one is given much broader scope to work with [in long poems] and, as I said before, the time that it takes to write and the changes in one's mood and one's ideas enrich the texture of the poem considerably in a way that couldn't possibly happen in a poem written all at once. And they are in a way diaries or logbooks of a continuing experience or, at any rate, of an experience that continues to provide new reflections and therefore it gets to be much closer to a whole reality than the shorter ones do.[8]

From this point of view, the sharp and gradual turns in a poem may reflect the interruptions and distractions we experience in everyday life, the opposing thoughts that suggest themselves even as we try to hold on to a single dis-cursive thread, the ways in which the world appears alternatively inscrutable and simple. Poetry "gets to be much closer to a whole reality" by changing in the way lived experience changes moment by moment and over extended periods of time. Conversely, the difficulty and the time involved in reading a long poem are themselves elements of the aesthetic experience.

Ashbery's aesthetic analogue to lived experience thus depends on the effect the poem produces rather than on the poem's argument or content per se. Ashbery has written in similar terms of the "almost physical pain with which we strive to accompany the evolving thought of one of James's or Gertrude Stein's characters": "As in life, perseverance has its rewards—moments when we emerge suddenly on a high plateau with a view of the whole distance we have come."[9] Of course, poetic effect itself relies to some extent on content, especially when the subject matter borders on the self-reflexive, as it frequently does in Ashbery:

> We have surprised him
> At work, but no, he has surprised us
> As he works. The picture is almost finished,
> The surprise almost over, as when one looks out,
> Startled by a snowfall which even now is
> Ending in specks and sparkles of snow.
>   *"Self-Portrait in a Convex Mirror"*

I was depressed when I wrote that. Don't read it. Still, if you must, take
note of certain exemptions in the
fourth paragraph where I was high . . .
   Flow Chart

If by chance you should be diverted or distracted for a moment from
awareness of your imprisonment by some pleasant or interesting occur-
rence, there is always the shape of the individual day to remind you. It
is a microcosm of man's life as it gently wanes, . . . the reminder that
time is moving on and we are getting older, not older enough to make
any difference on this particular occasion, but older all the same. Even
now the sun is dropping below the horizon; a few moment ago it was
still light enough to read but now it is no more, the printed characters
swarm over the page to create an impressionistic blur. Soon the page
itself will be invisible.
   "The System"[10]

None of the passages is exclusively self-referential. In the lines from "The
System," for example, the reflections on the waning of day and getting older
filter into the comments on the readability of the printed characters: "Soon
the page itself will be invisible" carries connotations of human and literary
mortality. And the confession from *Flow Chart* is patently a mock confession.
As is typical in Ashbery, metapoetic and poetic matter interpenetrate.[11] In
the otherwise regular, or not so regular, course of a poem, sudden switches
to the present tense and expressions like "even now," "this time," and "Don't
read it" point to the immediate present of the poem's composition or the
projected moment of reading. The resulting blur between interpretive levels
has affinities to the collapsing of surface and depth, and of object and subject,
in Elizabeth Bishop's poetry.[12]
   Ashbery's attempts to take into account how the poem is affecting the
reader lead him not only to make self-reflexive remarks on occasion but also
to give the reader indications of where the poem has been and is going. Thus,
in the opening pages of "The New Spirit," the narrator comments, "It's just
beginning" and "It's not easy at first."[13] A kind of "journey of life" progression
(already signaled by the Dantesque "middle of a journey") then takes over,
with its peak moments and low points. One recurrent image for the effort of
progression and its temporary rewards is climbing a mountain and resting on
the summit or looking down:

And gradually, as the air gets thinner as you climb a mountain, these things will stand forth in a relief all their own—the look of belonging. It is a marvelous job to do, and it is enough just to approximate it. Things will do the rest. Only then will the point of not having everything become apparent, and it will flash on you with such dexterity and such terribleness that you will wonder how you lived before—as though a valley hundreds of miles in length and full of orchards and all sorts of benevolent irregularities of landscape were suddenly to open at your feet, just as you told yourself you could not climb a step higher.[14]

The similarity of this passage to Ashbery's description of reading Stein ("As in life, perseverance has its rewards—moments when we emerge suddenly on a high plateau") makes the suppressed analogy between lived experience and the experience of reading the poem more evident.[15] Other internal references to progression include expository ("Let us assume for the sake of argument that the blizzard I spoke of earlier has occurred") and narrative cues ("Meanwhile he had taken the universal crisis on his own shoulders").[16] As with the contrasting connectives, whose use overlaps somewhat with these other cues, Ashbery's internal references can be, and often are, misdirective, rhetorically rather than logically or narratively motivated. Ashbery's poetry is, after all, especially striking in its apparent nonsequiturs. In general, however, the referencing is user-friendly, providing temporary direction and perspective that, even if false or presented as inadequate in the very act of articulation, allows the reader to continue. As Ashbery writes in "Self-Portrait in a Convex Mirror," "enough of a cover burnishes / To keep the supposition of promises together / In one piece on the surface, letting one ramble."[17]

Closural gestures are perhaps the most obvious feature of pacing in Ashbery's long poems. These gestures often precede the ending of the poem by a few pages or stanzas, as in "A Wave":

And already the sky is getting to be less salmon-colored,
The black clouds more meaningless (otter-shaped at first;
Now, as they retreat into incertitude, mere fins)
And perhaps it's too late for anything like the overhaul
That seemed called for, earlier, but whose initiative
Was it after all? I mean I don't mind staying here
A little longer, sitting quietly under a tree, if all this
Is going to clear up by itself anyway.[18]

After two more stanzas, the poem ends. But "A Wave" is already performing the poetic equivalent of a fade-out shot in a film with its talk of a cessation of struggle and resting under a tree. "The New Spirit" and "The System" in *Three Poems* anticipate their endings from an even longer way off, as if their argumentative or narrative momentum, building up slowly through pages of prose, propelled the poetry forward in such a way that rhetorical brakes had to be applied well in advance of the closing paragraphs. This staggered movement toward closure can be illustrated through selected quotation of the last ten pages of "The New Spirit":

> The note is struck, the development of its resonances ready to snap into place.

> But the light continues to grow, the eternal disarray of sunrise, and one can now distinguish certain shapes such as haystacks and a clocktower. So it was true, everything was holding its breath because a surprise was on the way.

> All this happened in April as the sun was entering the house of Aries, the Ram.

> Something *is* happening. The new casualness had been introducing itself, casually of course, but suddenly its credentials lay everywhere.

> Thus summed up, he felt sickened at the wholeness.

> It is very early.
> The heavens only seem to be in a state of ferment.

> He thought he had never seen anything quite so beautiful as that crystallization into a mountain of statistics.

> One day the thought occurred to him that it was still early, if you were to judge by how few events had actually taken place.

> But it dawned on him all of a sudden that there was another way, that this horrible vision of the completed Tower of Babel . . . could be shut out—and really shut out—simply by turning one's back on it.

> And this is again affirmed in the stars: just their presence, mild and unquestioning, is proof that you have got to begin in the way of choosing some one of the forms of answering that question.

Although it is hard to pinpoint where Ashbery begins to move definitively toward closure, if indeed he ever does, it is nevertheless clear that he is making gestures in that direction long before the poem's final paragraph. Even before the Ram character or "he" assumes a prominent role, phrases like "The note is struck" indicate that the poem's narrative has arrived at some new stage—"not a climax but a point"—which, even as its consequences are postponed in the following pages, initiates a series of forestalled closures.[19] The dialectical back and forth of the poem continues ("But the light continues to grow . . . All this happened . . . Something *is* happening"), but with something like the force of a slowing pendulum insofar as the poem's approaching close is making itself felt. (The Tower of Babel passage is, however, the closest thing to a climax in a poem that skirts epiphanic moments.) The expectation of closure that the poem's rhetoric elicits is offset by a rhetoric of resistance to closure and desire for open-endedness, "unravelings of all kinds, to be proposed but never formulated."[20]

Even this cursory discussion of some features of Ashbery's long poems underscores the ways in which *Three Poems* issues as much from general aspects of his style and interest in long poems as it does from his decision to experiment with writing poetry in prose.[21] From the perspective of today if not of 1972, *Three Poems* frames itself more as an Ashbery long poem than as a prose poem or prose-poem sequence. At the very least, its form and frame qualify the notion that prose poetry exists as its own genre. It is not as if *Three Poems*, Ashbery's one prose poem among his long poems, fails to present readers with unique interpretive challenges but rather that these challenges do not substantially differ in quality from those of other Ashbery long poems.[22] There is even a sense in which the flatly titled *Three Poems* frames itself as requiring no more interpretive apparatus than the generic poem, whether in prose or not.[23] In a related vein, *Three Poems* probably owes some of its success to the fact that Ashbery's verse poetry has qualities that adapt well to prose: poetry in prose versus poetry in verse is mostly a formal distinction in Ashbery's work.

•   •   •

Three Poems can be differentiated somewhat from Ashbery's other long poems in terms of its generic sources. Ashbery has directed interviewers to a miscellaneous set of prose texts: Thomas Traherne's *Centuries of Meditations*, Giorgio de Chirico's *Hebdomeros*, and W. H. Auden's "Caliban to the Audience" from *The Sea and the Mirror*.[24] John Shoptaw argues that these works are often more interesting in the ways they differ from Ashbery's prose poems than as source material in the usual sense.[25] Harold Bloom somewhat more boldly asserts that *Three Poems* is "written in a prose apparently without precursors."[26] "Precursor" has a significance for Bloom that perhaps justifies his assertion, but the hint that *Three Poems* is sui generis is misleading even if the poem's prose has no compelling literary ancestor. Shoptaw's approach is more practically helpful in situating and interpreting Ashbery's poems in this respect; it also lends itself to a discussion of generic influence. Some passages in *Centuries of Meditations*, for example, do resemble passages in *Three Poems*, but the genre of Traherne's work is probably the more important source for Ashbery:

> 1. . . . Certainly Adam in Paradice had not more sweet and Curious Apprehensions of the World, then when I was a child.

> 2. All appeared New, and Strange at the first, inexpressibly rare, and Delightfull, and Beatifull. I was a little Stranger which at my Enterance into the World was Saluted and Surrounded with innumerable Joys. My Knowledg was Divine. I knew by Intuition those things which since my Apostasie, I Collected again, by the Highest Reason. My very Ignorance was Advantageous. I seemed as one Brought into the Estate of Innocence.

> From the outset it was apparent that someone had played a colossal trick on something. The switches had been tripped, as it were; the entire world or one's limited but accurate idea of it was bathed in glowing love, of a sort that need never have come into being but was now indispensable as air is to living creatures. It filled up the whole universe, raising the temperature of all things. Not an atom but did not feel obscurely compelled to set out in search of a mate. . . .

> We have all or most of us had unhappy childhoods; later on we tried to patch things up and as we entered the years of adulthood it was a relief, for a while, that everything was succeeding. . . . It became a delight to enumerate all the things in the new world our maturity had opened up for us, as inexhaustible in pleasures and fertile pursuits as some more down-to-earth Eden.[27]

Both Traherne and Ashbery compare moments in life (childhood, falling in love) to earthly paradises. The two accounts are also alike in their recollection of the freshness and novelty of the experiences. Ashbery's prose is, of course, more ironic given its puns and its mixture of straightforward narration and off-the-cuff commentary: his Eden is "more down-to-earth." Nevertheless, the narrative and argumentative gestures that Traherne and Ashbery make are similar, especially when considered within the common context of meditative prose. Certain passages from *Centuries of Meditations* seem Ashberian in part because they appear within a work of loosely discursive writing not unlike that of *Three Poems*, where trains of thought and narratives are pursued and discontinued with hints of some progression. But as Margueritte Murphy has observed, Ashbery's emphasis on the meditational models for *Three Poems* should not obscure the fact that the poem is by no means conventional meditation.[28] *Three Poems* shifts from one discursive mode to another fairly frequently, sometimes in the middle of a sentence, and even when it remains within more or less meditative discourse for pages at a time it is often self-consciously playing with generic conventions.

Similar observations can be made about the relationship of *Three Poems* to *Hebdomeros* and "Caliban to the Audience": de Chirico's and Auden's works are models for Ashbery's prose poetry in the general and generic sense that they are hybrids of different literary kinds. In contrast to *Centuries of Meditations*, however, stylistic similarities need not be read backward from *Three Poems* into the prose of *Hebdomeros* and "Caliban to the Audience." A passage at the end of Ashbery's translation of the twenty-five-page central episode of *Hebdomeros*, for example, reads in its own context like an Ashbery fade-out:

> The evening was coming to an end; the last guests, and Hebdomeros with them, paid their respects to the master of the house and his children and left the villa whose park was already plunged in darkness. Outside, the sky offered an unforgettable spectacle: the constellations were laid out so perfectly that they formed real figures drawn with dotted lines, as in illustrated dictionaries. Hebdomeros, delighted, stopped and began to point them out, which was in fact quite simple for him since they were easily recognizable and someone completely devoid of astronomical learning would have recognized them without difficulty. One could see the Twins, leaning on each other in a classic pose of tranquility; one could see the Great Bear, obese and touching, dragging his pelt against the darkness of the profound ether; further on the Fish were slowly revolving . . . ; there was something there for everyone and even for the most exaggerated requirements. No one felt like going home.[29]

The astrological details in this passage are reminiscent of the zodiac and tarot images in the closing pages of "The New Spirit," and the mood evoked by de Chirico's description of the day's end and the "unforgettable spectacle" is remarkably similar to the atmosphere at the close of "The Recital," though Ashbery's spectators do go home and sleep. In other passages, de Chirico uses extralong quotations and run-on sentences in Ashberian ways, and the digressive afterthoughts of de Chirico's narrator arguably foreshadow some of Ashbery's midsentence turns to speculation.[30]

Certain passages in "Caliban to the Audience" read even more as prefigurations of Ashbery's prose:

> Yes, you have made a definite start; you *have* left your homes way back in the farming provinces or way out in the suburban tundras, but whether you have been hanging around for years or have barely and breathlessly got here on one of those locals which keep arriving minute after minute, this is still only the main depot, the Grandly Average Place from which at odd hours the expresses leave seriously and sombrely for Somewhere, and where it is still possible for me to posit the suggestion that you go no farther. You will never, after all, feel better than in your present shaved and breakfasted state which there are restaurants and barber shops here indefinitely to preserve; you will never feel more secure than you do now in your knowledge that you *have* your ticket, your passport *is* in order, you have *not* forgotten to pack your pyjamas and an extra clean shirt.[31]

The matter-of-fact tone with which this paragraph begins, hinting at some progression in thought or narrative development, is typical of Ashbery's prose, and the use of the pronoun "you" to refer ambiguously to the narrator, the reader, or some other addressee is a device Ashbery employs for a variety of effects in *Three Poems*.[32] Where Ashbery would be likely to switch discursive registers, however, the Auden passage expands into a critique of bourgeois love of creature comforts (the pyjamas, the clean shirt) and continues in that vein for some length. What ambiguity could be read into Caliban's "you" vanishes. As Shoptaw points out, Auden's style and stance also tend to be more classical than Ashbery's: there is relatively little that is misdirective in Auden's elaborate conceits, and the juxtaposition of the literary and the demotic in "Caliban to the Audience" is tame in comparison to what can be found in *Three Poems*.[33]

   •   •   •

It has become a kind of critical ritual to mention a handful of other general topics relating to Ashbery and *Three Poems*, issues that in direct or indirect ways involve postmodernism. Postmodernity means many and sometimes contradictory things in the world of academic criticism: I am concerned here only with the interpretive consequences of considering Ashbery's work to be postmodern. Ashbery, significantly, does not find the term very helpful: "As for postmodernity, I think I can recognize it in architecture and even in music, but I hardly see what it corresponds to in literature. My idea is to democratize all forms of expression, an idea which comes to me from way back, maybe from Whitman's *Democratic Vistas*—the idea that the most demotic and the most elegant forms of expression equally deserve to be taken into account. It seems to me that postmodernism is a little bit that."[34] He grants that his work is postmodern insofar as postmodernism implies a democratization of forms of expression—a weak sense of the term, especially when in the same breath he mentions that this idea may go back to *Democratic Vistas*. (Ashbery might as easily have cited Wordsworth's preface to *Lyrical Ballads*, though the context of the interview, conducted in French for a French audience, seems to have urged forward the issue of Americanness that comes up in his interviews in Poland and Britain as well.) Ashbery has also spoken of the democratization of discourses as a specific goal when writing *Three Poems*.[35] From this point of view, Ashbery's prose poetry is postmodern according to his own minimal notion, though the poetry itself arguably makes his general aims clear without depending on postmodernity as an interpretive framework.

Some critics have been more specific. Margueritte Murphy maintains that the prose poem in general fits Lyotard's definition of the postmodern, "the unpresentable in presentation itself," and that *Three Poems* is especially postmodern not only because it comes after the works of Stein and Williams but also because it subverts generic conventions and discourses in new ways. To illustrate her point, she discusses the ambiguity of the pronouns and related features of *Three Poems*, emphasizing the work's submergence of the "lyric I," the polyphonic character of its prose, and, in general, Ashbery's "poetics of inclusion."[36] Stephen Fredman also argues that Ashbery "chose to include"; he supports Robert Creeley's assessment of *Three Poems* as "a possible way out of the postmodern dilemma of the self" and discusses the poem's self-declared problem of selectivity and its ruminations on art's ability to mimic life's way of happening.[37] Marjorie Perloff routinely considers Ashbery postmodern and places his work in a tradition of a "poetics of indeterminacy."[38] Like Murphy, Perloff comments on the ambiguous pronouns of *Three Poems* in such a way as to suggest that they disrupt the notion of the self implicit in the romantic "lyric I"; unlike Murphy, her version of postmodernism is Jameson's, not Lyotard's: "In the consciousness of the postmodern poet, fragments of earlier poetry float to the surface, not to be satirized . . . but as the 'blank parody' Fredric Jameson has defined as pastiche, which is to say, the neutral mimicry that takes place when there is no longer a norm to satirize or parodize. When Ashbery's speaker asks, 'Have I awakened? Or is this sleep again?' he is not satirizing Keats's 'Ode to a Nightingale.'"[39] One dissenting voice among critics is John Shoptaw's, whose analysis of a passage near the beginning of "The New Spirit" ("For we judge not, lest we be judged, yet we are judged all the same") shows that "Jameson's blanket generalization [about parody and pastiche] blurs the textual specifics of postmodern poetry."[40] Shoptaw also comments that "not all of *Three Poems* is equally or similarly 'democratic': 'The New Spirit' emphasizes private and romantic discourse; 'The System' foregrounds public discourse; and 'The Recital' features both pragmatic and personal writing."[41] In a different vein altogether, Andrew Ross discusses Ashbery's work in the context of modernism.[42]

Leaving aside the question of whether Ashbery is postmodern, it is possible to tease out the interpretive effects of considering him as such. Critics who think of Ashbery as postmodern tend to locate and privilege qualities of his writing such as indeterminacy, democratization of discourses, subversion of generic constraints, self-referentiality (especially insofar as the poetry questions its own authority and, in general, deconstructs itself), antimonumentalism, polyphony, dialogism, and open-endedness. The resulting portrait may be an idealization of certain values and beliefs of our historical moment. At the same time, however, an emphasis on indeterminacy, antimonumentalism, and the like suggests something important about Ashbery's poetry and prose poetry, if necessarily via some distortion of literary history. As with the idea of a distinctly American prose poem, the idea of a postmodern Ashbery or a postmodern genre informs reading experiences through the attention it brings to bear on a particular set of interpretive issues and its propaganda value. The postmodern framework very likely affects interpretation in other ways as well, if not by a kind of grain-of-truth logic then negatively through the effort involved in overcoming the expectations that the category "postmodernism" carries with it.

The literary-historical cost of most postmodern Ashberys is a straw-man version of modernism. Bringing the prosaic into poetry, for example, is not only as long-standing a project of modern poetry as Ashbery intimates in his comment about *Democratic Vistas* but also an idea with which modernists like Eliot were particularly obsessed. Ashbery's poetry is, needless to say, very different from Eliot's, perhaps antithetical to it in some ways, but the difference between the two poets has little to do with reductive oppositions like dialogic versus monologic, open-ended versus closure-oriented, and perhaps even postmodern versus modernist when the former is used in any but its chronological sense. Ashbery's own comments on his poetic aims are illuminating in this regard. In a 1981 interview he claimed, "My mind wants to give clichés their chance, unravel them, and so in a way contribute to purifying the language of the tribe."[43] Four years later he asserted more forcefully, "Everybody knows Mallarmé's dictum about purifying the language of the tribe. In my case I don't feel it needs purifying. I try to encourage it."[44] The contradiction between Ashbery's statements need not imply a confusion or misrepresentation of aims nor even necessarily a change of opinion. By softening his claim about purifying language with the phrase "in a way contribute to purifying," Ashbery arguably expressed discomfort with the term if not the idea of purifying in 1981. From this perspective, the later assertion merely expands on the earlier. Alternatively and more interestingly, both sets of remarks show affinity with Eliot's project of bringing the prosaic into poetry: the Mallarmé dictum Ashbery alluded to is suggestively closer to Eliot's "purify the dialect of the tribe" from *Four Quartets* than to the original "Donner un sens plus pur aux mots de la tribu."[45] As Ashbery has suggested in comparing Eliot's and Auden's use of everyday language, Eliot's poetry may simply not go far enough in incorporating the prosaic into poetry.[46]

Generally speaking, however, postmodernism implies more than a difference in degree between itself and modernism, and it is from this perspective that an interpretation emphasizing Ashbery's postmodernism risks overlooking some of the most meaningful tensions in his work. The problem of selectivity evoked in the opening page of *Three Poems* illustrates this point:

> I thought that if I could put it all down, that would be one way. And next the thought came to me that to leave all out would be another, and truer, way.
>
> clean-washed sea
>
> The flowers were.
>
> These are examples of leaving out. But, forget as we will, something soon comes to stand in their place. Not the truth, perhaps, but—yourself. It

is you who made this, therefore you are true. But the truth has passed on

to divide all.

It is important to note, as most critics have, that the problem of selectivity has aesthetic, autobiographical, and philosophical implications. It is also crucial to observe that omission and inclusion are associated in some way with verse and prose.[47] Ashbery's solution to the problem, however, is much more ambiguous than the desire to include everything might indicate, especially if the choice of prose is supposed to imply this poetics of inclusion.[48] As Shoptaw points out, the opening statements of *Three Poems* reverse the expected sequence of inclusion and omission, "putting the way of total prose not after but before the 'truer' way of fragmented lyric."[49] It is furthermore not clear whether the desire to include in fact wins out over selectivity. A convincing argument can be made that the narrator of *Three Poems* deliberately chooses not to include everything or perhaps has no choice in the matter whatsoever.

An aesthetics of inclusion or a postmodern perspective is not an entirely inappropriate framework within which to interpret Ashbery's *Three Poems*, however. Nor is *Three Poems* an essentially exclusionary and modernist work. The emotional and argumentative movements in Ashbery's poetry are often dialectical. Ashbery's poems may, for example, swerve away from the monumentalism they evoke, but in the process they betray some attraction for the monumental and other things they apparently deny themselves, perhaps even create an atmosphere of desire through rhetorical denial. In either case, as Ashbery suggests in an early poem that questions the monumental, the poet or the reader builds "a mountain of something" merely by "pouring energy into this single monument" of the poem.[50] Monumentalism, nondemocratic discourse, and related qualities may, in other words, be secretly wished for in the short run and unavoidable in the long run, in spite or because of the poem's rhetoric. An exclusive emphasis on Ashbery's postmodernism tends to ignore these tensions and in effect short-circuits an important source of the poetry's energy.

. . .

Dialectical movement of narrative and argument is especially important for *Three Poems*. John Shoptaw develops this notion in detail in his discussion of *Three Poems*, noting that in the course of the poem "a number of dialectical changes are rung, if not rigorously pursued." His partial list of triads in *Three Poems* ranges from "the new, the old, and the renewed" to "potential, actual (kinetic), and pragmatic action" and beyond: in "The Recital," if not already in "The New Spirit" and "The System," Ashbery "self-consciously adopts the dialectic as a structural principle" for his three-poem book or three-movement poem.[51] Shoptaw provides a general description of the poem's dialectical progression:

> In a landscape as imposing and undifferentiated as *Three Poems*, changes in argument, discursive register, and even format are not readily discernible. Ashbery may very well have drawn up the blueprint for *Three Poems* as he went along. But a formal design and a dialectical argument are legible in the final product. *Three Poems* consists of two fifty-page poems and a ten-page resumption. Each poem differs minimally and significantly in format: "The New Spirit" is made up of "prose blocks" (unindented prose stanzas) and unindented verse, "The System" of prose blocks, and "The Recital" of regularly indented paragraphs. On the back cover of the Viking edition appears Ashbery's reworded summary of the work:
>
> "Meant as a kind of trilogy to be read in sequence, the book opens [in 'The New Spirit'] with a spiritual awakening to earthly things that also involves drawing the author's dilemma over selectivity in his work into a metaphor for man's ability to act either with or upon his destiny. Then [in The System'] Ashbery moves into wry, quasi-dialectical language to tell a love story with cosmological overtones, and [in 'The Recital'] he concludes with a poem that consolidates and fleshes out the themes of the previous two, balancing them with the sometimes harsh facts of his own autobiography."
>
> After discussing the problematic choice of a poetic "way" with his readers, the writer in "The New Spirit" turns to a particular reader, ostensibly a former lover, meditating on the history of their affair and on his consequent reintroduction to the world. Near the end of the poem these reflections coalesce into a character called "the Ram" or "he." This "new spirit," both character and persona in an allegorical narrative of prophetic "selection," takes the podium and pulpit in "The System," delivering first a religious history of the sixties and then a sermon on living out one's unknowable destiny. . . . "The Recital" begins brilliantly with the pointed sentence "All right." In ordinary usage this phrase would inaugurate a survey of what is to be done; but in the context of *Three Poems* it also reads as a contraction, "all is right," which readmits

the synthesizing "all" left out at the beginning of "The New Spirit." . . .
So "The Recital" synthesizes the old and the new in an inconspicuous
renewal. *Three Poems* subtly defamiliarizes the reader, who goes along
following each step but ends up completely lost.[52]

On the one hand, even slight formal differences can hint at a dialectical
progression. On the other hand, "Ashbery may very well have drawn up the
blueprint for *Three Poems* as he went along": there is a danger in making
too much of the dialectical movements of the poem. As several critics have
argued, taking their cues from some of Ashbery's comments on his poetry,
the dialectical movements of *Three Poems* can also be fruitfully compared to
musical progression and resolution.[53] Ashbery himself, after talking about the
"unity" and "progression" of *Three Poems* in one interview, throws a monkey
wrench into speculations about continuous—let alone dialectical—argument
in the poem by remarking that the resolution or attempt at resolution at the
end of all the poem's contradictions "in fact implies that the work is a series
of contradictions."[54]

But dialectical progression has an importance for *Three Poems* that goes
beyond the poem's triadic arguments and structures. It is here where the
notion of a negative dialectic is helpful.[55] Dialectical argument generally
implies a conscious and forward-oriented movement of thought, even when
the argument does not take the supposedly Hegelian and quasi-syllogistic
form of thesis, antithesis, synthesis. *Three Poems* plays with this expectation
and sometimes fulfills it. More often than not, however, the direction and
progression of the poem's arguments and narrated incidents are negatively
determined. Trains of thought and threads of narrative tend to shift directions at moments of impasse, not resolution or synthesis. The contrasting
connectives discussed earlier hint at this tendency; the poem also muses
metaphorically on a negative way of proceeding:

> There is probably more than one way of proceeding but of course you
> want only the one way that is denied you, the leaves over that barrier
> will never turn the sorrowful agate hue of the rest but only burnish
> perpetually in a colorless, livid explosion that is a chant of praise for
> your having remained behind to think rather than act. Meditation rains
> down on you to be sucked up in turn by the sun like a stream, making
> it all the more difficult to know where the branching out should occur.
> It is like approaching a river at night, uncertain of the direction of the
> current. But the pulsating of it leads to further certainties because,

bouncing off the vortexes to be joined, the cyclical force succeeds in defining its negative outline.[56]

The poem links the problem of choosing a direction to the ways in which desire and thought lead indirectly to action. The "river at night" sentence is motivated in part by the sentence preceding it, in which "meditation rains down" and then is "sucked up in turn by the sun like a stream," confusing matters of argumentative "branching out." At one level, the implied image of a delta or forks in a river is emblematic of decisions that need to be made. "Branching out" also has connotations of exploring new possibilities and turning away from narrow specialization. In such a context, the imagined scene of someone "approaching a river at night, uncertain of the direction of the current" invites self-referential readings. Just as a river leaves behind its course and finds its direction via the checks it receives to its forward motion, the plots and arguments of *Three Poems* are at the very least discernible in retrospect and tend to be negatively determined.

Negative dialectic need not imply a conscious structural principle. It is instead a way of accounting for the paradoxical senses of unity and confusion, forward progression and meandering, continuous and interrupted argument, that *Three Poems* evokes. A negative dialectic furthermore suggests there is a strong pragmatic streak in Ashbery's poetry and thought: when the poet reaches a dead-end, he shifts to a more propitious alternative he may not have discovered had he not reached the impasse. What progression emerges in *Three Poems* is quirky and antiteleological, though not directionless. Direction, or lack of it, is in fact a recurring motif of the poem, especially "The New Spirit":

> But it is hard, this not knowing which direction to take, only knowing that you are moving in one, not because no rest was decreed for you but because the force that shot you here remains through inertia, and even while contemplating the globe of seeming contradictions that grow out of your present standing you have begun to evolve in that other direction not included by the archer, a present time draped backward over the past, the appetites no longer chided, full in the expectation of becoming belief but just as surely periled by the negative of premature ripeness that haunts the joyous wilderness like the shadow of the grave.[57]

This long sentence enacts in microcosm the simultaneously forward and retrograde movements of the poem. The apparently digressive remarks of the narrator pull against the forward movement of the prose.[58] Along with the negatively proceeding argument ("But it is hard . . . not because . . . but because . . . and even while"), the prose itself continually points forward like a shot arrow in the sense that it measures time passing in the reading or composition of the poem. *Three Poems* not only contains typically Ashberian references to location and progress throughout the course of the poem, it also mentions specific months and tropes many sentences as moments of thought that are unraveling themselves in the process of articulation.[59] If that were not enough, past "could have been" and future "could be" experiences negatively determine the progression of thoughts and events via their ghost presence: "that other direction not included by the archer, a present time draped backward over the past, . . . full in . . . expectation . . . but . . . periled by the negative."

In another sense, the arrows propelling "The New Spirit" forward are Cupid's. Desire, or checked desire, is sometimes specifically mentioned as an impetus for forward movement:

> [W]e resumed our roles of progressive thinkers and builders of the art of love. Not that such a thing could exist, or if it did it would certainly not be anything like an art, which can only exist by coming into existence, and then the rules may be drawn up, though it makes very little difference since no one will ever play that game again. It lay there in the already clouded vision as we looked at each other, some dark beginning force that made it clear that the time for action was past and the time for making speeches had come. So, somewhat stimulated at the idea of not turning back but going forward, making virtue of necessity, no doubt, we proceeded to actually examine what there was left for us. (25–26)

Once again progression is negatively determined: not turning back seems the decisive precondition for going forward. Because too much thinking ahead and plotting spoil the experience of love, and yet longing keeps forcing us to be "progressive" thinkers, not action but a kind of active passivity results, as the reversed cliché "the time for action was past and the time for making speeches had come" implies.[60] The *ars amatoria* of this passage is in many ways the *ars poetica* of *Three Poems*. The poem backs into moving forward by searching for direction while questioning progression that is too plotted. When asked in an interview "What is the core of your *Three Poems*?" Ashbery first considered whether any writer knew what was at the heart of his or her own work and then replied, "I think probably looking for a core is the core."[61]

If *Three Poems* is continually displacing its core in the act of looking for it, then any distillation of the poem's narrative or argumentative content risks either the generality of a statement like "looking for a core" or the partiality of a recitation of selected details. The interpretive dilemma mirrors one of the poem's dilemmas, the problem of selectivity. Given the work's length and tenuous argumentative threads, critics have understandably gravitated toward less narrative-oriented approaches.[62] Moving beyond a general description of the poem's dialectical movements certainly has its risks: if not of reading continuity into passages to satisfy a will to coherence, then of minimizing the importance of the nonnarrative elements of *Three Poems*. From another perspective, however, a critical approach that emphasizes the ways in which the poem's meditations do not follow one another may be equally misguided, especially insofar as discontinuity is taken to be, in and of itself, a positive trait of a piece of writing—and therefore something absolutely rather than relatively present in the work in which we wish to find it. For all of the influx of different discourses into the poem, the paragraphs and prose blocks of *Three Poems* derail their discursive trains of thought less often than most long stanzas in Ashbery's verse poems. At the very least, much of the effect of *Three Poems* depends on the reader's attempt to follow the poem's "argument."

In short, interpreting *Three Poems* requires a more than usual amount of critical tact. The surest way of leaving something out of an account of the poem is tracing a single line of development, and yet the poetry also urges the reader to follow the logic of each narrative or argument as closely and as far as possible. "The New Spirit," for example, can be read as a meditation on the ability to act—"with or upon . . . destiny" as the back cover says, but often in the more particular sense "so as to find or be found by a beloved." As "The New Spirit" progresses, it almost seems as if desire calls love and the beloved into existence:

[T]he art of love. Not that such a thing could exist. . . . It lay there. . . . It was waiting for us . . .

For the time being you can go on pretending that it is enough to listen to those inner promptings, the voice of the soul, until that fatal day when the look of the beloved flashes on you with its intensity of fixed lightning.

[I]t is before us helplessly waiting:
It must exist once the idea of it exists.

He exists, but he is as a stranger for you in your own home.
(25–26, 32, 34, 360)

Eventually the Ram appears (43), a kind of incarnation of the beloved or perhaps desire itself: "The Ram is imbued with tremendous force which can easily turn into shouted obscenities if he doesn't get his way, as sometimes happens" (44).

Clearing the way for love to happen may be an important, negatively developed theme of "The New Spirit," but it, too, tells only one story of the poem. As is often the case in Ashbery's work, love-poem dilemmas tend to double for the problems of communication between poet and reader or spark reflections on solipsism. Similarly, the dilemmas over selectivity and choosing a direction can lead to speculation on fate and free will, action and quietism, and related issues. Searching for autobiographical or ontological truth is yet another possible framework of interpretation. All of these concerns and more are present in the poetry, often at once and sometimes in pointed or humorous contradiction with each other. In the "open field of narrative possibilities" (41) of *Three Poems*, story lines and arguments intertwine in such a way as to make it impossible to speak of a single and linear movement forward, excepting, perhaps, the march of the prose itself.

•   •   •

In discussing what argumentative and narrative developments occur in *Three Poems*, it is necessary to measure progression against a variety of recurring themes, images, phrases, and formal features. The "progression" and "unity" Ashbery claims for the work are relative, emerging gradually after extended engagement with the poetry. "The New Spirit," in particular, begins tentatively, as if it were groping its way toward everything from subject matter to prose form. In the opening pages of the poem there are a large number of short prose blocks, sentence fragments, enjambments across prose blocks, and switches between flat, free-verse stanzas and prose. The poem, however, eventually finds a rhythm. The free verse drops out of the poem for more than twenty pages after page 12. When it returns at three later moments (33, 39, 47), it takes on a kind of detached commentator role. The intervals between these free-verse passages are roughly equal, and each passage is approximately a page long. Meanwhile, the prose passages have also reached an equilibrium of sorts. The watershed moment is probably the long prose block beginning on page 19 ("However, / the honesty of this approach is eased") and ending on page 29 ("nothing here any longer bears your imprint"). After this passage,

202 *Negative Dialectics*

as the narrator says, "The problem becomes more definite" (29). Page 32 witnesses the poem's last enjambment across prose blocks, and no prose section of "The New Spirit" reaches beyond the length of two pages from this point on.

The poem's formal changes can be linked to some thematic development. The interrupted passages and the quick succession of prose and verse in the first half of "The New Spirit" suggest that Ashbery, in the fiction of the poem if not literally, is working out how to write the long poem in prose he is writing: the mimesis of life's way of happening is also a representation of the poem's way of happening. The formal equilibrium of the second half of the poem corresponds to a more sustained consideration of the imminence of the beloved. The reflections at the end of the long prose block in the middle of "The New Spirit" even suggest that the negatively proceeding meditation of the poem's first half has been progressive:

> The fact that you did all this—cleared away all the debris so that the created vacuum would expel you forward into an exact set of conditions replying to exact demands—fertilizes each instant as it is born, increases and dies, spontaneously generating the light that flushes through the silver-outlined mask of your face . . . . The problem becomes more definite. (28–29)

In spite of the poem's antiteleological and antimonumental stance, its rhetoric creates an air of expectation, apparently building toward the Tower of Babel passage. This movement necessitates the "new journey" (51) and eventual breakdown of "The System."

Though useful in isolating some themes, dividing up and describing "The New Spirit" in this way leaves out a host of other developments in the poem. A somewhat more nuanced narrative emerges when one pays attention to images like the moon:

> It is not easy at first. There are dark vacancies the light of the hunter's moon does little to attenuate. Ever thought about the moon, how well it fits what it has to light?

> Why its imperfections are just a token of how life moves along, haltingly but somehow always getting there in time, in our time. A cloak of somnolence, heavy and sticky as moonlight, translucent but imperfectly so . . . becomes the state of present affairs—one of erect passivity, polarized through hesitation and love . . .

There was no getting around it, the Moon had triumphed easily once again, Hecate and her brood of snarling mutts were always around messing up the place, and in the meantime the crayfish had glided unnoticed out of the water and begun its upward course, drawn by some baffling magnetism toward its mother, the moon, who places everything in a puzzling light from which a fraction of the truth is not altogether absent, for the moon does illuminate, though erratically. (8, 20, 46)

The moon's light and distance connect it to discussions of love and the beloved, especially the way in which the moon's glow pulls the narrator away from a more earthly (less platonic) love and potentially distorts the truth. The lunacy of love is not to be avoided, however: it not only will return no matter how much emphasis we place on realism but also provides its own perspective, fitting well what it has to light. The narrator ostensibly keeps trying to rid himself of idealizations but is attracted to them or views them as "a preparatory dream which seemed to have the rough texture of life, but which dwindled into starshine [read 'moonshine'] like all the unwanted memories" (7). The dialectical movement of the poem tries to settle on a middle ground, "some kind of rational beauty within the limits of possibility" (26). In the final pages of "The New Spirit," the "he" of the poem receives a vision of what this new state of being might be:

[O]ut of that river of humanity comprised of individuals each no better than he should be . . . a tonal quality detached itself that partook of the motley intense views of the whole gathering but yet remained itself, scrupulously fixed equidistant between earth and heaven, as far above the tallest point on the earth's surface as it was beneath the lowest outcropping of cumulus in the cornflower-blue empyrean. Thus everything and everybody were included after all. (48–49)

On the following page the "horrible vision of the completed Tower of Babel" suggests that the position "equidistant between earth and heaven" is probably too neat a resolution of problems like realism, individualism, and selectivity. Nevertheless, the poem considers its own progression through Neoplatonic stages of love as significant, though not necessarily as a progression:

It wasn't that any of the previous forms of life he had taken: the animalistic one, the aristocratic one in which sex and knowledge fitted together . . . or the others . . . culminating in the (for him) highest form of love, which recognizes only its own generosity—it was not that these seemed no longer viable, stages in a progression whose end is still unseen and unimaginable. They had not merely served the purpose but were the purpose—what population is to the world, that explains it as it uses it. (50)

What matters is the desire for upward movement and the experiences resulting from it, for the idea of progressing through a chain of being may turn out to be as natural as drawing a breath: "this progression that is built into us like the chain of breathing" (23).

As the "starshine" passage shows, moon imagery often blends indistinguishably into planet and star imagery, and the reflections on love and the beloved intersect both: the archer is as much the constellation and zodiac sign Sagittarius, "the healer" (42), as Cupid. Once again, allowing for overlaps and interruptions in narrative is an important part of reading Ashbery's long poems. But it is equally important to recognize when a train of thought or set of images takes on its own quasi-symbolic value, as the stars and constellations eventually do in "The New Spirit." The star images near the beginning of the poem are similar to the moon images in that they tend to beg questions regarding the degree to which love is solipsistic or narcissistic ("as you are, as you are to me"). The constellation images closer to the end of the poem function as figurative solutions to such problems as inclusion versus exclusion, a plotted versus an open-ended future, and action versus passivity in that they are able to glow "like the sum of all their possible positions, plotted by coordinates, yet open to the movements and suggestions of this new life of action without development" (37).

At the very end of "The New Spirit," the constellations also represent an alternative to the monumental Tower of Babel. After reviewing the different stages of love he has experienced and suggesting that shutting out the terror produced by the vision of "the completed Tower of Babel" may be as simple as "turning one's back on it," the narrator remarks: "In the other direction one saw the desert and drooping above it the constellations that had presided impassively over the building of the metaphor that seemed about to erase them from the skies" (50–51). These constellations, and the last two pages of the poem in general, have attracted an astonishing amount of critical commentary.[63] Indeed, it is difficult to avoid reading this last section of "The New Spirit" as a climax, if only because it is the last section, provides some answers to questions the poem has posed, and caps a rhetorical sequence that has arguably been building since the assertion "The problem becomes more definite." As the narrator comments, the constellations represent "the sum total of all the good influences and friendly overtures in your direction"; they "create the impression of a climate in which nothing can go wrong" (51). Unlike the dominating tower, the stars above have a calming effect, even as they urge the speaker forward to seek answers to new questions in the final lines of the poem.

But does the last section of "The New Spirit" really provide solutions to the dilemmas the poem has constructed for itself? The figure of the constellations does at least negotiate some of the poem's Scyllas and Charybdises: the stars represent a kind of direction or destiny but leave it to the individual to connect the dots; they are selected points but allow for an imaginative reconstruction of the whole; and so on. And it would be misleading to point out that the constellations are, in the end, a mere figure of speech even as they point to a possibility beyond the figurative, if only because the poem is aware of "the success or failure, depending on your point of view, of the project" (51). The apparent climax then fade-out of the poem's close is at odds with the manner in which the poem has progressed to this point, however. The dialectical movement of the poem guarantees some open-endedness—we are given the promise of a new journey—but the pull of the approaching end of the poem, initiated by the preceding pages of closure-oriented prose, exerts a force that is greater than any argumentative resolution, especially given that the latter is tentative. In other words, there is a sense in which the poem's rhetoric, not logic, brings the work to a close.

⋅ ⋅ ⋅

Unlike "The New Spirit," "The System" is more certain about the directions it chooses and the answers it works out for itself. As in "The New Spirit," the negative and dialectical impulse of the meditative prose continues in "The System," only with less anxiety about the method, or lack of method, of proceeding: "There is no need for setting out, to advertise one's destination. . . . Gradually one grew less aware of the idea of not turning back imposed as a condition for progress" (54, 63). "Setting out" or "striking out" had been a recurrent source of uneasiness and excitement in "The New Spirit."[64] After the opening pages of "The System," this concern vanishes, only to reemerge in the past tense ("when you were setting out") shortly before the question of how to use "the reality of our revelation, as well as to what end, has been resolved" (80) and then pointedly after the narrator remarks to himself and the reader that a "new arrangement is already guiding your steps and indicating the direction you should take without your realizing it": "But now to have absorbed the lesson, to have recovered from the shock of not being able to remember it, to again be setting out from the beginning—is this not something good to you?" (86). Clearly some change in approach or attitude has occurred since "the earlier days" of the poem. Accounting for this change is not simply a matter of following the poem's logic, however: rhetorical constraints and impulses are at least as important and hint at tensions between the prosaic and the poetic that come to a head in the middle poem of *Three Poems*.

"The System" begins in medias res: "The system was breaking down" (53) refers to a present state, which the narrator then "accounts for" with a thirty-page history and analysis that leads back to the present. Whatever tone of crisis might be read into this opening is instantly swept away by comments concerning the "playfulness" with which "we actually sit down to the business of mastering . . . the clotted sphere of today's activities" (54). The opening pages of "The System" also introduce some images that return later, the most important of which is the room:

> There is no need for setting out, to advertise one's destination. All the facts are here and it remains only to use them in the right combinations, but that building will be the size of today, the rooms habitable and leading into one another in a lasting sequence, eternal and of the greatest timeliness.

> This was outside reality. Inside there was like a bare room, or an alphabet, an alphabet of clemency. Now at last you knew what you were supposed to know. The words formed from it and the sentences formed from them were dry and clear, as though made of wood. (54, 55)

The narrator apparently wishes to avoid building the monumental Tower of Babel of "The New Spirit." The building he wants "will be the size of today," and it will contain habitable rooms. The desire for an eternal monument has not vanished: hope is expressed that the new building will be simultaneously enduring and responsive to each individual moment, a "lasting sequence . . . of the greatest timeliness." All this talk of rooms relates to poetic activity, as evidenced in the second passage cited here. The words and sentences formed from the "bare room" are "dry and clear, as though made of wood." We have moved out of the verse-poetry stanza to the spare, although still boxed, lines of prose. Significantly, the room portrayed here contrasts with "outside reality." Even a long prose poem has constraints and is not coextensive with the world, regardless of its relative success in mimicking life's way of happening.

The room images in "The System" spawn reflections on more subjects than writing poetry. A crucial passage involving a room occurs near the beginning of the poem, immediately following the introductory material and a description of falling in love:

> [G]lowing love . . . now indispensable as air is to living creatures. It filled up the whole universe, raising the temperature of all things. Not an atom but did not feel obscurely compelled to set out in search of a mate; not a living creature, no insect or rodent, that didn't feel the obscure twitchings of dormant love, that didn't ache to join in the universal hullabaloo that fell over the earth, roiling the clear waters of the reflective intellect, getting it into all kinds of messes that could have been avoided if only, as Pascal says, we had the sense to stay in our room, but the individual will condemns this notion and sallies forth full of *hubris*, bent on self-discovery in the guise of an attractive partner who is *the* heaven-sent one, the convex one with whom he has had the urge to mate all these seasons without having realized it. (56–57)

Pascal's room brings in suggestions of quietism and solipsism, temptations that the poem presents as real even as it attempts to work itself free of them. While it is probably no coincidence that Baudelaire and Ashbery both make use of the famous Pascal *pensée* in prose poems that are self-conscious about their form ("room" for "stanza" again: see the discussion of "La Solitude" in chapter 3), some lines near the end of Bishop's "Questions of Travel" are more immediately relevant for "The System":

> *Is it lack of imagination that makes us come*
> *to imagined places, not just stay at home?*
> *Or could Pascal have been not entirely right*
> *about just sitting quietly in one's room?*[65]

Bishop and Ashbery question the viability of Pascal's room while intimating some attraction for it. In "The System," leaving one's room may involve will and *hubris*, but may also be prompted by love. When the long sentence beginning "Not an atom" becomes run-on with the words "but the individual will condemns this notion," it is clear that the breathless and determined qualities of the prose suggest something about the experience it seeks to describe. The pun on breathlessness is submerged in the comparison of love to oxygen—"love is in the air," the thin air on mountaintops in "The New Spirit"—and there is a hint of coupling—Adam's mate and O_2—in all the poem's talk of atoms and molecules heating up.[66] In this context, "the convex one" looks forward to the reflections on the self and other, solipsism and love, and other dilemmas in "Self-Portrait in a Convex Mirror."[67]

The consistent block form and expository quality of the prose in "The System" make it relatively easy to map out the poem's surface argument and progression. The tidiness of this argument is more apparent than actual but nevertheless contrasts sharply to the uncertainties about form and direction in "The New Spirit." After the initial comments about the system breaking down and the lack of a need to set out (53–54), the narrator recounts a more or less personal history of emotional, religious, and philosophical development, sometimes set against the background of recent social history (62). Insofar as it is continuous, this recitation ends its first stage with a desire to avoid all self-centered approaches to one's relations to the world and a critique of those people who would lose the world "by skipping over the due process of elimination" (64), that is, those who would not go through the negative and dialectical process of questioning that the narrator is pursuing. The process of elimination then continues with a sermon-style review of the present situation ("On this Sunday"; 65–67), followed by discussions of the advantages and disadvantages of sensory perception and intellect (67–69), the "career notion" (69–70), the "life-as-ritual" concept (70–71), and frontal (71–73) and latent happiness (73–81)—where the latter turns out to be "a fleshed-out, realized version" of the former (81).[68] At the end of this series of discussions, the narrator struggles with conflicting desires "to act and remain at peace" (83) for a few pages, then speaks of a "new arrangement" (85) of desires and reality, tries to accept destiny without being fatalistic ("whatever was, is, and must be"; 85), and declares himself and the reader ready to set out from the beginning again (86). At this point we return to the poem's opening statement about the system breaking down: "And it was just here that philosophy broke down completely and was of no use. How to deal with the new situations that arise each day in bunches or clusters, and which resist categorization to the point where any rational attempt to deal with them is doomed from the start? And in particular how to deal with the one that faces you now, which has probably been with you always" (87). Problems involving selectivity and sensory experience resisting mental organization are not only still around, their reappearance seems inevitable. But now these issues seem secondary to those of love and communication.

It is hardly a surprise that love should be part of the subject matter of "The System," especially given its frequent appearance in "The New Spirit." The relative absence of the beloved in the thirty-page "history and analysis" section of "The System" is conspicuous, however. Love and hope for love may be the underlying motives for all the self-questioning as well as continuously present in recurrent conceits like "waiting for spring to arrive" and "the beautiful or mild day" (55, 63, 73, 75, 78). There is also at least one explicit reference to the imminence of love in the section on "latent happiness" (73). But the figure of the beloved does not really return until much later (94), when the poem speaks of a silence in which "he," the beloved, is waiting for the narrator, "you," to do or say something. In the meantime, much of the discussion has made reference to the dilemmas faced by the self—in particular, solipsism, as the room imagery sometimes suggests. It is significant that after all of the analysis and comments reiterating the breakdown of the new arrangement, the narrator exclaims: "How we move around in our little ventilated situation, how *roomy* it seems!" (88, my emphasis). Now the narrator gradually becomes aware of the eyes of the beloved fixed on him and accuses himself: "I know too that my solipsistic approach is totally wrong-headed and foolish" (94). By this stage the poem has cleared some space, and "there is air to breathe" (89): love is a real possibility again.

The return to the idea of the system breaking down thus parallels the narration of falling in love. It is even possible to reduce the remainder of the poem's plot to a kind of love story. As expectation builds, the narrator quickly reviews what has happened (90) and speaks of a choice that has to be made between moving and staying where one is (91). Desire or hope is being kept in check and yet reappears anyway, "for the reduced mode or scope must itself be nourished by a form of hope, or hope that doesn't take itself seriously" (90). The narrator then compares himself via a mock epic simile to a lost dog timidly approaching each passerby, only to upbraid himself for this "pitiable waif's stance" (91–92). Spring literally arrives at this moment—we are reminded of the poem's time of composition on pages 92 and 93—but turns out to be less impressive than the mild day in winter had seemed to promise. The "ominous hush" of the first day of spring threatens to become another dead-end, but as soon as the narrator contemplates the situation he starts to wonder whether the result, in spite of appearances, is in fact a positive development: "And who is to say whether or not this silence isn't the very one you requested so as to be able to speak? Perhaps it seems ominous only because it is concentrating so intensely on you and what you have to say" (93). Later this moment of silence is linked to a lull in conversation with the beloved in a room or a small restaurant (94–95, 97–

98, 101–02). The silence the narrator requested earlier was a productive but directionless absence of sound, vaguely connected with breathing, hence love: "Life became a pregnant silence, but it was understood that the silence was to lead nowhere. It became impossible to breathe easily in this constricted atmosphere" (63). Love and silence caused by love often trigger the negative and dialectical movement of the poem. It is shortly after the "Life became a pregnant silence" passage that the narrator remarks: "Gradually one grew less aware of the idea of not turning back imposed as a condition for progress."

As might be expected, "The System" continually postpones a declaration of love or break in the silence, even begins to muse on its postponements (98), and, as with the ending of "The New Spirit," the close of the poem seems initiated by rhetoric: after an interrupting voice ("You waited too long"; 99), the narrator picks up what he calls mislaid, as opposed to lost, threads, and the tone of the poem shifts.[69] Prose blocks begin with quasi-triumphant lines like "I know now that I am no longer waiting" (99) and "Today your wanderings have come full circle" (100). We are approaching a rhetorical climax. In a sense, the poem has been closing ever since the conclusion of the "history and analysis" section—silences, postponements, and reviews of what has transpired or been meditated upon notwithstanding. For a moment even the narrator's shifting uses of "I" and "you" collapse into the bold assertion that "We"—the poet and the beloved, the poet and the reader—"are alive and free" (102).

For about fourteen pages after he declares that his "ventilated situation" is "roomy" and that "there is air to breathe" (88–89), the narrator ponders old problems—fate, selectivity, solipsism—and arrives at new impasses that hint at some final overcoming. The rhetorical climax of "The System," comparable in intensity to the Tower of Babel passage in "The New Spirit," occurs near the poem's end:

> What place is there in the continuing story for all the adventures, the wayward pleasures, the medium-sized experiences that somehow don't fit in but which loom larger and more interesting as they begin to retreat into the past? There were so many things held back, kept back, because they didn't fit into the plot or because their tone wasn't in keeping with the whole. . . . The rejected chapters have taken over. For a long time it was as though only the most patient scholar or the recording angel himself would ever interest himself in them. Now it seems as though that angel had begun to dominate the whole story: he who was supposed only

to copy it all down has joined forces with the misshapen, misfit pieces that were never meant to go into it but at best to stay on the sidelines so as to point up how everything else belonged together, and the resulting mountain of data threatens us; one can almost hear the beginning of the lyric crash in which everything will be lost and pulverized, changed back into atoms ready to resume new combinations and shapes again, new wilder tendencies, as foreign to what we have carefully put in and kept out as a new chart of elements or another planet—unimaginable in a word. And would you believe that this word would possibly be our salvation? (103–4)

This passage depicts the breakdown of a system that has been sustaining the poet for some time now. The problem of selectivity has returned with a vengeance, as the "misfit pieces" of the narrative puzzle refuse to stay marginal. Chaos threatens in the form of a "mountain of data" not unlike the Tower of Babel. Oddly enough, however, the tone is hopeful: our inability to organize all the details of experience is potentially liberating.

Various narratives of "The System" come together at this moment. The mention of "atoms" and "elements" recalls passages such as the one where "Not an atom but did not feel obscurely compelled to set out in search of a mate." Falling in love, a sudden and unexpected event, foils completely any of the poem's progress toward self-sufficiency or holistic organization of experience. At the same time, what remains beyond our grasp or our ability to foresee, what is "unimaginable in a word," may provide us with something more important than what we are able to envision. From this perspective, the unimaginable saves us. But expressions such as "the word" and "lyric crash" point to other possibilities. The passage is ostensibly discussing an autobiographical variation on the problem of selectivity, what to do with the stories one has left out of one's story, yet the poetic and religious overtones of "the word" are difficult to ignore. The "atoms ready to resume new combinations and shapes again, new wilder tendencies" are the elements of a new poetry, appearing when the old lyric breaks down or is broken down on purpose. The allegory is self-referential: the new word or possible salvation of the poem is literally "unimaginable" but figuratively the poem's prose.

Although more obvious here given "lyric crash," connections between the form and argument of *Three Poems* have been present since the spatial illustrations of leaving out and inclusion on the first page of "The New Spirit." In the middle of "The System," the narrator expressed relief at finding prose more roomy than verse. At the end of "The System," the narrator describes himself walking out of another interior space, a movie theater, having yet again reached an impasse in his meditation: "And it is here that I am quite ready to admit that I am alone, that the film I have been watching all this time may be only a mirror, with all the characters including that of the old aunt played by me in different disguises. . . . I have been watching this film, therefore, and now I have seen enough; as I leave the theater I am surprised to find that it is still daylight outside (the darkness of the film as well as its specks of light were so intense); I am forced to squint; in this way I gradually get an idea of where I am."[70]

In this passage the narrator admits to himself that all of the action of the poem was, in a sense, a film in his head, and yet makes gestures toward a world outside. The movement is typical in a poem intent on incorporating new discourses into poetry and continuously swerving toward and away from self-referentiality. As with the close of "The New Spirit," one question that arises here is whether there is any progress in the poem's negative and dialectical process, and again the answer is that the poem provides figures and a rhetoric of forward movement but leaves open the question of argumentative progression. Instead of a static photograph (4, 15, 16, 29), "The System" gives us the metaphor of a motion picture, followed, literally and figuratively, by a fade-out. As "the memory of the film begins to fade," the narrator recognizes the necessity of "plunging into the middle of some other one," referring simultaneously to another movie, a new romantic relationship, and the next poem. Accommodations have been made with the past, room opens up, "and this incommensurably wide way leads to the pragmatic and kinetic future" (106).

• • •

As the brief coda to "The New Spirit" and "The System," "The Recital" generally gets short shrift from critics who discuss *Three Poems*. In the narrator's words near the opening of the poem, "The problem is that there is no new problem" (107). But if "The Recital" adds little to the arguments of the previous poems, reading for the argument, as before, needn't be more than a point of departure. For what it is worth, the poem's narrative or argument is fairly straightforward. Aware that dilemmas such as the reality of having to be selective versus the desire to "have it all" will inevitably recur, the narrator turns to the likely source of the problem, our ultimately childish impulses, asserting that "we ought to look into the nature of that childishness a little more, try to figure out where it came from and how, if at all, we can uproot it" (108). Most of the twelve-page finale to *Three Poems* is taken up with a discussion of the problems caused by the childishness of desire, a theme that had been alluded to earlier, in "The System": "Nor is today really any different: we are as childish as ever, it turns out, only perhaps a little better at disguising it, but we still want what we want when we want it and no power on earth is strong enough to deny it to us" (100). The "no power on earth" clause recalls passages in "The New Spirit" that discuss the pull of the moon and the narrator's alternate attractions to earthbound realism and heavenly idealism. The narrator of "The Recital" is similarly self-critical: "we are all like children sulking because they cannot have the moon" (108).

The terms of argument are familiar but with a difference. The discussion of the childish nature of desire leads the narrator into a quasi-autobiographical reflection on childhood, more specifically how an unhappy childhood lays the groundwork for adult relationships. Because we have learned to adjust our desires, our adult longing is for a "more down-to-earth Eden" (109). But problems remain. Our temporary truce with desire may even create new difficulties: "But as the days and years sped by it became apparent that the naming of all the new things we now possessed had become our chief occupation; that very little time for the mere tasting and having of them was left over" (109). Gradually we become Adam-like namers, a development that prompts the narrator to assert: "It becomes plain that we cannot interpret everything, we must be selective, and so the tale we are telling begins little by little to leave reality behind" (109). The necessity of selection returns once again, but there are hints that this situation is not merely a necessary evil. The expression "leave reality behind" is marvelously ambiguous. While it primarily means "depart from reality," it also takes on the sense of "leave traces of reality," as the poem later makes more explicit: "this time something real did seem to be left over" (117).

There are also formal differences between "The Recital" and the two other poems of *Three Poems*. The paragraphs of "The Recital" are in "standard prose": in contrast to the prose blocks of "The System," they are indented and there are no spaces between them. This prose is, needless to say, even further removed stylistically from the sometimes free-verse, sometimes fragmentary blocks of the first half of "The New Spirit." The paragraphs of "The Recital" rhetorically signal, and in part deliver, the straightforwardness of the poem's opening statements: "All right. The problem is that there is no new problem." The ruling pronoun, at least for the first nine pages of the poem, is the first person plural, a synthesis of the I-thou dialectic running through most of "The

New Spirit" and "The System." The narrator turns away from "we" and "us" at moments of impasse, just as in "The System" he would frequently turn to a outside scene: "You know now the sorrow of continually doing something that you cannot name, of producing automatically as an apple tree produces apples this thing there is no name for. And you continue to hum as you move forward, but your heart is pounding" (110). As Ashbery has suggested in an interview, some of the poignancy of this second-person aside relies on its self-reflexivity.[71] The desire to name something that cannot be named drives the poem forward, especially a poem that, among other things, describes its own process of becoming.

Immediately following the above aside, the poem returns to its opening concerns: "All right. Then this new problem is the same one, and that is the problem: that our apathy can always renew itself, drawing energy from the circumstances that fill our lives, but emotional happiness blooms only once, like an annual, leaving not even roots or foliage behind when its flower withers and dies" (110). Hints of either frustration or playful speculation creep into the narrator's latest attempt to name the problem. Perhaps because it is so concerned with naming, "The Recital" is especially rich in extended similes, as if the narrator were suggesting that he is only able to restate the problem in more expressive ways, not solve it definitively. The earlier comparison to an apple tree, with all of its lapsarian connotations, is an image of the poem, producing simile after simile out of some unspoken need forever on the verge of naming itself. The comparison of emotional happiness to an annual plant, like the simile of the sparrow flying near a cat on the next page, adds to the poem's sense that realization of desire is always a figure away. As the narrator once remarked of the system, "It was not a case of a spoiled child asking its mother for something for the nth time or of wishing on a star; it was a *new arrangement* that existed and was on the point of working" (85). In "The Recital," the narrator confronts his constant urge to use the phrase "It almost seems" (111).

The coda to *Three Poems* continues in this vein for a while, as the narrator keeps attempting to unburden himself of unrealistic desires and to state the result of his meditations and experiences. He eventually asserts that "any reckoning of the sum total of things we are is of course doomed to failure from the start" (113). What is more, he suspects that "no art, however gifted and well-intentioned, can supply what we were demanding of it" (113). Although these statements carry an air of authority, they do not conclude the poem. For the moment, they mark only another impasse that causes the poet to turn briefly away from his reflections: "The days fly by; they do not cease. By night the rain pelted the dark planet" (113). The poem's negative dialectic is still at work, as new questions arise ("Why, after all, were we not destroyed?"; 114) followed by new reassurances ("This single source of so much pleasure and pain is therefore a thing that one can never cease wondering upon"; 115), only to be followed by new questions ("What is it to you then?"; 115). "The Recital" slips out of the first-person plural for good by the bottom of page 115, temporarily settling on the second person before another series of questions and conclusions returns the narrator to his room, the poem's moment of composition, and the first-person singular: "As I thought about these things dusk began to invade my room" (116). The poem's end is near.

Examined in the context of *Three Poems*, the gestures toward review and summation in "The Recital" relate to rhetorical movements as far back as the close of "The New Spirit." The constant sense of imminence in the second half of that poem eventually led the narrator to a brief summary of his progression through stages of love (50) and a promise of a new journey (51). Then in "The System," the narrator stepped back to analyze what had brought him to his present state of affairs, as if to prepare himself for a conversation he nevertheless keeps postponing. Before "The System" could end, in fact, the narrator reviewed his thoughts and experiences on three separate occasions (90, 96, 101). By the opening of "The Recital," *Three Poems* is very much in the mode of "looking for its core," trying to gain some perspective on itself.

But it is one thing to evoke synthesis, another to deliver it. Like "The New Spirit" and "The System," "The Recital" provides figures of a kind of progress, as evidenced in such phrases as a "synthesis of very simple elements" (117) and "a single smooth anonymous matrix" (118). But the narrator assesses the forward movement of *Three Poems* more accurately when he writes a few pages earlier: "It always presents itself as the turning point, the bridge leading from prudence to 'a timorous capacity,' in Wordsworth's phrase, but the bridge is a Bridge of Sighs the next moment, leading back into the tired regions from whence it sprang" (115–16). "Timorous capacity," a phrase from the first book of *The Prelude*, describes Wordsworth's feelings about the pace and direction of his writing:

> Thus my days are past
> In contradiction; with no skill to part
> Vague longing, haply bred by want of power,
> From paramount impulse not to be withstood,

A timorous capacity from prudence,
From circumspection, infinite delay.[72]

While Ashbery's "timorous capacity" does not require a detailed knowledge of the original Wordsworth any more than his "Bridge of Sighs" requires Byron, the *Prelude* context of the phrase is apt. Wordsworth is searching for a subject for his long poem and is uncertain whether his delays come from timidity or prudence. Ashbery's long poem, or group of three long poems, also searches for its subject and discusses its own ambitions and doubts, tacking between opposing positions as it makes its way forward. The ebb and flow of *Three Poems* does result in some progress, if not argumentatively speaking then with regard to the atmosphere of possibility that the work leaves the narrator and reader—perhaps the more important sort of progress.

The final paragraphs of "The Recital" show that the narrator is aware that the synthesis of opposing elements "in a new and strong, as opposed to old and weak, relation to one another" could have been possible long ago, "in the earlier days of experimentation" (117). He speculates that gradual familiarity is an additional element necessary for the synthesis but discontinues this train of thought as he realizes that it is becoming harder to distinguish the new and old elements from each other. As the poem begins its fade-out, it comments on itself as a kind of performance complete with spectators: "The performance had ended, the audience streamed out; the applause still echoed in the empty hall" (118). This last image recalls the narrator's exit from the theater at the close of "The System." In both instances a whiff of expectation remains in the air. Given that "recital" refers simultaneously to a musical performance and the narration of the poem, in retrospect it seems as if the whole of *Three Poems* is the narrator's rehearsal for some real-life action. After all of the attempts at summation, reviews of what has happened, and figurative representations of dilemmas, the poem resists closure in closing: "But the idea of the spectacle as something to be acted out and absorbed still hung in the air long after the last spectator had gone home to sleep" (118). In a work filled with so many rhetorical postponements, it is telling that the passive formulation "to be acted out and absorbed" leaves room for more meditation before acting. With one last corrective "but," the poet urges the spectator-reader to allow time for everything to sink in.

Needless to say, the reader does need time to piece together what is going on in *Three Poems*. In tracing the different narratives of the poem, it is easy to forget the struggle with plain meaning Ashbery's work often demands. Even Harold Bloom has remarked: "At first reading of 'The New Spirit,' I felt considerable bafflement, not at the subject-matter . . . , but at the procedure, for it was difficult to see how Ashbery got from point to point, or even to determine if there were points."[73] Bloom immediately adds that "repeated reading uncovers a beautiful and simple design" in the poem, but the discrepancy between initial confusion and gradual familiarity is significant. In swerving back and forth between resistance to and desire for direction and self-definition, *Three Poems* encourages the sort of reading experience Bloom describes. The poem's allegories of meaning and confusion, of straightforward narrative and digression, and of fate and free will are furthermore played out on a formal level: the alternations between verse and prose in "The New Spirit" give way to the block prose of "The System," which in turn gives way to the indented paragraphs of "The Recital." But instead of confirming oppositions between the poetic and the prosaic, *Three Poems* ultimately suggests that prose has as many conventions and constraints as poetry.

Perhaps even more significantly, the poetry versus prose or meaning versus confusion allegory is a map of the poem's critical reception. *Three Poems* is unique among Ashbery's works in that it has been positively received both by critics who view Ashbery as a late romantic and by those who regard him as the paragon of postmodernity—roughly the supporters of the Harold Bloom and language-poet canons, respectively. Many poets and critics, without necessarily sharing Bloom's views on literary history, have a high regard for *Three Poems* and most of Ashbery's work outside of *The Tennis Court Oath*. In pointed contrast, as John Koethe has observed, "The more theoretically inclined poets who have responded to Ashbery's work tend to limit their enthusiasm to *The Tennis Court Oath* and *Three Poems*, often showing little interest in his later books and viewing Bloom's assimilation of his work to the main line of American poetry running through Whitman and Stevens less as a vindication of it than as an act of academic co-optation."[74] In other words, *Three Poems* owes its position among Ashbery's works in part to the different literary-historical frameworks to which it lends itself. It also owes some of its reputation to Ashbery's choice of prose. In 1972, a collection of long prose poems would have had an avant-garde aura it does not necessarily have today, for Ashbery's negative aim—to avoid "the poetic" in *Three Poems*—has since convinced more readers of the possibility of poetry in prose, so that now we can begin to think about prose poetry as a genre. Or a form rather, as my conclusion will argue.

Coda to Chapter 8: From Hollander to Hejinian

The reception of John Ashbery's work points to one of several false divides in contemporary American poetry, the division between "formal" and "experimental" poets. This divide is based on an essentializing logic, whether explicit or, more likely, implicit in evaluations: certain poetic features (such as rhyme and play with typography) signal one tendency or the other, for better or worse. Poetic form is the window to the soul of the poem, and that soul is either damned or saved by formal predestination. Without denying that formal features are important poetic signals or that some of the formal discrimination in contemporary poetry is based on personal allegiances and other factors that have little to do with poetic form, I would maintain that the division is worse than wrongly conceived: it actively hampers our understanding and enjoyment of all sorts of poetry. Examining two prose poems written in the wake of *Three Poems* can provide some perspective on the rhetoric of formalism and experimentalism, in part because prose poetry has itself been surrounded by a rhetoric of form, or lack of form, and experiment.

John Hollander's *In Place* (1978, as part of *In Time and Place* in 1986) and Lyn Hejinian's *My Life* (1980, in expanded form in 1987) might seem to have little in common other than prose poetry. After all, the poets' reputations precede them: Hollander has written many poems in meter and rhyme, has some fame for his shape poems, and has published *Rhyme's Reason*, a guide to verse; Hejinian sees herself as an heir to Stein, has tried to invent her own forms of composition in each of her books, and has been published by presses where many who have "join[ed] forces in the social, political, and aesthetic grouping of the 'Language' poets" have published their work.[75] The works themselves arguably further the impression of difference. In *In Time and Place*, the thirty prose poems of *In Place* appear after the thirty-five verse poems in *abba* quatrains of *In Time*, open and close with poems that reflect on form, and contain sentences that, whatever their complexity in thought and meaning, tend to follow each other rhetorically and logically.[76] With its title and format, *My Life* may suggest a "realist" narrative (one prose poem per year of life), but the text itself vigorously resists such a narrative, contains many sentences that do not follow each other either rhetorically or logically, and violates its own structural integrity in that Hejinian not only adds eight new sections in the expanded edition, corresponding to the eight years passed since completing the first version of the book, but also adds eight sentences to each of the original thirty-seven sections of thirty-seven sentences and mixes these sentences throughout each section. Given these considerations, contemporary critical rhetoric urges the label "formalist" for Hollander and "experimentalist" for Hejinian. But the labels are misleading, if not patently inaccurate, and perform a disservice to both poets.

As a first impulse, a critic skeptical of the formal-experimental distinction might point out how poets like Hollander and Hejinian are not diametrically opposed. *In Place* and *My Life* have striking similarities that could be placed alongside their differences. Taken as a whole, both volumes in which the prose poems appear obliquely suggest and resist biographical interpretations, and both sets or sections of prose poems obliquely imply a sequence. *In Place* and *My Life* furthermore point to artifice in all autobiographical writing: Hollander places a mock journal in prose, *In Between*, in between the verse poems of *In Time* and the prose poems of *In Place*; Hejinian often gestures toward specific events in her life while mixing their chronology, questioning their significance, and interrupting their narratives.

Perhaps most important, *In Place* and *My Life* both turn away from *Three Poems* as a model but in the process show some filiation to it. Unlike the long poems of *Three Poems*, the prose poems of *In Place* are relatively short and independent of each other, for all of the implied sequence. What is more, a few of them turn toward a French model, René Char's prose poetry, and most possess a single or double paragraph structure in which descriptions and brief narratives alternate throughout, though there is a slight tendency toward description in the one-paragraph poems and a tendency toward narrative or argument in the two-paragraph poems (where the second paragraph can function like a turn in a sonnet). All of these features may seem a far cry from the often misdirective yet rhetorically continuous prose of *Three Poems*. But *In Place* is as riddled with contrasting connectives as Ashbery's poetry: twenty-five of the thirty prose poems contain at least one "but" or "yet," and many depend on a structure of contrast even when the connectives are absent. The most Ashberian poems are the first and last poems of the sequence, "The Way We Walk Now" and "In Place of Place," texts that, among other things, reflect on writing poetry in prose. Hollander's poetry does not need Ashbery to be marked by the use of logical discourse and argumentative progression, but it is hard not to hear an Ashberian resonance in phrases like the following from "In Place of Place":

> First of all, the original enclosure within which was our everywhere: it became, when we had to leave it, nowhere that was or was not to be.

Well, then, To recapitulate: the earliest places are all taken away. . . .

So that everywhere we visited, every area wherein we may have been said to dwell, turned out in time to be bases we had to touch, acceptances. . . .

And, finally, there is something right about the vagrancy of the replacements. Nowhere can keep us for too long.

There must be some way of learning from this about the last replacement, which is not of picture for place nor of place for picture, which is not like filler . . . which is not, in fact, like anything occupying space at all.[77]

As in Ashbery, the rhetoric of argumentative progression is often marked by negative turnings and in some ways points more to a desire for resolution than the completion of a thought. "The Way We Walk Now" and "In Place of Place" were written after the other poems in *In Place*, but as frames they invite us to look for a sequence and to consider whether the other poems were consciously or unconsciously composed as alternatives to Ashbery's prose poetry.

The frequently paratactic sentences of *My Life* are even harder not to read as a self-conscious turn away from Ashbery's prose. The staccato effect of short sentences, isolated phrases, and a relative lack of subordinate clauses is especially apparent in the 1980 edition of *My Life*. In the opening section, "A pause, a rose, something on paper," for example, Hejinian writes:

The waves rolled over our stomachs, like spring rain over an orchard slope. Rubber bumpers on rubber cars. In every country is a word which attempts the sound of cats. "Everything is a question of sleep," says Cocteau, but he forgets the shark, which does not. Find a drawer that's not filled up.[78]

This effect, in part mimetic of how a child would process reality (or how an adult would remember childhood experiences), in part aimed at interrupting mimesis and realist narrative, is sometimes made more prominent with the addition of sentences in the 1987 edition, though Hejinian often makes her sentences or rhetorical train of thought more continuous. It is as if with time her need to resist a certain kind of sentence or trend toward narrative or argument diminishes or merges dialectically with its opposing trend. (The eight new sections are some of the longer sections in the book.) Hejinian rewrites the preceding passage as follows:

The waves rolled over our stomachs, like spring rain over an orchard slope. Rubber bumpers on rubber cars. The resistance on sleeping to being asleep. In every country is a word which attempts the sound of cats, to match an isolable portrait in the clouds to a din in the air. But the constant noise is not an omen of music to come. "Everything is a question of sleep," says Cocteau, but he forgets the shark, which does not. Anxiety is vigilant. Perhaps initially, even before one can talk, restlessness is already conventional, establishing the incoherent border which will later separate events from experience. Find a drawer that's not filled up.[79]

Although the addition of short phrases like "Anxiety is vigilant" may interrupt the flow of the passage, the passage seems if anything more rhetorically if not argumentatively continuous. "The resistance on sleeping to being asleep" reads as a difficult gloss on the lines before it and prefigures the comments on sleep that will follow. Hejinian "explains" why every country has a different word to mimic that sounds of cats ("to match an isolable portrait in the clouds to a din in the air"), then qualifies her explanation in the next phrase, "But the constant noise is not an omen of music to come." Though the exact sense of these lines is difficult to make out, the rhetorical gestures toward connection make themselves felt, and the long sentence beginning "Perhaps initially, even before one can talk" stands out not only because it seems stylistically and rhetorically appropriate in its context but also because it is semantically user-friendly: it reads as a retrospective comment on childhood restlessness. Like a synthesis brought about by a dialectical swerve away from an opposing train of thought, *My Life* arguably breaks away from the method of *Three Poems* only to join up with it later on.

However we frame comparisons between *In Place* and *My Life* or between both works and *Three Poems*, the question of formalism and experimentalism remains after the impulse to show that Hollander and Hejinian are not diametrically opposed passes. The poets may not be opposed per se, but the differences between them are nevertheless real. Here the skeptical critic might be tempted to turn the equation around: Hejinian is the formal poet because all of her books are obsessed with form; Hollander is the experimental poet in that his work shows a great deal of formal variety, as evidenced not only in the different sections of *In Time and Place*, but also in collections like *Powers of Thirteen*, where he constructs his own form (thirteen times thirteen poems of thirteen lines of thirteen syllables) as arbitrary or as motivated as the form of *My Life*. Reversing the formal-experimental equation shows how the terms that make up the equation depend on each other: both experimentalism and formalism ideally imply experimentation with forms. But still, it might be said, there are experiments and there are experiments, and there are forms and there are forms: perhaps it is a question of tameness and risk in formal experiment.

In exploring the rhetoric of formalism and experimentalism, one quickly reaches a point where the terms "formal" and "experimental" are more misleading than helpful, regardless of the differences between works like *In Place* and *My Life*. Whatever relative truth exists in the idea that one poet's work is more radically experimental than another's, when the poets in question are as concerned with poetic form and experimentation as Hollander and Hejinian clearly are, the two labels only impair understanding and open-mindedness. We need to be circumspect when arguing that a work or genre breaks with traditional form or lacks form: conventional forms have a way of reasserting themselves when we think we are rid of them, and sometimes working through conventions is the best way of working around those conventions that are in our way. As we all supposedly know by now, a poem cannot be judged by its cover, its extrinsic form, alone. The rhetoric of formalism and experimentalism shows that we may not have assimilated this idea, whatever lip service we pay to it.

With Hollander and Hejinian, at least, we can go a step further in deconstructing the opposition between formal and experimental poetry. If we read their prose poems with an eye to self-referential moments, we can test the degree to which they posit a dialectical view of form and experiment. It is easy to find such moments in Hollander's "The Way We Walk Now," because the poem asks to be read as an allegory about writing poetry in prose (in fact, it has been reprinted in Caws and Riffaterre's collection of essays on prose poetry, with the subtitle "A Theory of the Prose Poem"). The poem's title refers to the way in which poets now write poetry: they walk—that is, write—differently than they used to. Stately walks of yore have given way to dances, gallops, and roller-skating; we have moved outside of the "Great Palaces" with "interconnecting rooms": we no longer need even the room, or stanza, to write poetry. Still, the speaker remarks at the end of the poem's first paragraph, our current movement is "better for having started out in one of the great houses."[80] There is ideally some continuity between prose poetry and prior forms.

The allegory to this point is for formal experimentation with an awareness of tradition. The poem's second paragraph turns the argument up a dialectical notch: "But then it almost ceased to matter where we were." Having worked through tradition toward something new, there is no necessity for either a break from or a return to older forms, and the new way of walking generates its own forms. What is more, whatever nostalgia or "pathos" we have for the "old places" does not alter the fact that the distance "between us and the houses crammed full of chambers," the stanzaic poems, is "utter, like that between the starry heavens above and the text below us, on the opened page." Here the allegory refers as much to the "narrative" of *In Time and Place* as to writing prose poetry. The days of the quatrains of *In Time*, poems of personal loss addressed to people, in which the poet could "Bounce the black ball of [his] despair" off the "four walls" of his "narrow cell," have been replaced by prose poems of place.[81] The break is definitive; the season in hell, or the worst of it, is over. The utter distance between the stanzaic poems and these prose poems able to move all over the "opened page" suggests that prose poetry calls for a entirely new approach to writing. Such a perspective does not rule out the possibility that prose poetry has its own rules.

If Hollander's allegory moves from indoors to outdoors, from a form confined by the walls of the stanza to a form whose confines are of an entirely different sort, Hejinian's book begins by resisting traditional forms, such as the realist narrative, only to end like Ashbery's "New Spirit" by embracing a new form of realism. Self-referential moments can be found throughout *My Life*, but some of the most telling commentary on the poem occurs in the eight sections added to the 1987 edition. Up to this point, the whole effort of *My Life* has been mostly geared toward avoiding a teleological narrative of the self, a chronology of events that can be unproblematically documented by language (though Hejinian admits at one point that "Continuity, not so much of ideas as of assumptions, or attitudes" is "a style one simply can't break away from").[82] Even the text's periodic repetitions of the titles or quotations at the beginning of each section seem aimed toward resisting linear narrative. In the final eight sections, Hejinian appears to address issues of the poem more directly. In the section "Preliminaries consist of such eternity," she strikes a note of compromise: "Things are different but not separate, thoughts are discontinuous but not unmotivated (like a rose without pause)."[83] Events may not exist in a seamless narrative, but neither are they random. The parenthetical "like a rose without pause" gestures back to the opening section, "A pause, a rose, something on paper," as if to suggest that the events written about in her work are motivated, for all of their discontinuity, and may now be more continuous ("without pause"). A few sentences later, Hejinian writes: "Jameson speaks of a 'collective struggle to wrest a realm of Freedom from a realm of Necessity,' and I put pen to page scrupulously and write, 'I prefer the realm of Necessity.'"[84] Whatever the truth about causation, the speaker expresses a desire for determinism, a sentiment that, given the task *My Life* has set for itself, may be unexpected though not unmotivated.

While it may be an overstatement to say that *My Life* swings dialectically away from its initial position in the closing sections, it is hard to ignore the collective force of the self-referential statements calling for a kind of return to realism: "It is precisely a special way of writing that requires realism. This will keep me truthful and do me good."[85] It is also hard not to hear defensiveness in some comments:

> [T]hey accuse it of theory, they say it lacks feeling, where they want, instead, what they call "singing," i.e. contagion.

> "My client wants to know," said the public defender on behalf of Mr. S., who had been persistently whispering to him and passing him notes on scraps of paper, "what, in your opinion, is the meaning of the story of the Emperor's New Clothes."

> Night after night, in poetic society, line gathering and sentence harvesting. Of course I want things to be real!

> The story of the Emperor's New Clothes is about mass delusion and the power of advertising.

> Minute discriminations release poetic rather than cerebral effects.

> Realism, if it addresses the real, is inexhaustible.[86]

Perhaps worried about the reception of her poetry yet wanting to defend staunchly the intellectual element in her work, Hejinian expresses the desire for a poetry that addresses the real, meaning at the very least both the intellect and the senses. ("The page duplicates the head with genitals," Hejinian goes on to write.)[87] In general, the poet sees her work as a synthesis of various oppositions, including form and experiment. At one point she asserts, "Form, then be expressive," implying poetic form should come before subject matter, then quotes Zola in the wake of her comments on realism and "poets ranting": "We are experimental moralists showing by experiment in what fashion a passion behaves in a social milieu."[88] For Hejinian, form and experiment are intimately related. Through them, passion and, in general, poetic content come through the text.

Hollander's and Hejinian's prose poems may not share the same point of departure or converge dialectically toward the same goal, but they both play with oppositions in ways that explode some of the rhetoric surrounding them. It is probably no accident that the locus for this play with oppositions is prose poetry, whose very existence is predicated on overcoming the traditional opposition between poetry and prose. *In Time and Place* allegorizes the opposition by associating verse poems in rhyme and meter with the time element of poetry and poems in prose with the place or space element of poetry, only to suggest in the end that the distinction is relative and may be inadequate in some cases. The final poem of the collection, "In Place of Place," urges us to think of the dialectic as ongoing, even as it wonders about "the last replacement."[89] Hollander's allegory, as usual, exists on more than one level: the replacements or "places that follow" are, as he says, "themselves representations: of the lost places? Yes. Of people? Perhaps. Of ourselves? Usually." The poet is meditating on loss and elegy, among other things. It is only after going on for some time about what the "last replacement" is *not* that "In Place of Place" can conclude: "It is the replacement of space itself, of that space within which place has its being, with what will never again leave room." Leave room for what? Leave what room? The absence of space leaves no room for anything or room for nothing. But all the play on "room" in *In Time and Place* leaves the reader room to read a couple of puns into this last phrase, including the suggestion of a new kind of space beyond the verse-prose or stanza-paragraph opposition, a room that is not a room. Near the end of *My Life*, Hejinian similarly asserts, "A paragraph is a time and place."[90]

Like Hollander, Hejinian ends her collection of prose poems with reflections on mortality and filling space. Toward the close of "Skies are the terrains of this myopic," she writes, "The rejection of interruption—the only thing in its space at the time," recalling her own practice of interruption, rejecting it, and reestablishing the idea insofar as she must interrupt herself to make the point. At the end of "The world gives speech substance and mind (mile) stones," she gestures toward her new brand of realism, the space realism needs to accomplish its own ends, and the utopian quality of that space with an infinitive phrase: "To goggle at the blessed place that realism requires." The book then concludes with remarks about human fear of and the inability to comprehend mortality: "The fear of death is residue, its infinity overness, equivalence—an absolute. Reluctance such that it can't be filled." There may be events in life that cannot be filled in the space of the prose poem, perhaps even in the space of human thought.

In the interest of space if not thought, a gesture toward the variety of prose poetry in contemporary American literature has to suffice here. As Peter Johnson has remarked in a recent issue of *The Prose Poem*, we are arguably in the middle of a "prose-poem renaissance," of which the prose-poem journal itself is some proof.[91] Invoking Ashbery and the rhetoric of formalism and experimentalism should already suggest a wide range of practitioners, but the reader may be better off regarding this range as a small slice of poetry's pie or as only one way of slicing that pie. Some further range will be alluded to in passing when I discuss prose-poetry anthologies in the conclusion; here I want to stress how a false division of poets or kinds of poems—divides of this sort haunt the history of the prose poem—performs a major disservice to our understanding and evaluation of the poetry itself. Readers' opinions may vary regarding the function of literary criticism—whether it exists in the service of history, philosophy, or some other discipline or disciplines; whether, if it is its own discipline or has its own perspective among other disciplines, it exists mainly to elucidate texts or evaluate them; or whether its function is a combination of all or some of the above functions—but productive, if not clear, critical terms should be beyond methodological squabbles. Even if criticism is skeptically regarded as covert propaganda for ideological, aesthetic, or whatever ends, it helps to have some perspective on what is at stake. What is at stake in the formalist-experimentalist divide? Not much, from an informed theoretical perspective; perhaps a little bit of attention from the perspective of the poetry market; and maybe a great deal from a psychological or sociological point of view. This last story, interesting as it may be, would take us far away from prose poems.

Conclusion

All right. The problem is that there is no new problem. —John Ashbery, "The Recital"

What I really want to know is how this will affect me, make me better in the future? Maybe make me a better conversationalist? —John Ashbery, "The Ice Storm"

If criticism today urges opening with an apology for what could not be taken into consideration, it also recommends self-reflection when concluding, though of a different sort. Amid the summaries, the clarifications, and the tying together or unraveling of loose ends, some parting remarks on methodology are de rigueur, and a gesture at least should be made toward that sometimes refreshing, sometimes devastating question, "So what?" In the introduction I asserted that understanding prose poetry as a genre means exploring the interpretive consequences of what has been called the *poème en prose* or prose poem, as if it were a genre. At a minimum, more needs to be said about my emphasis on "interpretive consequences" and the skepticism lurking in the phrase "as if it were a genre." For reasons that will become clear in the telling, a brief look at French and Anglo-American anthologies of prose poetry provides a convenient way of exploring these and other issues that need to be addressed in conclusion.

The most striking fact about prose-poem anthologies in French is their scarcity. Suzanne Bernard lists only two anthologies in her encyclopedic study: Maurice Chapelan's *Anthologie du poème en prose* (1946, reprinted in 1959) and Guillaume and Silvaire's selection in the second volume of *Poésie vivante* (1954).[1] The latter is a small journal devoted to contemporary poets, the former an almost four hundred–page book covering more than a century of prose poetry and providing an introduction on the history and aesthetics of the *poème en prose*. Bernard's bibliography is comprehensive through the year of its publication (1959). Since then, only one book-length anthology has appeared in France, Luc Decaunes's *Le Poème en prose* (1984). Like Chapelan's anthology, *Le Poème en prose* includes work from as far back as the eighteenth century, though the cutoff dates on its title page are 1842—the publication of *Gaspard de la nuit*—and 1945. Decaunes's collection brings the number of French anthologies of the prose poem up to a total of three, a tiny number considering that the *poème en prose* became an accepted form early on in France and has played a significant role in that country's poetic tradition for the last 150 years.[2]

There is at least one other important anthology in French, only it will not turn up in card catalogs or database searches or even under "anthologies" in a bibliography as thorough as Bernard's. Towards the end of Huysmans's novel *À Rebours* (1884), the protagonist compiles a unique collection of prose poems:

> Des Esseintes reposa sur la table *L'Après-midi du faune* [*sic*], et il feuilleta une autre plaquette qu'il avait fait imprimer, à son usage, une anthologie du poème en prose, une petite chapelle, placée sous l'invocation de Baudelaire, et ouverte sur le parvis de ses poèmes.
>
> Cette anthologie comprenait un selectæ du *Gaspard de la nuit* de ce fantasque Aloysius Bertrand qui a transféré les procédés du Léonard dans la prose et peint, avec ses oxydes métalliques, des petits tableaux dont les vives couleurs chatoient, ainsi que celles des émaux lucides. Des Esseintes y avait joint *Le Vox populi*, de Villiers, une pièce superbement frappée dans un style d'or, à l'effigie de Leconte de Lisle et de Flaubert, et quelques extraits de ce délicat *Livre de Jade* dont l'exotique parfum de ginseng et de thé se mêle à l'odorante fraîcheur de l'eau qui babille sous un clair de lune, tout le long du livre.
>
> Mais, dans ce recueil, avaient été colligés, certains poèmes sauvés de revues mortes: *Le Démon de l'analogie, La Pipe, Le Pauvre Enfant pâle, Le Spectacle interrompu, Le Phénomène futur,* et surtout *Plaintes d'automne* [*sic*] et *Frisson d'hiver,* qui étaient les chefs-d'œuvre de Mallarmé et comptaient également parmi les chefs-d'œuvre du poème en prose, car ils unissaient une langue si magnifiquement ordonnée qu'elle berçait, par elle-même, ainsi qu'un mélancolique incantation, qu'une enivrante mélodie, à des pensées d'une suggestion irrésistible,

à des pulsations d'âme de sensitif dont les nerfs en émoi vibrent avec une acuité qui vous pénètre jusqu'au ravissment, jusqu'à la douleur. [Des Esseintes placed "The Afternoon of a Faun" back on the table and perused another booklet which he had had printed for his private use: an anthology of the prose poem, a little shrine whose patron saint was Baudelaire, and whose outer sanctuary opened onto that author's work.

The anthology included selections from the *Gaspard de la nuit* of Aloysius Bertrand, that poet of the fantastic who transferred Da Vinci's methods into prose by painting a series of small pictures with his metallic oxides—*tableaux* whose vivid colors shimmer like clear enamels. To these Des Esseintes had added Villiers's "Vox populi," a work superbly stamped in a gold style reminiscent of Leconte de Lisle and Flaubert, and some extracts from that delicate *Book of Jade*, whose exotic perfume of ginseng and tea blends with the fresh fragrance of water babbling in moonlight throughout the book.

But various poems saved from defunct journals had also been included in this collection: "The Imp of the Analogy," "The Pipe," "Poor Pale Child," "The Interrupted Spectacle," "The Future Phenomenon," and especially "Autumn Lament" and "Winter Shiver," Mallarmé's masterpieces, which were also among prose poetry's masterpieces. For they brought together a language so magnificently ordered that it lulled you through its own power like a melancholy incantation, an intoxicating melody, toward thoughts of an irresistible seduction, toward the pulsations of a sensitive soul whose quivering nerves vibrate with an acuteness which penetrates to the point of rapture, to the point of pain.][3]

As might be expected, Des Esseintes's anthology opens with Baudelaire and Bertrand, though the reversal of chronology indicates that Huysmans's path to the latter poet was through the former—a useful reminder of the prose poem's reception. The inclusion of Villiers de l'Isle-Adam's "Vox Populi," one of the shorter stories from *Contes cruels* (1883), and Judith Gautier's *Livre de Jade* (1867), a book of pseudotranslations from Chinese, might surprise some modern readers, as might the absence of Rimbaud and Lautréamont.[4] But Huysmans's novel is saturated with the aesthetic atmosphere of symbolism and decadence, and the important editions of *Illuminations* and *Les Chants du Maldoror* had not yet appeared at the time of the novel's composition. It is equally telling that Des Esseintes's highest praise of Mallarmé is reserved for the early nostalgia-haunted and lyrical prose poems, "Plainte d'automne" and "Frisson d'hiver." The deliberately prosaic style of a twentieth-century poet like Jacob, traced back to Baudelaire through Rimbaud, would not be an inevitable development from a fin de siècle perspective.

However tinged by the twilight colors of its age, Des Esseintes's aesthetic emphasizes brevity and intensity, two qualities that the later anthologies in French also champion. Decaunes is dogmatic about these traits, supporting his claims with references to Max Jacob's preface to *The Dice Cup* and a slogan, which in the fictional present of composing his introduction, he happens across in Chapelan's book: "I just opened up again Maurice Chapelan's beautiful *Anthologie du poème en prose*, published almost forty years ago now, and I find there, in three substantives, the very principals of the genre, outside of which there is hardly any health: BREVITY—INTENSITY—GRATUITOUSNESS."[5] While the brevity and intensity aesthetic informs Chapelan's commentary and selections, a search of his anthology will not turn up the "three substantives." They come from Suzanne Bernard: "[B]revity, intensity, [and] gratuitousness are not, as we have seen, possible elements of beauty for it [the prose poem], but really constitutive elements without which it does not exist."[6] Decaunes's misattribution is probably unintentional, a confusion between two critics he respects, but even or especially in this light, it shows how insistent he is about brevity and intensity. By including Bernard's gratuitousness and printing the three substantives in capitals, Decaunes also makes the revolutionary subtext (LIBERTY—EQUALITY—FRATERNITY) more explicit. Without this subtext, the third trait, gratuitousness, is almost literally gratuitous, though it does reinforce the notion of aesthetic autonomy. Decaunes, moreover, could have easily substituted related qualities for any of the three substantives without altering his general aesthetic—density for intensity, for example.[7] The ideal that emerges is similar to the American stereotype of the French *poème en prose* discussed in chapters 5 and 6: a short, intense, objectlike piece of prose.

The selections in the French anthologies tend to confirm Decaunes's aesthetic. Most of the prose poems in Chapelan's *Anthologie* are a page or less in length, though the book includes some longer works, such as Guérin's nine-page "Le Centaure," a seven-page selection from Ernest Renan's *Souvenirs d'enfance et de jeunesse*, and an eight-page extract from *Les Chants de Maldoror*. Chapelan also allows for the found prose poem, any prose text that elicits an intensity of response the reader associates with poetry: "Only the acquiescence of individual sensibility can provide proof of whether the prose poem is truly a poem: its poetic faculty does not exist in it, but in us."[8] This belief and Chapelan's practice of excerpting passages from longer works earn him a reproach from Decaunes: "I fear Maurice Chapelan has fallen into that confusion against which the author of *The Dice Cup* justly put us on our guard: POETIC PROSE IS NOT PROSE POETRY. . . . The fundamental law of the prose poem, which demands an autonomous object, a verbal body that is complete and closed off, is . . . not respected in these 'elegant extracts.'"[9] But Decaunes's criticisms of Chapelan's editorial methods in the end point to fundamental agreements on traits like intensity and brevity. The real difference between the two editors has to do with Decaunes's greater insistence on aligning editorial practice with theory: most of his selections take up less than a page, and none is more than two pages long. Des Esseintes's booklet and the Silvaire and Guillaume anthology also favor the short prose poem.

Whatever their degree of aesthetic consensus, the French anthologies map out histories of the prose poem that are (inevitably) partial, either because they do not seek to provide overarching narratives or the organization of any given history appears arbitrary when examined closely or compared with another. The Silvaire and Guillaume edition of *Poésie vivante* confines itself to contemporary poets and never claims to be broadly representative. Des Esseintes compiles his prose poems for private consumption, and though the fictional frame points to the anthology's public and published existence, it also marks the selections as representative of a period's aesthetic, not a genre's history. The Chapelan and Decaunes anthologies are more ambitious. Many of the same poets from the "first century" of prose poetry appear in these books, but the editors organize their selections differently. Chapelan divides the history of the prose poem into "L'âge classique" (The classical age) and "Le foisonnement contemporain" (The contemporary flowering), two periods of roughly fifty years each. The "classical" period stretches back to writers like Parny ("a sort of prefiguration") and Lammenais ("proposed *at first* to enchant the reader, but") and forward to Rimbaud, though the editor's introduction makes it clear that Bertrand and Baudelaire are the points of departure for this history.[10] As the word "foisonnement" indicates (with its overtones of "swarming" and "abundance"), the shape of Chapelan's contemporary period is not fixed but emerging: it stretches from Laurent Tailhade and Émile Verhaeren to Francis Ponge and beyond, including along the way the work of poets who consciously wrote *poèmes en prose*, like Stuart Merrill and Paul Claudel, as well as selections from Gide and Proust.

Decaunes subtly corrects Chapelan's history in *Le Poème en prose*. Instead of two divisions there are three: *Four Predecessors, The First Age*, and *The Second Age*.[11] In the *Four Predecessors*, Decaunes surgically removes poets like Parny from his history proper of the prose poem. The first age of this history then begins with Bertrand, but Lefèvre, Baudelaire's unacknowledged predecessor, is ceded first position in the collection by virtue of biographical chronology. In other words, the history traced is as Baudelairean in origin as Chapelan's or Des Esseintes's. Decaunes's "first age" is, however, longer than Chapelan's "classical age": it closes with Paul Claudel, Pierre Louÿs, and Alfred Jarry for no apparent reason other than the editor's desire to begin the "second age" with Max Jacob, "the uncontested master of the prose poem."[12] Decaunes's commentary and selections here suggest that the aesthetic of "brevity, intensity, and gratuitousness," for which Jacob is presented as the paragon, cracks a little under the pressure of absolute enforcement. Jacob wrote a variety of short and intense prose works, but Decaunes limits his selections to prose poems from *The Dice Cup*:

> I had first envisioned joining to the extracts of this masterpiece the disturbing text entitled "L'Amour du prochain" . . . which figures in the *Last Poems*, published in the wake of the poet's death. But this prose text makes use of emotional elements *which are exterior to it*; it alludes to circumstances and facts to which the reader must refer if he wants the poem to have a meaning, including a poetic meaning. Its lack makes the poem "gape" like an empty pocket. We touch on one of the fundamental laws of the prose poem here. That is why I did not retain this terrifying text in the end.[13]

This insistence on the "fundamental law" of gratuitousness goes far beyond anything Bernard intended in her tripartite formula. But Decaunes cannot entirely seal off Jacob's work from its historical circumstances and reception. Though he does not include "L'Amour du prochain" in his anthology, Decaunes lists the place and year of the poet's death as "the infirmary of the [concentration] camp of Drancy, 1944."[14] The events surrounding Jacob's death "gape" in part because the editor attempts to avoid mentioning them.

Faulting an anthology editor for omissions is as easy as faulting a translator for not equaling the original—and as potentially beside the point. The ways in which the editors organize their anthologies and explain their principles are much more revealing.[15] Des Esseintes, Chapelan, and Decaunes all place Baudelaire at the beginning of prose poetry's history, even or especially when precursors appear in their anthologies. Baudelaire is an organizational principle in virtually every narrative of prose poetry because he was responsible for giving "poème en prose" its modern generic sense, and yet, as I have argued, it is worth remembering that he was not alone in his efforts. Needless to say, my own argument reinforces the tendency to begin conceptually, if not literally, with Baudelaire, even when resisting the approach. The question mark I place after histories of prose poetry helps make them visible as narratives—competing interpretive frameworks rather than authoritative accounts—without necessarily canceling their perspectives. Such questioning also resists teleological thinking about the prose poem, whether in the form of aesthetic development toward a type ("the short and intense"; "the prosaic") or with regard to essences (the prose poem as inevitably subversive).

. . .

Viewed in retrospect, my skepticism and questioning arise in part from my comparative approach. The importance that comparison possesses for my argument can be illustrated via a survey of British and American anthologies of prose poetry and a discussion of how the French and Anglo-American traditions differ. Here is a list of British and American anthologies of the last hundred years, beginning with an 1890 collection discussed in chapter 5 and continuing through 1996:

> *Pastels in Prose*, trans. Stuart Merrill, ed. William Dean Howells (1890)
>
> *New Directions 14*, "A Little Anthology of The Poem in Prose," ed. Charles Henri Ford (1953)
>
> *A Prose Poem Anthology*, ed. Duane Ackerson (1970)
>
> *Pebble 11*, "Fifty-four prose poems," ed. Greg Kuzma and Duane Ackerson (1974)
>
> *The Prose Poem: An International Anthology*, ed. Michael Benedikt (1976)
>
> *Epiphanies: The Prose Poem Now*, ed. George Myers, Jr. (1987)
>
> *The Anatomy of Water: A Sampling of Contemporary American Prose Poetry*, ed. Steve Wilson (1992)
>
> *Models of the Universe*, ed. Stuart Friebert and David Young (1995)
>
> *A Curious Architecture*, ed. Rubert Loydell and David Miller (1996)
>
> *The Party Train: A Collection of North American Prose Poetry*, ed. Robert Alexander, Mark Vinz, and C. W. Truesdale (1996)

This list is conservative and among other things does not include a number of dissertations, many special issues of journals, and some limited-edition anthologies.[16] Even in its trimmed version, it is far longer than the most expansive list of French prose-poetry anthologies, a curious fact given the prose poem's general acceptance and importance in France and its historically marginal status in Britain and America. It also suggests periods of renewed interest in the prose poem, one in the late 1960s and early 1970s and then another in the mid 1980s and 1990s.[17]

Though a useful place to begin, a list of anthologies does not say much about their content, organization, or publishing context. The first anthology, *Pastels in Prose*, consists of translations from French and, like Des Esseintes's booklet, is marked by a fin de siècle aesthetic. Its editor, William Dean Howells, talks about how the prose poem's "wonderful refinement, which is almost fragility, is happily expressed in the notion of 'Pastels.' "[18] Charles Henri Ford's "Little Anthology" is the first anthology of the prose poem to include a wide range of poems composed in English, though it also includes many translations from French and languages as diverse as Arabic, German, and Chinese. Passages from Shakespeare and the Koran mingle with parables from Poe and Kafka and poems of Rimbaud and Aiken. Most twentieth-century and many nineteenth-century selections are surrealist—if not by dint of a conscious, or rather unconscious, aesthetic, then via general atmosphere—including Ashbery's "A Dream" and the French poems by Char, Colinet, and Gracq. As Parker Tyler explains in his introduction to the anthology, Ford's interest in the prose poem has everything to do with an interest in the unconscious. One of the anthology's assumptions is that prose is a freer form than verse and hence allows easier access to thoughts and emotions that lie below or on the other side of consciousness.[19] In explaining Ford's critical and aesthetic claims, Tyler distances himself somewhat from them, but both he and Ford consistently approach the prose poem as a poetic form, not a genre.[20]

As noted in chapter 5, all the English-language anthologies after Ford's are "of the prose poem" in the sense that the term "poem in prose" drops out of general use. It is tempting to view the shift in terminology as a shift to a new claim about generic status, but it is not as if the issue of genre was absent from *Pastels in Prose*, and the editors of and contributors to the later anthologies are as likely to call prose poetry a form as a genre without much concern for clear distinction. In a brief note in the back of the *Pebble* anthology, Donald Hall talks about prose poetry as a form; in his afterword to *A Curious Architecture*, David Miller favors genre; in *The Party Train*, Robert Alexander and C. W. Truesdale alternately refer to prose poetry as a form and a genre, as does Steve Wilson in *The Anatomy of Water*; and Michael Benedikt opens *The Prose Poem* by calling the prose poem a form but then defines it as a genre a few pages later.[21] The lack of consistent terminology is as much a sign of struggle against narrow definitions as an indication of uncertainty or casual usage, and the increasing appearance of the term "genre" in introductions and afterwords is arguably a result of recent editors' familiarity with the critical literature on prose poetry.[22] In other words, a discussion of prose poetry "as a genre" may be academic in more than one sense.

The British and American anthologies from the 1970s onward fall broadly into two types: polyglot and Anglophone. Benedikt's *The Prose Poem* is clearly one of the former and probably the most ambitious prose-poem anthology to date. In addition to its British and American sections, this six hundred–page collection includes translations of poems from a broad array of foreign languages, including French, German, Spanish, Portuguese, Swedish, Russian, and Japanese. The selections in Duane Ackerson's 1970 anthology are mostly French and American. *Models of the Universe* includes many American and French poets, as well as translations from Russian, German, Italian, Spanish, Greek, Swedish, and Hebrew. *Epiphanies* is American-centered but also contains a few prose poems from non-Americans with international reputations, such as Julio Cortázar and Czeslaw Milosz. The other English-language anthologies—the *Pebble* issue, *The Anatomy of Water*, *A Curious Architecture*, and *The Party Train*—are American, Anglo-American, or North American in their focus.

Whether focused on many languages or one, a driving impulse behind the British and American anthologies has been to reintroduce the prose poem to an English-speaking audience. Editors' comments range from bewilderment to outrage at the lack of attention the prose poem has received in the United Kingdom and the United States:

> The prose poem is an international form that has been explored by major poets abroad for almost two centuries. Although a well-known, even venerable genre world-wide, it is only recently that English-speaking poets, particularly Americans, have "discovered" the prose poem.
> *Michael Benedikt (1976)*

> It seems timely to anthologize prose poets. There is still a deficit of work in this area being published, and little in the way of any historical or literary overview or acceptance.
> *Rupert Loydell (1996)*

> Why this critical neglect—and even hostility—has occurred is a mystery to me.
> *C. W. Truesdale (1996)*

> To me the question is, Why all this critical brouhaha about the prose

poem now, at the end of the century—when I thought all these questions had been settled once and for all at the beginning of it?
Robert Alexander (1996)[23]

As the tones of these remarks indicate, even the recent surge of interest in the prose poem and all the new anthologies are not signs of wide acceptance. On the contrary: the impassioned pleas, the sensed need for anthologies, and the fact that all the recent collections come from small presses suggest that the prose poem has had limited critical and popular success.

Anthology editors offer a variety of reasons for the continuing lack of attention given to prose poetry. Two recent editors have argued that the prose poem is subversive:

> Most important for us to note, however, is that prose poetry was born in America as part of the underground. It was, and often still is, fiercely anti-establishment.
> *Steve Wilson (1992)*

> [W]hen poetry subverts even its own norms, its dependence on the line of verse for identity, it is probably at its most subversive, opening up possibilities that sound whimsical at the same time that they provoke anger and distrust. If anyone thought that all this had long since become non-controversial, they had only to follow the recent award of a Pulitzer Prize to a book of prose poems (by Charles Simic) and the protests by certain prosaic poets and stuffy reviewers.
> *David Young (1995)*[24]

The argument that prose poetry defies categorization is closely related to notions of its being subversive, for it implies that critics, magazine editors, publishers, and readers have had difficulty placing prose poems within some framework of poetry or prose literature.[25] Of course, neither of these arguments explains why French poets and readers have had fewer difficulties with the *poème en prose*. Benedikt claims that an isolationist strain, stemming from T. S. Eliot, "the virtual beginning . . . of the fundamentally English-based, anti-internationalist critical approach which dominated America until the early 1960's," is the fundamental source of resistance to the prose poem in the United States.[26] According to Alexander, "the answer lies somewhere in the dominance of free verse for the last seventy-five years or so. In essence, in America at any rate . . . , free verse has forced the prose poem . . . to the sidelines, has marginalized it as a genre."[27] As I argued in chapters 5 and 6, a reexamination of the comparison with the French tradition helps here. A lack of prestige figures among Anglophone prose poets and the existence of not only free verse but also forms like the modern long poem go a long way toward explaining why the prose poem was often not so much resisted as not seen as necessary—if seen at all—in Britain and America. These explanations beg some further questions—about the sort of resistance that a lack of interest or awareness may belie or concerning the lack of prestige figures in the first place—but they also make it clear that historical contingency plays an important role in the French and Anglophone responses to prose poetry.

In reintroducing the prose poem to their audiences, the British and American anthologies are more concerned than their French counterparts with clearing some space for contemporary prose poets. The strategy of early collections like Ford's "Little Anthology" and Ackerson's *A Prose Poem Anthology* is to mix English-language poems with translations of foreign texts.[28] Even Benedikt's *The Prose Poem* fits this model in the sense that the American and British sections come at the end of the volume and are dominated by contemporary writers—the oldest English-language poets are Kenneth Patchen and Karl Shapiro (both born after 1910). The *Pebble* anthology is devoted exclusively to contemporary poets, as are almost all anthologies from the 1980s and 1990s: *Epiphanies*, *The Anatomy of Water*, and *A Curious Architecture*. The clear exception to this trend is Friebert and Young's *Models of the Universe*, which "shows you the successes" in the history of the prose poem, with a "tilt, if any, toward the representation of the essential craziness and exuberant inventiveness . . . of the genre, from Bertrand on."[29] *The Party Train* provides a small section on precursor figures ("Pathfinders and Desperadoes"), but the collection's emphasis is on contemporary poets, especially in comparison to the historical mapping and selections in French anthologies like Decaunes's *Le Poème en prose* and Chapelan's *Anthologie du poème en prose*.[30]

Overtly or covertly plugging writers is, of course, one of the many time-honored uses of the anthology. As Decaunes's battle cry of brevity, intensity, gratuitousness suggests, the French anthologies are no more aesthetically neutral than the Anglophone collections. No anthology is or should be. But editorial approaches also point to ways in which anthologies construct literary histories within and across national literatures. Decaunes and Chapelan are able to talk about the *poème en prose* as a definable tradition and to provide historical narratives whose central figures match, whatever the differences in selection and organization. There is nothing approaching this kind of consensus among the English-language anthologies, though names like Stein,

Williams, Edson, and Bly recur fairly often in general discussions. British and American anthologies either define prose poetry in English in relation to a French or an international genre (Ford, Benedikt, Ackerson, Young), construct a native tradition (Alexander, Vinz, and Truesdale), or emphasize formal issues (most anthologies of contemporary poets). The French anthologies are better able to construct histories because the national tradition they represent has recognizable reference points—"poème en prose" coming into being as a simple abstraction with Baudelaire and the generation after him, obvious candidates for precursor figures to Baudelaire, and a line of highly regarded practitioners often in dialogue with their predecessors.

. . .

The ability to construct a history around an abstraction is perhaps a necessary condition for a genre, but it is by no means a sufficient one. It is more than possible to write histories and publish anthologies of the sonnet, for example, even though "sonnet" has arguably come to refer more to a form than a genre.[31] The small number of French prose-poem anthologies could thus indicate that the *poème en prose* has already "proved itself" regardless of whether it is or was a genre. Prose poems in fact appear frequently in general anthologies of French poetry, whereas they either are absent from or make only cameo appearances in comparable British and American collections.[32] Once the prose poem is widely accepted, each substantiation of it becomes literally a poem in prose. But if prose poetry remains marginal, as it has in America, "prose poem" is primarily a figure of speech. It would appear that prose poetry must hover somewhere between figure of speech and literal fact in order to become a genre.

Once again, "prose poetry as a genre" threatens to become an issue more of semantics than of interpretation. What is genre anyway, and why is it important? Some of the arguments of chapters 1 and 4, in particular the distinction between mode and genre, are of use here. Modal terms tend to be adjectival and generic terms substantive—"lyric" as opposed to "the lyric," for example—because, as Alastair Fowler explains, "Modes have always an incomplete repertoire, a selection only of the corresponding kind's features, and one from which overall external structure is absent."[33] My own position is that genre, too, always has an incomplete repertoire of features in the sense that a complete list of generic traits is at best an ideal, and even a list of operative traits, determined by the reading context, would be potentially expandable. If all this seems a bit abstract, it is because genre is an abstraction, an interpretive framework that reading presupposes—an invisible fence whose boundaries, however constantly redrawn, are never absent when we read. Whether or not prose poetry is a genre, it is a simple abstraction: once "prose poetry" comes into being as a term and an idea, it can begin to attract adherents and detractors, create histories and theories about itself, and spawn critical literature and anthologies regardless of whether the term refers to diverse material that cannot be reduced to a definition.

Throughout my discussion, I have stressed that genres are negatively defined: they take on their identities in relation to other genres. The generic features of the prose poem vary according to the historical and cultural milieu and even within more narrow literary contexts. Moreover, traits of a genre are not limited to formal or textual properties like meter, size, and subject matter but may include such apparently extrinsic constraints as publishing context and readership. Any generalizable aspect of reading is potentially a generic signal. Prose poetry may not be a genre—judged by its American readership, for example, its generic status is doubtful, in spite of the recent flurry of anthologies—but considering it from a generic perspective puts the interpretive consequences of genre into relief.[34] When considered as a genre, prose poetry forces one to pay greater attention to literary-historical context, including reception history, and makes this context more visible as an interpretive framework. Even if, in the end, the term "genre" falls away from a discussion of prose poetry, generic considerations never do.

The semantic issue now shifts to a new plane. Have I expanded the concept of genre so much that I have emptied it of explanatory power? If any generalizable aspect of reading can be a generic signal, my discussion virtually equates genre with interpretive framework, and "generic" becomes less and less the adjective of genre as it is pulled toward its everyday meaning, "descriptive of a type." Something like a truism results: generic signals are generic aspects of reading. To understand why genre does not collapse completely into some catch-all category requires a turn to the critical context of my project. In concentrating on genre and, in general, "invisible fences," I am countering approaches that see prose poetry as necessarily subversive, constraintless, open-ended, postmodern. Within the current debates about prose poetry, my emphasis is meant to provide a corrective force, a sharpening of focus through negative differentiation, not (or not simply) a refutation of opposing critical viewpoints but a dialectical swing away from them. "Genre" is thus not entirely synonymous with "interpretive framework": it is a way of pointing toward a process of reading informed by, among other things, literary-historical and formal considerations.

But genre does more than indicate the general tenor and direction of my argument: it represents a response both to the interpretive challenges raised by my subject matter and to what I perceive as a missing element in the theory and practice of literary criticism that, like my own, seeks to go beyond traditional notions of formalism. As I wrote in chapter 3, *poème en prose* has the notion of differentiation built into its generic label. Even to begin interpreting prose poems requires a familiarity with neighboring forms and genres. If I have expanded the concept of genre in exploring its significance for prose poetry, the concept still remains bound to the central point of departure for my ideas about genre: negative differentiation. In practice, this means that generic concerns are bound by literary-historical context, especially literary, linguistic, and reception history. Genre forces an engagement with literary history, not a retreat into cataloging formal feature. And in linking issues of literary form to literary history, genre allows for meaningful connections to cultural—or historical, or whatever—concerns that literature is informed by and informs.

The trajectory of my chapters runs from negative differentiation to negative dialectics. The introduction displaced the search for a definition of prose poetry in favor of generic considerations and their interpretive consequences. Genre theory and literary-historical context followed, interspersed with many brief and a few extended readings of prose poems. Within the context of the general argument, my readings of "La Solitude," the modernist poems, and *Three Poems* provide a gloss on "exploring the interpretive consequences" of prose poetry as a genre. In "La Solitude," the poem's negative differentiation on the level of genre parallels the poet's struggle to distinguish his voice among a multitude of voices—city crowds, poetic predecessors, the contemporary literary market. Ashbery's prose poem, which in part sets out to avoid "a posture, a certain rhetorical tone" of the *poème en prose*, draws on meditational prose and the modern long poem for much of its generic form and incorporates throughout a wide variety of prose discourses. *Three Poems*, moreover, proceeds rhetorically if not argumentatively by a negative dialectic, revealing philosophical, amatory, and other concerns through its narrative misdirections and redirections.

The conceptual movement "outward" to an abstraction like genre or to literary-historical context is as inevitable as the movement "back toward" a particular poem, which in turn necessitates further searches for interpretive frames and returns to the poem. This systole-diastole motion, played out in the conceptual movement between literary theory and literary history on the one hand and both of these and readings of individual works on the other, is, of course, a general interpretive pattern—the hermeneutic circle. The version of the hermeneutic circle outlined by my chapters is dynamic in that the interpretive framework can shift rapidly like the tone of an Ashbery sentence but also retains focus via inevitable returns to individual poems and concerns like genre. As with the narrative of *Three Poems*, initial questions and points of concentration help explain the path the argument takes, whatever detours result from discoveries and impasses.

My general model of reading may also help explain why the desire for a definition of prose poetry returns regardless of whether the definition is necessary or important for interpretation. To begin any discussion presupposes some agreement on subject matter. Arguably a vague, almost tautological notion suffices, such as "some species of poetry" or "poetry written in prose" for a discussion of prose poetry. This initial notion will not be arbitrary in that it will take its cue from the history of the term or subject matter in question. To continue discussion may require more precision, but how much or in what sense depends on our aims. I have opted for negative definition, arguing that literary-historical context is important for interpreting prose poetry. The process of negative definition, however thorough, creates a desire for a more complete definition because it is inevitably open-ended yet organized around an abstraction. This desire for a more comprehensive framework may be what drives all interpretation forward—we feel the need to place what we are reading in some context—but the resulting framework depends a lot on the sort of questions we seek to answer in the first place and may not have anything to do with comprehensiveness. The process of interpreting creates some of the desire for itself.

Whether my ideas about genre overemphasize interpretation is a matter the reader must decide. After all, genre has functions that are not easily accommodated by the label "interpretive": it draws attention to certain works, potentially at the expense of others, and it has a classificatory dimension even if, as I argue, it primarily helps guide interpretation. The reader must also decide whether my initial "vague notion" of prose poetry is an adequate point of departure and whether the ways in which I flesh out this notion in the course of my discussion are compelling. Even granting my method of negative differentiation, the reader may feel my arguments converge too obliquely on what is or is not prose poetry or how considering a work a prose poem affects how we read it (just as there are many methods of calculating the value of pi, but some converge so slowly they are at first less accurate than commonplace approximations). The reader should also interrogate my notion of "operative" contexts or traits, because the notion that negative differentiation pinpoints the generic traits most important for interpretation still leaves open the question of deciding what the neighboring genres are, leading us back to literary history and also inevitably back to some decision-making that cannot be derived from the theory governing the general method of inquiry. Interpretation is ultimately a rhetorical act: making my case is as much convincing the reader that a certain set of questions is important as answering them.

My model of reading can be concretely expressed via an image from *Cyrano de Bergerac*. In a scene near the end of the play's third act, Cyrano is trying to prevent the count De Guiche from discovering and breaking up the marriage of Roxane and Christian. In order to prevent De Guiche from interrupting the ceremony, Cyrano pretends he has just fallen from the moon and goes on to boast that he has invented six ways to travel through space. To De Guiche's increasing astonishment, Cyrano explains each of his methods. The count has just yelled out "Five!" in acknowledgment of the fifth explanation when Cyrano exclaims:

> Lastly, lie down on an iron board or chair,
> Take a strong magnet, and throw it in the air!
> Now that's a fine method: for the iron will pursue
> The magnet upward as it hurtles toward the blue.
> Then throw the magnet up again, and abracadabrix!
> You can ascend indefinitely thus.

Which "makes six," as De Guiche replies, "Six excellent methods." The reader is like this moon voyager lying on an iron board and continually throwing a magnet upward, catching it, and throwing it up again. The interpretive frameworks we project from a work in our attempt to understand it are continually threatening to collapse, so we adjust our frames of reference, continue onward, then adjust our perspectives again. We are searching for some ultimate interpretive framework (asking for the moon, as it were), but do we ever get there? What is the theoretical ground for this process? Meanwhile, something like reading occurs.

Notes

1. Origins of the Prose Poem

1. All translations are mine unless otherwise noted. When the original, foreign-language text is a poem or a work I discuss in some detail, I include the original version and a translation in the text. For other foreign-language texts, I provide a translation without the original for works that are relatively available and otherwise include the original in a footnote. Left out of these considerations are epigraphs like the one for this chapter, which are not accompanied by the original texts.

2. Bernard, *Le Poème en prose*, 22. Bernard traces the term back to a remark the abbé du Bos made in 1700: "ces poèmes en prose que nous appelons Romans" (these prose poems that we call *Novels*). In *La Tradition française*, Pierre Moreau quotes the same phrase as coming from a letter of Boileau to Charles Perrault (3). Moreau also quotes a 1688 use of "poème en prose" and a 1663 example of "poète en prose."

3. Cervantes, *Don Quixote*, 479.

4. See, for example, the *Poetics*, section 1447b. There are also several passages in the *Rhetoric* that suggest something like poetry in prose, and Quintilian's *carmen solutum* ("loosed poem") is of some interest in this matter (*Institutiones Oratoriae*, Book 10, section 1).

5. For the eighteenth-century usage of "poème en prose" as primarily figurative, see Bernard, *Le Poème en prose*, 22–23.

6. See Watt, *Rise of the Novel*, 52.

7. Terdiman, *Discourse/Counterdiscourse*. Terdiman makes this point clear by quoting a November 1882 letter from Huysmans to Flaubert that indicates that the prose poem, more than poetry in general, was a terrifying notion to the average bourgeois (272).

8. From the preface to *Lyrical Ballads* (Wordsworth, *Selected Poems*, 451).

9. Abrams, *Mirror and the Lamp*, especially chapters 4, 8, and 11.

10. Clayton, *Prose Poem in French Literature*, 151.

11. See Bernard, *Le Poème en Prose*, 25, and Clayton, *Prose Poem in French Literature*, especially 75. See also Tieghem, *Ossian en France*. The emphasis on the primitive receives a classic expression in Schiller's notion of "naïve" poetry.

12. See Tieghem, *Le Préromantisme*.

13. Clayton, *Prose Poem in French Literature*, 75.

14. Lyons, "Les best-sellers."

15. "Béni soit le Dieu d'Israël! si sa colère est terrible au méchant endurci, sa miséricorde est infinie pour le pécheur repentant. Humilions nos fronts devant lui, et il tournera son visage vers nous; pleurons sur nos péchés, et il nous en lavera; demandons grace, et nous l'obtiendrons: pour tous les bienfaits qu'il nous prodigue, il ne demande que notre amour, et n'est-ce pas un bienfait de plus?" Cottin, "La Prise de Jéricho," 1:55.

16. See, for example, Louis Sébastien Mercier's "Hymne au printemps" (1784), a five-page work that Vista Clayton (81) argues may be a response to Reyrac's forty-page *Hymne au soleil*.

17. "On trouvera dans le premier volume [des *Mélanges de littérature*] un petit poëme en prose, intitulé: *La Prise de Jéricho*, écrit par madame Cottin, auteur de *Claire d'Albe, de Malvina et d'Amélie Mansfield*. Le succès général et mérité qu'ont obtenu ces trois romans, rendrait ici superflu l'éloge de l'auteur. J'oserai dire cependant que la lecture de *La Prise de Jéricho* peut ajouter encore à l'opinion qu'on a dû concevoir de son rare talent. Au mérite d'une action intéressante, de la peinture fidèle et animée des sentimens et des mœurs, ce poëme en réunit un autre, qui suppose beaucoup de goût, c'est celui d'avoir imité avec vérité, mais sans aucune exagération, le style figuré qu'on appelle oriental, et qui caractérise les écrits qui nous restent du peuple juif" (Suard, in Cottin, *Mélanges*, ix–x). I am indebted to Leah Price for the reference to "petit poëme en prose" in the 1824 edition of Cottin's works that led me to this 1803 reference.

18. "Dans l'espace de huit ans, madame Cottin a publié cinq romans. *La Prise de Jéricho*, qui parut en 1802 [*sic*], dans les *Mélanges de Littérature* de M. Suard, doit être considérée comme le premier ouvrage de cette femme célèbre, quoique nous ne sachions pas précisément à quelle époque il fut composé. C'est un petit poëme en prose, que se distingue par le style et par les détails, mais dont le plan est faiblement tracé, et dont les situations principales manquent de vraisemblance. C'était sans doute une de ces ébauches que faisait madame Cottin dans le mystère, avant que ses amis lui eussent révélé à elle-même son génie, et à laquelle elle avait mis plus tard la dernière main. "Au mérite d'une action intéressante, dit M. Suard, de la peinture fidèle et animée des sentimens et des mœurs, ce poëme en réunit un autre, qui suppose beaucoup de goût, c'est celui d'avoir imité avec vérité, mais sans aucune exagération, le style figuré qu'on appelle oriental, et qui caractérise les écrits qui nous restent du peuple juif." Le tort de l'auteur est d'avoir introduit l'amour dans un sujet qui ne pouvait en comporter, ni par la durée prescrite de l'action, ni par la position et le caractère des personnages." Cottin, *Œuvres completes*, 41–42.

19. See Max Millner's introduction to his edition of Bertrand's *Gaspard de la nuit*.

20. Bernard, *Le Poème en prose*, 777. *Télémaque* continued to be a best-seller into the early 1850s. See Lyons, "Les Best-sellers," 379.

21. For the popularity of Cottin's works see Lyons "Les Best-sellers," 373–77. There was at least one eighteenth-century work referred to by its author as a "petit poème en prose." Rousseau called his *Chants des Lévites d'Ephraïm* "une manière de petit poème en prose" (a kind of small prose poem). See Michel Sandras, *Lire le poème en prose*, 50.

22. The use of the *tréma* in the word "poëme" became archaic during the course of the nineteenth century, though it still had some currency in the 1850s and 1860s. See Robert and Rey, *Le Grand Robert*, 523. Baudelaire himself varied his spellings of "poète" and "poème," but, as Claude Pichois notes with regard to the poet's correspondence, the phrase "[petits] poëmes en prose" is almost always written with the *tréma*. See Baudelaire, *Correspondance* [hereafter *Cor*], 1:xx n.1. In a note on the title *Petits Poëmes en prose* (Baudelaire, *Œvres complètes* [hereafter *oc*], 1:1294), Pichois suggests that Baudelaire may have been contrasting his poems to the relatively large philosophical work of Poe, *Eureka*, which bears the subtitle "Poem in Prose." The Pléiade edition of Baudelaire consistently modernizes the spelling of "poëme" to "poème" except in the two-page explanation of the variant titles of the *Petits Poëmes en prose* (Baudelaire, *oc*, 1:1298–99).

23. In *The Prose Poem as a Genre in Nineteenth-Century European Literature*, John Simon discusses why the *poème en prose* attracted only minor romantic poets before Baudelaire (149).

24. See Kittay and Godzich, *Emergence of Prose*.

25. Clayton, *Prose Poem in French Literature*, 6–7. Dacier argued that prose renders the original's beauty more faithfully than verse. Similar defenses appear in Trocheau's preface to his translations of various English poems (1749).

26. Clayton, *Prose Poem in French Literature*, 7. The first translations of Ossian were published in fragmentary form and thus appeared more like lyrics than epics in prose. Though it became more common to translate verse into prose during the course of the eighteenth century, there were also instances in which the English prose of Macpherson's Ossian was translated into French alexandrine couplets.

27. Bernard, *Le Poème en prose*, 37–38.

28. Hass, *Essay*. For Hass's mention of the dialogic, see 49; for open-endedness, see 51; for inner freedom of form, see 55. Jonathan Monroe, Richard Terdiman, and, to a lesser extent, Margueritte Murphy make use of Bakhtin in their analyses of the prose poem. A good summary of the claims critics make regarding the novel's form is given by Michael McKeon in *The Origins of the English Novel*: "Many critics have been sensitive to the unique status of the novel as the *modern* genre, the newcomer that arrives upon a scene already articulated into conventional generic categories and that proceeds to cannibalize and incorporate bits of other forms—the traditional and canonic genres as well as aberrant, 'nonliterary' writings—in order to compose its own conventionality. To some it has seemed that these conventions of origin may even render problematic the status of the novel *as* a genre. Indeed, this sense of the novel's

lack of 'internal' rules, its resistance to the authority of traditional convention, its self-creation through the negation of other forms—these apprehensions of the novel's generic incoherence are easily assimilable to the archetypolist view of the novel as a deterioration or a displacement of essential form and structure" (11).

29. McKeon, *Origins*, 163.

30. McKeon, *Origins*, 164.

31. McKeon, *Origins*, 19.

32. As McKeon puts it: "Genres provide a conceptual framework for the mediation (if not the 'solution') of intractable problems, a method for rendering such problems intelligible. . . . Genres fill a need for which no adequate alternative method exists. And when they change, it is also as part of a change both in the need they exist to fill and in the means that exist for its fulfillment" (*Origins*, 20).

33. Jameson, *Political Unconscious*, 106. See also Cohen, "History and Genre," 208.

34. I would direct the reader unfamiliar with genre criticism not only to Fowler's book but also to such works as Paul Hernadi's *Beyond Genre*, Joseph P. Strelka's collection of essays *Theories of Literary Genre*, Heather Dubrow's *Genre*, Adena Rosmarin's *The Power of Genre*, André Lefevre's "Systems in Evolution," Ralph Cohen's "History and Genre," Mary Gerhart's *Genre Choices, Gender Questions*, and Thomas O. Beebee's *The Ideology of Genre*, which contain useful summaries of various critical perspectives and outline some of the general issues. David Fishelov's *Metaphors of Genre* also provides a useful perspective on the field by exploring the "role of analogies" in genre theory.

35. Fowler, *Kinds of Literature*, 38.

36. Fowler compares genre theory to linguistics only to reject the analogy as limited due to the "extended repertoire of forms" that a literary kind possesses (*Kinds of Literature*, 20–21, 49). Here my disagreement with Fowler may be more a question of emphasis than substance: Fowler either assumes a narrow definition of grammar or is overly concerned with disassociating his thought from structuralism.

37. Fowler, *Kinds of Literature*, 28.

38. Fowler, *Kinds of Literature*, 45.

39. What I have to say about the undesirability of algorithmic definitions is similar to what Fowler says about "recursive functions" (*Kinds of Literature*, 46–47) and generic labels (especially 147–48).

40. Fowler, *Kinds of Literature*, 16.

41. Fowler, *Kinds of Literature*, 41. For family resemblance, see 40–44. The critics Fowler cites are Robert Elliott, Maurice Mandelbaum, and Graham Hough.

42. Fowler, *Kinds of Literature*, 41–42. For an additional qualification to theories of "family resemblance," see Fowler's note 17 on page 288 and chapter 3 of Fishelov's *Metaphors of Genre*.

43. Fowler, *Kinds of Literature*, 43.

44. Fowler, *Kinds of Literature*, 49.

45. Fowler, *Kinds of Literature*, 106–7.

46. Fowler, *Kinds of Literature*, 112.

47. See Fowler, *Kinds of Literature*, 113.

48. Fowler occasionally hints at a negatively defined notion of genre in *Kinds of Literature*. See his treatment of counterstatement (and in particular "antigenre") in the chapter on transformations of genre (especially 174–79). His discussion of "antinovel" is especially relevant for prose poetry. But here, as elsewhere, Fowler treats negative definition as a special case, whereas I see it as fundamental to an understanding of what constitutes genre.

49. Fowler, *Kinds of Literature*, 108.

50. Rosmarin, *Power of Genre*, 21. Rosmarin draws on philosopher Hans Vaihinger and art critic E. H. Gombrich.

51. Rosmarin, *Power of Genre*, 20–22. As Rosmarin points out, the terminology of error can be misleading: she prefers to speak of difference seeking similitude (44–45). One might also say one is always "in error" or "in the process of correction" (where the process is open-ended) or "in the process of interpretation" (where the ideas of mistakenness and correctness are deferred).

52. The hermeneutic circle has its roots in Hans-Georg Gadamer's *Truth and Method*. Rosmarin draws on E. D. Hirsch's *Validity in Interpretation* to discuss its ramifications for genre but also mentions that Karl Viëtor and René Wellek have treated genre as "a special case of the hermeneutic circle" (*Power of Genre*, 27).

53. Rosmarin, *Power of Genre*, 40.

54. Rosmarin, *Power of Genre*, 42–43.

55. Cohen, "History and Genre," 217.

56. Cohen, "History and Genre," 204. Cohen is discussing Foucault's *Archaeology of Knowledge* and Derrida's "Law of Genre."

57. From Derrida's "Law of Genre"; qtd. in Cohen, "History and Genre," 205.

58. Cohen, "History and Genre," 205.

59. Cohen, "History and Genre," 207.

60. At least one critic, Thomas O. Beebee, stresses the importance of negative differentiation: "I argue that, since a 'single' genre is only recognizable as difference, as a foregrounding against the background of its neighboring genres, every work involves more than one genre, even if only implicitly" (*Ideology of Genre*, 28, see also 257).

61. Cohen, "History and Genre," 210.

62. Cohen, "History and Genre," 210.

63. Cohen, "History and Genre," 211.

64. Cohen, "History and Genre," 213.

65. Cohen, "Reply," 229.

66. Fishelov, *Metaphors of Genre*, 12.

67. Fishelov, *Metaphors of Genre*, 27, 26.

68. In a note, Fishelov gives the page reference to the relevant section in *Kinds of Literature* (149–90), but his objections are directed at Fowler's article (*Metaphors of Genre*, 25).

69. Fishelov, *Metaphors of Genre*, 8.

70. Fishelov, *Metaphors of Genre*, 6–8, 49.

71. Fishelov, *Metaphors of Genre*, 60. Chevalley's "une fiction en prose d'une certaine étendue" is quoted by E. M. Forster in *Aspects of the Novel*.

72. Fishelov, *Metaphors of Genre*, 60–61.

73. Fishelov, *Metaphors of Genre*, 61.

74. "Still, Jameson's argument that g[enre] theory has been discredited by modern thinking about lit[erature] seems now largely convincing" (Preminger and Brogan, *New Princeton Encyclopedia*, 458).

75. My brief overview of genre criticism has itself been selective. In particular, I do not do justice to Fishelov's insightful discussions of the four common analogies of genre: his many observations and suggestions would almost have to be taken up individually. Other "post-Fowler" critics of genre include: Paul Alpers, Earl Miner, Jean-Marie Schaeffer, Fowler himself, Mary Gerhart, and Thomas O. Beebee. In *What is Pastoral?* Alpers reworks Fowler's concept of mode, claiming that the latter's insistence that modes are historical phenomena "leads to his undue emphasis on the details of 'outer form,' at the expense of the feelings and attitudes that motivate them" (48). Alpers goes on to assert that mode is "the term that suggests the connection of 'inner' and 'outer' form" (49) and "the literary manifestation, in a given work, . . . of its assumptions about man's nature and situation" (50). Alpers's view of mode makes use of Kenneth Burke's notion of the "representative anecdote," which, Alpers suggests, may have advantages over terms like "paradigm" (13). Miner and Schaeffer are both interested in the insights comparative studies bring to genre. In *Comparative Poetics* and "Some Issues of Literary 'Species, or Distinct Kind,'" Miner draws on his knowledge of Japanese and other non-Western literatures to extend some of Fowler's insights and reconceptualize others. In spite of the promise of this approach, Miner disappointingly falls back on the tripartite division of genre into lyric, narrative, and dramatic (see Fowler, *Kinds of Literature*, 235–39). In "Literary Genres and Textual Genericity," Schaeffer divides genre theory into historicist and structuralist camps, apparently in an attempt to bridge the gap between them, though he himself is historically inclined and strongly antiessentialist. He points out that "generic terms are at least partially pragmatic; they do not solely describe literary phenomena, they also enter into their constitution" (178) and argues that "the study of relationships between texts and genres must be preceded by the study of relationships between texts and genre names" (179). Fowler has published several genre-oriented pieces since *Kinds of Literature*, including "The Future of Genre Theory" (1989), in which he restates some of his earlier arguments but also suggests new "metaphors of organic energy" for genre

(301) and in general argues that the study of genre "offers a way round several of the issues that divide deconstructionists and traditionalists" (291). Gerhart must not have had access to this last article when she dubbed Fowler a traditionalist in "The Dilemma of the Text" (1989), but even so her characterization of Fowler as a traditionalist seems based on a highly misleading if not misinformed reading of *Kinds of Literature*: her only citation of "Alasdair [*sic*] Fowler" is a misquotation of a passage on the first page of his book (357). More important, her critique of the "traditionalist" position boils down to an "overemphasis on the uniqueness of the literary text" (359), a criticism that may fit Bernadetto Croce but not anyone interested in regenerating genre theory for use in interpretation. Gerhart's summaries of the "ideological" and "deconstructionist" views of genre—the other two of the "three major options" she finds in contemporary critical discourse—are more even-handed, though her claim that the ideological approach reverses the traditionalist trend toward uniqueness may be questioned insofar as such approaches often suspect that groupings of texts are no more than constructions (in this sense, she may have the impulses behind traditionalist and ideological approaches backward). Gerhart's expansion of her article in *Genre Choices, Gender Questions* (1992) maintains the same emphasis, including the misquotation from the first page of *Kinds of Literature*, only now the book is labeled "Alistair [*sic*] Fowler's introduction to genre theory" (104). As the title implies, *Genre Choices, Gender Questions* explores the relations between genre and gender. Thomas O. Beebee's *The Ideology of Genre* is more difficult to summarize succinctly. His general emphasis is similar to Fowler's in that he views genre as inescapably part of our reading experience. Beebee stresses, as I do, that genre is negatively defined or differentiated; drawing on D. S. Rosenberg, he locates "the ideological component in generic choice . . . not so much in the content of the genre, as in its opposing itself to other genres" (263). In short, "Genres must be defined recursively: genres are made out of other genres" (264).

The "pre-Fowler" critics of genre are too numerous to list, let alone discuss at any length. Among the better-known critics, one might mention Frye, Jameson, Derrida, and Foucault (all taken up earlier), and Benjamin, Bakhtin, Wellek, Guillén, Hernadi, Genette, Todorov, and Jauss. As I stated previously, I believe Fowler's book corrects, synthesizes, and extends most genre criticism that precedes *Kinds of Literature*. Bakhtin deserves special mention, if only because many prose-poetry critics have been drawn to his "dialogism" (see note 28). In my view prose poetry (or the novel, for that matter) is not inherently more dialogic than verse poetry, though it may be useful to speak of historical moments when certain genres drew on a relatively wide range of discourses. Left out of this summary is the entire German "morphological" approach that has its origins in Goethe's concept of "Naturformen." Morphological critics would include Karl Viëtor, Emil Staiger, Wolfgang Kayser, Käte Hamburger, and Walter Muschg; they attempt to connect genres with aspects of human experience, especially psychological, linguistic, and philosophical attitudes or positions. See the essays in Strelka, *Theories of Literary Genre* (especially Klaus

Weissenberger's "A Morphological Genre Theory," 229–53), and Gerhart, *Genre Choices, Gender Questions* 59–62.

76. Fowler, *Kinds of Literature*, 48, 63. The phrase "poème en prose" also appears on page 239 in a quotation of another critic. In this context, prose poetry is implied to be an intermediate genre like Menippean satire.

77. Fowler, *Kinds of Literature*, 112.

78. Fowler, *Kinds of Literature*, 181–88.

79. Kittay and Godzich, *The Emergence of Prose*, 3.

80. At this point the reader may wonder what is wrong with the commonplace division of genres into narrative, dramatic, and lyric. As Fowler points out, these divisions in fact only describe "one of many elements in a work or genre," namely "representational mode. . . . Moreover, it is usual for several representational modes to combine or alternate or mix within a single work" (*Kinds of Literature*, 236). Fowler traces the historical evolution of the triad "narrative, dramatic, lyric" from Plato and Aristotle through Renaissance theorists such as Minturno (see especially 235–36). He then argues against "discourse" approaches and generic divisions based solely on language function, on the grounds that they, too, focus on a single generic feature (237–39). The German morphological critics sometimes distinguish between the three "genres" (lyric, epic, and dramatic) and the historical "types" (elegy, ode, tragedy, and so on).

81. See Fowler, *Kinds of Literature*, 46–47.

82. Fowler, *Kinds of Literature*, 268.

83. Fowler, *Kinds of Literature*, 269.

84. Fowler, *Kinds of Literature*, 159.

85. For Fowler's discussion of paradigms, see *Kinds of Literature*, 151–55. Like Fishelov's "prototypical members," Fowler's "paradigms" may be indebted to Kuhn.

2. A Wide Field of Prose Possibilities

1. See especially Bernard, *Le Poème en Prose*, 19–93; Sandras, *Lire le poème en prose*; and the opening chapters of Simon, *Prose Poem*.

2. Chateaubriand, *Atala*, 60–61.

3. See the dedicatory letter to the *Petits Poëmes en prose* (Baudelaire, *oc*, 1:275–76).

4. Given the number of prose poem doublets of verse lyrics in his œuvre, Baudelaire may have from time to time literally translated verse into prose.

5. Nerval, "Les Poésies de Henri Heine."

6. Baudelaire, *oc*, 1:284–85.

7. For a comparison of "Le Joujou du pauvre" (and "Morale du joujou," Baudelaire's first version of what was to become the prose poem) and Rousseau's ninth *promenade*, see Chase, "Paragon, Parergon." For the Rousseau sources of "Le Gâteau," see the first of Zimmerman, "Trois Études sur Baudelaire et Rousseau."

8. Rousseau, *Les Rêveries*, 42.

9. Rousseau *Les Rêveries*, 121: "Quelquefois mes rêveries finissent par la méditation, mais plus souvent mes méditations finissent par la rêverie."

10. Rousseau *Les Rêveries*, 99–100.

11. Nerval, *Œuvres complètes* 3:1010.

12. Nerval, *Œuvres complètes* 3:1010.

13. Compare Baudelaire's remarks on Poe's decision to write short stories (*oc*, 2:329–30): "That is why this genre of composition, which is not placed at as a high a level as pure poetry, can supply products which are more varied and easily appreciated by the mass of readers. The author of a short story, moreover, has a multitude of tones and nuances of language at his disposition—the reasonable tone, the sarcastic, the tone of the humorist—which poetry repudiates, and which are as it were dissonances, outrages to the idea of pure beauty. But this is also what puts the author who pursues a simple aim of beauty in a short story at a great disadvantage, deprived as he is of the most useful tool, rhyme. I know that all literatures have made efforts, sometimes successful, to create purely poetic stories; Edgar Allan Poe himself wrote some very beautiful ones. But these are struggles and efforts which only serve to illustrate the power of true methods adapted to analogous ends, and I am not far from believing that for some authors, the greatest one might pick, these heroic attempts are born from despair." As I discuss in the next chapter, Baudelaire associated Nerval with Poe. Also compare Houssaye's preface (35–36) from his *Œuvres poétiques* (1857), which seems inspired by Baudelaire's sonnet "Le Tonneau de la Haine" (*oc*, 1:71): "Journalism, that cask of the Danaïdes, into which all the imaginations of our time have poured their amphorae, will end by devouring the intelligences which God had destined for poetry in its horrific nightly revelry. Some of them, however, struggling against this brutal thirst, have preserved, while playing the role of monster, the wine of the ideal vine which flowers in their hearts for another cask."

14. Nerval, *Œuvres completes*, 3:399. Another version of this dedication appears at the beginning of *La Bohême galante* (3:235).

15. Robb, "Les Origines." For Baudelaire and journalism, see also chapters 1 and 3 in Monroe, *Poverty of Objects*.

16. *L'Artiste* (15 September 1864), 142.

17. For a similar argument and a more general discussion of the importance of caricature for Baudelaire, see McLees, *Baudelaire's "Argot Plastique."* See also Terdiman, *Discourse/Counterdiscourse*, 153. For Baudelaire's own interest in caricature, see his "Du l'Essence du rire" (*oc*, 2:525–43), "Quelques caricaturistes Français" (*oc*, 2:544–63), and "Quelques caricaturistes étrangers" (*oc*, 2:564–74).

18. For a general discussion of the development and popularity of the *physiologie*, see Lhértier, "Les Physiologies."

19. Huart, *Physiologie du flâneur*, 10–11.

20. Baudelaire, *oc*, 1:291. The title of the prose poem and its subject matter seem inspired by Poe; the phrase "bath of multitude" is De Quincey's. For more complete

references to the Poe and De Quincey sources, see Kopp's edition of the *Petits Poëmes en prose*, 222–23.

21. "Le véritable flaneur ne s'ennuie jamais, il se suffit à lui-même et trouve dans tout ce qu'il rencontre un aliment à son intelligence" (Huart, Physiologie, 124). The phrase "poète actif et fécond" occurs in the second paragraph of Baudelaire's "Les Foules" (*oc*, 1:291), "ne pouvoir pas se supporter eux-mêmes" in the second to last paragraph of "La Solitude" (*oc*, 1:314).

22. In his discussion of caricature's potential for ideological critique, Terdiman observes that *physiologies* developed in the wake of censorship laws that forbade outright caricatures of Louis Philippe and his government, such as the pear-head representations of the king in the early 1830s. Rather than attacking the ruling ideology directly, the *physiologies* caricatured it piecemeal by ridiculing its superstructural manifestations (*Discourse/Counterdiscourse*, 163).

23. The phrase "mystérieux et brillant modèle" is from Baudelaire's dedicatory letter to Arsène Houssaye (*oc*, 1:276). Bernard and Simon are among the critics who have compared Bertrand and Baudelaire. See also Nies, *Poesie in Prosaischer Welt*.

24. Bertrand, Gaspard de la nuit, 47–48. Bernard (*Le Poème en prose*, 61) compares the final version of "Octobre" to an earlier version that is in block text.

25. Bernard, for example, asserts in a teleological future tense that Bertrand is personally responsible for establishing prose poetry as a genre: "Bertrand's role will be precisely to rescue the prose poem from the constraints of imitation or pastiche, and to give it the same authenticity, the same poetic virtues, as the poem in verse" (*Le Poème en prose*, 39). She also remarks: "Bertrand is the true creator (and this point has, I believe, never been contested) of the prose poem as a literary *genre*" (51).

26. See, for example, Bernard, *Le Poème en prose*, 91, 120; Kopp's introduction to his edition of *Petits Poëmes en prose*, (especially xix, n. 2); and Ruff's introduction to his edition of *Petits Poëmes en prose*, 16. For further instances of Lefèvre echoes in Baudelaire, see Fongaro, "Aux Sources de 'Recueillement.'" Some of Lefèvre's prose poems appear earlier than 1854 in various journals and in his collection of poetry *Les Vespres de l'abbaye du val* (1845).

27. Lefévre, *Le Livre du promeneur*, 453.

28. The best example of this sort of sentence in Baudelaire occurs in *Fusées* 8.11 (*oc*, 1:655): "Ces beaux et grands navires, imperceptiblement balancés (dandinés) sur les eaux tranquilles, ces robustes navires, à l'air désœuvré et nostalgique, ne nous disent-ils pas dans une langue muette: Quand partons-nous pour le bonheur?" (These large, beautiful vessels, imperceptibly balanced [bobbing] on peaceful waters, these robust vessels with an air of idleness and nostalgia, aren't they saying to us in a mute language: "When will we embark for happiness?"). Also compare the following lines from the prose poem "L'Invitation au voyage" (*oc*, 1:303): "Fleur incomparable, tulipe retrouvée, allégorique dahlia, c'est là, n'est-ce pas, dans ce beau pays si calme et si rêveur, qu'il faudrait aller vivre et fleurir?" (Incomparable flower, sought after tulip,

allegorical dahlia, it is there, is it not, in that beautiful country, so peaceful and so dreamy, that one should go live and flourish?).

29. Baudelaire, *oc*, 1:275.

30. Guiette, "Le Titre des 'Petits Poèmes en Prose,'" 167. The Lefèvre poems with Baudelairean titles include "Le Port," "L'Horloge," and "Le Miroir." On Baudelaire's knowledge of and possible acquaintance with Lefèvre, see Bernard, *Le Poème en Prose*, 120.

31. For a bibliography of prose-poem-like works written before Baudelaire's *Petits Poëmes en prose*, see Bernard, *Le Poème en prose*, 776–77. For a discussion of some of these works, see Bernard, "Aperçu historique," 19–93.

32. Guérin, *Poésie*, 214.

33. Rabbe, *Album d'un pessimiste*, 107, 114–15.

34. Houssaye, *Œuvres poétius*, 287–88.

35. Champfleury (Jules Fleury), *Chien-Caillou*, 115–16. "Chien-Caillou" is the nickname of the engraver Rudolphe Bresdin (Baudelaire, *oc*, 2:1089). See also Baudelaire's review of Champfleury (*oc*, 2:21–23).

36. Compare the poems of Baudelaire's contemporaries Pierre Dupont and Auguste Barbier. Baudelaire's innovation may lie in his nonsatirical treatment of urban subjects: unlike Barbier and poets in a tradition that stretches at least as far back as Horace, the poet of the "Tableaux Parisiens" sought to discover beauty in the modern city. Baudelaire's reputation as a city poet or the first modern poet is nevertheless overemphasized and ultimately based on only one aspect of his poetry and thought.

37. For a discussion of ekphrastic writing and the prose poem, see Shattuck, "Vibratory Organism." Shattuck argues that a passage from Baudelaire's *Salons* is a prose poem *avant la lettre*. On the importance of *salon* writing for the prose poem, see Simon, *Prose Poem*, 96. As Simon points out, it is probably significant that Diderot's *Salons* were first published in complete form in 1821. For a discussion of the *Tableau de Paris*, see Stierle, "Baudelaire's 'Tableau parisiens.'" The notes to Lemaitre's and Kopp's editions of *Petits Poèmes en prose* are the best places to begin to sort out the importance of the short story and other genres for Baudelaire. One might also compare works that mix poetry and prose (a tradition going as far back as Dante's *Vita Nuova* and Boethius's *Consolation of Philosophy*) and extracts from longer works published in anthologies and miscellanies.

38. Murphy, *Tradition of Subversion*, 69. See also Sandras's thematic groupings of prose-poem-like works in *Lire le poème en prose* (especially 33–41 and 106–43).

39. Baudelaire, *oc*, 1:129; Bossuet, *Sermon sur la mort*, 138.

40. Baudelaire, *oc*, 1:134. Bossuet, *Sermon sur la mort*, 133. Section 6 of "Le Voyage," with its description of "Le spectacle ennuyeux de l'immortel péché" (*oc*, 1:132), is especially sermonlike in its moralizing tone. Baudelaire's poem is dedicated to an avowed believer in human progress, Maxime Du Camp, and, like Bossuet's "Sermon sur la Mort," questions the belief in human progress.

41. See especially the "Tableaux Parisiens" poems dedicated to Hugo: "Le Cygne," "Les Sept Vieillards," and "Les Petites Vieilles." If we take at face value Baudelaire's assertions that these poems were written with Hugo in mind (see the notes to "Le Cygne" [*oc*, 1:1007]), some of the rhythmical dislocation I speak of may be linked to Hugo's experimentation with the alexandrine.

42. Hugo, *Œuvres poétiques*, 491, 499.

43. "Prends garde à Marchagny! La prose poétique/ Est une ornière où gît le vieux Pégase étique." From "À un écrivain" (*Les Quatre Vents de l'Esprit*); qtd. in Bernard, *Le Poème en prose*, 40.

44. Johnson speaks in particular of a "code struggle" between traditional and nontraditional lyric discourse (*Critical Difference*, 25).

45. "En somme c'est encore *Les Fleurs du mal*, mais avec beaucoup plus de liberté, et de détail, et de raillerie" (Baudelaire, *Cor*, 2:615).

3. Poetry in a Prosaic World

1. Baudelaire, *oc*, 1:275–76.

2. See Kopp's and Ruff's editions of *Petits Poëmes en prose* and Johnson, *Défigurations*, 18–28. For Baudelaire's strategic use of dedications, see Chambers, "Baudelaire et la pratique de la dédicace."

3. The caricature of Baudelaire in the first issue of *Le Boulevard* (1 December 1862) is a good example of the popular image of Baudelaire that Gautier was combating in his preface. "Les Nuits de M. Baudelaire" (The nights of Mr. Baudelaire) shows an upturned bed with the poet's bare left foot out and his right leg sticking up from under the covers. A skeleton, at least two black cats, a skull, and what look like alchemical flasks can be seen in the background. Books and some clothes are strewn on the floor in front. Gautier's description of Baudelaire as a consummate artist owes much to Baudelaire's articles on Gautier.

4. "On voit que Baudelaire prétendait toujours diriger l'inspiration par la volonté et introduire une sort de mathématique infaillible dans l'art. Il se blâmait d'avoir produit autre chose que ce qu'il avait résolu de faire, fût-ce, comme au cas présent, une œuvre originale et puissante" (Gautier, *Portraits et souvenirs littéraires*, 300).

5. In his 18 February 1866 letter to Ancelle, Baudelaire writes that he will swear up and down that his poetry is all art, even though it actually comes from his life (Baudelaire, *Cor*, 2:610).

6. For a related discussion, see Brombert, "Will to Ecstasy." Brombert examines the relationship between will and intoxication.

7. Baudelaire, *oc*, 1:5, 82.

8. Baudelaire, *oc*, 1:82, 26.

9. Baudelaire, *oc*, 1:186, 184.

10. Baudelaire, *oc*, 1:361.

11. Reprinted in Sainte-Beuve, *Portraits littéraires II*, 343–64.

12. Baudelaire, *Cor*, 2:196.

13. Baudelaire, *Cor*, 1:116–18, 343.

14. Qtd. in Kamerbeek, "Sainte-Beuve et Baudelaire," 101. See also Baudelaire, *oc*, 1:790, and a related passage in one of Baudelaire's articles on Gautier (*oc*, 2:117).

15. Qtd. in Kamerbeek, "Sainte-Beuve et Baudelaire," 98–99.

16. Baudelaire, *Cor*, 2:474.

17. Baudelaire, *Cor*, 2:457–85.

18. Baudelaire, *Cor*, 2:493.

19. Baudelaire, *Cor*, 2:583.

20. Sainte-Beuve's affair with Madame Hugo was the inspiration for the relationship between Amaury and Madame de Couaën in *Volupté*.

21. Balzac, *Comédie humaine* 4:672–73. Kamerbeek quotes from the 1839 text, which varies somewhat from the 1843 version.

22. See Monroe, *Poverty of Objects*, 93–98.

23. Baudelaire, *Cor*, 1:177, and *Cor*, 1:444.

24. Baudelaire, *oc*, 1:438–39.

25. Balzac, *Comédie humaine*, 11:387. Raphaël de Valentin, the protagonist of *La Peau du Chagrin*, also writes a treatise on the will. Valentin refers to will as a substance, or rather a "material force similar to vapor" (*Comédie humaine*, 9:103).

26. From Sainte Beuve, *Nouveaux Lundis III* (1862); qtd. in Kamerbeek, "Sainte-Beuve et Baudelaire," 104.

27. From Sainte-Beuve, *Joseph Delorme* (1829) in *Poésies complètes*, 124; qtd. in Kamerbeek, "Sainte-Beuve et Baudelaire," 104.

28. Ashbery uses the opening phrase of this sonnet ("Moi, je suis la tulipe") as the title of one of the poems in *Shadow Train*, a collection of fifty "sonnet-sized" poems.

29. Baudelaire, *oc*, 1:558.

30. "Il doit être démontré maintenant par assez d'exemples que le mouvement poétique de 1824–1828 n'a pas été un simple engouement de coterie. . . . Il suffisait dans chaque ville de deux ou trois jeunes imaginations un peu vives pour donner l'éveil et sonner le tocsin littéraire. Au XVIe siècle, les choses s'étaient ainsi passé lors de la révolution poétique proclamée par Ronsard et Du Bellay: le Mans, Anger, Poitier, Dijon, avaient aussitôt levé leurs recrues et fourni leur contingent. Ainsi, de nos jours, l'aiglon romantique (les ennemis disaient l'orfraie) parut voler assez rapidement de clocher en clocher, et, finalement, à voir le résultat en gros après une quinzaine d'années de possession de moins en moins disputée, il semble qu'il y ait conquête" (Sainte-Beauve, *Portraits Littéraires II*, 343–44).

31. With Sainte-Beauve, however, Baudelaire jealously guarded his reputation as a son of romanticism. In 1858 and 1859 letters to his "cher protecteur," Baudelaire took pains to clear himself first of the charge, leveled at him by the author of a 6 June 1858 letter in the *Figaro*, of denying and defaming his romantic predecessors (*Cor*, 1:500–501), then of some satiric comments on romanticism made by his friend

Hippolyte Babou in the 10 February 1959 issue of the *Revue française* (*Cor*, 1:553). The fear of offending Sainte-Beuve indicates that Baudelaire risked being perceived as antiromantic in the wake of the publication of *Les Fleurs du mal*, if not because of the content of the book perhaps because of his earlier association with Champfleury and realism (a movement Baudelaire would take some pains to distance himself from). See his notes for the article "Puisque réalisme il y a" (Since realism exists; *oc*, 2:56). In the *Salon de 1846*, Baudelaire refers to romanticism in Stendhalian terms: "For me romanticism is the most recent, most current, expression of beauty" (*oc*, 2:420). In later life, he goes so far as to call Flaubert, Barbey d'Aurevilly, and himself "old romantics" (*Cor*, 2:471). It is perhaps most accurate to say that, while rejecting certain aspects of romanticism such as nature poetry, Baudelaire remained essentially romantic in his aesthetics, but Baudelaire disliked being labeled any one thing, be it romantic, realist, or member of the "art for art's sake" movement.

32. Sainte-Beuve writes of the sonnet: "Neither Lamartine nor Hugo wrote anything of the sort. Nor did Vigny. The swans and the eagles, if they wished to enter this cage, would have broken their wings there." Qtd. in Kamerbeek, "Sainte-Beauve et Baudelaire," 104.

33. Balzac, *Comédie humaine*, 4:464.

34. Balzac, *Comédie humaine*, 4:1033.

35. Baudelaire, *oc*, 2:134–35.

36. Baudelaire, *Cor*, 2:459–60.

37. See Burton, *Baudelaire in 1859*.

38. Baudelaire, *oc*, 2:130.

39. Delesalle, "Baudelaire rival de Jules Janin?" 41. My discussion of *Le Gâteau des rois* is highly indebted to this article.

40. Janin, *Les Gâteau des rois*, 55–56.

41. Janin, *Les Gâteau des rois*, 2.

42. For Baudelaire's response to the 1865 article, see *oc*, 2:231–40; for the "éreintage absolu," see *oc*, 2:50.

43. Delesalle, "Baudelaire rival de Jules Janin?" 42.

44. Baudelaire, *oc*, 2:24.

45. Janin, *Les Gâteau des rois*, 50–53; Delesalle, "Baudelaire rival de Jules Janin?" 47.

46. Janin, *Les Gâteau des rois*, 14.

47. Baudelaire, *Cor*, 2:238.

48. It is possible that Baudelaire intended the title "Les Deux crépuscules" to refer only to the verse poems. "Le Soir" and "Le Matin" are later published with slight revisions in the *Les Fleurs du mal* as "Le Crépuscule du soir" and "Le Crépuscule du Matin."

49. Leakey, *Collected Essays*, 211.

50. *Fontainebleau*, 73–74.

51. See Leakey, *Collected Essays*, 212. See also Leakey, *Baudelaire and Nature*.

52. *Fontainebleau*, 84.

53. *Fontainebleau*, 71, 80–83.

54. The *Fontainebleau* versions of the two poems can be found in Baudelaire, *oc*, 1:1327–29. Until their 1861 versions, the poems were textually linked to each other (*oc*, 1:1329).

55. *Fontainebleau*, 79.

56. Baudelaire, *oc*, 1:313–14.

57. For the argument that Jules Janin is the "gazetier philanthrope," see Delesalle, "Baudelaire rival de Jules Janin?" 52.

58. The original text of La Bruyère reads "Tout notre mal vient de ne pouvoir être seuls" (All our evil comes from not being able to be alone) (Baudelaire, *oc*, 1:1330).

59. See Baudelaire, *oc*, 1:1330.

60. When Baudelaire was in Belgium, he wrote of La Bruyère: "French author, very slighted in Belgium" (*oc*, 2:873).

61. The original lines of Pascal are: "Quand je m'y suis quelquefois à considérer les diverses agitations des hommes . . . , j'ai découvert que tout le malheur des hommes vient d'une seule chose, qui est de ne savoir pas demeurer en repos, dans une chambre" (When I've started thinking sometimes about the different troubles of men . . . , I have discovered that all of the misfortune of men comes from a single thing, which is not knowing how to remain at rest, in a room) (390).

62. See Kopp's edition of *Petits poëmes en prose*, 277, and M. J. Pommier, *Dans les chemins de Baudelaire*, 146.

63. Sainte-Beuve, *Volupté*, 210.

64. Sainte-Beuve, *Volupté*, 211.

65. Sainte-Beuve, *Volupté*, 212.

66. Baudelaire, *oc*, 1:1319.

67. Baudelaire, *oc*, 1:336. "Le Thyrse" is commonly read as an allegory of the prose poem. See Johnson, *Défigurations*, chapter 3.

68. Balzac, *Comédie humaine*, 4:667.

69. Balzac, *Comédie humaine*, 4:1032.

70. Balzac, *Comédie humaine*, 5:705.

71. Balzac, *Comédie humaine*, 5:1064.

72. Baudelaire, *oc*, 1:365. For a similar observation, see Evans, *Baudelaire and Intertextuality*, 55–56.

73. Baudelaire, *oc*, 1:275.

74. Baudelaire, *oc*, 1:182. According to Kopp, the projected preface dates from 1859 to 1860 and the revision of the closing lines of "La Solitude" to something close to the final version occurs between November 1861 and October 1862 (*Petits Poëmes en prose*, 278).

4. The Makings of a Genre

1. See especially chapter 4 in Bernard, *Le Poème en prose* and its bibliography. Many of the collections of prose poems in the 1890s and the first decade of the twentieth century are labeled simply "poèmes en prose."

2. See Bernard, *Le Poème en prose*, 383–90.

3. Huysmans, *À Rebours*, 221–23.

4. See especially Bernard's bibliography on this period (*Le Poème en prose*, 783–86). For comparisons between free verse and prose poetry, see Bernard, *Le Poème en prose*, 401–5, 408.

5. Mallarmé, *Œuvres complètes*, 360–68. Mallarmé does not discuss prose poetry in this lecture but refers in general to contemporary experiments in verse. He also mentions Wagner and the poetic ideal of music (365).

6. Breunig, "Why France?" 11. See also Simon, *Prose Poem*, 622.

7. Breunig, "Why France?" 12. For Hugo's "loosening" of the alexandrine, see chapter 2.

8. Kahn, *Premiers Poèmes*, 20. Bernard points out that Kahn also claimed that the prose poem was more important in Baudelaire's time than his own and that free verse could fulfill all of the functions of the *poème en prose* (*Le Poème en prose*, 468).

9. Banville, *Petit Traité de poésie française*, 8–9.

10. The French is "long, immense et raisonné *dérèglement de tous les sens.*" From Rimbaud's 15 May 1871 letter to Paul Demeny, *Œuvres complètes*, 251.

11. Simon, *Prose Poem*, 271–72.

12. Bernard, *Le Poème en prose*, 463–65.

13. Monroe, *Poverty of Objects*, 153.

14. The Boileau phrase ("Finally Malherbe came") is from the *Art Poétique*. The Hugo phrase ("Then . . . I came") is from "Réponse à un acte d'accusation" in *Les Contemplations* (*Œuvres poétiques*, 2:496).

15. Rimbaud, *Œuvres complètes*, 121–22.

16. For the anecdote of Létrange, see Rimbaud, *Œuvres Complètes*, 979. At the pleading of her son, Madame Rimbaud rented a piano that, because of the narrowness of the stairway in her house, had to be hauled up to the second floor through the outside window. The line in "Après le Déluge" would therefore represent an exaggeration of the height required to haul the piano. For the possible allusion to Madame Bovary, see Rimbaud, *Illuminations*, 89–90. As with the biographical explanation, Madame Bovary's founding or installing a piano in the Alps is associated with a quixotic impulse. "Le Splendide-Hôtel" was a hotel in Paris that burned down in 1872. From Rimbaud, *Œuvres complètes: Correspondance*, 503.

17. For the association of Eucharis with the bucolic, see Adam's notes in Rimbaud, *Œuvres complètes*, 979; for sexual imagery, see Adam's summary of a Yves Denis article, 978. Forestier suggests that Eucharis represents an outmoded kind of poetry (Rimbaud, *Œuvres complètes: Correspondance*, 503).

18. Forestier cites Suzanne Bernard for the connection between the rainbow and the seal of God (Rimbaud, *Œuvres complètes: Correspondance*, 503).

19. For a discussion of some of these readings, see Adam's notes to the poem in Rimbaud, *Œuvres complètes*, 978.

20. See Forestier's notes in Rimbaud, *Œuvres complètes: Correspondance*, 503. Osmond also speculates about the revolutionary edge to the echo of Madame de Pompadour's "Après nous, le déluge" (Rimbaud, *Illuminations*, 89).

21. The order of the poems in *Illuminations* may not be Rimbaud's. See Osmond's introduction in Rimbaud, *Illuminations*.

22. Sonnenfeld, "*L'Adieu suprême*, 210. Sonnenfeld's argument about "the boundaries of the prose poem" is in the same spirit as my "invisible fences." Unlike Sonnenfeld, I am interested in boundaries that are not immediately recognizable as relating to a work's formal construction: anything, in short, that frames a poem, especially its literary reception. Another important difference between Sonnenfeld's arguments and my own is his insistence on the prose poem's conservatism: "But it is my contention that the *prose poem* . . . is formally a profoundly conservative and traditional structure in its ceremonials of entrance and exit; that no matter how radical its content, how relentless its striving for apparent or real incoherence, the prose poem undergoes the secondary elaboration of syntactical coherence and its boundaries most often are clearly defined and marked" (200). While this assertion is a valuable corrective to claims made on behalf of the prose poem's radical open-endedness and subversive nature, it is itself engaged in an essentializing logic. My position is that form alone does not make a work conservative or revolutionary and that the categories "conservative" and "revolutionary" obfuscate more issues than they help explain.

23. Mallarmé, *Œuvres complètes*, 512–19. Mallarmé has very little to say about Rimbaud in his correspondence, though he does salute the appearance of an edition of Rimbaud's works in a June 1898 letter to Paterne Berrichon (Mallarmé, *Correspondance*, 10:230).

24. For the idea that the prose poem is a short and concentrated form, see Bernard, *Le Poème en prose*, 9–17, and the introductions to Chapelan, *Anthologie*, and Decaunes, *Le Poème en prose*. Simon avoids generalizing about prose poetry by calling Rimbaud's "short, or very short poem in prose or verses . . . not an epigram," but a "new poetic genre" (*Prose Poem*, 286).

25. For the association of Lautréamont and Rimbaud, see Bernard *Le Poème en prose*, 215. Bernard points out that Rimbaud and Lautréamont were both young writers who wrote their prose poems in the early 1870s before abandoning poetry and that they died at relatively early ages. On the history of the datings of *Une saison en enfer* and *Illuminations*, see Bernard, *Le Poème en prose*, 156–62, and Rimbaud, *Œuvres complètes*, 949–52, 976–77. As Adams points out in his notes to *Œuvres complètes*, *Une Saison en enfer* was generally viewed as Rimbaud's farewell

to poetry until Henri de Bouillane de Lacoste's 1949 article "Rimbaud et le problème des Illuminations."

26. Lautréamont, *Lautréamont*, 169–70. The English translation is, with minor changes, Paul Knight's, from *Maldoror and Poems*, 159–62.

27. The reader is addressed as "enhardi et devenu momentanément féroce" (Lautréamont, *Lautréamont*, 45).

28. See Bürger, *Theory of the Avant-Garde*, especially 41, 47.

29. See Bernard, *Le Poème en prose*, 248.

30. See Mondor's and Jean-Aubry's notes to Mallarmé's prose poems in Mallarmé, *Œuvres complètes*, 1550–51.

31. Baudelaire, *oc*, 2:831. Although written in 1864, "Le Phénomène futur" was not published until 1875. Baudelaire apparently knew of the poem through an intermediary (see Mallarmé, *Œuvres complètes*, 1554–55). For a more detailed analysis of the poetic relationship between Baudelaire and Mallarmé as it regards their prose poetry, see Johnson, *Défigurations*, and the chapter "Les Fleurs du mal armé," in *A World of Difference*, 116–33.

32. See especially the first section of this essay, "Le Beau, la mode et le bonheur" (The beautiful, fashion, and happiness; Baudelaire, *oc*, 2:683–86).

33. Mallarmé, *Œuvres complètes*, 269–70.

34. For the publication history of Mallarmé's prose poems, see Mallarmé, *Œuvres complètes*, 1547–52.

35. The prose poems are on pages 134–35.

36. Baudelaire's prose poem "Le *Confiteor* de l'artiste" (1:278–79) laments the finite individual's plight in the face of the infinite but turns away from this sort of brooding at the end. The final line of the poem is epigrammatic: "L'étude du beau est un duel où l'artiste crie de frayeur avant d'être vaincu" (The study of beauty is a duel in which the artist screams in terror before being defeated).

37. Cros, *Charles Cros*, 157. "Effarement" was originally published in *Le Coffret de santal* under the subheadings "Fantaisies en prose" and "Sur Trois aquatintes de Henry Cros." Bernard suggests that Cros knew of Mallarmé's posthumously published *Igitur* (*Le Poème en prose*, 354).

38. If "Effarement" was based on Henry's art work, the etching has not survived. The text of the poem was published without accompaniment of a pictorial image. See Bernard, *Le Poème en prose*, 354.

39. Claudel, *Connaissance de l'Est*, 140.

40. *Connaissance de l'Est* was not the first book entirely composed of prose poems, but it is telling that the author did not feel the need to provide a generic title or subtitle (as compared to the *Petits Poëmes en prose*; *Divagations, ou anecdotes en prose*; and *Fantaisies en prose*).

41. Bernard also claims that at a certain point in literary history the prose poem ceased to be treated as a genre *à part* and became "one of the forms, and not the least

employed, that is capable of staking claims on a gestating work" (*Le Poème en prose*, 700). But she asserts that this did not occur until after 1930 and never acknowledges that there may be a sense in which the prose poem never was a genre.

42. See, for example, "Les petits poissons rouge dans leur bocal, ou Anatomie du poème en prose" (The little red fish in their fish tank, or Anatomy of the prose poem), a collaborative effort of René de Gourmont, Alfred Vallette, and Albert Aurier, published under the pseudonym "Quasi" in 1892 (qtd. in Bernard, *Le Poème en prose*, 503).

43. Bernard's argument is in part based on the quantity of prose poems in small journals. For the prose poem and free verse, see Bernard, *Le Poème en prose*, especially 373–400; for the proliferation of mixed and hybrid forms, see 418.

44. Jacob, *Le Cornet à dés*, 21. The 1916 preface is on pages 19–24.

45. Buffon's "Le style c'est l'homme même" is cited by Jacob, *Le Cornet à dés*, 19.

46. Jacob states that "l'art est la volonté de s'extérioriser par des moyens choisis: les deux définitions coïncident et l'art n'est que le style" (art is the will to make oneself exterior though chosen means: the two definitions coincide and art is nothing but style) (*Le Cornet à dés*, 21).

47. Jacob, *Le Cornet à dés*, 22.

48. See Jacob, *Le Cornet à dés*, 22: "le poème en prose pour exister doit se soumettre aux lois de tout art, qui sont le style ou volonté et la situation ou émotion" (in order to exist the prose poem has to be subject to the laws of all art, which are style, or will, and situation, or emotion).

49. Jacob, *Le Cornet à dés*, 22.

50. "Le poème est un objet construit et non la devanture d'un bijoutier . . . le poème en prose est un bijou" (Jacob, *Le Cornet à dés*, 23). Jacob's comments on the "little shock" a work of art produces and the "margin" or "special atmosphere" surrounding it are similar to Walter Benjamin's notions of shock and aura.

51. Jacob, *Le Cornet à dés*, 22.

52. Jacob, *Le Cornet à dés*, 22–23.

53. Bernard suggests Jacob was exasperated by his contemporaries' praise of Rimbaud as the master of the prose poem (*Le Poème en prose*, 636). Monroe describes Baudelaire and Rimbaud as "a kind of Scylla and Charybdis in the tradition of the prose poem between which Jacob's sense of his own identity as a prose poet . . . is most threatened" (*Poverty of Objects*, 161).

54. See Sandras, *Lire le poème en prose*, 80. Journalistic surveys of literary and other issues (*enquêtes*) were in vogue in the early twentieth century.

55. "C'est à Baudelaire qu'on doit d'avoir imposé, avec éclat, mais non sans avoir hésité, le titre de 'poème en prose' pour une livraison de proses courtes dans *La Revue fantaisiste* du 1er novembre 1861. Cette expression, dont l'usage se répand entre 1860 et 1920, tend à disparaître dans les décades suivantes, avant de faire retour, au moins chez les lecteurs, grâce à la publication de proses brèves dans la collection 'Poésie' des

Éditions Gallimard. De nos jours, si l'expression a un parfum de désuétude, l'objet qu'elle désigne est toujours bien vivant, mais aussi difficile à saisir qu'il l'était à l'époque du *Spleen de Paris*" (Sandras, *Lire le poème en prose*, 16).

56. "Les œuvres de Saint-John Perse, de Michaux, de Char et de Ponge ont contribué à modifier la représentation de la poésie. Dans les années soixante, la prose est non seulement reconnue comme l'une des écritures possibles du poème, mais comme la forme majeure de l'expression poétique. Et les écrivains n'éprouvent pas la nécessité de préciser sur la couverture de l'ouvrage s'il est en vers ou en prose. . . . Aujourd'hui, la situation n'est plus la même. Depuis vingt ans, le vers a fait retour" (Sandras, *Lire le poème en prose*, 91).

57. One indirect proof of this comes from the series of textbooks edited by Lagarde and Michard used in most French high schools. In the volume on the nineteenth century, the *poème en prose* has its own section; in the volume on the twentieth century, prose poems are scattered among verse poems.

58. Fishelov, *Metaphors of Genre*, 13.

59. Fowler, *Kinds of Literature*, 112. Fowler most likely considers the sonnet a genre. In discussing size as a generic feature, Fowler remarks that "genre often determines length precisely" and gives as examples the sonnet and computistic verse (62).

60. Genres of the prose poem also exist in English, such as Edson's and Fixel's "fabulist" poems. See Sandras, *Lire le poème en prose*, and Delville, *American Prose Poem*, for some groupings if not genres of prose poems.

5. The Emergence of Prose Poetry in English

1. From "Advice to an Author," section 1 of Shaftesbury, *Characteristics of Men, Manners, Opinions, Times, etc.*, 1:108. The OED is also my source for the references below to the *Daily Chronicle* and Arthur Symons.

2. Qtd. in Rosmarin, *Power of Genre*, 29.

3. Coleridge, *Complete Works*, 301–6. When collecting his works, Coleridge felt the need to explain why he included "The Wanderings of Cain" with his poems and wrote an apologetic preface to the work (301–02).

4. Kingsley, *Alton Locke*, 96.

5. Qtd. in Price, "George Eliot," 146.

6. Review of *Poetical Works*, *Edinburgh Review* 59 (1834): 327–41. I am indebted to Leah Price for this quotation.

7. Emerson, *Selections from Ralph Waldo Emerson*, 304.

8. Poe, "Review of New Books." Although the column is unsigned, the OED lists Poe as author.

9. Poe, *Selected Prose, Poetry, and Eureka*, 484. The title of the Auden edition indicates a certain amount of ambiguity about the generic status of *Eureka*. Apparently it is neither poetry nor prose.

10. Poe, "Review of New Books," 69. Contrary to Poe's indication, the original passage appears as the preface to volume 2. The preface is signed "Cornelius Matthews, Evert A. Duyckinck. New York, Nov. 1, 1841." Matthews wrote this preface as a general plea for the wide range of the modern critic—a writer who, he asserts, does much more than make a "mere decision upon a book" and compliment or not compliment the author "on its binding, its pages, its spelling, its typography" (iv).

11. Dickens, "The Old Church-yard Tree."

12. Dickens, "The Old Church-yard Tree."

13. Cather, *Professor's House*, 33. Near the end of chapter 8, the narrator remarks, "The lake winds were scouring the town, and Scott [the professor's son-in-law] had laryngitis and was writing prose poems about the pleasures of tending your own furnace when the thermometer is twenty below" (80).

14. Woolf, *Roger Fry*, 106. Also compare a later passage: "How, without any of Ruskin's or Pater's skill, in words [Fry] arouses sensation [in *Vision and Design*]; how he brings colour onto the page, and not only colour but forms and their relations; how without anecdote or prose poetry he wakes the eye to qualities that it has never seen before, are problems for the literary critic to solve at leisure" (227).

15. Wilson, *Axel's Castle*, 203.

16. Dowson's *Decorations in Prose* was published along with his *Decorations in Verse*. Merrill, who translated the prose poems that appear in *Pastels in Prose*, was an American expatriate who wrote and published poetry in French.

17. Howells, introduction to *Pastels in Prose*, v–vi, vi, vi, vii.

18. Howells, introduction to *Pastels in Prose*, v.

19. Eliot, "Prose and Verse"; Manning, "Poetry in Prose"; Aldington, "A Note on Poetry in Prose."

20. Eliot, "Prose and Verse," 3.

21. Aldington, "A Note on Poetry in Prose," 16.

22. Edson, Bly, and Shapiro all published books in the 1960s consisting entirely of prose poems.

23. Every English-language anthology since Ford's has had the word "prose poem" somewhere in its title.

24. I am referring to Williams's *Kora in Hell* (1920) and Fredman's *Poet's Prose* (1983, 1990).

25. De la Mare, *Poetry in Prose*, 52, 8.

26. See, for example, Simon, *Prose Poem*, 645, and Baudelaire's conclusion to *Un mangeur d'opium*, where he talks of the "tableaux poétiques" of De Quincey (*oc*, 1:515).

27. Yeats breaks Pater's prose into lines in his edition of the *Oxford Book of Modern Verse* (1936). France has a similar tradition of prose style, to which writers like Bossuet and Chateaubriand would belong.

28. Hawthorne, *American Travel Sketches*, 47–48.

29. Hawthorne, "Sketches"; Hawthorne, "Fragments."

30. Hunt, "Dreams."

31. Hunt, "Dreams," 239–40. For commentary on Hunt's work in the context of ekphrastic poetry, see Hollander, *Gazer's Sprit*, 88–90.

32. Emerson, *Journals and Miscellaneous Notebooks* (Journal D, entry 365).

33. The actual quotation reads "Tis not every day that I / Fitted am to prophesy" (248). For Emerson's speculation about his inability to write verse, see his 1831 entry (in "Blotting Book III") in *Journals and Miscellaneous Notebooks*, vol. 3, 295.

34. Lazarus, *Poems*, 58–56. One remote possibility of French inspiration for Lazarus's prose poems would be the tradition of the biblical poem in prose, that is, works like Cottin's *La Prise de Jéricho* (see chapter 1).

35. Wilde, *Works*, 15–16.

6. American Prose Poem, Take One

1. Pound's letter, whose "dialect" French translates "Yes, I've already seen that— that's Rimbaud!!" is in Pound, *Selected Letters*, 124. Williams's rejoinder is in *Imaginations*, 11.

2. Edson, "Prose Poem," 321.

3. Fredman, *Poet's Prose*, 10.

4. Fredman, *Poet's Prose*, xiii (preface to the first edition).

5. Ashbery, "Craft Interview," 92. I date the year of the interview based on interview questions and answers that reveal that *Three Poems* (February 1972) was not yet published (83) and that Ashbery had recently finished "The Recital" (93). When asked later about his views on French prose poetry, Ashbery wrote that he would considerably modify his earlier statement, asserting that when he spoke of "a posture, a certain rhetorical tone" he may have had the *Petits Poëmes en prose* in mind (though he now believed Baudelaire's poems do not deserve this reproach) or perhaps the high moral tone of Péguy, Crevel, or some of Perse. He also spoke of his fondness for Jacob, Lautréamont, and Rimbaud (letter to author, 22 June 1995).

6. As Sandras argues (citing a 1910 remark by Gide and a 1924 passage by Jacques Rivière), the symbolist prose poem also became a target of twentieth-century French poets (*Lire le poème en prose*, 80).

7. This sense of "poeticized prose" is similar to Murphy's description of Eliot's, Williams's, and Stein's attempts to "resist 'poeticizing' prose in the manner of the Decadents or of minor imagists" (*Tradition of Subversion*, 166).

8. The *Daily Chronicle* remark is quoted from the OED entry on the prose poem. Symons's remark is from *Dramatis Personae*, 346–47; Simon's is from *Prose Poem*, 622–23; and Edson's is from "Prose Poem," 321.

9. For Banville, see chapter 4. Arthur Symons, author of the influential *The Symbolist Movement in Literature* (1899), was very familiar with late-nineteenth-century French poetry.

10. For a discussion of pseudotranslation in France, see chapter 1.

11. Upward, "Scented Leaves."

12. *Poetry* 2.6 (September 1913):228.

13. *Poetry* 2.3 (June 1913): 81.

14. *Poetry* 2.3 (June 1913): 115.

15. For mixtures of prose and verse, see Cannell, "Poems in Prose and Verse," 171–76, and Lowell, *Sword-blades and Poppy Seed*. In his review of *Sword-blades and Poppy Seed*, Fletcher refers to the form as "polyphonic prose."

16. Stein, "Advertisement." As Stein's title indicates, this poem is in the form of an advertisement.

17. Henderson, "Poetic Prose"; Lowell, "Vers libre"; and Fletcher, "Miss Lowell's Discourse."

18. Simon, *Prose Poem*, 666.

19. Murphy, *Tradition of Subversion*, 47–48. In the pages preceding this passage, Murphy gives an account of Wilde's trials.

20. Aldington, "A Note on Poetry in Prose," 16.

21. De la Mare, *Poetry in Prose*, 53.

22. De la Mare, *Poetry in Prose*, 52. As he suggests, the dictionary referred to does not include a specific reference to prose poetry or poetry in prose.

23. De la Mare, *Poetry in Prose*, 53.

24. Murphy, *Tradition of Subversion*, 59–60.

25. Eliot, "Borderline of Prose," 159. In *A Tradition of Subversion*, Murphy suggests that Eliot's dislike of the term is related to Babbitt's mistrust of mixed or feminized genres (48–51, 59–60). Eliot also registers his mixed feelings about the prose poem in "The Post Georgians," an unsigned review in the 11 April 1919 issue of *The Athenaeum*. He writes of Aldous Huxley: "In his prose poems . . . he has made the mistake of going for a model to Laforgue instead of to Rimbaud. The prose poem is an aberration which is only justified by absolute successes" (171). As strong as the label "aberration" is, Eliot seems more frustrated by the practice than the idea of poetry in prose.

26. Eliot, "Borderline of Prose," 158–59. Eliot does, however, allow Aldington's poems "great merit" (159). As I mention, Eliot's later opinions of Mallarmé are much more favorable, through these generally refer to the French poet's verse poems: see Eliot's 1942 "The Music of Poetry" (*On Poetry and Poets*, 30), his second Milton article (1947; *On Poetry and Poets*, 154), and the echoes of Mallarmé in *Four Quartets*.

27. Eliot, "Prose and Verse," 3.

28. Eliot, "Prose and Verse," 9.

29. Eliot, "Prose and Verse," 9.

30. Eliot, "Borderline of Prose," 158.

31. From section 2 of "Little Gidding." All quotations of Eliot's poetry are from *Complete Poems*.

32. Dante's verse about the refining fire, which closes canto 26 of the *Purgatorio* and appears near the end of *The Waste Land*, is also somewhere in the background here (as is the biblical image on which it is based). Mallarmé's line is "Donner un sens plus pur aux mots de la tribu" (To give a purer sense to the words of the tribe) ("Le Tombeau d'Edgar Poe," *Œuvres completes*, 70). Eliot's "purify" gives the line the connotation of a refining process, and his use of the word "dialect" implies that this process socializes—Eliot might say "civilizes"—language.

33. Eliot, "Prose and Verse," 10.

34. Eliot, preface to *Anabasis*, 11.

35. Eliot, "Prose and Verse," 5.

36. For the dangers of relying on the musical element of poetry, see Eliot's essay "The Music of Poetry" (*On Poetry and Poets*, 26–38). Eliot does not reject the musical element in poetry but cautions against an exclusive reliance on it (32). See also Eliot's criticism of Milton for letting "musical significance" rather than "actual speech or thought" guide his syntax ("Milton I," *On Poetry and Poets*, 142). For Valéry's analogy and Eliot's commentary on it, see Eliot's introduction to *Collected Works of Valéry*, xv–xvi.

37. Eliot, introduction to *Collected Works of Valéry*, xvi.

38. Eliot, *To Criticize the Critic*, 33–34.

39. Eliot seems to have very consciously applied the principle of alternation between the poetic and the prosaic in *Four Quartets*. Each quartet, for example, contains a short "lyric section" (section four) followed and preceded by more discursive free-verse meditations.

40. Eliot makes use of his rationale for the long poem in other essays, such as "Poetry and Drama" (1951): "But if our verse is to have so wide a range that it can say anything that has to be said, it follows that it will not be 'poetry' all the time. . . . It is indeed necessary for any long poem, if it is to escape monotony, to be able to say homely things without bathos, as well as take the highest flights without sounding exaggerated. And it is still more important in a play, especially if it is concerned with contemporary life" (*On Poetry and Poets*, 74). The argument remains very much the same as in "From Poe to Valéry," only the context has shifted slightly, to the use of verse in drama. In general, Eliot is likely to bring the subject of the long poem up in any context of poetry versus ordinary speech (or prose), a tendency that suggests a link between his thoughts on the long poem and his criticism of prose poetry.

41. Eliot, "Prose and Verse," 5.

42. See, for example, Eliot, "Prose and Verse," 5, and various passages in "Milton (II)," an essay of 1947 (*On Poetry and Poets*, 153–54).

43. See, for example, Eliot's criticism of a Valéry passage implying that a philosophical poem is no longer possible, in the "Dante" essay in *Sacred Wood*, 159–60. For Swinburne and Pater, see Eliot, "Prose and Verse," 7; see also Eliot's 1920 article on

"Swinburne as a Poet" (*Sacred Wood*, 144–50). Eliot's criticism of these figures does not preclude admiration.

44. Dickie asserts: "After *The Waste Land*, and probably because of Eliot's success, his contemporaries began to announce their intentions to write long, public poems" (*On the Modernist Long Poem*, 6).

45. Eliot's influence continued into the next generation of poets. In fact, many of the poets who published their first books after the Second World War attended the "From Poe to Valéry" lecture, even if, as Elizabeth Bishop points out in a letter, most of them were drunk. See her letter to Carley Dawson (26 November 1948) in *One Art*, 177.

46. Dickie, *On the Modernist Long Poem*, 162.

47. Eliot, *Inventions*, 90.

48. As noted, the dating of "The Engine" is uncertain, but the ship going down could recall the sinking of the *Titanic* (1912) or even the *Lusitania* (1915).

49. See Christopher Ricks's notes on Vildrac's *Découvertes* in Eliot, *Inventions*, 297.

7. American Prose Poem, Take Two

1. Stein, *Writings*, 2:307–8.

2. Hoffman, *Development of Abstractionism*, 174.

3. Stein, *Writings*, 2:195, 313.

4. Stein, *Writings*, 2:195.

5. Stein, *Writings*, 2:196.

6. Stein, *Writings*, 2:218. I have in mind Woolf's essays "Mr. Bennett and Mrs. Brown" and "Character in Fiction."

7. Stein, *Writings*, 2:198.

8. Stein, *Writings*, 2:202.

9. Stein, *Writings*, 2:203.

10. Stein, *Writings*, 2:217.

11. Stein, *Writings*, 2:218.

12. Stein, *Writings*, 2:198.

13. Stein, *Writings*, 2:315.

14. Stein, *Writings*, 2:326.

15. Stein, *Writings*, 2:322. Meyer picks up on Stein's ideas of Englishness and Americanness in "Stein and Emerson." He points out how Stein believed that Americans, unlike the British, were not settled in their ways and how this perceived quality of American life finds its way into her writing insofar as "words [are] detached from the solidity of things" (89), to take one example.

16. Stein, *Writings*, 2:305–8.

17. Stein, *Writings*, 2:326.

18. Stein, *Writings*, 2:327.

19. Stein, *Writings*, 2:326.

20. Stein, *Writings*, 2:329–30.

21. Stein, *Writings*, 2:334.

22. When Stein discusses her struggle with nouns, the problem of narrative arises, only to be postponed to a later date (*Writings*, 2:328). Stein wrote her four lectures on *Narration* shortly after *Lectures in America*.

23. Stein, *Writings*, 2:328.

24. Stein, *Writings*, 2:331.

25. In *The Autobiography of Alice B. Toklas*, Toklas remarks that she was surprised "never to see a french book on her [Stein's] table, although there were always plenty of english ones, there were even no french newspapers. But do you never read french, I as well as many other people asked her. No, she replied, . . . there is for me only one language and that is english" (Stein, *Writings*, 1:729). See also Stein's preface to *Everybody's Autobiography* (xxiv).

26. One critic of the first type is Allegra Stewart, who reads *Tender Buttons* as a mandala, a "magic circle" or enclosure for the unconscious mind (*Gertrude Stein*, 72). Marianne DeKoven best represents the second type. In *A Different Language*, she argues, "There is no reason to struggle to interpret or unify either the whole of *Tender Buttons* or any part of it, not only because there is no consistent pattern of meaning, but because we violate the spirit of the work in trying to find one" (76). Other interpretations of *Tender Buttons* include work by Richard Bridgman, Michael J. Hoffman, Neil Schmitz, Pamela Hadas, Harriet Chessman, Jayne L. Walker, Lisa Ruddick, Jonathan Monroe, Margueritte S. Murphy, Margaret Dickie, Michael Edward Kaufmann, and Mena Mitrano.

27. Bridgman, *Gertrude Stein*, 126.

28. Hadas, "Spreading the Difference," 61.

29. DeKoven, *Different Language*, 81, 76.

30. Murphy, *Tradition of Subversion*, 136, 57. Recipes could be considered potential narratives in that they imply the act of cooking. Murphy hints at a narrative of formal progression by purposely placing her Stein chapter after her Williams chapter, thereby reversing the chronology of composition and publication.

31. Bridgman, *Gertrude Stein*, 130.

32. Here I am following the edition of *Tender Buttons* in Stein's *Writings*, which is based on her typescript version. In other versions, the item "Dirt and Not Copper" contains two paragraphs.

33. Dydo, "Reading the Handwriting."

34. Hoffman, *Development of Abstractionism*, 193–95. Hoffman reconstructs Stein's method in *Tender Buttons* as a combination of focused attention on an object, mental associations, drifts of thought away from and back to the object, and interruptions of daily life. DeKoven offers a similar reconstruction (*Different Language*, 78–79). Both critics seem to draw on Stein's comments in "Portraits and Repetition"

where she speaks of mixing inside and outside (*Writings*, 2:302–3). See also a similar passage in *The Autobiography of Alice B. Toklas* (*Writings*, 1:814).

35. The notebooks and manuscripts are in the Stein collection in the Beinecke Library at Yale. It is likely that Stein composed at least some of *Tender Buttons* in the notebooks, though they may contain material copied from elsewhere. Stein writes in *The Autobiography of Alice B. Toklas* that she frequently "wrote on scraps of paper in pencil, copied it into french school note-books in ink and then often copied it over again in ink" (*Writings*, 1:712; see also Dydo, "Reading the Handwriting," 86–87). The manuscripts of *Tender Buttons* are in pencil and contain sections that are crossed out.

36. DeKoven incorrectly states that "none of [the notebooks] is filled" (*Different Language*, 164).

37. For the paragraph beginning "A tribune," see Stein, *Writings*, 1:350.

38. Stein, *Writings*, 1:782.

39. Stein, *Writings*, 1:814.

40. In "Rooms," Stein writes "Every room is open when there are not four, there were there and surely there were four, there were two together" (*Writings*, 1:346). In *The Autobiography of Alice B. Toklas*, she notes: "The house at 27 rue de Fleurus consisted then [1907] as it does now of a tiny pavilion of two stories with four small rooms, a kitchen bath, and a very large atelier" (*Writings*, 1:662). The lines "Currents, currents are not in the air and on the floor and in the door and behind it first" may refer, among other things, to the fact that Stein and Toklas did not have electricity installed in their home until June 1914 (*Writings*, 1:351, 801; see "A Long Dress" in "Objects" for current as electricity). For the break between Stein and her brother, see Hadas, "Spreading the Difference," and Wineapple, *Sister Brother*, especially 378–79.

41. As DeKoven suggests, it is also possible to conclude that there was some simultaneous composition of the sections or that the order of composition, whatever it is, is not that of the published version, for otherwise Stein would not have had trouble remembering (*Different Language*, 164).

42. See Hoffman, *Development of Abstractionism*, 199–207.

43. DeKoven, *Different Language*, 79; Monroe, *Poverty of Objects*, 200; Dickie, *Stein, Bishop, and Rich*, 24, 26–27 (also in Dickie and Travisano, *Gendered Modernisms*, 8–9, 11); Murphy, *Tradition of Subversion*, 166. As Dickie points out, "Rooms" also "does not have the same status as the other sections" in Lisa Ruddick's reading of *Tender Buttons* (*Stein, Bishop, and Rich*, 213; Dickie and Travisano, *Gendered Modernisms*, 23).

44. Gass, *World*, 101; Bridgman, *Gertrude Stein*, 129; and Shoptaw, "Lyric Cryptography."

45. Stein, *Writings*, 2:333.

46. Stein, *Writings*, 1:350–51.

47. Bridgman, *Gertrude Stein*, 120.

48. The frequency of the prefix "ex" is especially apparent in the notebook manuscript, where Stein almost always uses the shorthand "x" for "ex."

49. Stein, *Writings*, 1:346–47.

50. Stein, *Writings*, 1:351.

51. Stein, *Writings*, 1:585.

52. Stein, *Writings*, 1:333. For related arguments about "center" and "custom," see Bridgman, *Gertrude Stein*, 132–34, and Monroe, *Poverty of Objects*, 196–97.

53. Stein, *Writings*, 1:348.

54. Stein, *Writings*, 1:326. The transformation of noun into verb is doubly present in "aider" (French "to help"). Shortly before "This is this dress, aider," there is an often-cited instance in which Stein literally changes a noun into a verb while making an erotic pun. The description for "Peeled pencil, choke" is extremely short—"Rub her coke"—where "Rubber" is split into two words, and it appears as if "h" from "choke" has been placed in front of the "er."

55. Stein, *Writings*, 1:351–52. I have corrected the text slightly here. In *Writings* the passage concludes: "why is it when it is *and is* and there is no doubt, there is no doubt that the singularity shows" (my emphasis). The extra "and is" does not appear in any other published version of *Tender Buttons*.

56. Stein, *Writings*, 1:347, 349, 355.

57. Stein, *Writings*, 1:354, 355.

58. Other "hints at narrative" might include the references to hurting, breaking, and mending throughout *Tender Buttons*. There are suggestive relations in meaning and sound in words like "tender" and "mend her" that may be germane to my discussion of "center." Also compare "rent," "rend," and similar words.

59. Stein, *Writings*, 1:344.

60. Stein, *Writings*, 1:354.

61. Unless otherwise noted, I have retained the Library of America's spellings. Center is consistently spelled with "er" in Stein's notebook manuscripts and type-scripts. Neither the notebooks nor the typescripts should be assumed to be definitive, however. The typescript of "Rooms," for example, spells "color" with "our," whereas the typescripts of "Objects" and "Rooms" use the "or" spelling. The typescripts and the first edition of *Tender Buttons* (1914) moreover contain errors that have for the most part been reproduced in every published edition since. The major exception is the *Tender Buttons* published in the fall 1928 issue of *transition*. Stein herself wrote a note detailing the errors in the first edition, which must have been used by the editors of *transition* because the one obvious error in this edition ("any's is welcome" for "any's is unwelcome" in "Glazed Glitter"; compare "any is unwelcome" in Stein, *Writings*, 1:313) seems to have been introduced by a misreading of Stein's handwriting. Stein's handwritten corrections are significant in part because they do not correct the British spellings of center used in the first edition. In fact, Stein even retains the British spelling in the one correction in which "center" appears. It is therefore

possible that Stein either introduced the alternative spellings of the first edition herself or, having noticed the variants, decided to retain them. Needless to say, she simply may not have cared. *A Dictionary of American English* (1938) and Mencken's *The American Language* (1937) confirm that American and British spellings of "center" had diverged by 1914, though one can find some obstinate exceptions, such as the editorial policy of the *Atlantic Monthly* throughout the 1920s (Mencken, *American Language*, 393). Edmund Wilson's use of "centre" in *Axel's Castle* (1931) is another noteworthy exception.

62. Williams, *Imaginations*, 95.

63. Williams, *Imaginations*, 116–17, 133, 145.

64. Williams, *Imaginations*, 31.

65. Williams, *Imaginations*, 31.

66. The first versions of Hemingway's stories from *In Our Time* were published as *in our time* (without the capitals). For a history and analysis of both versions, see Tetlow, *Hemingway's "In Our Time."* For Crane's "Havana Rose," compare the poem as printed in Weber's edition of Crane's *Complete Poems* to that in Simon's *Poems of Hart Crane*. Weber's version is in two prose paragraphs; Simon's version contains lines numbered and broken at irregular intervals in accordance with Crane's manuscript. For Toomer, see "Nora" and "Calling Jesus."

8. Negative Dialectics

1. Bly has published several collections containing prose poems, starting in 1962 (*Silence in the Snowy Fields*) and including a volume collecting his prose poetry. Edson's poetic reputation rests on writing prose poetry. His first book of prose poems, *The Very Thing That Happens*, was published in 1964. See also his article "The Prose Poem in America" cited in chapter 5.

2. Perloff's comment is from the back cover of the Viking edition of *Three Poems*.

3. Silliman, "New Prose." My number of fifty is conservative. Silliman's list includes all sorts of prose-poem-like works but does not include volumes by authors "in which prose is not substantially represented" (170).

4. Ashbery, *Rivers and Mountains*, 39. As discussed later, "The New Spirit" opens with a meditation on selectivity. See Shoptaw, *On the Outside*, 127, and Fredman, *Poet's Prose*, 122. Bloom (*John Ashbery*) also notes that the tower of Babel passage seems an echo of "The Skaters."

5. See Ashbery, "Craft of John Ashbery," 90; Ashbery, "Interview with John Murphy," 24; and Ashbery, "Experience of Experience," 253. Ashbery, "Interview by Ross Labrie," contains a parenthetical remark about not quite avoiding repetition (32), as does Ashbery, "Interview with John Ashbery" (181).

6. Ashbery, *The Double Dream of Spring*, 81; Ashbery, *Three Poems*, 19.

7. Perhaps the most striking examples in Stevens occur in "An Ordinary Evening in New Haven." The opening stanzas of the poem talk of the "and yet, and yet, and yet"

in relation to the eye's or the poet's "never-ending meditation." Later Stevens closes section XX with "He may evade / Even his own will and in his nakedness / Inhabit the hypnosis of that sphere" only to begin section XXI with "But he may not" (Stevens, *Collected Poems*, 465, 480).

8. Ashbery, "Craft Interview," 93, see also 83–84; Ashbery, "Interview in Warsaw," 305; Ashbery, "Interview with John Ashbery," 184–85; Ashbery, "Experience of Experience," 245; and Fredman, *Poet's Prose*, 102–3.

9. Ashbery, "The Impossible," 252.

10. Ashbery, *Self-Portrait in a Convex Mirror*, 74; Ashbery, *Flow Chart*, 60; Ashbery, *Three Poems*, 65–66.

11. Ashbery has remarked: "It seems to me that poetry has to be self-referential in order to refer to something else. . . . Self-referentiality is not a sign of narcissism, but actually is a further stage of objectivity" (Ashbery, "Imminence of Revelation," 70–71).

12. Ashbery has stated that he likes Bishop's poetry because it is unlike his and that Bishop is "someone who doesn't resemble [him] in the least" (Ashbery, "Interview with John Ashbery," 180). While Ashbery's early sestinas may be his only poems that closely resemble some of Bishop's work, the two poets have more in common than Ashbery's statements may lead one to believe. A strong strain of pragmatism and what might be called "epistemological skepticism" inform both of their work. Bishop and Ashbery have also steered away from overtly confessional and political poetry.

13. Ashbery, *Three Poems*, 7, 8.

14. Ashbery, "The New Spirit," in *Three Poems*, 9.

15. Ashbery uses the mountain-climbing imagery in similar ways in other poems: "Moving on we approached the top / Of the thing, only it was dusk and no one could see, / Only somebody said it was a miracle we had gotten past the / Previous phase" (Ashbery, "A Wave," in *A Wave*, 73). As I suggest later with my comments on "timorous capacity," this move is Wordsworthian. Compare the opening of Wordsworth's "Michael": "If from the public way you turn your steps / Up the tumultuous brook of Green-head Gyhll, / You will suppose that with an upright path / Your feet must struggle; in such bold ascent / The pastoral mountains front you, face to face. / But, courage! for around that boisterous brook / The mountains have all opened out themselves, / And made a hidden valley of their own" (*Selected Poems*, 146).

16. Ashbery, *Three Poems*, 82–83, 45.

17. Ashbery, *Self-Portrait in a Convex Mirror*, 72.

18. Ashbery, *A Wave*, 88.

19. Ashbery, *Three Poems*, 8.

20. Ashbery, *Three Poems*, 51.

21. Fredman has remarked in a related vein, "*Three Poems* unites the two extreme forms of American poetry, the long poem and poet's prose" (*Poet's Prose*, 114).

22. Ashbery has other prose poems that are long, but they are not framed as "long poems" per se.

23. When asked what he was trying to achieve in *Three Poems*, Ashbery laconically replied, "I think I was trying to write three long prose poems" (Ashbery, "Craft of John Ashbery," 90). There may be a vague generic signal implied by the title of *Three Poems*, along the lines of Stein's *Three Lives* and Flaubert's *Trois Contes*, though Ashbery does not recall any specific connection (letter to author, 22 June 1995).

24. See Ashbery, "Interview with Richard Kostelanetz," 103, and Ashbery, "Interview in Warsaw," 303.

25. Shoptaw, *On the Outside*, 132–34, 141, 146.

26. Bloom, *John Ashbery*, 73.

27. Traherne, *Centuries*, 110; Ashbery, "The System" and "The Recital," in *Three Poems*, 56–57, 108–9.

28. Murphy, *Tradition of Subversion*, 172.

29. Chirico, "From *Hebdomeros*," 34. Shoptaw discusses some of this passage in relation to the ending of "The New Spirit" (*On the Outside*, 146).

30. For an example of a run-on sentence, see Chirico, "From Hebdomeros"; for examples of long quotations, see 15 and 29.

31. Auden, *Collected Poems*, 335.

32. The "other addressee" of "you" often appears to be an imagined or actual lover. For a discussion that places Ashbery's use of pronouns in critical perspective, see Shoptaw, *On the Outside*, 139–41.

33. Shoptaw, *On the Outside*, 132.

34. Ashbery, "Entretien," 7 (my translation). Ashbery is responding to the question: "In your opinion is poetry still a specific genre in the era of postmodernity?"

35. See Ashbery, "Interview by Ross Labrie," 31, and Ashbery, "Art of Poetry," 55.

36. Murphy, *Tradition of Subversion*, 170–72.

37. Fredman, *Poet's Prose*, 117. Fredman borrows the phrase "He chose to include" from Stevens's "Notes toward a Supreme Fiction." The remark about the dilemma of the postmodern self is Fredman's paraphrase of Creeley.

38. See the Ashbery chapters in Perloff, *Poetics of Indeterminacy*.

39. Perloff, *Poetic License*, 282.

40. Shoptaw, *On the Outside*, 133

41. Shoptaw, *On the Outside*, 133.

42. Ross, *Failure of Modernism*. In "An Interview with John Murphy," Ashbery remarks that when he started writing he felt he was "probably going to be a Modernist poet" (21).

43. Ashbery, "Imminence of a Revelation," 72.

44. Ashbery, "Interview with John Murphy," 20.

45. I discuss these lines in chapter 5.

46. See Ashbery, "Interview with Ross Labrie," 30; Ashbery, "Art of Poetry," 38–9;

Ashbery, "Craft of John Ashbery," 93; and Ashbery, "Interview with John Murphy," 23. See also Shoptaw's remarks on Ashbery's undergraduate thesis on Auden (*On the Outside*, 132). In "Craft of John Ashbery," Ashbery remarks, "In Eliot, the language of 'The Tribe' always strikes me as a kind of an appendage rather than something that is part of the core of the poetry as in early lyrical Auden" (93). From an Ashberian perspective, there is also a sense in which Auden does not go far enough toward introducing the prosaic into poetry. In framing this issue as one of going or not going far enough, we should be careful not to view poetry from within a narrative of progression toward "freedom" or "natural speech" or "more direct revelation." In *Modern Poetry after Modernism*, James Longenbach cautions against reading twentieth-century poetry through what he calls a "breakthrough" narrative. In his chapter "John Ashbery's Individual Talent," Longenbach points out that Ashbery sometimes makes use of this narrative. As his chapter title suggests, Longenbach follows Shoptaw in arguing that "Ashbery's poetry can hardly be discussed without almost constant reference to an extraordinarily wide range of precursors (among whom Eliot looms prominently)," so that "even if the poems seem . . . more 'advanced' than Eliot's—more open to demotic language, more accommodating to popular culture, more suspicious of the lyric's unified voice—the poems are nonetheless unthinkable without Eliot's example" (88).

47. See Bloom, *John Ashbery*, 74; Murphy, *Tradition of Subversion*, 168–69; and Shoptaw, *On the Outside*, 126.

48. Ashbery has talked about his urge to cover the page with words (Ashbery, "Interview in Warsaw," 302). For "inclusionism," see Murphy, *Tradition of Subversion*, 168–69, and Fredman, *Poet's Prose*, 117.

49. Shoptaw, *On the Outside*, 126.

50. Ashbery, "These Lacustrine Cities," in *Rivers and Mountains*, 9. The full quotation is "you see // You have built a mountain of something, / Thoughtfully pouring all your energy into this single monument."

51. Shoptaw, *On the Outside*, 136. For a reading emphasizing Hegelian ideas and dialectic, see Staiger, "Hitherside of History."

52. Shoptaw, *On the Outside*, 134–36. The bracketed additions in the quotation of the back-cover blurb are Shoptaw's.

53. See Shoptaw, *On the Outside*, 136–37; Murphy, *Tradition of Subversion*, 175–76; and Fredman, *Poet's Prose*, 109. For Ashbery's comments on the relationship of music to his poetry see Ashbery, "Pleasures of Poetry," 82; Ashbery, "Craft of John Ashbery," 95–96; and Ashbery, "Interview in Warsaw," 304. In "Interview in Warsaw," Ashbery talks of the progression in *Three Poems* as a Neoplatonic allegory of love "going from, you know, the physical up to the spiritual": "the underlying theme is a kind of progression which I didn't know because I didn't know I was going to meet somebody and fall in love while I was in the middle of it" (304).

54. Ashbery, "Interview in Warsaw," 304.

55. Readers may be reminded of Theodor Adorno's concept of "negative dialectics" in works such as *Negative Dialectics* and *The Dialectics of Enlightenment*. My use of the term does not depend on his ideas and should be considered in light of my own arguments.

56. Ashbery, "The New Spirit," in *Three Poems*, 31.

57. Ashbery, *Three Poems*, 29–30. All subsequent quotations of *Three Poems* list the page number in parenthesis after the quotation.

58. See Murphy, *Tradition of Subversion*, 174, and Shoptaw, *On the Outside*, 138, for discussions of the etymology of "prose" (from *provertere*, to turn forward).

59. On the composition and publication dates of *Three Poems*, Shoptaw notes: " 'The New Spirit,' begun in November 1969 and mostly written between January and April 1970, was published in *The Paris Review* (Fall 1970); 'The System,' written between January and March 1971, was published in *The Paris Review* (Winter 1972); 'The Recital,' written in April 1971 appeared both in *The Poetry Review* (Winter 1971–72) and, significantly, in *Fiction* (Spring 1972)" (*On the Outside*, 362).

60. In a related vein, Fredman argues that "Ashbery seems to counsel a Rilkean active passivity as the wisest course for the human will in its encounter with its own destiny" (*Poet's Prose*, 120). As is typical with Ashbery, the reversal of the cliché does not completely negate it. Among other things, speech-making is invested with an active quality.

61. Ashbery, "Experience of Experience," 254.

62. The major exception is David Shapiro's paragraph-by-paragraph reading of *Three Poems*, "Meditations on Probability," in *John Ashbery*, 133–74. Fredman significantly places his narrative material in a three-page footnote, providing a "set of descriptive titles as a summary of the book" for "the reader anxious for some heuristic device" (*Poet's Prose*, 178).

63. See Bloom, *John Ashbery*, 75–76; Fredman, *Poet's Prose*, 124–25; Murphy, *Tradition of Subversion*, 191–92; Shapiro, *John Ashbery*, 153–54; and Shoptaw, *On the Outside*, 145–47.

64. See 10, 28, 35, and 44. As Shoptaw remarks, "Drawing on the sense of failure in the all-American game of baseball . . . Ashbery's 'idea of striking out' (TP 10) means canceling a portion of text, losing at love, and beginning a journey" (*On the Outside*, 137).

65. Bishop, *Complete Poems*, 94.

66. Shoptaw discusses "the 1960s refrain" of "love is in the air" in relation to a passage on page 10 of "The New Spirit" (*On the Outside*, 142). Scientific imagery is extremely important for "The System" (also for "The New Spirit" in light of the moon and other astronomical references). For examples of atom or element imagery, see 61, 86, 88, and 104; for conservation of matter and energy, see 85 and 91; for motion and movement, see 4, 5, 20, 27, and 31 in "The New Spirit" and 74, 86, 90, 100, and 106 in "The System."

67. On the previous page, the narrator talks of "a point of view like the painter's: in the round." This "round view" of things, often associated with painting, recurs in "The System" (93, 99) and "The Recital" (113). Roundness of view relates to themes like holistic understanding and inclusion.

68. For an illuminating discussion of Ashbery's "frontal and latent happiness" in relation to Freud's pleasure and reality principles, see Shoptaw, *On the Outside*, 152–53.

69. Thread imagery appears elsewhere in "The System" (77, 84) as do variants of the image, such as following a trail of crumbs (81) and references to "the whole warp and woof of the design" (77).

70. Ashbery, *Three Poems*, 105. For other examples of turning to an outside space when encountering an impasse, see 72, 80, and 82.

71. Ashbery, "Craft Interview," 93–94.

72. Wordsworth, *Prelude*, 41, 43. The corresponding lines of the 1805 version are even more self-critical.

73. Bloom, *John Ashbery*, 75.

74. Koethe, "Absence of a Noble Presence," 86.

75. Hejinian, *My Life* (1987), 116. The experimental-traditional distinction is widespread, if not always acknowledged. Jerome McGann has made what may be the most overt declaration of the distinction: "L=A=N=G=U=A=G=E Writing is distinctively experimental, while poets like Pinsky, Louise Glück, and John Hollander are traditionalists" ("Contemporary Poetry," 255).

76. As I note later, a mock journal, *In Between*, comes in between *In Time* and *In Place*. The juxtaposition of these sections emphasizes different kinds of form.

77. Hollander, *In Time and Place*, 99–100.

78. Hejinian, *My Life* (1980), 6.

79. Hejinian, *My Life* (1987), 8.

80. Hollander, *In Time and Place*, 69; Caws and Riffaterre, *Prose Poem*, 231–32.

81. Hollander, "Others Who Have Lived in This Room," *In Time and Place*, 37. Hollander plays with the etymological meaning of stanza as room in several poems in the collection.

82. Hejinian, *My Life* (1980), 26; Hejinian, *My Life* (1987), 27.

83. Hejinian, *My Life* (1987), 96.

84. Hejinian, *My Life* (1987), 97. Hejinian is drawing on a passage in Jameson's *The Political Unconscious*: "[Long-dead issues] can recover their original urgency for us only if they are retold within the unity of a single great collective story; only if, in however disguised and symbolic a form, they are seen as sharing a single fundamental theme—for Marxism, the collective struggle to wrest a realm of Freedom for a realm of Necessity; only if they are grasped as vital episodes in a single vast unfinished plot" (19–20). Later Jameson discusses the new models of causation Marxist critics should try to embrace (moving away from "billiard ball" or deterministic models).

85. Hejinian, *My Life* (1987), 101.

86. Hejinian, *My Life* (1987), 99–101.

87. Hejinian, *My Life* (1987), 101.

88. Hejinian, *My Life* (1987), 98, 101.

89. Hollander, *In Time and Place*, 100.

90. Hejinian, *My Life* (1987), 96.

91. Johnson, "Interview," 68. Appearing first in 1992, *The Prose Poem: An International Journal* owes its name from an anthology edited by Michael Benedikt in 1976. In addition to prose poems, interviews, book reviews, and essays, the journal includes an up-to-date bibliography of criticism on the prose poem.

Conclusion

1. Bernard, *La Poème en prose*. Chapelan opens his anthology with the remark: "As incredible as it seems, and seemed to me the instant I had an inkling of it, [before this] not one anthology of the prose poem existed in France" (Si peu croyable qu'il paraisse, et nous parût dès l'instant que nous le soupçonnâmes, il n'existait point en France d'anthologie du poème en prose) (*Anthologie*, vii).

2. In the back of *Lire le poème en prose*, Sandras includes a minianthology of the *poème en prose*, which I do not discuss. This anthology is typical in that the history outlined here places Baudelaire and Bertrand at its beginning.

3. Huysmans, *À Rebours*, 221–22. For more on Huysmans, see chapter 4.

4. "Vox Populi" had also been published in *L'Étoile française* (14 December 1880) and *La Comédie humaine* (24 December 1881). The story arguably appears more like a prose poem when published alone in a journal.

5. "Je viens de rouvrir sa [Maurice Chapelan's] belle *Anthologie du poème en prose*, publiée voici bientôt quarante ans, et j'y trouve en trois substantifs les principes même du genre, en dehors desquels il n'y a guère de salut: BRIÈVETÉ — INTENSITÉ — GRATUITÉ" (Decaunes, *Le Poème en prose*, 15).

6. "[B]rièveté, intensité, [et] gratuité sont pour lui [le poème en prose], nous l'avons vu, non des éléments de beauté possibles, mais vraiment des éléments constitutifs sans lesquels il n'existe pas" (Bernard, *Le Poème en prose*, 793). Bernard discusses the aesthetics of the prose poem more fully on pages 435–44.

7. In her extended discussion of the aesthetics of prose poetry, Bernard in fact talks about density, not intensity, as the corollary of brevity (*Le Poème en prose*, 444).

8. "Que le poème en prose soit véritablement un poème, l'acquiescement de la sensibilité de chacun peul seul en apporter la preuve: sa vertu poétique, ce n'est pas en lui, c'est en nous" (Chapelan, *Anthologie*, xvi).

9. "Maurice Chapelan est tombé, je le crains, dans cette confusion contre laquelle, justement, nous met en garde l'auteur du *Cornet à dés*. LA PROSE POÉTIQUE N'EST PAS LE POÉME EN PROSE. . . . La loi fondamentale du poème en prose, qui veut un objet autonome, un corps verbal complet et bien clos, dans ces 'morceaux choisis' n'est . . . pas respectée" (Decaunes, *Le Poème en prose*, 16–17).

10. For the phrases "une sorte de préfiguration" and "proposé *d'abord* d'enchanter le lecteur, mais . . . ," see Chapelan, *Anthologie*, 3 and 4; for Chapelan's remarks about Bertrand and Baudelaire, see 3.

11. The French titles are *Quatre précurseurs*, *Première époque*, and *Deuxième époque*. The anthology also includes a fourth section (*Post-Scriptum*) in which Decaunes's own prose poems appear.

12. "Le maître incontesté du poème en prose" (Decaunes, *Le Poème en prose*, 139). Though the order of individual poets in *Le Poème en prose* is determined by birth date, Decaunes does not provide a clear rationale for his two epochs. He comes closest to an explanation when he writes in his introduction that Jacob's preface to *Cornet à dés* was "un texte sans précédent, à partir duquel il n'a plus été possible de tomber, autrement que par inadvertance ou mauvais vouloir, dans les confusions et les amalgames qu'on avait à déplorer jusque-là" (a text without precedent, after which it was no longer possible—other than by inadvertence or ill will—to fall into the confusions and amalgams which were to be deplored up until then) (13).

13. "J'avais envisagé de joindre aux extraits de ce chef-d'œuvre le texte bouleversant intitulé "L'Amour du prochain" . . . qui figure dans les *Derniers Poèmes* publiés au lendemain de la mort du poète. Mais ce texte en prose met en œuvre des éléments émotionnels *qui lui sont extérieurs*; il fait allusion à des circonstances et des faits auxquels le lecteur doit se référer s'il veut que le poème ait un sens, y compris un sens poétique. Faute de quoi le poéme 'bâille' comme un poche vide. Nous touchons là à une des lois fondamentales du poème en prose. Voilà pourquoi je n'ai finalement pas retenu ce texte terrible" (Decaunes, *Le Poème en prose*, 139).

14. "Infirmerie du camp de Drancy, 1944" (Decaunes, *Le Poème en prose*, 139). Decaunes normally only lists the city in which the poet died.

15. As far as coverage of historical periods goes, Chapelan's and Decaunes's selections are impressive if one makes allowances for their tendencies to exclude longer prose works and to favor texts consciously composed as prose poems. The complete absence of women poets is perhaps the most glaring omission from Chapelan's and Decaunes's anthologies, at least to an American reader. This sort of omission is not unusual in discussions and anthologies of French poetry, whether in prose or verse.

16. For anthologies in dissertations, see Alexander, *American Prose Poem*, and Katz, *Contemporary Prose Poems in French*. Additional anthologies of prose poetry in journals are listed *The Prose Poem: An International Journal* 4 (1995). They include *Madrona* (2 [1973]: 7), *Arion's Dolphin* (3 [summer-autumn 1974]: 3–4), *Indiana Review* (9 [2 November 1986]: 4), *Denver Quarterly* (25 [spring 1981]: 4), and *lift* ([August 1991] 7). In his introduction, Benedikt claims that "over the past several years [the early 1970s], after a virtual silence on the subject, some twenty U.S. literary magazines have published issues devoted fully or in part to the prose poem" (*Prose Poem*, 39). As for limited-edition anthologies, I have in mind publications like Godbert's *Anywhere Out of the World*, which collects four poems.

17. It is possible to see these trends as resulting from, on the one hand, an "aesthetic of liberation" and emphasis on accessing the unconscious (late 1960s and early 1970s), and, on the other hand, a postmodern aesthetic and language-poet influence (1980s and 1990s). Needless to say, both explanations are very rough. The scholarly arguments about the prose poem's subversive nature, though touched on by early French critics like Bernard and Decaunes, have been put forward most noticeably by American critics since the 1970s.

18. Howells, introduction to *Pastels in Prose*, viii.

19. See especially Tyler's remarks in Ford, "A Little Anthology," 330, 336.

20. Near the opening of his introduction, Tyler quotes Ford: "The poem in prose is the form of the future" ("A Little Anthology," 330). Though Tyler is skeptical about the claim "form of the future," his ensuing discussion concerns the prose poem as a form.

21. Hall's comments are entitled "Some Ideas About Prose Poems" (*Pebble* has no page numbers). Hall seems to be replying to Ford (see note 20) when he writes, "By no means is prose the form of the future. Prose poems . . . are a station on the journey. Everything is a station on the journey" (Kuzma and Ackerson, "Fifty-four prose poems"). For Miller, see Loydell and Miller, *Curious Architecture*, 162–63; for Alexander and Truesdale, see Alexander, Vinz, and Truesdale, *Party Train*, xix, xx, and xxxi; for Wilson, see *Anatomy of Water*, 8. Benedikt opens The *Prose Poem* with the assertion, "The prose poem is an international form " (39). His definition of prose poetry is tentative: "The best working definition . . . in the midst of such widespread exploration of the form—is that it is a genre of poetry" (46–47).

22. All of the anthologies published in the 1990s make references to prose poetry criticism in their introductions or afterwords.

23. Benedikt, *Prose Poem*, 39; Loydell and Miller, *Curious Architecture*, 7; Alexander, Vinz, and Truesdale, *Party Train*, xix (Truesdale citing Alexander).

24. Wilson, *Anatomy of Water*, 8, and Freibert and Young, *Models of the Universe*, 18.

25. See, for example, Wilson, *Anatomy of Water*, 6, and Alexander, Vinz, and Truesdale, *Party Train*, xix.

26. See Benedikt, *Prose Poem*, 39–40. In making Eliot a kind of villain in the story of the American prose poem, Benedikt's narrative is similar to Margueritte Murphy's (see chapter 6). Strictly speaking, Murphy and Benedikt are concerned with Eliot's influence (via New Criticism and other paths), though they both argue that his resistance to the prose poem—its disturbing mixture of genre, its lack of restraint—can be found in his critical writings.

27. Qtd. in Alexander, Vinz, and Truesdale, *Party Train*, xix.

28. Ford's anthology also includes older poems in English (from writers like Wilde and Shakespeare), as if it were constructing a kind of pedigree for the prose poem.

29. Freibert and Young, *Models of the Universe*, 18, 19. The most recent poet in the anthology is Tomas Tranströmer (b. 1931).

30. The "Pathfinders and Desperadoes" section of *The Party Train* is about fifty pages and includes work from writers as various as Hawthorne, Whitman, Stein, Williams, Toomer, Hemingway, Faulkner, and Patchen. The entire book is over three hundred pages.   •

31. See my comparison of "sonnet" and "novel" at the end of chapter 4.

32. Prose poems have appeared frequently in French anthologies of poetry since the 1950s (see chapter 4). Very few prose poems appear in the best-selling American anthologies like *The Norton Anthology of Modern Poetry*. There are a few prose poems in specialized anthologies like Berg and Mezey's *The New Naked Poetry: Recent American Poetry in Open Forms*. And some prose pieces, which writers like Russell Edson publish elsewhere as prose poems, appear in anthologies of genres related to prose poetry, like the collection in Schwartz, *Imperial Messages*.

33. Fowler, *Kinds of Literature*, 107.

34. To the degree that the readership of prose poetry is a subset of the readership of poetry, the prose poem might be a "subgenre," as Fowler describes it. Readership is only one trait, however, and the desire to subdivide may be more of a classificatory than interpretive impulse. See my remarks on subgenre in chapter 1.

Bibliography

Abrams, M. H. *The Mirror and the Lamp: Romantic Theory and the Critical Tradition*. New York: Oxford UP, 1953.

Ackerson, Duane, ed. *A Prose Poem Anthology*. Pocatello, Idaho: Dragon Flying, 1970.

Aldington, Richard. "A Note on Poetry in Prose." *The Chapbook* 22 (April 1921): 16–20.

Alexander, Robert. "The American Prose Poem, 1890–1980." Ph.D. dissertation, University of Wisconsin–Milwaukee, 1982.

Alexander, Robert, Mark Vinz, and C. W. Truesdale, eds. *The Party Train: A Collection of North American Prose Poetry*. Minneapolis: New Rivers, 1996.

Alpers, Paul. *What Is Pastoral?* Chicago: U of Chicago P, 1996.

Ashbery, John. "The Art of Poetry XXXIII." Interview with Peter Stitt. *Paris Review* 25.90 (1983): 30–76.

———. "Craft Interview with John Ashbery." With Janet Bloom and Robert Losada. *The Poet's Craft: Interviews from "The New York Quarterly."* Ed. William Packard. New York: Paragon House, 1987. 79–97. Revised version of interview from *The Craft of Poetry: Interviews from "The New York Quarterly."* Ed. William Packard. Garden City, N.Y.: Doubleday, 1974. 111–32.

———. "The Craft of John Ashbery." Interview with Louis A. Osti. *Confrontations* 9.3 (1974): 84–96.

———. *The Double Dream of Spring*. New York: Ecco, 1970.

———. "Entretien avec John Ashbery." Interview with André Bleikasten. *La Quinzaine littérarire* 16.28 (February 1993): 7–8.

———. "The Experience of Experience: A Conversation with John Ashbery." With A. Poulin Jr. *Michigan Quarterly Review* 20.3 (1981): 242–55.

———. *Flow Chart*. New York: Knopf, 1991.

———. "The Imminence of a Revelation." Interview with Richard Jackson. *Acts of Mind: Conversations with Contemporary Poets*, by Richard Jackson. University: U of Alabama P, 1983. 69–76.

———. "The Impossible." Review of *Stanzas in Meditation*, by Gertrude Stein. *Poetry* 90 (July 1957): 250–54.

———. "An Interview in Warsaw." With Piotr Sommer. *Code of Signals: Recent Writings in Poetics*. Ed. Michael Palmer. Berkeley, Calif.: North Atlantic, 1983. 294–314.

———. "An Interview with John Ashbery." Conducted by John Koethe. *SubStance* 37/38 (1983): 178–86.

———. Interview with Richard Kostelanetz. *The Old Poetries and the New*, by Richard Kostelanetz. Ann Arbor: U of Michigan P, 1981. 87–110. Rpt. of "How to Be a Difficult Poet." *New York Times Magazine* (23 May 1976).

———. Interview with Sue Gangel. *American Poetry Observed: Poets on Their Work*. Ed. Joe David Bellamy. Chicago: U of Illinois P, 1984. 9–20. Revised version of interview in the *San Francisco Review of Books* (November 1977).

———. "John Ashbery: An Interview by Ross Labrie." *American Poetry Review* 13.3 (May/June 1984): 29–33.

———. "John Ashbery: An Interview with John Murphy." *Poetry Review* 75.2 (August 1985): 20–25.

———. "The Pleasures of Poetry." Interview with David Lehman. *New York Times Magazine* (16 December 1984).

———. *Rivers and Mountains*. New York: Ecco, 1966.

———. *Self-Portrait in a Convex Mirror*. New York: Viking, 1975.

———. *Shadow Train*. New York: Viking, 1981.

———. *Three Poems*. New York: Viking, 1972.

———. *A Wave*. New York: Viking, 1984.

Auden, W. H. *Collected Poems*. Ed. Edward Mendelson. London: Faber and Faber, 1976.

Auster, Paul, ed. *The Random House Book of Twentieth-Century French Poetry*. New York: Random House, 1982.

Balzac, Honoré de. *La Comédie humaine*. Ed. Marcel Bouteron. Vols. 4, 9, and 11. Paris: Gallimard, 1952–62.

Banville, Théodore de. *Petit Traité de poésie française*. 1872. Paris: Alphonse Lemerre, 1891.

Barlow, Norman H. *Sainte-Beuve to Baudelaire: A Poetic Legacy*. Durham, N.C.: Duke UP, 1964.

Baudelaire, Charles. *Correspondances complètes*. Ed. Claude Pichois and Jean Ziegler. 2 vols. Paris: Gallimard, 1973.

———. *Œuvres complètes*. Ed. Claude Pichois. 2 vols. Paris: Gallimard, 1975–76.

———. *Petits Poëmes en prose*. Ed. Marcel Ruff. Paris: Garnier-Flammarion, 1967.

———. *Petits Poëmes en prose*. Ed. Robert Kopp. Paris: José Corti, 1969.

———. *Petits Poèmes en prose (Le Spleen de Paris)*. Ed. Henri Lemaitre. Paris: Garnier Frères, 1962.

Beebee, Thomas O. *The Ideology of Genre: A Comparative Study of Generic Instability*. University Park: Pennsylvania State UP, 1994.

Benedikt, Michael, ed. *The Prose Poem: An International Anthology*. New York: Dell, 1976.

Benjamin, Walter. *Charles Baudelaire: A Lyric Poet in the Era of High Capitalism*. Trans. Harry Zohn. New York: New Left Books, 1973.

Berg, Stephen, and Robert Mezey. *The New Naked Poetry: Recent American Poetry in Open Forms*. Inidanapolis, Ind.: Bobbs-Merrill, 1976.

Bernard, Suzanne. *Le Poème en prose de Baudelaire jusqu'à nos jours*. Paris: Nizet, 1959.

Bertrand, Louis (Aloysius). *Gaspard de la nuit: Fantaisies à la manière de Rembrandt et de Callot*. Paris: Gallimard, 1980.

Bishop, Elizabeth. *The Complete Poems, 1927–1979*. New York: Farrar, Straus, Giroux, 1979.

———. *One Art*. Ed. Robert Giroux. New York: Farrar, Straus, Giroux, 1994.

Bloom, Harold, ed. *John Ashbery*. New York: Chelsea House, 1985.

Bossuet, Jacques-Bénigne. *Sermon sur la Mort et autres sermons*. Paris: Garnier-Flammarion, 1970.

Breunig, Leroy C. "Why France?" Caws and Riffaterre, *Prose Poem*, 3–20.

Bridgman, Richard. *Gertrude Stein in Pieces*. New York: Oxford UP, 1970.

Brombert, Victor. "The Will to Ecstasy: The Example of Baudelaire's 'La Chevelure.'" *Yale French Studies* 50 (1974): 55–64.

Bruss, Elizabeth W. *Autobiographical Acts: The Changing Situation of Literary Genre*. Baltimore: Johns Hopkins UP, 1976.

Bürger, Peter. *Theory of the Avant-Garde*. Trans. Michael Shaw. Minneapolis: U of Minnesota P, 1984.

Burton, Richard. *Baudelaire and the Second Republic: Writing and Revolution*. Oxford: Clarendon, 1991.

———. *Baudelaire in 1859: A Study in the Sources of Poetic Creativity*. New York: Cambridge UP, 1988.

Cannell, Skipwith. "Poems in Prose and Verse: A Sequence." *Poetry* 2.5 (August 1913): 171–76.

Cather, Willa. *The Professor's House*. New York: Vintage Classics, 1990.

Caws, Mary Ann, and Hermine Riffaterre, eds. *The Prose Poem in France: Theory and Practice*. New York: Columbia UP, 1983.

Cervantes, Miguel de. *Don Quixote*. Trans. Walter Starkie. New York: Signet, 1964.

Chambers, Ross. "Baudelaire et la pratique de la dédicace." *Saggi e richerche de letteratura francese* 24 (1985): 121–40.

Champfleury (Jules Fleury). *Chien-Caillou: Fantaisies d'hiver*. Paris: La Librairie Pittoresque de Martinon, 1847.

Chapelan, Maurice. *Anthologie du poème en prose*. 1946. Paris: Juilliard, 1959.

Chase, Cynthia. "Paragon, Parergon: Baudelaire Translates Rousseau." *Difference in Translation*. Ed. Joseph Graham. Ithaca, N.Y.: Cornell UP, 1985. 63–80.

Chateaubriand, François René. *Atala, René, Les Aventures du dernier Abencérage.* Ed. Fernand Letessier. Paris: Garnier Frères, 1958.

Cherel, Albert. *La Prose poétique française.* Paris: Artisan du Livre, 1940.

Chessman, Harriet Scott. *The Public Is Invited to Dance: Representation, the Body, and Dialogue in Gertrude Stein.* Stanford, Calif.: Stanford UP, 1989.

Chirico, Giorgio de. "From *Hebdomeros,* by Giorgio de Chirico, translated by John Ashbery." *Art and Literature: An International Review* 4 (spring 1965).

Claudel, Paul. *Connaissance de l'Est.* Paris: Gallimard, 1974.

Clayton, Vista. *The Prose Poem in French Literature of the Eighteenth Century.* New York: Institute of French Studies, 1936.

Cohen, Ralph. "History and Genre." *New Literary History* 17.2 (winter 1986): 203–18.

———. "Reply to Dominick LaCapra and Richard Harvey Brown." *New Literary History* 17.2 (winter 1986): 229–32.

Cohen, Ralph, ed. *The Future of Literary Theory.* New York: Routledge, 1989.

———. *New Directions in Literary History.* Baltimore: Johns Hopkins UP, 1974.

Coleridge, Samuel Taylor. *The Complete Works of Samuel Taylor Coleridge.* Vol. 7 (Poems). Ed. W. G. T. Shield. New York: Harper & Brothers, 1884.

Cottin, Sophie Ristaud. *Œuvres complètes.* Tome 1, *Claire d'Albe.* Paris: Ménard et Dusenue, fils, 1824.

———. "La Prise de Jéricho." *Mélanges de Littérature.* Ed. J. B. A. Suard. Tome 1. Paris: Dentu, 1803.

Crane, Hart. *The Complete Poems and Selected Letters and Prose of Hart Crane.* Ed. Brom Weber. New York: Liveright, 1966.

———. *The Poems of Hart Crane.* Ed. Marc Simon. New York: Liveright, 1986.

Cros, Charles. *Charles Cros, Tristan Corbière, Œuvres complètes.* Ed. Louis Forestier and Pierre-Olivier Walzer. Paris: Gallimard, 1970.

Decaunes, Luc, ed. *Le Poème en prose.* Paris: Seghers, 1984.

DeKoven, Marianne. *A Different Language: Gertrude Stein's Experimental Writing.* Madison: U of Wisconsin P, 1983.

De la Mare, Walter. *Poetry in Prose.* Warton Lecture on English Poetry 1935. London: Humphrey Milford Amen House, 1935. Rpt. Folcroft, Pa.: Folcroft, 1969.

Delesalle, Jean-François. "Baudelaire rival de Jules Janin?" Patty and Pichois, *Études,* 41–53.

Delville, Michel. *The American Prose Poem: Poetic Form and the Boundaries of Genre.* Gainesville: UP of Florida, 1998.

Derrida, Jacques. "The Law of Genre." *Glyph* 7 (1980): 202–29. Rpt. in *Critical Inquiry* 7.1 (autumn 1980): 55–81.

Dickens, Charles. "The Old Church-yard Tree." *Household Words* 16 (13 July 1850): 377–78. Rpt. in *Harper's New Monthly Magazine* (September 1850): 483.

Dickie, Margaret. *On the Modernist Long Poem.* Iowa City: U of Iowa P, 1986.

———. "Recovering the Repression in Stein's Erotic Poetry." Dickie and Travisano, *Gendered Modernisms*, 3–25.

———. *Stein, Bishop, and Rich: Lyrics of Love, War, and Peace.* Chapel Hill and London: U of North Carolina P, 1997.

Dickie, Margaret, and Thomas Travisano, eds. *Gendered Modernisms: American Women Poets and Their Readers.* Philadelphia: U of Pennsylvania P, 1996.

Dubrow, Heather. *Genre.* New York: Methuen, 1982.

Dydo, Ulla E. "Reading the Handwriting: The Manuscripts of Gertrude Stein." Kellner, *Gertrude Stein Companion*, 84–96.

Edson, Russell. "The Prose Poem in America." *Parnassus: Poetry in Review* 5.1 (fall/winter 1976).

Eliot, T. S. "The Borderline of Prose." *New Statesman* 9 (19 May 1917): 157–59.

———. *The Complete Poems and Plays, 1909–1950.* New York: Harcourt, Brace & World, 1971.

———. Introduction to *Collected Works of Valéry.* Vol. 7. New York: Bollingen Foundation, 1958.

———. *Inventions of the March Hare: Poems 1909–1917.* Ed. Christopher Ricks. New York: Harcourt Brace, 1996.

———. *On Poetry and Poets.* Boston: Faber and Faber, 1957.

———. Preface to *Anabasis*, by St.-John Perse. Trans. T. S. Eliot. 1938. New York: Harcourt, Brace, 1949.

———. "Prose and Verse." *The Chapbook* 22 (April 1921): 3–10.

———. *The Sacred Wood.* New York: Methuen, 1920.

———. *To Criticize the Critic.* New York: Farrar, Straus & Giroux, 1965.

Emerson, Ralph Waldo. *The Journals and Miscellaneous Notebooks of Ralph Waldo Emerson.* Vols. 3 and 7, 1838–42. Ed. William H. Gilman and Alfred Ferguson. Cambridge: Belknap Press of Harvard UP, 1963.

Evans, Margery. *Baudelaire and Intertextuality: Poetry at the Crossroads.* Cambridge: Cambridge UP, 1993.

Fishelov, David. *Metaphors of Genre: The Role of Analogies in Genre Theory.* University Park: Pennsylvania State UP, 1993.

Fletcher, John Gould. "Miss Lowell's Discovery: Polyphonic Prose." Review of *Swordblades and Poppy Seed*, by Amy Lowell. *Poetry* 6.1 (April 1915): 32–36.

Fongaro, Antoine. "Aux Sources de 'Recueillement.'" Patty and Pichois, *Études*, 158–77.

Fontainebleau, hommage à C. F. Denecourt. Paris: Hachette, 1855.

Ford, Charles Henri, ed. "A Little Anthology of the Poem in Prose." *New Directions* 14 (1953).

Fowler, Alastair. "The Future of Genre Theory: Functions and Constructional Types." Cohen, *Future of Literary Theory*, 291–303.

————. *Kinds of Literature: An Introduction to the Theory of Genres and Modes.* Cambridge: Harvard UP, 1982.

————. "The Life and Death of Literary Forms." *New Literary History* 2.2 (1971): 199–216. Rpt. in Cohen, *New Directions*, 77–94.

Fredman, Stephen. *Poet's Prose: The Crisis in American Verse.* 1983. Cambridge: Cambridge UP, 1990.

Friebert, Stuart, and David Young, eds. *Models of the Universe.* Oberlin, Ohio: Oberlin College P, 1995.

Gass, William. *The World within the Word.* New York: Knopf, 1978.

Gautier, Théophile. *Portraits et souvenirs littéraires.* Paris: Charpentier, 1881. Rpt. in *Œuvres complètes* 9. Geneva: Slatkine Reprints, 1978.

Gerhart, Mary. "The Dilemma of the Text: How to 'Belong' to a Genre." *Poetics* 18.4–5 (1989): 355–73.

————. *Genre Choices, Gender Questions.* Norman and London: U of Oklahoma P, 1992.

Godbert, Geoffrey. *Anywhere Out of the World: Prose Poems Selected by Geoffrey Godbert.* Warwick, England: Grenville Press Pamphlets, 1993.

Guérin, Maurice de. *Poésie.* Paris: Gallimard, 1984.

Guiette, Robert. "Le Titre des 'Petits Poèmes en Prose.'" *Romanica Gandensia* 12 (1972): 165–72.

Guillaume, L., and A. Silvaire, eds. *Poésie vivante.* Tome 2. Paris: Librairie Les Lettres, 1954.

Hadas, Pamela. "Spreading the Difference: One Way to Read Gertrude Stein's *Tender Buttons.*" *Twentieth Century Literature* 24.1 (spring 1978): 57–75.

Hass, Gerhard. *Essay.* Stuttgart: J. B. Metzlershe Verlagsbuchhandlung, 1969.

Hawthorne, Nathaniel. "Fragments from the Journal of a Solitary Man." *American Monthly Magazine* 4 (July 1837).

————. *Hawthorne's American Travel Sketches.* Ed. Alfred Weber, Beth L. Lueck, and Dennis Berthold. Hanover, N.H.: UP of New England, 1989.

————. "Sketches from Memory by a Pedestrian. No. 2." *New England Magazine* (December 1835).

Hejinian, Lyn. *My Life.* Providence, R.I.: Burning Deck, 1980. Expanded and rpt. Los Angeles: Sun & Moon, 1987.

Henderson, Alice Corbin. "Poetic Prose and Vers Libre." *Poetry* 2.2 (May 1913): 70–72.

Hernadi, Paul. *Beyond Genre: New Directions in Literary Classification.* Ithaca, N.Y.: Cornell UP, 1972.

Hoffman, Michael J. *The Development of Abstractionism in the Writings of Gertrude Stein.* Philadelphia: U of Pennsylvania P, 1965.

Hollander, John. *The Gazer's Spirit.* Chicago: U of Chicago P, 1995.

————. *In Time and Place.* Baltimore: Johns Hopkins UP, 1986.

Houssaye, Arsène. *Œuvres poétiques*. Paris: Hachette, 1857.

Howells, W. D. Introduction to *Pastels in Prose*, by Stuart Merrill. New York: Harper & Brothers, 1890.

Huart, Louis. *Physiologie du flâneur*. Illustrated by Adolphe, Daumier, and Maurisset. Paris: Aubert et Companie; Lavigne, 1841.

Hugo, Victor. *Œuvres poétiques de Victor Hugo*. Ed. Pierre Albouy. Vol. 2. Paris: Gallimard, 1967.

———. *Les Orientales, Les Feuilles d'automne*. Paris: Gallimard, 1966.

Hunt, Leigh. "Dreams on the Borders of the Land of Poetry." *The Keepsake of 1828*. London: Thomas Davison, 1828. 234–40.

Huysmans, J. K. *À Rebours*. Paris: Garnier-Flammarion, 1978.

Jacob, Max. *Le Cornet à dès*. Paris, Gallimard, 1945.

Jameson, Fredric. *The Political Unconscious*. Ithaca, N.Y.: Cornell UP, 1982.

Janin, Jules. *Le Gâteau des rois, symphonie fantastique*. Paris: D'Amyot, 1847. Rpt. and annotated by Joseph-Marc Baibé. Paris: Lettres Modernes, Minard, 1972.

Johnson, Barbara. *The Critical Difference: Essays in the Contemporary Rhetoric of Reading*. Baltimore: Johns Hopkins UP, 1980.

———. *Défigurations du langage poétique, la seconde révolution baudelairienne*. Paris: Flammarion, 1979.

———. *A World of Difference*. Baltimore: Johns Hopkins UP, 1987.

Johnson, Peter. "Interview [with Robert Bly]." *The Prose Poem: An International Journal* 7 (1998): 68–86.

Kahn, Gustave. *Premiers Poèmes*. Paris: Mercure de France, 1897.

Kamerbeek, J., Jr. "Sainte-Beuve et Baudelaire entre Velleius et Valéry." Patty and Pichois, *Études*, 91–113.

Katz, Doris. "Contemporary Prose Poems in French: An Anthology with English Translations and an Essay on the Prose Poem." Ph.D. dissertation, University of Michigan, 1970.

Kaufmann, Michael Edward. "Gertrude Stein's Re-vision of Language and Print in *Tender Buttons*." *Journal of Modern Literature* 15.4 (spring 1989): 447–60.

Kellner, Bruce, ed. *A Gertrude Stein Companion: Content with Example*. New York: Greenwood, 1988.

Kinglsley, Charles. *Alton Locke, Tailor and Poet: An Autobiography*. Ed. Elizabeth A. Cripps. Oxford: Oxford UP, 1983.

Kittay Jeffrey, and Wlad Godzich. *The Emergence of Prose: An Essay in Prosaics*. Minneapolis: U of Minnesota P, 1987.

Koethe, John. "The Absence of a Noble Presence." *The Tribe of John: Ashbery and Contemporary Poetry*. Ed. Susan M. Schultz. Tuscaloosa: U of Alabama P, 1995.

Kuzma, Greg, and Duane Ackerson, eds. "Fifty-four prose poems." *Pebble* 11 (1974).

LaCapra, Dominick. "Comment" [on Ralph Cohen's "History and Genre"]. *New Literary History* 17.2 (winter 1986): 219–22.

Lautréamont, Comte de. *Lautréamont, Germain Nouveau, Œuvres complètes*. Ed. Pierre-Olivier Walzer. Paris: Gallimard, 1970.

———. *Malador and Poems*. Trans. Paul Knight. New York: Penguin, 1988.

Lazarus, Emma. *The Poems of Emma Lazarus*. Vol. 2, *Jewish Poems: Translations*. Cambridge: Houghton Mifflin, 1888.

Leakey, F. W. *Baudelaire and Nature*. Manchester: Manchester UP, 1969.

———. *Collected Essays, 1953–1988*. Ed. Eva Jacobs. Cambridge: Cambridge UP, 1990.

Lefevere, André. "Systems in Evolution: Historical Relativism and the Study of Genre." *Poetics Today* 6.4 (1985): 665–79.

Lefèvre, Jules. *Le Livre du promeneur, ou les mois et les jours*. Paris: Librairie D'Amyot, 1854.

Lewalski, Barbara, ed. *Renaissance Genres*. Cambridge: Harvard UP, 1986.

Lhértier, André. "Les Physiologies." Martine, Chartier, and Vivet, *Le Temps des éditeurs*, 380–81.

Longenbach, James. *Modern Poetry after Modernism*. New York: Oxford UP, 1997.

Lowell, Amy. *Sword-blades and Poppy Seed*. Cambridge, Mass.: Riverside, 1914.

———. "Vers Libre and Metrical Prose." *Poetry* 3.6 (March 1914): 213–20.

Loydell, Rupert, and David Miller, eds. *A Curious Architecture*. Devon, England: Stride, 1996.

Lyons, Martyn. "Les best-sellers." Martine, Chartier, and Vivet, *Le Temps des éditeurs*, 369–97.

Mallarmé, Stephane. *Correspondance de Stéphane Mallarmé*. Ed. Henri Mandor. 11 vols. Paris: Gallimard, 1959–85.

———. *Œuvres complètes*. Eds. Henri Mondor and G. Jean-Aubry. Paris: Gallimard, 1945.

Manning, Fredric. "Poetry in Prose." *The Chapbook* 22 (April 1921): 10–16.

Martine, Henri-Jean, Roger Chartier, and Jean-Pierre Vivet, eds. *Le Temps des éditeurs: Du Romantisme à la belle époque*. Tome 3 of *Histoire de l'édition française*. Paris: Promodis, 1985.

Matthews, Cornelius. Preface. *Arcturus: A Journal of Books and Opinion* 2.6 (June 1841): iii–vi.

McGann, Jerome. "Contemporary Poetry, Alternate Routes." Von Hallberg, *Politics*, 253–76.

McKeon, Michael. *The Origins of the English Novel*. Baltimore: Johns Hopkins UP, 1987.

McLees, Ainslie Armstrong. *Baudelaire's 'Argot Plastique,' Poetic Caricature and Modernism*. Athens: U of Georgia P, 1989.

Mencken, H. L. *The American Language*. New York: Knopf, 1937.

Meyer, Steven J. "Stein and Emerson." *Raritan* 10.2 (fall 1990): 87–119.

Miner, Earl. *Comparative Poetics*. Princeton, N.J.: Princeton UP, 1990.

———. "Some Issues of Literary 'Species, or Distinct Kind.' " Lewalski, *Renaissance Genres*, 15–44.

Mitrano, Mena. "Linguistic Exoticism and Literary Alienation: Gertrude Stein's *Tender Buttons*." *Modern Language Studies* 28.2 (spring 1998): 87–102.

Monroe, Jonathan. *A Poverty of Objects: The Prose Poem and the Politics of Genre*. Ithaca, N.Y.: Cornell UP, 1987.

Moreau, Pierre. *La Tradition française du poème en prose avant Baudelaire*. Paris: Archives des Lettres Modernes nos. 19–20, 1959.

Morson, Gary Saul. *The Boundaries of Genre: Dostoevsky's "Diary of a Writer" and the Traditions of Literary Utopia*. Austin: U of Texas P, 1981.

Murphy, Margueritte. *A Tradition of Subversion: The Prose Poem in English from Wilde to Ashbery*. Amherst: U of Massachusetts P, 1992.

Myers, George, ed. *Epiphanies: The Prose Poem Now*. Westerville, Ohio: Cumberland, 1987.

Nerval, Gérard de. *Œuvres complètes*. Ed. Jean Guillaume et Claude Pichois. 3 vols. Paris: Gallimard, 1993.

———. "Les Poésies de Henri Heine." *Revue des Deux Mondes* 23 (15 juillet 1848): 224–43.

Nies, Fritz. *Poesie in Prosaischer Welt: Untersuchungen zum Prosagedicht bei Aloysius Bertrand und Baudelaire*. Heidelberg: Carl Winter Universitätsverlag, 1964.

Parent, Monique. *Saint-John Perse et quelques devanciers: Études sur le poème en prose*. Paris: Librairie C. Klincksieck, 1960.

Pascal, Blaise. *Pensées et Opuscules*. Ed. Léon Brunschvicg and Pierre Boutroux. Paris: Classiques Hachette, 1959.

Patty, James S., and Claude Pichois, eds. *Études baudelairiennese*, hommage à W. T. Bandy. Neuchâtel, Switzerland: À la Bacconière, 1973.

Perloff, Majorie. *Poetic License: Essays on Modernist and Postmodernist Lyric*. Evanston, Ill.: Northwestern UP, 1990.

———. *The Poetics of Indeterminacy: Rimbaud to Cage*. Princeton, N.J.: Princeton UP 1981.

Poe, Edgar Allan. "Review of New Books." *Graham's Lady's and Gentleman's Magazine* 20.1 (1842): 69.

———. *Selected Prose, Poetry, and Eureka*. Ed. W. H. Auden. New York: Holt, Rhinehart, and Winston, 1950.

Pommier, M. J. *Dans les chemins de Baudelaire*. Paris: J. Corti, 1945.

Pound, Ezra. *Selected Letters, 1907–1941*. Ed. D. D. Paige. 1950. New York: New Directions, 1971.

Preminger, Alex, and T. V. F. Brogan, eds. *The New Princeton Encyclopedia of Poetry and Poetics*. Princeton, N.J.: Princeton UP.

Price, Leah. "George Eliot and the Production of Consumers." *Novel* (winter 1997).

Rabbe, Alphonse. *Album d'un pessimiste*. Paris: Plasma, 1979.

Rauhut, Franz. *Das französische Prosagedicht*. Hamburg: Friederichsen, de Gruyter, 1929.

Review of *The Poetical Works of Anne Radcliffe*. *Edinburgh Review* 59 (1834): 327–41.

Rimbaud, Arthur. *Illuminations, Coloured Plates*. Ed. Nick Osmond. London: Athlone, 1976.

———. *Œuvres complètes*. Ed. Antoine Adam. Paris: Gallimard, 1972.

———. *Œuvres complètes: Correspondance*. Ed. Louis Forestier. Paris: Laffont, 1992.

Robb, Graham. "Les Origines journalistiques de la prose poétique de Baudelaire." *Les Lettres romanes* 44.1–2 (February–May 1990): 15–26.

Robert, Paul, and Alain Rey, eds. *Le Grand Robert de la langue française*. Tome 8 (P-Raisi). Paris: Le Robert, 1985.

Rosmarin, Adena. *The Power of Genre*. Minneapolis: U of Minnesota P, 1985.

Ross, Andrew. *The Failure of Modernism: Symptoms of American Poetry*. New York: Columbia UP, 1988.

Rousseau, Jean-Jacques. *Les Rêveries du promeneur solitaire*. Ed. S. de Sacy. Paris: Gallimard, 1972.

Ruddick, Lisa. *Reading Gertrude Stein: Body, Text, Gnosis*. Ithaca, N.Y.: Cornell UP, 1990.

Sainte-Beuve, Charles Augustin. *Poésies complètes*. Paris: Charpentier, 1890.

———. Preface to *Gaspard de la nuit*. Rpt. in *Portraits Littéraires II*. Paris: Garnier Frères, 1862. 343–64.

Saintsbury, George. *A History of English Prose Rhythm*. 1912. London: Macmillan, 1922.

Sandras, Michel. *Lire le poème en prose*. Paris: Dunod, 1995.

Schaeffer, Jean-Marie. "Literary Genres and Textual Genericity." Cohen, *Future of Literary Theory*, 167–87.

Schmitz, Neil. "Gertrude Stein as Post-Modernist: The Rhetoric of *Tender Buttons*." *Journal of Modern Literature* 3.5 (July 1974): 1206–18. Rpt. in *Critical Essays on Gertrude Stein*. Ed. Michael J. Hoffman. Boston: G. K. Hall, 1984.

Schwartz, Howard. *Imperial Messages: One Hundred Modern Parables*. Woodstock, N.J.: Overlook, 1991.

Sebeok, Thomas, ed. *Style in Language*. Cambridge: MIT P, 1966.

Shaftesbury, Anthony Ashley Cooper, third earl of. *Characteristics of Men, Manners, Opinions, etc.* Indianapolis, Ind.: Bobbs-Merrill, 1964.

Shapiro, David. *John Ashbery: An Introduction to the Poetry*. New York: Columbia UP, 1979.

Shattuck, Roger. "Vibratory Organism: *crise de prose*." Caws and Riffaterre, *Prose Poem*, 21–35.

Shoptaw, John. "Lyric Cryptography." *Poetics Today* 21.1 (spring 2000): 221–62.

————. *On the Outside Looking Out: John Ashbery's Poetry*. Cambridge: Harvard UP, 1994.

Silliman, Ron. "New Prose, New Prose Poem." *Postmodern Fiction: A Bio-Bibliographical Guide*. Ed. Larry McCaffery. Movements in the Arts, No. 2. New York: Greenwood, 1986. 161–74.

Simon, John. *The Prose Poem as a Genre in Nineteenth-Century European Literature*. Ph.D dissertation, Harvard, 1959. Rpt. New York: Garland, 1987.

Skinner, B. F. "Has Gertrude Stein a Secret?" *Atlantic Monthly* 153 (January 1934): 50–57.

Sonnenfeld, Albert. "*L'Adieu suprême* and Ultimate Composure: The Boundaries of the Prose Poem." Caws and Riffaterre, *Prose Poem*, 198–211.

Staiger, Jeff. "The Hitherside of History: Tone, Knowledge, and Spirit in John Ashbery's 'The System.'" *Texas Studies in Literature and Language* 39.1 (spring 1997): 80–95.

Stein, Gertrude. "Advertisement." *Pagany* 1.3 (summer 1930) 40.

————. *Everybody's Autobiography*. London: Virago, 1985.

————. *Tender Buttons*. 1914. New York: Haskell, 1970.

————. *Tender Buttons. transition* 14 (fall 1928): 13–55. Rpt. New York: Kraus Reprint Collection, 1967.

————. *Writings 1903–1932*. (*Writings* 1). Ed. Catharine R. Stimpson and Harriet Chessman. New York: Library of America, 1998.

————. *Writings 1932–1946*. (*Writings* 2). Eds. Catharine R. Stimpson and Harriet Chessman. New York: Library of America, 1998.

Stevens, Wallace. *The Collected Poems of Wallace Stevens*. New York: Vintage Books, 1982.

Stewart, Allegra. *Gertrude Stein and the Present*. Cambridge: Harvard UP, 1967.

Stierle, Karlheinz. "Baudelaire's 'Tableau parisiens' und die Tradition des 'tableau de Paris.'" *Poetica* 6 (1974): 285–322. Rpt. and trans. as "Baudelaire and the Tradition of the *Tableau de Paris*." *New Literary History* 11.2 (1980): 345–61.

Strelka, Joseph P., ed. *Theories of Literary Genre*. Yearbook of Comparative Criticism 8. University Park: Pennsylvania State UP, 1978.

Symons, Arthur. *Dramatis Personae*. Freeport, N.Y.: Bobbs-Merrill, 1971.

Terdiman, Richard. *Discourse/Counterdiscourse: The Theory and Practice of Symbolic Resistance in Nineteenth-Century France*. Ithaca, N.Y.: Cornell UP, 1985.

Tetlow, Wendolyn E. *Hemingway's "In Our Time": Lyrical Dimensions*. Lewisburg, Pa.: Bucknell UP, 1992.

Tieghem, Paul van. *Ossian en France*. 2 vols. 1917. Geneva: Slatkine Reprints, 1967.

————. *Le Préromantisme*. 2 vols. Paris: Alcan, 1924.

Toomer, Jean. "Calling Jesus." *Cane*. New York: University Place, 1923. 102–3.

————. "Nora." *Double Dealer* 4.21 (September 1922): 110.

Traherne, Thomas. *Centuries, Poems, and Thanksgivings*. Vol. 1 of *Introduction and Centuries*. Oxford: Clarendon, 1958.

Upward, Allen. "Scented Leaves from a Chinese Jar." *Poetry* 2.6 (September 1913): 191.

Von Hallberg, Robert, ed. *Politics and Poetic Value*. Chicago: U of Chicago P, 1987.

Walker, Jayne L. *The Making of a Modernist: Gertrude Stein from "Three Lives" to "Tender Buttons."* Amherst: U of Massachusetts P, 1984.

Watt, Ian. *The Rise of the Novel*. Berkeley: U of California P, 1957.

Weissenberger, Klaus. "A Morphological Genre Theory: An Answer to a Pluralism of Forms." Strelka, *Theories*, 229–53.

Wesling, Donald. *The New Poetries: Poetic Form since Coleridge and Wordsworth*. Lewisburg, Pa.: Bucknell UP, 1985.

Wilde, Oscar. *The Works of Oscar Wilde*. Vol. 9, *Poems in Prose*. 1894. Rpt. New York: AMS, Sunflower Edition, 1909.

Williams, William Carlos. *Imaginations*. Ed. Webster Schott. New York: New Directions, 1970.

Wilson, Edmund. *Axel's Castle: A Study in the Imaginative Literature of 1870 to 1930*. New York: Charles Scribner's Sons, 1931.

Wilson, Steve, ed. *The Anatomy of Water: A Sampling of Contemporary American Prose Poetry*. Decatur, Ga.: Linwood, 1992.

Wineapple, Brenda. *Sister Brother: Gertrude and Leo Stein*. New York: G. P. Putnam's Sons, 1996.

Woolf, Virginia. *The Complete Shorter Fiction of Virginia Woolf*. Ed. Susan Dick. 2nd ed. New York: Harcourt Brace Jovanovich, 1989.

——. *Roger Fry: A Biography*. London: Hogarth, 1940.

Wordsworth, William. *The Prelude: 1799, 1805, 1850*. Ed. Jonathan Wordsworth, M. H. Abrams, and Stephen Gill. New York: Norton, 1979.

——. *Selected Poems and Prefaces*. Ed. Jack Stillinger. Riverside Editions. Boston: Houghton Mifflin, 1965.

Zimmerman, Melvin. "Trois Études sur Baudelaire et Rousseau." *Études Baudelairiennes IX: Baudelaire, Rousseau et Hugo*. Neuchâtel, Switzerland: Éditions de la Baconnière, 1981. 31–71.

Index

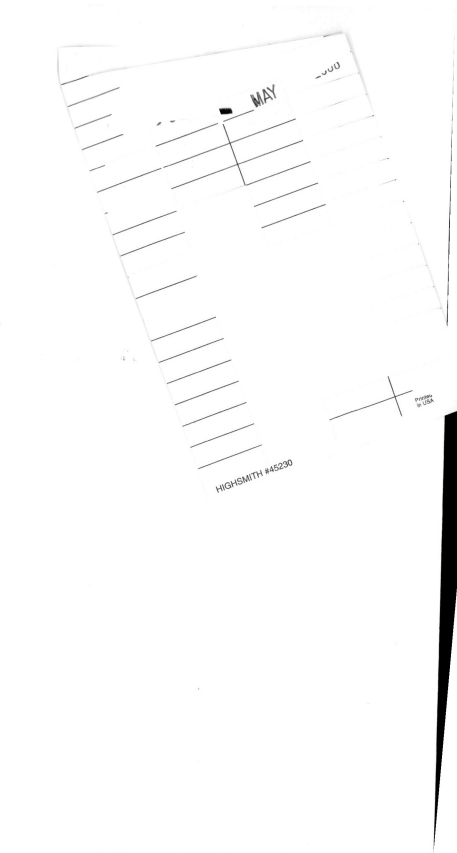

MAY

HIGHSMITH #45230

Printed in USA